Employee Benefits

Employee Benefits

A Primer for Human Resource Professionals

Fourth Edition

Joseph J. Martocchio
University of Illinois

 McGraw-Hill
Irwin

EMPLOYEE BENEFITS: A PRIMER FOR HUMAN RESOURCE PROFESSIONALS

Published by McGraw-Hill/Irwin, a business unit of The McGraw-Hill Companies, Inc., 1221 Avenue of the Americas, New York, NY, 10020. Copyright © 2011, 2008, 2006, 2003 by The McGraw-Hill Companies, Inc. All rights reserved. No part of this publication may be reproduced or distributed in any form or by any means, or stored in a database or retrieval system, without the prior written consent of The McGraw-Hill Companies, Inc., including, but not limited to, in any network or other electronic storage or transmission, or broadcast for distance learning.

Some ancillaries, including electronic and print components, may not be available to customers outside the United States.

This book is printed on acid-free paper.

2 3 4 5 6 7 8 9 0 DOC/DOC 1 0 9 8 7 6 5 4 3 2 1 0

ISBN 978-0-07-353052-9
MHID 0-07-353052-2

Vice president and editor-in-chief: *Brent Gordon*
Publisher: *Paul Ducham*
Director of development: *Ann Torbert*
Managing development editor: *Laura Hurst Spell*
Editorial coordinator: *Jane Beck*
Vice president and director of marketing: *Robin J. Zwettler*
Associate marketing manager: *Jaime Halteman*
Vice president of editing, design and production: *Sesha Bolisetty*
Senior project manager: *Bruce Gin*
Lead production supervisor: *Carol A. Bielski*
Design coordinator: *Joanne Mennemeier*
Media project manager: *Suresh Babu, Hurix Systems Pvt. Ltd.*
Cover design: *Joanne Mennemeier*
Cover images: *Getty Images, Jupiter Images, PictureQuest*
Typeface: *10/12 Palatino*
Compositor: *Glyph International*
Printer: *R. R. Donnelley*

Library of Congress Cataloging-in-Publication Data

Martocchio, Joseph J.
   Employee benefits : a primer for human resource professionals / Joseph J. Martocchio.—4th ed.
      p. cm.
   Includes bibliographical references and index.
   ISBN-13: 978-0-07-353052-9 (alk. paper)
   ISBN-10: 0-07-353052-2
  1. Employee fringe benefits—United States. 2. Compensation management—United States. I. Title.
  HD4928.N62U637 2009
  658.3′25—dc22
                                            2009044312

www.mhhe.com

For Brad

About the Author

Joseph J. Martocchio is the Associate Dean for Academic Affairs and Professor in the School of Labor and Employment Relations, University of Illinois at Urbana-Champaign. He earned his Master's degree and PhD in human resource management from Michigan State University's School of Labor and Industrial Relations. Professor Martocchio's research and teaching interests include employee compensation, employee benefits, and the influence of generational diversity on preferences for employee benefits. He has researched extensively, placing him in the top 5 percent of the most productive researchers published in premier applied psychology journals for the 1990s, according to a survey conducted by the Society for Industrial and Organizational Psychology (SIOP). Martocchio is a fellow of SIOP and the American Psychological Association and a fellow of the Employee Benefits Research Institute. He is the co-editor of the annual research series *Research in Personnel and Human Resources Management* (Emerald Insight Publishing). Martocchio is the author of a textbook titled *Strategic Compensation: A Human Resource Management Approach* (Pearson Education).

Preface

Employee benefits are an increasingly important element of employee compensation packages. The term *employee benefits* refers to compensation other than hourly wage, salary, or incentive payments. Examples of just a few specific employee benefits include paid vacation, medical insurance coverage, retirement plans, and tuition reimbursement. The federal and state governments mandate specific benefits based on a variety of laws (e.g., the federal Social Security Act of 1935 and subsequent amendments) and specify minimum standards to qualify for favorable tax treatment (thanks to the Employee Retirement Income Security Act of 1974). Government-mandated benefits usually focus on protection against loss of income for a variety of reasons (e.g., disability benefits for workers and family members). Employers also choose to offer several benefits to employees that fall into three categories:

- Protection programs
- Paid time-off
- Services

Despite the importance of employee benefits, this segment of compensation packages is not very well understood, mainly because of the vast array of regulations that govern employee benefits practices. In addition, many employers tailor benefits to the needs and preferences of their workforces, making it difficult to stay abreast of all the possible practices. Further, employee benefits historically were treated as a response to government regulations. In many respects, mandated benefits were simply taken for granted. Finally, companies offer benefits because their competitors do. Except for government-mandated benefits, companies offer many benefits to receive favorable tax treatment by reducing taxable income and to avoid competitive disadvantage by attracting and retaining the best-qualified employees.

The fourth edition of this book—*Employee Benefits: A Primer for Human Resource Professionals*—was written to promote an understanding of employee benefits programs among current human resource practitioners, employees who simply wish to gain a fuller understanding of employee benefits practices, and among students enrolled in college-level compensation and benefits courses. For practitioners, this book will serve as an introductory reference guide. It will help practitioners put benefits practices into the appropriate context and to orient them toward asking the right questions of experts related to employee benefits (company accountants, attorneys, managers of benefits, the federal government, etc.). For instance, "Why do we reduce company-sponsored retirement benefits for retirees who also receive Social Security benefits?"

Employees will gain a more complete understanding of how and why employers provide benefits as they do. They will find answers to important questions such as "Why do more companies favor defined contribution plans over defined benefit plans?" and "How do companies determine vacation eligibility?"

For students, HR majors and other business majors at the undergraduate and graduate levels will benefit from this book. There are no prerequisites. It can be used in courses on employee compensation, employee benefits, and human resource management. This book contains 12 chapters, organized into four parts:

- Part 1: Introduction to Employee Benefits
- Part 2: Retirement, Health, and Life Insurance
- Part 3: Services
- Part 4: Extending Employee Benefits: Design and Global Issues

Each chapter contains a chapter outline, learning objectives, key terms, and discussion questions.

NEW TO THE FOURTH EDITION

All the chapters have been thoroughly revised to capture the ever-changing field of employee benefits—and the employee benefits field changes at a breakneck pace, too! One new chapter has been added and another deleted:

- Added to the fourth edition is a newly written chapter, Psychology of Employee Benefits, which describes the psychological foundation of employee benefits from both the employer and employee perspectives. Key concepts such as the psychological contract between the employee and employer set the context for examining employee reactions to benefits practices such as various types of fairness perceptions and job satisfaction, helping to provide employee benefits professionals with a deeper understanding of effective benefits practices. This chapter provides a complementary perspective to the economic foundations for employee benefits already included in this book.
- Deleted from this edition is the chapter on nonqualified plans for highly compensated employees and executives. This particular area of employee benefits was in great flux when the fourth edition was being prepared. It was anticipated that the material would have been out-of-date by the time you received the fourth edition. It is anticipated that the dust will settle in the coming years and a timely chapter will be included in subsequent editions of this book.

SUPPLEMENTAL MATERIALS FOR INSTRUCTORS AND STUDENTS

All supplements are available from the book Web site at www.mhhe.com/martocchio4e. Given the rapid and substantial changes in the benefits area, the website will also offer updates to text coverage of important benefits topics and issues.

Instructor supplements:
Web site: Instructor's manual/testbank/PowerPoint

Student supplements:
Web site: Quizzes/chapter review material/text updates

ACKNOWLEDGMENTS

Many individuals made valuable contributions to this edition. I am indebted to the reviewers who provided thoughtful remarks on chapter drafts during the development of this textbook: James C. Coulson from Chapman University, Lori Olson from Western Technical College, and Joel Rudin from Rowan University.

At McGraw-Hill, I thank the following individuals for their support: Laura Spell, Heather Darr, Sara Hunter, Bruce Gin, Debra Sylvester, Matt Baldwin, and Lynn Bluhm. At Carlisle Publishing Services, I thank my developmental editor, Lori Bradshaw, for her excellent ideas, professionalism, and eye for details!

Joseph J. Martocchio

Brief Contents

Table of Contents

Part **One**

Introduction to Employee Benefits

Introducing Employee Benefits

Chapter Outline

Learning Objectives

In this chapter, you will gather information about

1. Origins of employee benefits practice.
2. Various legally required and discretionary benefits.
3. Legal and regulatory influences on employee benefits practices.
4. The strategic importance of benefits and approaches to strategically planning the benefits program.
5. Various types of information used to develop strategic benefit plans.

Congratulations! You've graduated and now been hired for your first job at a great salary. Before you embark on what undoubtedly will be a rewarding career, your new company, like most companies, requires you to attend a new-employee orientation, including a presentation about the company's employee benefits. Upon arrival at orientation, you are handed a large packet of materials and the speaker tells you that you will have to make a variety of choices, including which health insurance coverage to elect, whether to choose life insurance protection and at what amount, and whether to participate in the company's defined benefit or defined contribution retirement plan. For the next 90 minutes, you hear about the various features of your new company's employee benefits program.

At the end of the presentation, the speaker informs you that you must choose among the options from A to Z within two weeks; otherwise, you will be enrolled in the default options or forfeit eligibility to receive a particular benefit until the next calendar year. As you make your way from the benefits orientation to meet with your new boss, you think, "How will I go about making such critical choices?" You begin reading the cover page. "Aha!" you exclaim. The cover sheet contains information that encourages you to meet with your employee benefits representative to discuss numerous choices. As you read this book, you will learn a variety of information about employee benefits practices in the United States and around the world. You will find the information useful as a new or current employee who participates in a company's employee benefits program and as a human resource professional who is knowledgeable about plan design and administration.

DEFINING AND EXPLORING EMPLOYEE BENEFITS

This illustrative vignette describes the experiences of most newly hired employees. Employee benefits professionals assist employees in their choices by educating them about the various features of benefits plans and the implications of opting for one option versus another. Also, employee benefits represent an important component of total compensation packages offered by employers, which requires employee benefits professionals to understand the complexity of benefits so they may help employees get the most from their programs. Establishing benefits programs is not a straightforward proposition. As we discuss later in this chapter, employee benefits professionals must take into account several factors when shaping the benefits program.

Despite the importance of employee benefits, this segment of compensation packages is not very well understood, mainly because of the vast array of regulations that govern employee benefits practices. In addition, many employers tailor benefits to the needs and preferences of their workforces, making it difficult to stay abreast of all the possible practices. Further, employee benefits historically were treated as a response to government regulations. In many respects, mandated benefits were simply taken for granted. Finally, companies offer benefits because their competitors do. Except for government-mandated benefits, companies offer many benefits to receive favorable tax treatment by reducing taxable income, to promote a positive public image, and to avoid competitive disadvantage by attracting and retaining the best qualified employees. This book was written to promote an understanding of employee benefits programs among current human resource practitioners, among employees who simply wish to gain a fuller understanding of employee benefits practices, and among students enrolled in college-level compensation and benefits courses.

Let's start off with a brief definition of employee benefits. Next, we will put employee benefits in the context of total compensation systems in companies (Exhibit 1.1) and from there expand the definition of employee benefits. Finally, we will examine strategic considerations essential for effective employee benefits programs.

Defining Employee Benefits

The term **employee benefits** refers to compensation other than an hourly wage or salary. Examples of specific employee benefits include paid vacation, medical insurance coverage, and tuition reimbursement, but the number of employee benefits can be staggering. To organize the vast benefits information efficiently, most benefits professionals group them by two attributes: the role the benefit serves recipients and the source of the benefit.

Three fundamental roles characterize benefits programs: protection, paid time-off, and accommodation and enhancement. **Protection programs** provide family benefits, promote health, and guard against income loss caused by catastrophic factors like unemployment, disability, or serious illnesses. **Paid time-off** policies compensate

EXHIBIT 1.1
Employee Benefits in the Total Compensation Scheme

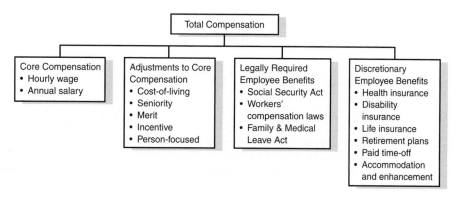

Total Compensation			
Core Compensation • Hourly wage • Annual salary	Adjustments to Core Compensation • Cost-of-living • Seniority • Merit • Incentive • Person-focused	Legally Required Employee Benefits • Social Security Act • Workers' compensation laws • Family & Medical Leave Act	Discretionary Employee Benefits • Health insurance • Disability insurance • Life insurance • Retirement plans • Paid time-off • Accommodation and enhancement

employees when they are not performing their primary work duties. **Accommodation and enhancement benefits** promote opportunities for employees and their families. A wide variety of programs exist, including stress management classes, flexible work schedules, and tuition reimbursement.

Employee benefits derive from two broad sources. The U.S. government requires that most employers provide particular sets of benefits to employees. We refer to these as legally required benefits. Such laws as the Social Security Act of 1935 mandate a variety of programs designed to provide income to retired workers, monetary benefits to the beneficiaries of deceased workers, and medical protection for older Americans. Companies may offer additional benefits on a discretionary basis. We refer to these benefits as discretionary benefits.

Exhibit 1.2 lists typical employee benefits offered in U.S. companies. As this exhibit shows, protection programs are required by law, and companies may choose to offer additional protection programs. U.S. employers, excluding the government, offer paid time-off benefits and services on a discretionary basis. In contrast, as we discuss in Chapter 12, other countries mandate paid time-off.

Employee Benefits in the Total Compensation Scheme

Employee benefits are a part of a company's total compensation system. **Total compensation** represents both the monetary and nonmonetary rewards. As shown

EXHIBIT 1.2
Typical Employee Benefit Offerings in the United States

Legally Required Benefits	
Old-Age, Survivor, and Disability Insurance (OASDI)	Unemployment insurance
	Workers' compensation
Medicare	Family and medical leave

Discretionary Benefits	
Protection Programs	Jury duty and witness duty leaves
Medical insurance	Military leave
Dental insurance	Nonproduction time (e.g., lunch
Vision insurance	periods)
Life insurance	
Prescription drugs	*Accommodation and Enhancement*
Mental health and substance abuse	*Programs*
Maternity care	Employees' and family members'
Disability insurance (short- and	mental and physical well-being
long-term)	Employee assistance programs
Pension programs (defined benefit,	Wellness programs
defined contribution, hybrid plans)	Family assistance programs
	Educational benefits for employees
Paid Time-Off	Educational assistance programs
Holidays	Tuition reimbursement programs
Vacation	Scholarship programs
Sick leave	Support programs for daily living
Personal leave	Transportation services
Bereavement or funeral leave	Physical fitness
Sabbatical leave	

in Exhibit 1.1 monetary compensation includes core compensation, adjustments to core compensation, legally required benefits, and discretionary benefits. Compensation professionals establish monetary compensation programs to reward employees according to their job performance levels or for learning job-related knowledge or skills. As we will discuss shortly, monetary compensation represents core compensation. Nonmonetary rewards include protection programs (for example, medical insurance), paid time-off (for example, vacations), and services (for example, day care assistance). Most compensation professionals refer to nonmonetary rewards as employee benefits. We will address the origins of employee benefits practice in the United States later in this chapter and in subsequent chapters where relevant to specific benefits practices.

Core Compensation

Employees receive **base pay,** or money for performing their jobs. Companies disburse base pay to employees in one of two forms. Employees can earn hourly pay, or a wage, for each hour worked, or they can earn a salary for performing their jobs, regardless of the actual number of hours worked. Companies measure salary on an annual basis.

Adjustments to Core Compensation

Over time, employers adjust employees' base pay to recognize increases in the cost of living, differences in employees' performance, or differences in employees' attainment of job-related knowledge and skills. We define these core compensation elements next.

Cost-of-living adjustments (COLAs) represent periodic base pay increases that are based on changes in prices as indexed by the consumer price index (CPI). COLAs enable workers to maintain their purchasing power and standards of living by having their base pay adjusted for inflation. Over time, most everything we buy costs more money, such as the price of a gallon of gasoline. In February 1999, the average price of gas was $0.96 per gallon and has risen substantially since then to approximately $2.05 per gallon in April 2009—a 113 percent increase! How exactly does inflation affect us? Let's assume, for example, that a local grocery store employs college students to stock shelves on a part-time basis and pays the federal minimum hourly wage rate, which has been $7.25 since 2009. Let's also assume that a student typically works 10 hours per week. This means that the total weekly pay is $72.50 ($7.25 per hour × 10 hours per week). Further, let's assume a student typically drives his car 50 miles per week between home and work and the car's gas mileage is only 10 miles per gallon. Considering these data, in 2009 the student spends $10.25 for gas [(50 miles/10 miles per gallon) × $2.05 per gallon]. Let's assume that the price of gasoline in 2013 is $4.00 per gallon. The student will spend a whopping $20.00 for gas—in other words (50 miles/10 miles per gallon) × $4.00 per gallon—$9.75 more ($20.00 − $10.25) in 2013 than in 2009. As long as the grocery store owner maintains the hourly wage rate and limits the number of weekly work hours to 10 and gas continues to rise in price, the student will have less money available for other pursuits in 2013.

Seniority pay systems reward employees with periodic additions to base pay according to an employee's length of service performing his or her job. Over time, employees presumably refine existing skills or acquire new ones that enable them to work more productively. This rationale comes from human capital theory, which states that employees' knowledge and skills generate productive capital known as human capital. A person employed in a company for a long time knows the rules and procedures from which she develops the skill (i.e., human capital) to perform a job more quickly in an exemplary fashion than newly hired employees.

Merit pay programs assume that employees' compensation over time should be determined, at least in part, by differences in job performance. Employees earn permanent increases to base pay according to their performance, which rewards excellent effort or results, motivates future performance, and helps employers retain valued employees. Merit pay increases are expressed as a percentage of current base pay, with higher percentage increases for better performers. For instance, an employee currently earning $25,000 annually receives a 10 percent merit pay increase, making her total $27,500 after her pay raise takes effect: $25,000 + (10 percent × $25,000).

Incentive pay rewards employees for partially or completely attaining a predetermined work objective. Incentive pay is defined as compensation (other than base wages or salaries) that fluctuates according to an employee's attainment of some standard based on individual or group goals (e.g., $1,000 to customer sales representatives whose customer service ratings increased each month over a six-month period), or company earnings (for instance, employees share 2 percent of company profits when the company substantially exceeds its performance projections).

Person-focused pay rewards employees for learning new knowledge and skills through designated curricula sponsored by an employer. This approach rewards employees for the range, depth, and types of skills or knowledge they are *capable* of applying productively to their jobs following training. This feature distinguishes pay-for-knowledge plans from merit pay and incentive pay, which rewards actual job performance.

THE FIELD OF EMPLOYEE BENEFITS PRACTICE

The field of employee benefits practice is essential to companies. Virtually every company offers at least one benefit to employees, and most companies offer several. In this book, we emphasize the importance of benefits in achieving legal compliance and competitive advantage and how companies achieve these goals. Meeting these imperatives requires benefits specialists who work in departments within the broader human resource functions or as external consultants offering expert advice. Employees in benefits departments usually span the organizational hierarchy, including clerical staff members, managerial employees, and executives.

So, with which issues do employee benefits professionals work? Employee benefits managers and specialists handle the company's employee benefits program, notably its health insurance and pension plans. Expertise in designing and administering benefits programs continues to take on importance as employer-provided benefits account for a substantial proportion of overall compensation costs and as benefit plans increase in number and complexity. For example, pension benefits might include savings and thrift, profit-sharing, and stock ownership plans; health benefits might include long-term catastrophic illness insurance and dental insurance. Familiarity with health benefits is a top priority for employee benefits managers and specialists, as more firms struggle to cope with the rising cost of health care for employees and retirees. In addition to health insurance and pension coverage, some firms offer employees life and accidental death and dismemberment insurance; disability insurance; and relatively new benefits designed to meet the needs of a changing workforce, such as parental leave, child and elder care, long-term nursing home care insurance, employee assistance and wellness programs, and flexible benefits plans. Benefits managers must keep abreast of changing federal and state regulations that may affect employee benefits.[1]

Employee benefits professionals can stay abreast of pertinent developments in the field through a variety of associations. Professional associations for the benefits field signal the importance of the benefits function. These associations offer a variety of services to help benefits professionals stay abreast of innovative company practices, changes in legal requirements, and tools to assist in the development and implementation of benefits. The International Foundation of Employee Benefit Plans (IFEBP, www.ifebp.org) is an example of an association of benefits professionals. The Society for Human Resource Management (www.shrm.org) and WorldatWork (www.worldatwork.org) are also excellent professional organizations that address employee benefits issues as well as other human resource management issues. The Employee Benefit Research Institute (EBRI, www.ebri.org) is a nonprofit, nonpartisan organization committed exclusively to data dissemination, policy research, and education on economic security and employee benefits.

Legally Required Benefits

Legally required benefits are mandated by the following laws: the Social Security Act of 1935 (Chapter 8), various state workers' compensation laws (Chapter 8), and the Family and Medical Leave Act of 1993 (Chapter 9). All provide protection programs to employees and their dependents. We review the basics of each benefit here, deferring detailed treatment to the designated chapters.

The Social Security Act of 1935

The economic devastation of the Great Depression era prompted the federal government into action, because most people used up their life savings to survive and opportunities for gainful employment were scarce. The **Social Security Act of 1935** set up two programs: a federal system of income benefits for retired workers and a system of unemployment insurance administered by the federal and state governments. Amendments to the Social Security Act in 1965 established the disability insurance and Medicare programs. The term **Old-Age, Survivor, and Disability Insurance (OASDI)** refers to the programs that provide retirement income, income to the survivors of deceased workers, and income to disabled workers and their family members. **Medicare** serves nearly all U.S. citizens aged at least 65, as well as disabled Social Security beneficiaries, by providing insurance coverage for hospitalization, convalescent care, major doctor bills, and prescription drug coverage.

State Compulsory Disability Laws (Workers' Compensation)

Workers' compensation insurance came into existence during the early decades of the 20th century, when industrial accidents were very common and workers suffered from occupational illnesses at alarming rates.[2] During the early years of industrialization of the U.S. economy, no laws required employers to ensure the health and safety of employees. Seriously injured and ill workers were left with virtually no recourse because social insurance programs to protect such workers were nonexistent. **State compulsory disability laws** created workers' compensation programs. **Workers' compensation** insurance programs, run by the individual states, are designed to cover employee expenses incurred in work-related accidents or injuries. These programs have six objectives:

1. Provide sure, prompt, and reasonable income and medical benefits to work-accident victims or income benefits to their dependents, regardless of fault.
2. Provide a single remedy and reduce court delays, costs, and workloads arising from personal injury litigation.
3. Relieve public and private charities of financial drains.
4. Eliminate payment of fees to lawyers and witnesses, as well as time-consuming trials and appeals.
5. Encourage maximum employer interest in safety and rehabilitation through appropriate experience-rating mechanisms.
6. Promote frank study of the causes of accidents (rather than concealment of fault), reducing preventable accidents and human suffering.

The Family and Medical Leave Act of 1993

The **Family and Medical Leave Act (FMLA)** provides job protection to employees in cases of a family or medical emergency. FMLA permits eligible employees to take up to 12 workweeks of unpaid leave during any 12-month period. These employees retain the right to return to the position they left when the leave began or to an equivalent position with the same terms of employment, including pay and benefits. The passage of the FMLA reflects growing recognition that the parents of many employees are becoming elderly, rendering them susceptible to a serious illness or medical condition. The passage of the FMLA also recognizes the increasing prevalence of two-income families and the changing role of men regarding child care.

Discretionary Benefits

Companies can choose to offer a wide variety of benefits to employees. Discretionary benefits fulfill three main roles. The first, *protection programs*, most closely parallels legally required benefits by offering protections to employees and family members due to income loss or ill health. The second, *paid time-off,* affords employees time off with pay for many purposes, including illness or to celebrate designated holidays. The third variety, *accommodation and enhancements,* offers improvements to employees and their families in many ways. Wellness programs and educational assistance programs are examples of accommodation and enhancement benefits.

Income Protection Programs

Disability Insurance Disability insurance replaces income for employees who become unable to work on a regular basis because of an illness or injury. Employer-sponsored disability insurance is more encompassing than workers' compensation because these benefits generally apply to work- and nonwork-related illness or injury. We will review disability insurance programs in greater detail in Chapter 7.

Life Insurance Employer-sponsored **life insurance** protects family members by paying a specified amount to an employee's beneficiaries upon the employee's death. Most policies pay some multiple of the employee's salary—for instance, benefits paid at twice the employee's annual salary. Employees usually have the option of purchasing additional coverage. Frequently, employer-sponsored life insurance plans also include accidental death and dismemberment claims, which pay additional benefits if death was the result of an accident or if the insured incurs accidental loss of a limb. We review life insurance in Chapter 7.

Retirement Plans **Retirement plans,** sometimes referred to as pension plans, provide income to individuals and beneficiaries throughout their retirement. Individuals may participate in more than one pension plan simultaneously. We discuss retirement plans in Chapter 5. Companies may establish their retirement plans as defined contribution plans, defined benefit plans, or hybrid plans that combine features of defined contribution and defined benefit plans. Under a **defined contribution plan,** employers and employees make annual contributions to separate accounts established for each participating employee, based on a formula contained in the plan document. The amount each participant receives in retirement depends on the performance of the selected investment vehicle (for example, company stock, government bonds). Typically, formulas call for employers to contribute a given percentage of each participant's annual pay each year. Employers invest these funds on behalf of the employee in any of a number of ways, such as company stocks, diversified stock market funds, or federal government bond funds. A **defined benefit plan** guarantees the retirement benefits specified in the plan document. This benefit usually is expressed in terms of a monthly sum equal to a percentage of a participant's preretirement pay multiplied by the number of years he or she has worked for the employer. Although the benefit in such a plan is fixed by a formula, the level of required employer contributions fluctuates from year to year. The contribution depends on the amount necessary to make certain the benefits promised will be available when participants and their beneficiaries are eligible to receive them.

Health Protection Programs

Health protection programs refer to a host of practices geared toward promoting sound health. Health protection programs subsume health insurance (Chapter 6), as well as a variety of additional programs designed to promote physical and mental health. Employers refer to these programs, often set up to promote healthier lifestyles, as **wellness programs** (Chapter 10). Examples of wellness programs include stress management programs. Benefits professionals usually designate wellness programs as an accommodation and enhancement benefit, which we review later in this chapter.

Health insurance covers the costs of a variety of services that promote sound physical and mental health, including physical examinations, diagnostic testing (X-rays), surgery, and hospitalization. Companies can choose from four broad classes of health insurance programs, including **fee-for-service plans, managed care plans, point-of-service plans,** and **consumer-driven health care.** Companies may offer additional specialized insurance: **Dental insurance** benefits may cover routine preventative procedures (e.g., cleanings once every six months) and necessary procedures to promote the health of teeth and gums. **Vision insurance** plans usually cover eye examinations, lenses, frames, and fitting of glasses. **Prescription drug plans** cover the costs of drugs. These plans apply exclusively to drugs that state or federal laws require be dispensed by licensed pharmacists. **Mental health and substance abuse plans** cover the costs to treat mental health ailments such as clinical depression and the abuse of alcohol or chemical substances (e.g., addictions to cocaine or prescribed narcotic medications). We discuss health protection programs in Chapter 6.

Paid Time-Off

The second type of discretionary benefits is paid time-off. Paid time-off policies compensate employees when they are not performing their primary work duties. Companies offer most paid time-off as a matter of custom, particularly paid holidays, vacations, and sick leave. In unionized settings, paid time-off provisions are specified within the collective bargaining agreement. The paid time-off practices that are most typically found in unionized settings are jury duty, funeral leave, military leave, clean-up time, preparation, travel time, rest period, and lunch period. Exhibit 1.2 includes typical paid time-off benefits. We address these benefits in greater detail in Chapter 9.

Accommodation and Enhancement Programs

Accommodation and enhancement benefits promote opportunities for employees and family members. We discuss these benefits in Chapter 10. Following are four specific objectives of accommodation and enhancement benefits, with a corresponding benefit stated in parentheses:

- Mental and physical well-being of employees and family members (stress management).
- Family assistance programs (child care).

- Skills and knowledge acquisition through educational programs (tuition reimbursement).
- Opportunities to manage daily challenges (transportation services).

Basic Design Considerations for Discretionary Benefits

Of course, benefits professionals possess substantial leeway when designing the set of discretionary benefits. We review numerous design considerations throughout this book as we examine specific benefits in detail, and general design considerations in Chapter 11. As we discuss later in this chapter and in Chapters 2 and 3, companies strive to offer cost-effective benefits that will promote the recruitment and retention of highly qualified employees. Chapter 2 addresses these issues from a psychological perspective, and Chapter 3 addresses these issues from an economic perspective. The following is a basic introduction to these common features.

- *Eligibility provisions.* Companies must decide whether to limit participation to current employees, their dependent family members, and survivors of deceased current or retired employees. Companies may also decide to limit participation among current employees. For instance, many companies exclude part-time employees because it reduces a company's total cost of benefits.
- *Kinds of benefits.* Which benefits do companies offer to eligible individuals? Companies may sponsor a variety of broad benefits, including retirement plans, health insurance, and paid time-off. Then they select specific benefits from these broad categories. Defined contribution retirement plans are often preferred because these plans are more cost-effective than defined benefit plans.
- *Level of benefits.* Companies choose benefits based on maximum benefit limits. For example, health insurance benefits specify **maximum benefit limits,** expressed as a dollar amount over the course of one year or over an insured's lifetime. In many cases, insurance policies specify both annual maximums (e.g., $25,000) and lifetime maximums ($1,000,000). They may also choose not to set any dollar limit to benefits. A maximum lifetime benefits provision protects employers from the costs of long-term or catastrophic claims and repeated incidences of illness.
- *Waiting period.* Waiting periods specify the minimum number of months or years an employee must remain employed before becoming eligible for one or more benefits. Waiting periods often correspond with the length of probationary periods. Companies impose probationary periods to judge a newcomer's job performance, and they explicitly reserve the right to terminate employees who demonstrate low job performance.
- *Financing benefits.* Employers choose from four approaches—noncontributory, contributory, and employee-financed programs, or some combination thereof. **Noncontributory financing** means that the company pays the total costs for each discretionary benefit. Under **contributory financing,** the company and its employees share the costs. Under **employee-financed benefits,** employers do not contribute to the financing of discretionary benefits as employees bear the entire cost. The majority of benefit plans today are contributory, largely because the costs of benefits have risen so dramatically.

- *Employee choice.* Traditionally, a company offered the same set of benefits to most or all employees. Increasingly, companies offer employees varying degrees of choice. **Flexible benefits,** or **cafeteria plans,** enable employees to choose from among a set of benefits and different levels of these benefits (Chapter 11). The increasing diversity of the workforce has made standardized benefits offerings less practical: Demographic diversity is associated with greater differences in needs and preferences for particular benefits. For instance, workers with pre-school-age children find day care assistance programs most appealing, and workers nearing retirement age find value in company-sponsored retiree health care insurance.

- *Communication.* Oftentimes, employees either are unaware of or undervalue their benefits. Communicating the features and costs of benefits is essential. Effective communications create an awareness of, and appreciation for, the way current benefits improve the financial security and physical and mental well-being of employees (Chapter 11).

Origins of Employee Benefits

Different forces led to the rise of legally required and discretionary employee benefits. The U.S. government established programs to protect individuals from catastrophic events such as disability and unemployment. As highlighted earlier, legally required benefits are protection programs that attempt to promote worker safety and health, maintain family income streams, and assist families in crisis.

Historically, legally required benefits provided a form of social insurance. Prompted largely by the rapid growth of industrialization in the United States during the late 19th and early 20th century as well as the Great Depression of the 1930s, initial social insurance programs were designed to minimize the possibility of destitution for individuals who were unemployed or became severely injured while working. In addition, social insurance programs aimed to stabilize the well-being of dependent family members of injured or unemployed individuals. Further, early social insurance programs were designed to enable retirees to maintain subsistence income levels. These intents of legally required benefits remain intact today.

The first signs of contemporary discretionary employee benefits were evident in the late 1800s when large companies such as American Express offered their employees pension plans. For the next few decades, most of the development in employee benefits practice resulted from government legislation, as previously noted. Then, discretionary benefits offerings became more prominent in the 1940s and 1950s due in large part to federal government restrictions placed on increasing wage levels. Employee benefits were not subject to those restrictions. Companies expanded their discretionary benefits as an alternative to wage increases or as a motivational tool. During that period, the term *welfare practices* described employee benefits. **Welfare practices** were "anything for the comfort and improvement, intellectual or social, of the employees, over and above wages paid, which is not a necessity of the industry nor required by law."[3]

The opportunities available to employees through welfare practices varied. For instance, some employers offered libraries and recreational areas while others provided financial assistance for education and home improvements. In addition, employer sponsorship of medical insurance coverage became common. Employee unions also contributed directly to the increase in employee welfare practices. As we will address shortly, the National Labor Relations Act of 1935 (NLRA) legitimized bargaining for employee benefits. Union workers tend to participate more in benefits plans than nonunion employees.[4] Unions also contributed indirectly to the rise in benefits offerings in nonunion settings. Nonunion companies tend to minimize the likelihood of unionization by offering their employees benefits comparable to those received by employees in union shops.

Employees typically view employer-sponsored benefits as entitlements. Anecdotal evidence suggests that most employees still feel this way: Company membership entitles them to benefits. Until recently, companies have also treated virtually all elements of benefits as entitlements. They have not questioned their role as social welfare mediators. However, both rising benefits costs, increased foreign competition, and a deep economic recession have led companies to question this entitlement ethic; most companies are shifting responsibility for the cost of some benefits to employees. For example, in Chapter 6, we discuss employer-sponsored high-deductible health plans.

LEGAL AND REGULATORY INFLUENCES ON DISCRETIONARY BENEFITS PRACTICES

While employers are free to offer discretionary benefits, specific laws influence the application of these practices. To understand these influences, it is necessary to distinguish between "private sector" employers and governmental employers because different regulations influence discretionary benefits practices in these sectors of the U.S. economy. The private sector refers to nongovernmental employers that strive to maximize profits or offer charitable services to the public in need (nonprofit companies). Ford and General Electric are examples of for-profit companies, and the American Red Cross and the United Way are examples of nonprofit companies. As of March 2009, private sector companies employed about 110 million persons—all U.S. civilian employees, and most for-profit. Profit maximization is the foundation of the U.S. economy. Private sector employers strive to increase profits, market share, and returns on investment for the owners and investors of companies. Employers expect workers to be as productive as possible to promote these goals. At the same time, containing pay and benefits costs contributes to profit maximization.

Conflicting goals between employees and profit-oriented employers necessitate regulations to protect employees from unfair treatment. The following excerpt captures the natural clash between employers and employees, employer profit maximization goals, and employee desires for equitable and fair treatment:

> As competition increased in the textile industry, the original concern of the mill owners for their employees gave way to stricter controls which had nothing to do with the well-being of the workers. Employers reduced wages, lengthened hours, and intensified work. For a workday from 11.5 to 13 hours, making up an

average week of 75 hours, the women operatives were generally earning less than $1.50 a week (exclusive of board) by the late 1840s, and they were being compelled to tend four looms whereas in the 1830s they had only taken care of two . . . [The manager] ordered them [the female textile workers] to come before breakfast. "I regard my work-people just as I regard my machinery. So long as they can do my work for what I choose to pay them, I keep them, getting out of them all I can."[5]

The fundamental goals of employees are to attain high wages, comprehensive benefits, safe and healthful work conditions, and job security. Prior to the 1930s, employees did not possess the right to negotiate with their employers over terms and conditions of employment. As a result, many workers were subjected to unsafe and unhealthful working conditions, inadequate pay and benefits, and excessive work hours. Today, employment legislation and labor unions protect the rights and status of workers. Thus, employer abuses are much less prevalent than before the passage of legislation and the rise in labor unions. Prior to the passage of the Employee Retirement Income Security Act of 1974 (ERISA, Chapters 4 and 5), employees could easily lose company retirement benefits after decades of service simply if the employer chose to use retirement funds for other purposes that benefited company profits. Also, employees did not possess the right to keep their retirement assets if they left a company before reaching retirement age. Years of congressional testimony and investigations led to the passage of ERISA based on the conclusion that employer-sponsored retirement plans were essential to the country's economic security and as an essential supplement to government-sponsored retirement programs through the Social Security Act of 1935.

Public sector employers include the U.S. federal government, state, and local entities. Approximately 23 million individuals are employed in the federal government's three branches—executive, judicial, and legislative. Public sector employers work on behalf of its citizens, and none of them exists to make profits. Rather, their role is to provide service to citizens who pay taxes and, in many cases, for citizens who are unable to pay taxes because they are unemployed. Examples of public sector employers include local police forces, community colleges, state colleges and universities, court systems, social service agencies, and public works departments (such as road maintenance). Although government employers do not seek profits, they still must operate within a budget to provide pay and benefits to employees and services to citizens. ERISA does not apply to public sector retirement plans. Instead, federal, state, and local laws establish the rules and protections for public sector employment.

Also, the government is a buyer and consumer of the products and services that private sector companies produce. Indeed, government spends more than $1 trillion each year on these items. The government uses energy to run its buildings, and it engages in contracts with private sector companies for a multitude of goods and services ranging from building construction to multimillion-dollar defense systems. Various laws require the government to pay contract employees the customary wage in the local area. This is important because many benefits, such as retirement plans, are tied to pay levels.

STRATEGIC PLANNING FOR THE BENEFITS PROGRAM

The development of successful benefits programs matches the priorities of ongoing strategic planning efforts within companies. Many U.S. companies build their success through creating and marketing innovative products and services to customers. Increasingly, companies emphasize the importance of employing diverse workforces to promote the inventive processes necessary for innovation.

For instance, Bristol-Myers Squibb pledges to "foster a globally diverse workforce and a companywide culture that encourages excellence, leadership, innovation, and a balance between our personal and professional lives."[6]

Basic Strategic Planning Concepts

Strategic planning entails a series of judgments, under uncertainty, that companies direct toward achieving specific goals. Companies base strategy formulation on environmental scanning activities. Discerning threats and opportunities is the main focus of environmental scanning. Strategic management is an inexact process because companies distinguish between threats and opportunities based on their interpretation of environmental factors. Business periodicals, daily newspapers, and online news outlets such as *BusinessWeek, The Wall Street Journal,* and CNN highlight critical threats or opportunities facing companies. For example, the number of defaults on home mortgage obligations has risen dramatically since 2007 and is expected to continue at least for the next few years. The rise in defaults is due in large part to the subprime mortgage lending business that has given home mortgages to millions of individuals without checking on their ability to make payments over the long term and the deep economic recession that has led to widespread unemployment. In most cases, those lenders issued mortgages despite credit reviews of applicants that showed a regular tendency not to meet their financial obligations. As a consequence, many of the subprime lenders are facing bankruptcy and many once-profitable homebuilders are stuck with unsold homes because there are fewer financially qualified people to buy homes. The large inventory of unsold new homes contributed to a dramatic drop in home prices.

Business professionals make two kinds of decisions—strategic decisions and tactical decisions. Briefly, strategic decisions guide the activities of companies in the market. **Tactical decisions** support the fulfillment of strategic decisions, which we discuss shortly. Exhibit 1.3 shows the relationship between strategic decisions and tactical decisions. We will look at ExxonMobil Corporation to illustrate these practices in the following paragraphs.

Strategic planning supports business objectives. Company executives communicate business objectives in competitive strategy statements. **Competitive strategy** refers to the planned use of company resources—technology, capital, and human resources (HR)—to promote and sustain competitive advantage. The time horizon for strategic decisions may span two or more years. ExxonMobil's competitive strategy is expressed as follows:

EXHIBIT 1.3
Relationship
between
Strategic and
Tactical
Benefits
Decisions

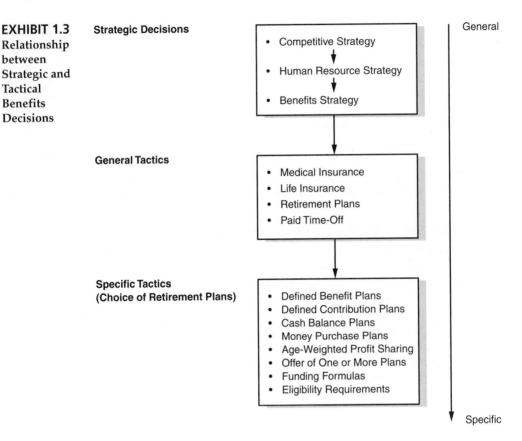

Strategic Decisions

- Competitive Strategy
- Human Resource Strategy
- Benefits Strategy

General

General Tactics

- Medical Insurance
- Life Insurance
- Retirement Plans
- Paid Time-Off

**Specific Tactics
(Choice of Retirement Plans)**

- Defined Benefit Plans
- Defined Contribution Plans
- Cash Balance Plans
- Money Purchase Plans
- Age-Weighted Profit Sharing
- Offer of One or More Plans
- Funding Formulas
- Eligibility Requirements

Specific

> ExxonMobil is the world's leading petroleum and petrochemical company—global, entrepreneurial, and growing. We explore for and produce oil and natural gas on 6 of the 7 continents. We operate refineries and chemical plants in every region. And we market lubricants, fuels, petrochemicals, and other products across the globe. [7]

Human resource executives collaborate with other company executives to develop human resource strategies. **Human resource strategies** specify the use of multiple HR practices. These statements are consistent with a company's competitive strategy:

> ExxonMobil is a dynamic, exciting place to work. We hire exceptional people, and every one of them is empowered to think independently, to take initiative, and be innovative. Our employees thrive on change, new technology, and synergistic partnerships both inside and outside our company. And while the work is exciting and ever changing, we know there's a time when work ends and life kicks in.[8]

Compensation and benefits executives work with the lead HR executive and the company's chief budget officer to prepare total compensation strategies. **Total compensation strategies** describe the use of compensation and benefits practices that support both human resource strategies and competitive strategies. Benefits professionals craft **benefits strategies** based on information contained in strategic benefit plans.

Strategic benefit plans detail different scenarios that may reasonably affect the company, and these plans emphasize long-term changes in how a company's benefit plan operates.[9] Companies establish strategic benefit plans on the interpretation of pertinent information in the external and internal environments, which we discuss shortly. ExxonMobil explicitly endorses the strategic importance of benefits, and ExxonMobil's benefits strategy flows from its competitive strategy:

> In return for your intelligence, ingenuity, and passion, here are the rewards that await you at ExxonMobil: Outstanding compensation, benefits, and employee programs as well as a satisfying balance between career pursuits and personal interests outside of work. Resources and support for ongoing development, growth, and success.[10]

As Exhibit 1.3 shows, managers throughout a company make tactical decisions to specify policy for promoting competitive advantage. Benefits tactics answer two questions: Does offering particular benefits (e.g., paid vacation) support the company's benefits strategy? and what is the optimal design (of vacation benefits)? Descriptions of six employee benefits tactics at ExxonMobil follow.[11]

> *Education assistance*—After employment, ExxonMobil reimburses 100 percent of college-related expenses for approved courses to maintain or improve your skills.

> *Education matching fund*—Three-to-one matching funds for employee and alumni donations to their alma mater.

> *Volunteer involvement program*—Grant moneys awarded for volunteering at eligible nonprofit organizations.

> *Adaptable work arrangements*—Options for adjustable work hours, telecommuting, part-time extensions for family-care needs, and personal time-off.

> *Resource referral*—For child care, elder care, adoption, teen issues, stress, and a variety of other issues.

> *Survivorship counseling*—Counseling for surviving spouses or children of active regular employees.

Approaches to Strategic Benefit Planning

We will begin this section with a review of two approaches to strategic benefit planning. Afterward, we will touch upon the kinds of information companies use in this planning process. In most companies, either compensation or benefits program executives (in some companies, one person is responsible for both) take the lead in strategic benefit planning. Two possible general approaches characterize strategic benefit planning: top-down and backing-in.[12] The **top-down approach** represents a proactive process: Companies regularly review the entire benefits program or particular parts of the program. This process may lead to a reformulation of the entire program or specific parts. Exhibit 1.4 illustrates how the

EXHIBIT 1.4   A Top-Down Approach to Strategic Benefit Planning: A Conceptual Framework

Source: V. Barocas. *Strategic Benefits Planning* (New York: The Conference Board, 1992), p. 15.

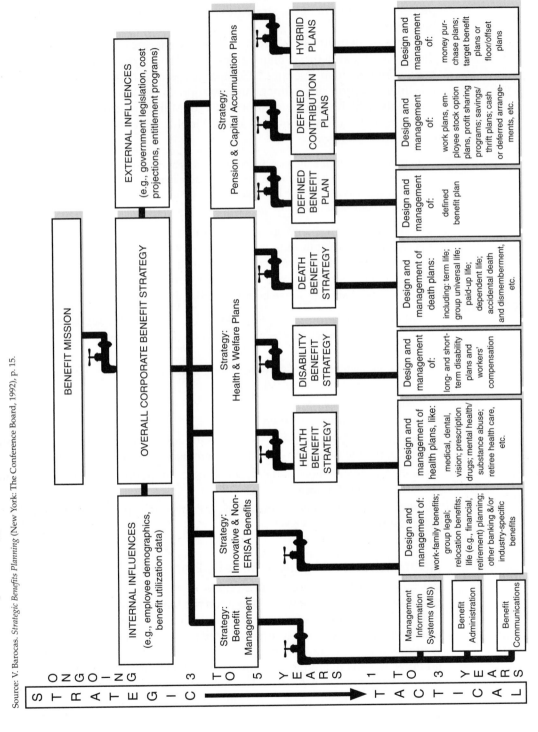

EXHIBIT 1.5   **A Backing-in Approach to Strategic Benefit Planning**

Source: V. Barocas, *Strategic Benefits Planning* (New York: The Conference Board, 1992), p. 16.

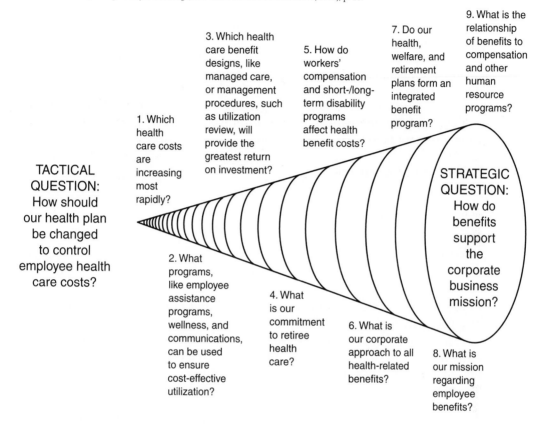

top-down approach unfolds and shows the representative time frames for particular stages of this process.

The **backing-in approach** is a reactive process because companies evaluate the benefits program only when unexpected problems arise. Exhibit 1.5 illustrates how the backing-in approach unfolds, along with the representative time frames for particular stages of this process. For instance, Company A, a manufacturing company, built a reputation as a great place to work for many reasons, including competitive pay and benefits. Recently, excessive turnover has occurred among its assembly line employees who have taken jobs at another local manufacturing company. Company A's HR staff conducted exit interviews to identify possible causes of turnover. Most exit interviews revealed significant dissatisfaction with wage freezes, steep rises in employee contributions for health insurance coverage, and the termination of dental benefits. Company management instituted these changes in response to inflated raw material costs. Its goal was to maintain profits while keeping the prices for company products constant. Intense economic pressures necessitated cuts, and these cuts made it difficult for the company to reduce turnover.

INFORMATION USED IN STRATEGIC BENEFIT PLANNING

Companies review and interpret several types of information for strategic benefits planning. This process permits business professionals to understand their company's standing in the market. For example, companies with strong potential to increase sales levels tend to be in better standing than companies with weak potential to maintain or increase sales. Companies in strong standing should be able to devote more financial resources to fund benefits programs than companies in a weak standing. Two sources of information include the external market environment and the internal company environment. We comment on the types of information for both sources, followed by brief, illustrative cases.

External Environment

External environmental factors include:

- Industry prospects, economic conditions, and forecasts
- Employer costs for compensation and benefits
- Government regulation of employee benefits
- Changing demographics of the labor force

Industry Prospects, Economic Conditions, and Forecasts

The first two factors, industry prospects along with current and anticipated economic conditions, set the backdrop for establishing strategic benefits plans. Industry prospects and economic forecasts set the backdrop for strategic benefits planning because these factors are indicators of the future of companies. Forecasts indicating growth possibly call for strengthening discretionary benefits offerings and levels to help recruit and retain the most qualified employees. Pessimistic forecasts emphasize the need to save costs by shifting more of the responsibility on employees. For example, more and more companies require that employees share a greater percentage of the cost of health insurance. Also, there has been a shift away from employer-sponsored defined benefit retirement plans to employer-sponsored defined contribution plans, which makes it easier for companies to predict their costs for retirement plan benefits. Further, negative outlooks may lead companies to expand outplacement services (i.e., helping unwanted employees find jobs elsewhere) in anticipation of large-scale layoffs.

Employers will very likely continue to sponsor employee benefits despite economic conditions for two reasons. First, the Internal Revenue Code and the Employee Retirement Income Security Act create tax advantages for companies that offer qualified benefits plans (see Chapter 4). Employers may exclude limited contributions to these plans from taxable annual income, leading to reduced tax payments to the federal government. Second, generous benefits offerings facilitate a company's attempt to attract and retain the best qualified employees. Although employer-sponsored benefits costs are significant at any point in time, well-qualified workforces presumably create lucrative advantages for companies as evidenced by high-quality customer service, competent business functions such as innovative marketing, and research and development.

Virtually every industry faces challenges in the coming years as competition increases. Long-standing commercial airlines (such as Delta) continue to struggle to maintain financial solvency with increasing fuel costs, competition from lower-cost start-up airlines (such as Jet Blue), and fewer passengers because of the recent economic recession. U.S. automobile makers continue to struggle for sales and profits as Japanese automakers prevail with high-quality reasonably priced cars. The U.S. housing market has been tremendously weak as borrowers find it difficult to secure mortgage loans because criteria have become stricter after a spate of mortgage loan defaults that resulted from some mortgage lenders issuing mortgages to individuals who could not afford them. Related businesses such as home improvement have slowed down tremendously because home values have fallen, eliminating equity many individuals once possessed. While these prospects might have changed since the fourth edition of this employee benefits book was written, these examples nevertheless illustrate the kinds of challenges facing U.S. industries. We know that financial woes in the automobile industry and commercial airline industry have influenced employer-sponsored retirement practices, shutting down traditional pension plans in favor of defined contribution savings plans such as 401(k) plans (Chapter 5).

Employer Costs for Compensation and Benefits

The U.S. Bureau of Labor Statistics (BLS) regularly publishes current information about employer costs for compensation and benefits in the United States (and changes in these costs over time) on its Web site at www.bls.gov. Benefits professionals may use these data to benchmark current benefits costs against reported averages or as a starting point for budget planning. The following paragraphs are excerpted from a BLS news release, based on December 2008 data.

> Employer costs for employee compensation for civilian workers averaged $29.18 per hour worked in December 2008, the U.S. Department of Labor's Bureau of Labor Statistics reported today. Wages and salaries, which averaged $20.37, accounted for 69.8 percent of these costs, while benefits, which averaged $8.81, accounted for the remaining 30.2 percent. Employer costs for legally required benefits averaged $2.27, or 7.8 percent of total compensation per hour worked in December 2008. Legally required benefits—which include Social Security, Medicare, federal and state unemployment insurance, and workers' compensation—is only one of several benefit categories included in Employer Costs for Employee Compensation, along with wages and salaries. Employer Costs for Employee Compensation is a product of the National Compensation Survey, which measures employer costs for wages and salaries, and employee benefits for nonfarm private and state and local government workers. Employer costs for insurance benefits—life, health, and disability—averaged $2.45 per hour (8.4 percent of total compensation). Paid leave benefits (vacations, holidays, sick leave, and personal) averaged $2.06 (7.1 percent); retirement and savings averaged $1.29 (4.4 percent); and supplemental pay averaged 74 cents (2.5 percent) per hour worked.[13]

The BLS presents the data for average hourly pay and specific benefits for the entire civilian workforce, private industry, state and local governments, and by particular categories: industry, occupational group, region, establishment size, and worker characteristics such as bargaining status and full- or part-time status. Employer costs per hour worked are available for five major occupational groups. Employer compensation costs also varied by industry, region, and establishment size. Exhibit 1.6 shows employer costs for employee compensation in the private sector, based on major occupational group.

Overall, benefits accounted for approximately 30 percent of total compensation costs. At first glance, the cost of specific benefits does not appear to be particularly high. For example, service industry employers spent an average of $8.46 per employee per hour to provide discretionary and legally required benefits. However, aggregating these costs for a one-year period (per employee) paints a different picture. Assume a typical service employee works 1,850 hours per year (37 hours a week × 50 weeks a year). An employer spends $15,651 for each employee annually just for discretionary benefits (1,850 hours per year × $8.46 per employee per hour).

Government Regulation of Employee Benefits

Four broad forces contribute to an employer's choice of discretionary benefits and its ability to fund them. The first two, adequacy of legally required benefits and employee expectations, directly influence an employer's choice. The third, the cost of legally required benefits, influences a company's ability to fund discretionary benefits. The fourth entails a variety of economic considerations, which we will take up in Chapter 3.

First, the workers' plight during the industrialization of the U.S. economy and the Great Depression promoted the rise of many legally required benefits. Examples include workers' compensation and both retirement income and medical insurance under the Social Security Act (Chapter 8). Federal and state governments mandated modest benefits, which were never intended as the sole means of support. After all, the U.S. economy is based on free market principles, not on socialist principles more commonly found in many eastern European countries and in large segments of the People's Republic of China. In addition, the cost of living has risen more quickly than government benefits. Finally, legislators during the early part of the 20th century could not anticipate the very high costs of health care due, in large part, to advances in medicine and health care technology. The entire structure of the health care industry is fundamentally different now than in the 1930s. Since then, medical research and development has led to the ability to diagnose diseases in the early stages and so life expectancy of individuals born in recent years has increased notably. These changes make the funding formulas inadequate to meet today's realities.

Second, the federal government's imposition of wage freezes during World War II gave rise to many present-day discretionary benefits. Employers withdrew costly offerings after the government ended the wage freeze. The withdrawal of these benefits created discontent among employees: Many viewed employer-sponsored benefits as an entitlement. For instance, employees strongly reacted to the withdrawal

EXHIBIT 1.6 Employer Costs per Hour Worked for Employee Compensation and Costs as a Percent of Total Compensation: Civilian Workers, by Major Industry Group, December 2008

Source: U.S. Department of Labor (March 12, 2009). Employer Costs for Employee Compensation—December 2008 (USDL: 09-0247), online at www.bls.gov.

Compensation Component	All Workers*		Occupational Group										Industry Group			
			Management, Professional, and Related		Sales and Office		Service		Natural Resources, Construction, and Maintenance		Production, Transportation, and Material Moving		Goods-Producing†		Service-Providing‡	
	Cost	Percent	Cost	Percent	Cost	Percent	Cost	Percent	Cost	Percent	Cost	Percent	Cost	Percent	Cost	Percent
Total compensation	$29.18	100.0%	$48.49	100.0%	$21.76	100.0%	$15.79	100.0%	$30.97	100.0%	$23.33	100.0%	$32.15	100.0%	$28.60	100.0%
Wages and salaries	20.37	69.8	34.07	70.3	15.42	70.9	11.22	71.1	20.99	67.8	15.57	66.7	21.54	67.0	20.14	70.4
Total benefits	8.81	30.2	14.43	29.7	6.34	29.1	4.57	28.9	9.98	32.2	7.76	33.3	10.61	33.0	8.46	29.6
Paid leave	2.06	7.1	4.00	8.2	1.44	6.6	.89	5.6	1.62	5.2	1.41	6.0	2.06	6.4	2.06	7.2
Vacation	.98	3.4	1.84	3.8	.70	3.2	.42	2.7	.85	2.7	.72	3.1	1.10	3.4	.96	3.4
Holiday	.67	2.3	1.28	2.6	.47	2.2	.28	1.8	.53	1.7	.50	2.1	.74	2.3	.66	2.3
Sick	.32	1.1	.68	1.4	.21	.9	.14	.9	.17	.6	.16	.7	.18	.6	.34	1.2
Personal	.09	.3	.20	.4	.06	.3	.04	.2	.07	.2	.04	.2	.05	.1	.10	.3
Supplemental pay	.74	2.5	1.16	2.4	.50	2.3	.29	1.8	.98	3.2	.85	3.7	1.26	3.9	.64	2.2
Overtime and premium§	.26	.9	.16	.3	.15	.7	.17	1.1	.66	2.1	.52	2.2	.58	1.8	.20	.7
Shift differentials	.06	.2	.10	.2	.02	.1	.05	.3	.05	.2	.10	.4	.09	.3	.06	.2
Nonproduction bonuses	.42	1.4	.90	1.9	.33	1.5	.07	.5	.27	.9	.23	1.0	.59	1.8	.38	1.3
Insurance	2.45	8.4	3.65	7.5	1.98	9.1	1.35	8.5	2.68	8.7	2.40	10.3	2.92	9.1	2.36	8.3
Life	.05	.2	.10	.2	.03	.2	.02	.1	.06	.2	.04	.2	.07	.2	.05	.2
Health	2.31	7.9	3.39	7.0	1.88	8.7	1.30	8.2	2.51	8.1	2.26	9.7	2.72	8.4	2.23	7.8
Short-term disability	.05	.2	.07	.2	.03	.2	.02	.1	.08	.3	.06	.3	.09	.3	.04	.1
Long-term disability	.04	.1	.09	.2	.03	.1	¶	α	.03	.1	.04	.2	.04	.1	.04	.1
Retirement and savings	1.29	4.4	2.43	5.0	.72	3.3	.60	3.8	1.59	5.1	.90	3.9	1.48	4.6	1.25	4.4
Defined benefit	.78	2.7	1.47	3.0	.32	1.5	.46	2.9	1.10	3.5	.52	2.2	.84	2.6	.76	2.7
Defined contribution	.51	1.8	.96	2.0	.40	1.8	.14	.9	.49	1.6	.38	1.6	.64	2.0	.49	1.7

(continued)

EXHIBIT 1.6 Employer Costs per Hour Worked for Employee Compensation and Costs as a Percent of Total Compensation: Civilian Workers, by Major Industry Group, December 2008 *(Continued)*

Compensation Component	Occupational Group													Industry Group			
	All Workers*		Management, Professional, and Related		Sales and Office		Service		Natural Resources, Construction, and Maintenance		Production, Transportation, and Material Moving		Goods-Producing†		Service-Providing‡	
	Cost	Percent	Cost	Percent	Cost	Percent	Cost	Percent	Cost	Percent	Cost	Percent	Cost	Percent	Cost	Percent
Legally required benefits	2.27	7.8	3.18	6.6	1.70	7.8	1.44	9.1	3.10	10.0	2.19	9.4	2.89	9.0	2.15	7.5
Social Security and Medicare	1.65	5.7	2.65	5.5	1.29	5.9	.94	6.0	1.76	5.7	1.33	5.7	1.83	5.7	1.62	5.6
Social Security§	1.32	4.5	2.08	4.3	1.04	4.8	.76	4.8	1.42	4.6	1.07	4.6	1.47	4.6	1.29	4.5
Medicare	.33	1.1	.56	1.2	.25	1.2	.19	1.2	.34	1.1	.26	1.1	.36	1.1	.33	1.2
Federal unemployment insurance	.03	.1	.02	α	.03	.1	.03	.2	.03	.1	.03	.1	.03	.1	.03	.1
State unemployment insurance	.14	.5	.13	.3	.13	.6	.11	.7	.18	.6	.16	.7	.20	.6	.12	.4
Workers' compensation	.45	1.6	.38	.8	.25	1.2	.35	2.2	1.14	3.7	.67	2.9	.84	2.6	.38	1.3

*Includes workers in the private nonfarm economy, excluding households and the public sector, excluding the federal government.

†Includes mining, construction, and manufacturing. The agriculture, forestry, farming, and hunting sector is excluded.

‡Includes utilities; wholesale trade; retail trade; transportation and warehousing; information; finance and insurance; real estate and rental and leasing; professional and technical services; management of companies and enterprises; administrative and waste services; educational services; health care and social assistance; arts, entertainment and recreation; accommodation and food services; other services, except public administration; and public administration.

§Includes premium pay for work in addition to the regular work schedule (such as overtime, weekends, and holidays).

¶Cost per hour worked is $0.01 or less.

αLess than .05 percent.

βComprises the Old-Age, Survivors, and Disability Insurance (OASDI) program.

of medical insurance. Legal battles followed based on the claims of employees that health protection was a fundamental right. Health insurance benefits subsequently became a mandatory subject of collective bargaining in union settings.

Third, the federal government requires companies to support legally required benefits. A variety of laws requires employer contributions with payroll taxes. For example, the **Federal Insurance Contributions Act (FICA)**[14] helps support the Social Security Old-Age, Survivor, and Disability Insurance program (OASDI). Unemployment insurance benefits are financed by federal and, sometimes, state taxes levied on employers. A federal tax is levied on employers under the **Federal Unemployment Tax Act (FUTA).**[15] We discuss both laws more fully in Chapter 8. Of course, limited financial resources necessarily force employers to reduce the number and level of discretionary benefits. For example, legally required benefits in private industry equaled more than 30 percent of total benefits expenditures.

Changing Demographics of the Labor Force

According to the Bureau of Labor Statistics, labor force diversity will continue to increase based on gender, age, race, and ethnicity. An employer-sponsored benefits program is most effective when the workforce is relatively similar in terms of needs and preferences. For example, let's assume a company's workforce has 60 percent women and 40 percent men. Most of the women are of child-bearing age and most of the men range in age between their 50s and 60s. On the surface, one could say that this workforce is not very similar in terms of needs and preferences for benefits because its composition varies considerably by gender and age. Below the surface, one could reasonably conclude that there will be substantial differences in the needs and preferences for benefits. Chances are that most of the women may place a high value on day care benefits while most of the men will not have a need for such benefits because their children are likely to be near or at adulthood.

Employees are more likely to endorse employer-sponsored benefits as long as these benefits fulfill their needs and preferences. Also, employees should believe that contributions to receive benefits are determined fairly. Workforce diversity will challenge a company's quest to establish benefits that satisfy the needs and preferences of workers. For example, the younger segment of the workforce may benefit from family assistance programs and educational assistance programs while the older segments of the workforce rely on generous health insurance benefits and pension plans that support progressive retirement income streams. Health insurance benefits may be redundant for some dual-income families. One spouse or partner will not elect health insurance benefits because he or she already receives coverage as a family member under the spouse's plan. As differences in employee needs and desire for benefits become apparent to workforce members, some employees will likely protest benefits they believe disproportionately suit co-workers. Certainly, differences in employee preferences and needs based on life stage and life circumstances call for flexible benefits offerings, which we discuss shortly.

Internal Environment

Internal environmental factors include workforce demographics and collective bargaining agreements.

EXHIBIT 1.7
Likely
Preferred
Benefits
According to
Demographics
and Life
Events

Demographics	Life Events Benefits
Unmarried male and female employees (uncoupled employees)	Physical fitness programs Generous vacation allowances
Employees with dependent elderly parents or relatives	Elder care benefits Flexible work schedules
Married male and female employees	Flexible work schedules
Employees with children, male or female, coupled or uncoupled	Day care assistance Life insurance Health insurance with dependent coverage Education benefits for children
Older workers (nearing retirement)	Retirement plans with accelerated benefits accumulation Health insurance coverage with prescription drug benefits Generous sick-leave allowances Disability insurance Retiree health care benefits

Workforce Demographics

The workforce characteristics of companies usually represent the characteristics of the broad labor force. Over time, company workforces have become more demographically diverse as labor force diversity has increased. Not surprisingly, workforce diversity has created challenges for companies establishing benefits programs. Demographic characteristics to a large extent symbolize employee needs and preferences, often associated with life events. Exhibit 1.7 shows typical benefits preferred by employees, indicating demographic characteristics and probable life events.

Should companies presume needs and preferences? Probably not. Benefits professionals may use surveys once every year or two to collect information about employee demographics, needs, preferences, recent or anticipated life changes, and the extent to which they find particular benefits useful. Statistical analyses will show whether there is an association among these factors. Benefits professionals may compare current offerings with survey results. Over time, they can check whether changes in age, family status, needs, and preferences influence employees' views of benefits. In Chapter 11, we will highlight a critical type of demographic diversity—age or generational diversity—that has already begun to create challenges for employee benefits design given the different needs and preferences for benefits based on generational affiliation.

Collective Bargaining Agreements

Collective bargaining agreements specify terms of employment, including pay, benefits, and working conditions. These agreements arise out of negotiations between management and labor unions that represent some or all employees in the company. As we discuss in Chapter 4, the National Labor Relations Act of

1935 established that both labor unions and employers possess a duty to bargain with the other party over terms of employment. Also, this act sets forth mandatory subjects of bargaining in the benefits area, including pension plans, health insurance, and paid time-off. Over the years, unions have successfully negotiated generous benefits for employees. Private sector employers with unionized workforces spend more money on benefits per hour worked than do their nonunion counterparts.

PLAN FOR THE BOOK

The key objective of this book is to assist college-level students, HR practitioners, and employees at-large to become well educated about the main features of employee benefits programs in U.S. companies. It is also designed to inform you about important issues surrounding benefits. As a primer, this book will not contain exhaustive details regarding every law, regulation, or company practice pertaining to employee benefits. But this book will provide a solid foundation for learning more about employee benefits issues, and the design and administration of effective benefits programs. It should enable you to possess an informed frame of reference for interactions with tax and legal experts.

Key Terms

employee benefits, 5
protection programs, 5
paid time-off, 5
accommodation and enhancement benefits, 6
total compensation, 6
base pay, 7
cost-of-living adjustments (COLAs), 7
seniority pay, 8
merit pay, 8
incentive pay, 8
person-focused pay, 8
Social Security Act of 1935, 9
Old-Age, Survivor, and Disability Insurance (OASDI), 9
Medicare, 10
state compulsory disability laws, 10
workers' compensation, 10
Family and Medical Leave Act (FMLA), 10

life insurance, 11
retirement plans, 11
defined contribution plan, 11
defined benefit plan, 11
health protection programs, 12
wellness programs, 12
health insurance, 12
fee-for-service plans, 12
managed care plans, 12
point-of-service plans, 12
consumer-driven health care, 12
dental insurance, 12
vision insurance, 12
prescription drug plans, 12
mental health and substance abuse plans, 12
maximum benefit limits, 13
noncontributory financing, 13
contributory financing, 13

employee-financed benefits, 13
flexible benefits, 14
cafeteria plans, 14
welfare practices, 14
strategic planning, 17
tactical decisions, 17
competitive strategy, 17
human resource strategies, 18
total compensation strategies, 18
benefits strategies, 19
strategic benefit plans, 19
top-down approach, 19
backing-in approach, 21
Federal Insurance Contributions Act (FICA), 27
Federal Unemployment Tax Act (FUTA), 27
collective bargaining agreements, 28

Discussion Questions

1. Describe how employee benefits fit into the total compensation function.

2. Offer some suggestions for how companies might lessen the entitlement mentality among employees toward employee benefits.

3. Companies possess limited budgets to fund employee benefits. From an employee's perspective, which employee benefits practices should be funded? Which are easily dispensable? Now respond to these questions as a company representative. Explain your answers.

4. Describe the differences between strategic benefits plans and benefits tactics. Should strategic benefits plans be developed before setting benefits tactics? Explain your answer.

5. Consider the varieties of internal and external information companies consider when planning the benefits program. Which piece of information do you believe is most important to this planning process? Least important? Explain your answers.

Endnotes

1. U.S. Bureau of Labor Statistics. 2008. Human Resources, Training, and Labor Relations Managers and Specialists. *Occupational Outlook Handbook, 2008–2009 Edition.* Online at www.bls.gov/oco/home.htm. Accessed: April 18, 2009.

2. F. R. Dulles and M. Dubofsky. 1993. *Labor in America: A History.* Arlington Heights, IL: Harlan Davidson.

3. U.S. Bureau of Labor Statistics. 1919. Welfare Work for Employees in Industrial Establishments in the United States. *Bulletin #250:* 119–23.

4. U.S. Department of Labor. August 2008. *Employee Benefits in the United States, March 2008 (08-1716).* Accessed: April 18, 2009.

5. F. R. Dulles and M. Dubofsky. 1984. *Labor in America: A History,* 6th ed., 1999. Arlington Heights, IL: Harlan Davidson.

6. Bristol-Myers Squibb's statement on workforce diversity. 2009. Online at www.bms.com/static/diversity/data/pres.pdf. Accessed April 18, 2009.

7. ExxonMobil's competitive strategy statement. 2009. Online at www.exxonmobil.com. Accessed April 18, 2009.

8. ExxonMobil's careers statement. 2009. Online at www.exxonmobil.com. Accessed April 18, 2009.

9. V. S. Barocas. 1992. *Strategic Benefit Planning: Managing Benefits in a Changing Business Environment.* Report Number 1012. New York: The Conference Board.

10. ExxonMobil's compensation and benefits strategy statement. Online at www.exxonmobil.com. Accessed April 18, 2009.

11. Description of some ExxonMobil benefits tactics. Online at www.exxonmobil.com. Accessed April 18, 2009.

12. Barocas, *Strategic Benefit Planning.*

13. U.S. Department of Labor. March 12, 2009. Employer Costs for Employee Compensation–December 2008. USDL: 09-0247. Online at www.bls.gov. Accessed April 18, 2009.

14. 26 U.S.C. §§3101–3125.

15. I.R.C. §3121(d); Treas. Reg. §§31.3121(d)-2; 31.3121(d)-1.

Chapter **Two**

The Psychology of Employee Benefits*

Learning Objectives

In this chapter you will gain an understanding about:

1. The employment relationship as an exchange relationship and the psychology behind why firms provide employee benefits.

2. Employee benefits as part of the psychological contract and how some employee expectations about benefits might be formed.

3. How violations by the organization of employees' expectations can lead to perceptions of injustice.

4. How employee benefits can be used by organizations as tools for generating perceptions of fairness and organizational support and lead to organizational citizenship behaviors.

* This chapter was prepared by Professor Niti Pandey, Krannert School of Management, Purdue University, and edited for this edition by Joseph Martocchio.

After the collapse of Digital Equipment Corp. cost him a 16-year career, Larry Millette started over, taking an entry-level factory job at the IBM plant in his Vermont village. The pay wasn't great. But to Millette, then in his late 40s, IBM offered something more valuable: a generous pension. By working another 15 years or so, then cobbling together his IBM and Digital pensions, Millette figured he could yet enjoy a decent retirement. But Millette's hopes have vanished in recent years as IBM all but abandoned the pension first promised to him. Today, after 11 years of 12-hour shifts, Millette has just $30,000 in his IBM pension account. He also has a new retirement strategy: "Work until I can't work anymore." Millette, now 59, is among hundreds of thousands of workers whose dreams of long, comfortable retirements are getting upended as US corporations shed both the costs and responsibilities of traditional pensions. Faced with intense competition in a global economy, and huge obligations as baby boomers retire, many of the nation's biggest companies are rewriting the social contract that for 60 or more years has bound them to workers.

The Boston Globe

September 17, 2006

The opening example illustrates not only the economic challenges, but also the psychological basis of employee benefits practices. Millette worked for IBM for 15 years, demonstrating loyalty and commitment. In exchange, he held a certain expectation of his employer, that of a generous pension. While IBM expected Millette to work hard and be a committed employee, IBM's inability to fulfill Millette's expectation is likely to have an impact on his performance, motivation, and commitment.

Companies take economic matters into account when making decisions about employee benefits practices, and we will address many of these considerations in Chapter 3. However, these employer practices also have a psychological basis in terms of how employees view these practices and react to them. In Chapter 1 we provided an overview of the origins and types of employee benefits practices. In this chapter we will look at the psychological basis of employee benefits.

The purpose of this chapter is to gain an understanding of employee benefits from the employees' perspective and to understand how employee benefits influence important employee attitudes such as commitment, motivation, and satisfaction. By understanding the psychological basis of employee benefits, employers can understand how employee benefits influence the attitudes and performance of their employees. Doing so will be useful because it will help employers to develop and maintain an effective benefits program aimed at maintaining a satisfied, committed, and productive workforce.

EMPLOYMENT RELATIONSHIP AS SOCIAL EXCHANGE

Most voluntary human behavior is driven, in part, by some expectation of outcomes. Work behavior is no exception. In fact, work behaviors are some of the most deliberated and goal-directed behaviors. In the most general terms, the employment relationship consists of clusters of human resource practices offered to a group of employees along with the resulting employee contributions to the employer or company.[1]

The basis for understanding the employment relationship lies in the concept of **social exchange**—the most basic concept explaining social behavior. All social behavior can be seen as "an exchange of activity (*work effort*), tangible (*visible performance*) or intangible (*motivation and commitment*), and more or less rewarding or costly (*pay and benefits*), between at least two persons (*employee and employer*)."[*2] Thus, social exchange in the employer–employee relationship is one where the employer offers inducements (e.g., wages, employee benefits) in return for employee contributions (e.g., performance, commitment).[3]

How Employee Benefits Constitute Social Exchange

For companies, employee benefits not only offer cost advantages and tax incentives, but also act as a recruitment tool for attracting and retaining desired employees. Employee benefits provide employees with economic and income security and personal and family welfare. People choose to work in exchange for remuneration. While wages or salary act as basic remuneration, employee benefits act as remuneration for the welfare of employees and fulfill such needs as health care, dependent care, retirement planning, vacations, and education. As such, in exchange they elicit increased motivation and commitment from employees toward the company and its goals.

The employment relationship can be said to constitute both economic exchange and social exchange.[4] **Economic exchange,** as with wages and salary, is one where the nature of the exchange has been specified at the time of employment. (Of course, economic exchange can also be renegotiated at any time during employment, such as yearly pay raises). Explicit company policies and procedures help to ensure that each party (i.e., the employer and the employee) fulfills the obligations in the exchange relationship. In other words, in exchange for continued employments and wages, employees are obligated to work for the employer. Certain employee benefits can fall under the category of economic exchange. For example, health insurance can be viewed in monetary terms, since it costs

---

*All words in italics in this quote are illustrative examples added for relevance to the employment relationship and employee benefits.

employers to pay for employees to have health insurance and is usually a part of the explicit agreement at the time of employment.

Social exchange tends to evolve over the employment period and is not necessarily established at the time of employment. The nature of the social exchange is left to the discretion of the employer and employee. As employees become aware of policies or use various employer practices over the period of their employment, they reciprocate with increased or decreased job effort and commitment. Employee benefits practices are numerous and versatile, as indicated by the range and variety of practices presented in Chapter 1. Employees' needs change over the duration of their employment with a company. This change may be in terms of personal career needs or self and family health and welfare needs. Different employee benefits are likely to be relevant to employees at different circumstances and stages of their life and career. If an employer can provide an employee with benefits suitable to the employee's evolving needs, the employee is likely to reciprocate with increased work effort and commitment. Hence, employee benefits are an especially relevant component of the social exchange between the employer and employee.

Workforce Changes and the Employment Relationship

To understand the importance of employee benefits for both employees and employers, it is important to understand the dynamic nature of the employment relationship. The nature of the employment relationship, especially in developed economies, has undergone several changes over the past few decades. Jobs are no longer characterized by traditional job security, strong loyalty to the organization, or the patriarchal role of the organization in the life of the employee. Instead, work arrangements and careers have become more flexible. There has been an increase in part-time and contingent workers. Regular layoffs have been taking place, especially in certain industries such as auto manufacturing.

To remain competitive, companies have started shifting the costs of employee benefits to their employees and retirees. A recent example of such a change in the employment relationship is the deal between GM and the United Auto Workers (UAW) labor union set in 2007.[5] This agreement created a UAW-run health care trust known as a Voluntary Employee Benefit Association (VEBA). GM agreed to transfer about 70 percent of its $55 billion (for the period of 80 years) employee and retiree health care debt to the trust and transferred the responsibility of administering retiree health care to the union. This allowed GM to remove a substantial amount of debt to become competitive again. The VEBA was described as insurance against losing retiree health care benefits should the automaker file for bankruptcy. GM is heavily embroiled in the economic crisis that began in the fall of 2008. Since GM's payments to the VEBA were to be made over a period of many years, its current financial direness is likely to affect the agreement made in 2007 with the UAW. Thus, the employment relationship is constantly changing and being defined by factors external to the company. In fact, the economic crises in 2008 and 2009 have depleted GM's cash resources, raising questions about whether it will be able to honor this agreement. Events at GM were still unfolding at the time this book went to press.

TABLE 2.1
Civilian Labor
Force by Age,
Gender, Race,
and Hispanic
Origin for
1984, 1994,
2004, and
Projected to
2014

Source: M. Toosi,
2005. "Labor Force
Projections to 2014:
Retiring Boomers,"
*Monthly Labor
Review,* pp. 25–44.

	1984	1994	2004	2014
Age 16–24 years	23,989	21,612	22,268	22,158
Age 25–54 years	74,661	93,898	102,122	105,627
Age 55 and older	14,894	15,546	23,011	34,315
Men	63,835	70,817	78,980	86,194
Women	49,709	60,239	68,421	75,906
White	98,492	111,082	121,086	129,936
Black	12,033	14,502	16,638	19,433
Asian	3,019	5,472	6,271	8,304
Hispanic origin	7,451	11,975	19,272	25,760
All other groups	—	—	3,406	4,427

Apart from economic and market challenges, the workforce in America and other developed economies is becoming increasingly diverse. Diversity in the workforce is stemming from an aging population[6] poised on the brink of retirement,[7] increased labor force participation by those over the age of 60,[8] decreasing age cohorts,[9] an increase in the proportion of racial and ethnic minorities and immigrants,[10] and an increase in single-person households.[11] Some of these trends and projections for the future are presented in Table 2.1.

Earlier, the design of compensation and benefits packages had assumed similarity of attitudes, needs, and expectations. The design of benefits practices had been premised on a white, married male workforce, typically from a single-earner household. The changing demographics, as presented in Table 2.1, indicate that companies can no longer afford to do so. Earlier employee benefits were also seen as entitlements by employees and employers. However, as the GM example suggests, companies today are being forced to shift costs to employees. Thus, two strong contingencies are shaping the employment relationship in terms of employee benefits today. The first is the economic challenges faced by the company. The second is the changing composition of the workforce. Both of these will determine the emerging role of employee benefits practices in the social exchange relationship between employers and employees.

So far in this chapter, we have examined the basic concepts surrounding economic and social exchange in the employment relationship. We have examined how employee benefits practices are a part of the social exchange relationship. And we have examined how the employment relationship (and employee benefits practices) is constrained by economic and workforce characteristics.

Companies today invest a lot in employee benefits practices to attract diverse employees. Thus, any measure of success that employee benefits would have in ensuring employee satisfaction, performance, and commitment would depend on employee attitudes toward benefits practices. This makes it important to understand the psychology of employee benefits. Next, we will examine some well-established psychological concepts that are relevant for explaining the importance, role, and impact of employee benefits for employees and employers.

PSYCHOLOGICAL CONTRACTS

Psychological contracts are an articulation of the exchange relationship between the employer and the employee. A psychological contract has been defined as an employee's subjective perceptions of the relationship of mutual obligations with the employer and company.[12] Employee benefits can be a part of the psychological contract employees hold about the employer's obligations to them in exchange for their work efforts. (Similarly, employers can expect employees to work and be committed to the company in exchange for the benefits they provide.)

Psychological contracts implicitly establish terms of employment. This is in contrast to more explicit economic exchange agreements such as wage or salary levels. Thus, as an example, company policies might imply that an employee will be eligible for educational assistance after five years of continuous employment and satisfactory levels of performance. An employee who is interested in making use of this benefit would reciprocate by remaining with the company and working hard. Thus, the employee's psychological contract with the company would include the employee's obligations (five years of hard work) and the employer's obligations (educational assistance). Recall the discussion earlier in the chapter about the evolving nature of social exchange. Psychological contracts are a part of the social exchange process in the employment relationship. Psychological contracts result in employees holding a range or continuum of expectations of the employer, ranging from pay and promotions to career development and family welfare.

The continuum of expectations that employees hold from an employer can be seen as having two poles: **transactional psychological contracts** and **relational psychological contracts.** Toward the transactional end of the continuum, employees' expectations of the employer are more economic and extrinsic in nature. Thus, employees' expectations of high pay and promotions or career advancement in exchange for hard work would represent transactional types of expectations in the psychological contract. On the other hand, toward the relational end, employees' expectations of the employer might be either economic or noneconomic, but are also emotional, subjective, and intrinsic in nature. Thus, employees' expectations of job security in exchange for loyalty to the employer would represent relational types of expectations in the psychological contract.

Psychological contracts that are transactional in nature can be understood with an example of short-term employment. An independent contractor or consultant hired by a firm is more likely to have transactional expectations of the hiring firm. The independent consultants or contractors would expect the firm to provide good pay as well as the opportunity to build their marketability by adding the firm to their client portfolio. Once the project or assignment for which the independent contractor was hired is completed, the exchange relationship with the firm might end. Relational expectations can be understood by looking at the employee–employer relationship. Employees hired by a company or firm with the understanding of full-time employment are more likely to hold both transactional and relational expectations of their employer. For instance, not only will such employees expect pay, promotion, and career advancement in exchange for work efforts, they will also expect job security, recognition, and support in exchange for

TABLE 2.2
Psychological
Contract
Continuum

Source: Rousseau
1990.

	Transactional Contract	Relational Contract
Focus	Economic, extrinsic	Economic and noneconomic, socioemotional, intrinsic
Time frame	Close-ended, specific	Open-ended, indefinite
Stability	Static	Dynamic
Scope	Narrow	Pervasive
Tangibility	Public, observable	Subjective, understood

commitment and loyalty to the employer. The main features of the continuum of expectations in psychological contracts can be summarized in Table 2.2.

Employee benefits practices can be seen to fulfill both transactional and relational expectations of employees. Some employee benefits might fulfill more transactional expectations. For example, as suggested earlier, American employees might expect employers to provide health insurance in addition to wages. There might also be legally required benefits (as we briefly discussed in Chapter 1) that the employer would be required to provide to employees. Thus, health insurance and other legally required benefits would form a part of employees' transactional expectations of the employer. Employee benefits might also fulfill employees' relational expectations. For instance, employee benefits such as the paid time-off and accommodation and enhancement benefits examined in Chapter 1 might help fulfill employees' relational expectations. An employee might expect paid vacation for completing a certain length of continuous employment or might start expecting family welfare practices provided to employees who have been with the firm for more than one year.

Additionally, some employee benefits might fulfill both transactional and relational expectations of employees. Retirement plans would be a good example of employee benefits that fulfill both transactional and relational expectations. For instance, employees might not only expect an employer to enroll them in a retirement plan when they are hired but also to make increasingly larger contributions as they stay committed and loyal to the company. This would increase their sense of security from the employment relationship. Similarly, educational assistance benefits aimed at rewarding continued employment as well as career development would help fulfill both transactional and relational expectations. Exhibit 2.1

EXHIBIT 2.1
Transactional–
Relational
Continuum of
Employee
Expectations
(Employee
Benefits as
Examples)

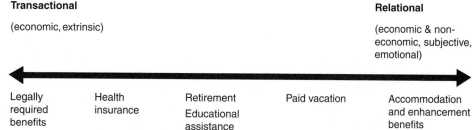

presents the transactional–relational continuum of employee expectations in the exchange relationship with some examples of employee benefits.

Psychological contracts develop and change over time. If employees have unrealistic expectations of the employer, they are likely to anticipate that the employer will fulfill obligations that may be beyond the employer's scope. For instance, a sense of entitlement might lead employees to expect the company to provide them with certain employee benefits. However, because of rising costs and other constraints, the company might not be able to do so. The company may terminate its defined benefits retirement plan. Or the company might be compelled to change the employee benefits it offers. If it previously did not require employee contributions toward health care coverage, it may choose to do so to offset the rapidly rising costs of health insurance. In such instances, it becomes important that employees are apprised of the changed expectations in a realistic manner. If employee benefits are understood to be a part of employees' psychological contracts, then communication and education about the employee benefits practices of the company is critical in establishing reasonable employee expectations. We will discuss approaches to benefits communications in Chapter 11.

Psychological Contract Development

Most psychological contracts take shape in the preemployment phase, when people seek information during recruitment and selection. Employees might seek information about both transactional and relational expectations of their potential employer. For instance, employees might address their transactional expectations by seeking information about a company's health insurance plan and promotion policies before accepting employment. And they might address their relational expectations by seeking more information about the company's employee assistance or family welfare policies. Ultimately, what the employee learns about the employer's benefits practices will form a part of the employee's expectations of this exchange relationship along this transactional–relational continuum.

Through direct inquiry, monitoring, and negotiation, employees may gather information from various sources in the company about these issues. It is expected that, over time, the expectations of the employee and employer will match.[13] Employees can form expectations that comprise their psychological contracts from two sources: their interactions with other members of the company and their perceptions of the company's culture.[14] If either of these sources of information is inaccurate, employees might form unrealistic expectations.

Psychological contracts are flexible in nature,[15] undergoing constant change based on the interactions employees have with the company and other employees. This flexibility allows employees to adapt to changes in the company's practices. If employees hold relatively stable expectations of employers, any changes in the policies and practices of the company will lead to the employee feeling betrayed unless changes entail offering more rather than less. However, if the employees have flexible expectations, they are more likely to change their psychological contracts to adjust for the changes the employer is compelled to make. The relevance of flexibility of psychological contracts can be driven home with a real-world example.

A 2008 *BusinessWeek* article provides an excellent example of how changes in employer practices might influence employee expectations about an employee benefits practice.[16] To control health care costs, in 2007 Toyota spent $9 million to build an on-site medical center at its truck factory in San Antonio, Texas. Now, for a $5 co-pay per doctor's office visit (as opposed to a $15 co-pay per visit off-site), employees can easily visit the clinic and receive health care. This move has allowed Toyota to slash its projected health insurance costs by millions. An added advantage has been increased productivity since employees don't have to leave the factory premises for medical care. While initially there was employee skepticism to a new practice, now the workers find little reason to venture outside the factory.

If the employees at the Toyota factory in San Antonio had flexible expectations of Toyota with regard to health care practices, they will adjust their expectations of the company to reflect the changes in Toyota's practices. Thus, regular renegotiation and evaluation of employer and employee expectations can help make employees' psychological contracts more explicit and changeable without fear of violation.[17]

Psychological Contract Violation

A violation of the psychological contract occurs when the employee perceives a discrepancy between the promises made by the employer and the actual fulfillment of the promises.[18] For example, in the United States, employers usually provide health insurance. A UC Berkeley Center for Labor Research and Education report states that between November 2007 (the designated start of the current economic recession) and February 2009, 3.7 million American adults are estimated to have lost their health insurance benefits.[19] Thus, employers' inability to continue to provide health insurance to employees will result in a violation of the employees' psychological contract. If a company withdraws or changes certain benefits, and those practices are an employee's psychological expectation of the company, then that employee will feel that the contract has been violated.

Violations of psychological contracts are different from unmet expectations. The responses to the violation of psychological contracts are likely to be more intense.[20] Violation of employees' expectations by the employer can cause feelings of betrayal and loss of trust. There may be two basic causes for violations of psychological contracts: reneging and incongruence.[21] When a company deliberately breaks a promise to employees, either willingly or because of circumstances, reneging is said to occur. Incongruence violations occur when the employee and the employer have different conceptualizations of the employment relationship. In other words, the employee might hold certain expectations of the employer. However, if the employee's actual experiences are different from these expectations, then the employee will feel that the psychological contract has been violated.[22] Violations of employees' psychological contracts can be quite expensive for companies as the following example illustrates.

A recent news report found that Wal-Mart's hourly employees were promised lunch and other breaks by the company, in addition to these breaks being required by law. When Wal-Mart reneged on these promises and forced employees to work unpaid off the clock, the aggrieved employees sued the company. The result was that, in late 2008, Wal-Mart had to agree to a settlement of $352 million for these violations.[23] Wal-Mart's employment practices have been much publicized. To create a more positive image with regard to its health and benefits practices, a few years ago the company announced a new health care plan and stated that it paid its employees above minimum wage.[24] Recent reports, however, suggest that Wal-Mart might not have delivered these promises in reality. If employees used the information publicized by the company to form expectations about the company and the reality they experienced was different, then they would experience contract violation. Some of the main effects of contract violation can be intentions to leave, actual turnover, low trust, low commitment, dissatisfaction, and bad citizenship.

Employee Benefits as Constituting Psychological Contracts

If employee benefits are a part of employees' psychological contract, then it is important for employers to ensure that employee expectations about benefits are clearly articulated and flexible. This will allow employers to avoid any psychological contract violations and the associated costs (lawsuits, lost trust, low morale, turnover, etc.). Sometimes employees may not be affected by minor contract violations. In the course of adjusting to the work environment, employees might also overlook certain violations. However, any serious violations can be avoided by clear communication and education about the nature and scope of the employee benefits practices offered by the company. For instance, a company with a large Spanish-speaking workforce might be well served by providing information about their benefits practices in both English and Spanish to ensure that all its employees fully understand its practices. And companies can hold training sessions where they explain the design, features, and use of the various benefits employees are eligible for. This will allow employees to form clear and accurate expectations about employee benefits as part of their psychological contracts.

Just as employees have expectations of the employer, the employer is also likely to have expectations of the employee. Incomplete effort, bad citizenship behavior, voluntary turnover, and low motivation can all be perceived by the organization as breaches of contract by the employee. The actions of the employee might also in some way contribute to the violations by the organization.[25] Thus, if the organization feels that employee performance is not what is expected, it can decide to withhold certain employee benefits, especially discretionary benefits. Once again, effective communication on the part of the organization could ensure that the psychological contract consists of explicit, rather than implicit, promises.[26]

Employee benefits have over the years become a growing source of employees' psychological contract violations.[27] As benefit costs increase, especially health care costs, an increasing number of companies are shifting benefit costs to the employees. As the employee cost burden associated with benefits increases, employee satisfaction decreases.[28] Additionally, how benefits are administered is also important. Employees will perceive a benefit as unfair if they are not receiving it according to either their needs or perceptions of entitlement.[29] Thus, expectations about employee cost burden, employee needs, and benefits design will all affect employee satisfaction. While some benefits may not be the most cost-effective way to meet employee needs, to avoid perceptions of psychological contract violations, companies will need to find lower-priced alternatives without sacrificing employee satisfaction.[30]

EMPLOYEE ATTITUDES AND EMPLOYEE BENEFITS

A company's policies and practices not only form a part of employees' psychological contract, they also influence employee attitudes. Perceptions of justice or fairness are especially important to understanding how pay and benefits practices influence employee attitudes. The employment relationship can be viewed as contract-based, that is, reflecting the mutual obligations of the employer and employee.

These contracts can be implicit, such as psychological contracts, and explicit, such as documented compensation packages. Employee benefits can be a part of both, with some benefits likely to be more explicitly offered and others more implicitly available. Congruence between employees' and the employer's expectations will lead to a greater fit between the employee and the employer as well as a sense of fairness. Violations of contracts will lead to perceptions of injustice.

Justice and Perceived Organizational Support

The concept of justice is concerned with the distribution of conditions and goods that affect an individual's well-being. In a work setting, the distribution of rewards (such as pay and benefits), information, and other resources will all lead to perceptions of justice. Perceptions of justice may be based on the rules by which distributions are made, the way rules are implemented, or the way decisions are made. The basis on which employees are eligible for benefits, the value of those benefits, how the benefits are administered, and employer decisions about which benefits to offer to employees would all influence employees' justice perceptions.

There are four types of justice perceptions. **Distributive justice** is perceived fairness about how rewards are distributed; **procedural justice** is the perceived fairness of processes; **informational justice** is the fairness of the accounts given for certain procedures; and **interpersonal justice** is perceived fairness of the interpersonal treatment people receive from others.[31] Job satisfaction, organizational commitment, evaluation of authority, organizational citizenship behavior, withdrawal, and performance are all affected by employees' perceptions of justice along these dimensions.[32]

Distributive justice is employees' perceptions of fairness of the outcomes they receive.[33] Where employee benefits are concerned, employees will form perceptions of fairness based on the benefits they are eligible for. If employees believe that the employer should provide them with certain benefits in exchange for their work efforts, and the employer fails to do so, then employees will conclude that the employer is being unfair. As a result, they might withhold effort and lower their commitment to the employer.

Procedural justice deals with employees' perceptions of fairness of the process by which decisions are made and includes the extent to which employees can participate in the process as well as the rules followed.[34] Thus, for example, by establishing rules for eligibility and contributions to retirement plans, employers can ensure procedural justice perceptions. Additionally, allowing employees to have a voice in the use of such benefits as self-development and education can also enhance their perceptions of procedural fairness.

Interpersonal justice is the perception of the degree to which the employer demonstrates concern and social sensitivity toward employees.[35] Thus, to illustrate, managers' awareness and concern for employee development and needs and recommending employees to be eligible for relevant benefits is likely to lead to fairness perceptions about interpersonal justice.

Informational justice deals with perceptions about the quality of information used to explain organizational decision making.[36] Thus, if an employer decided to offer certain benefits or to change or withhold others, the degree to which accurate and timely information is provided to employees will influence their perceptions of informational justice. For example, recent reports suggest that to save costs, some employers are now suspending their matching of employees' 401(k) savings.[37] If companies decide to change their policies and don't inform and educate their employees about such decisions, they might be perceived by employees as being unfair.

Changes in salary over time can alter the fairness perceptions established at the time of hiring.[38] Fairness perceptions are also affected when employers make changes to their practices; however, these can be mitigated by effective communication.[39] While earlier human resource practices were standardized, today there has been a shift toward nonstandardized, idiosyncratic work arrangements.[40] This is largely driven by the increased competition to attract and retain top talent on the part of companies,[41] as well as increased expectations of involvement from employees.[42] Employee benefits can be a part of this new individualized employment relationship.

The increasing diversity of the workforce implies varying employee expectations of the employer. As employees become more in charge of their own career development and seek to achieve work–life balance, employee benefits practices such as educational assistance, employee development initiatives, and family-friendly policies can potentially become the basis for unique employment contracts.

In addition to perceptions of justice and fairness, employees can also form perceptions of organizational support based on the human resource practices they encounter. **Perceived organizational support** is an employee's perception of the degree to which the employer values the employee's contributions and well-being.[43] Organizational support can act as an implicit inducement offered to employees as part of the social exchange relationship.

Certain employee benefits practices can act to signal organizational support. Employee benefits that signal the organization's concern for the well-being of the employee, such as mental health benefits, wellness programs, smoking cessation programs, and stress management, as well as those aimed at recognizing the employees' contributions such as recognitions and rewards, will help in fostering perceptions of perceived organizational support.

Emotionally committed employees have increased performance, reduced absenteeism, and decreased likelihood of turnover. Employers can ensure commitment by showing support to employees in the form of pay and promotion, approval and respect, and other aids needed to be effective in the company.[44] Certain rewards and job conditions are more likely to lead to perceived organizational support, such as recognition, pay, promotions, job security, autonomy, and training.[45]

Those human resource practices that indicate investment in human capital and demonstrate recognition of employee contributions will certainly promote perceptions of organizational support.[46] For instance, educational assistance programs are an example of investment in human capital, and pay raises and promotions recognize employee contributions. Thus, these practices will lead to employees feeling supported by the company.

From a social exchange perspective, employees will value the employer's discretionary efforts more highly than those that are beyond the employer's control.[47] Thus, discretionary employee benefits, offered to employees at the employer's own choice, are more likely to generate perceptions of organizational support than legally required benefits. Additionally, those discretionary benefits that address most closely the employee's needs for well-being and development are more likely to elicit perceptions of organizational support. The importance of flexible benefits practices, suited to the diverse necessities of the changing workforce, can hence be understood in terms of critical employee attitudes such as perceptions of fairness and perceived organizational support.

Organizational Citizenship Behavior

Employees' discretionary behavior, not explicitly or directly recognized by the formal reward system of the employer, but in aggregate promoting organizational effectiveness, is termed **organizational citizenship behavior**.[48] Thus, behaviors such as helping other employees, looking out for the employer's interests, and going beyond job requirements to help achieve company goals are all examples of organizational citizenship behavior. Satisfied employees engage in good citizenship behavior. A company's employee benefits practices can influence employees' satisfaction.

Organizational citizenship behavior is discretionary—it is not enforceable but rather a matter of personal choice. Citizenship behaviors tend to go beyond the formal job requirements. Such behaviors are not easily governed by individual incentive schemes since they are often difficult to discern and measure.[49] For instance, an employee who is helping a co-worker to succeed without any motive of recognition or reward from the employer is exhibiting citizenship behavior. Organizational citizenship behavior is a deliberate attempt by the employee to maintain the balance in the social exchange between the employee and the employer and is directly intended to benefit the employer.[50] If employees perceive their employer as generous and fair, they will seek to reciprocate by showing good citizenship behavior (in addition to job performance and commitment).

Employees' perceptions of both distributive and procedural justice are likely to affect citizenship behavior. If employees perceive that the employer is unfair, they will withhold good citizenship behavior.[51] For instance, if an employer decides to stop offering flextime benefits to an employee, and the employee perceives this as unfair, the employee can decide to stop putting in extra hours of work that she was previously doing to finish a project faster. Employee benefits practices that lead to perceptions of injustice or feelings of contract violations might also lead not only to poor performance, reduced commitment, and increased likelihood of turnover, but also to a reduction in extra-role, prosocial behaviors to help the employer be effective.

As stated earlier, job satisfaction can lead to organizational citizenship behavior that has effects on job performance.[52] There could be two reasons why job satisfaction would lead to organizational citizenship behaviors. It could be because people tend to reciprocate those who benefit them. Hence, if satisfaction comes largely from work, then employees may reciprocate with helping behaviors in the workplace. Also, employees who are satisfied and experience positive mood states tend to engage in good citizenship behaviors.

The concept of organizational citizenship behavior is based in social exchange. As such, employee benefits can be seen as eliciting job satisfaction and citizenship behaviors. In exchange for generous benefits and human resource practices, employees can use good citizenship behaviors to reciprocate and signal commitment and loyalty to the employer. Thus, employee benefits are an important part of the social exchange process that characterizes the employment relationship. They can be an important component of employees' psychological contract with the employer.

How companies design, communicate, and implement employee benefits affects employees' perceptions of fairness and organizational support. As a result of these attitudes, employees will engage in related organizational outcomes such as job performance, commitment, and citizenship behavior. Thus, the role of employee benefits in eliciting organizational effectiveness is undeniable.

Summary

This chapter discusses the psychological basis of employee benefits practices from the point of view of employees. Employee benefits practices can fulfill employees' transactional and relational expectations of the employer and the employment exchange relationship. If employees view their employer's benefits program as fair and meeting their expectations, then those employees will be satisfied and productive. When employees are satisfied and happy with the way the employer is treating them, they will be committed to the employer and even engage in good citizenship behaviors. Hence, it is important for employers to understand employee perceptions and attitudes about employee benefits. This will allow employers to design and communicate a benefits program that can attract and retain productive and committed employees.

Key Terms

social exchange, *33*
economic exchange, *33*
psychological contracts, *36*
transactional
psychological contracts, *36*

relational psychological
contracts, *36*
distributive justice, *41*
procedural justice, *41*
informational justice, *41*

interpersonal justice, *41*
perceived organizational
support, *42*
organizational citizenship
behavior, *43*

Discussion Questions

1. Discuss the concept of social exchange as it relates to the employment relationship. How does this concept apply to employee benefits practices?

2. Discuss how changes in the demographic composition of the American workforce will affect the employment relationship from the employer's perspective. What possible impact will these changes have on employee benefits practices?

3. What are psychological contracts? Discuss the main features of psychological contracts and how they develop.

4. How do employee benefits form a part of employees' psychological contracts? Discuss how employees' psychological contracts might be violated and the consequences of these violations for employers.

5. Discuss the different types of justice perceptions employees hold about the employer and the firm. How do a firm's employee benefits practices contribute to employees' justice or fairness perceptions?

6. What is organizational citizenship behavior? Discuss some of the employer outcomes of organizational citizenship behavior. How can employers use employee benefits practices to encourage employee citizenship behaviors?

Endnotes

1. A. S. Tsui, J. L. Pearce, L. W. Porter, and J. P. Hite. 1995. "Choice of employee-organization relationship: Influence of external and internal organizational factors." In G. R. Ferris (ed.), *Research in Personnel and Human Resource Management,* vol. 13, Greenwich, CT: JAI Press, pp. 117–151.

2. G. C. Homans. 1961. *Social Behavior: Its Elementary Forms.* New York: Harcourt, Brace, & World, Inc.

3. J. G. March and H. A. Simon. 1993. *Organizations,* 2ed, Cambridge, MA: Blackwell,

4. P. Blau. 1964. *Exchange and Power in Social Life.* New York: Wiley.

5. www.nytimes.com/2007/09/27/business/27auto.html?scp=1&sq=GM%20UAW%20VEBA&st=cse.

6. C. E. Weller. 2004. "Retirement benefits: The increasingly diverse labor force," *Employee Benefits Journal,* vol. 29, pp. 16–21.

7. E. E. Gordon. 2005. "The 2010 meltdown: Where will we find workers?" *Employee Benefit News,* vol. 19, p. 9.

8. M. Gendell. 2008. "Older workers: Increasing their labor force participation and hours of work," *Monthly Labor Review,* January, pp. 41–54.

9. M. F. Riche. 2003. "The demographics of tomorrow's workplace." In O. S. Mitchell et al. (eds.), *Benefits for the Workplace of the Future.* Philadelphia, PA: University of Pennsylvania Press.

10. Ibid.

11. Ibid.

12. D. M. Rousseau. 1990. "New hire perceptions of their own and their employer's obligations: A study of psychological contracts," *Journal of Organizational Behavior,* vol. 11, pp. 389–400.

13. Ibid.

14. W. H. Turnley and D. C. Feldman. 1999. "The impact of psychological contract violations on exit, voice, loyalty, and neglect," *Human Relations,* vol. 52, pp. 895–922.

15. N. Anderson and R. Schalk. 1998. "The psychological contract in retrospect and prospect," *Journal of Organizational Behavior,* vol. 19, pp. 637–647.

16. www.businessweek.com/magazine/content/08_32/b4095000246100.htm.

17. H. D. C. Thomas and N. Anderson. 1998. "Changes in newcomers' psychological contracts during organizational socialization: A study of recruits entering the British army," *Journal of Organizational Behavior,* vol. 19, pp. 745–767.

18. N. Anderson and R. Schalk. 1998. "The psychological contract in retrospect and prospect," *Journal of Organizational Behavior,* vol. 19, pp. 637–647.

19. www.sfgate.com/cgi-bin/article.cgi?f=/c/a/2009/04/01/BUFL16QRAO.DTL.

20. S. L. Robinson and D. M. Rousseau. 1994. "Violating the psychological contract: Not the exception but the norm," *Journal of Organizational Behavior*, vol. 15, pp. 245–259.

21. W. H. Turnley and D. C. Feldman. 1999. "The impact of psychological contract violations on exit, voice, loyalty, and neglect," *Human Relations*, vol. 52, pp. 895–922.

22. J. S. Bunderson. 2001. "How work ideologies shape psychological contracts of professional employees: Doctors' responses to perceived breach," *Journal of Organizational Behavior*, vol. 22, pp. 717–741.

23. www.nytimes.com/2008/12/24/business/24walmart.html?hp.

24. www.washingtonpost.com/wp-dyn/content/article/2005/10/28/AR2005102802079 .html.

25. L. McFarlane Shore and L. E. Tetrick. 1994. "The psychological contract as an explanatory framework in the employment relationship." In C. L. Cooper and D. M. Rousseau (eds.), *Trends in Organizational Behavior*, vol. 1, New York: John Wiley and Sons.

26. D. E. Guest and N. Conway. 2002. "Communicating the psychological contract: An employer perspective," *Human Resource Management Journal*, vol. 12, pp. 22–38.

27. M. A. Lucero and R. E. Allen. 1994. "Employee benefits: A growing source of psychological contract violations," *Human Resource Management*, vol. 33, pp. 425–446.

28. G. F. Dreher, R. A. Ash, and R. D. Bretz. 1988. "Benefit coverage and employee cost: Critical factors in explaining compensation satisfaction," *Personnel Psychology*, vol. 41, pp. 237–254.

29. E. Kossek and V. Nichol. 1992. "The effects of on-site child care on employee attitudes and performance," *Personnel Psychology*, vol. 45, pp. 485–509.

30. M. A. Lucero and R. E. Allen. 1994. "Employee benefits: A growing source of psychological contract violations," *Human Resource Management*, vol. 33, pp. 425–446.

31. R. Cropanzano, Z. S. Byrne, D. R. Bobocel, and D. R. Rupp. 2001. "Moral virtues, fairness heuristics, social entities, and other denizens of organizational justice," *Journal of Vocational Behavior*, vol. 58, pp. 164–209.

32. J. A. Colquitt, D. E. Conlon, M. J. Wesson, C. O. Porter, and K. Y. Ng, "Justice at the millennium: A meta-analytic review of 25 years of organizational justice research," *Journal of Applied Psychology*, vol. 86, pp. 425–445.

33. J. Greenberg, M. Roberge, V. T. Ho, and D. M. Rousseau. 2004. "Fairness in idiosyncratic work arrangements: Justice as an I-Deal." In J. J. Martocchio (ed.), *Research in Personnel and Human Resource Management*, vol. 23, pp. 1–34.

34. Ibid.

35. Ibid.

36. Ibid.

37. www.businessweek.com/magazine/content/08_47/b4109032466871.htm.

38. Y. Cohen-Charash and P. E. Spector. 2001. "The role of justice in organizations: A meta-analysis," *Organizational Behavior and Human Decision Processes*, vol. 86, pp. 278–321.

39. C. Lee, K. S. Law, and P. Bobko. 1999. "The importance of justice perceptions on pay effectiveness," *Journal of Management*, vol. 25, pp. 851–873.

40. J. Greenberg, M. Roberge, V. T. Ho, and D. M. Rousseau. 2004. "Fairness in idiosyncratic work arrangements: Justice as an I-Deal." In J. J. Martocchio (ed.), *Research in Personnel and Human Resource Management*, vol. 23, pp. 1–34.

41. M. D. Lee, S. M. MacDermid, and M. L. Buck. 2000. "Organizational paradigms of reduced-load work: Accommodation, elaboration, and transformation," *Academy of Management Journal*, vol. 43, pp. 1211–1226.

42. J. W. Budd. 2004. *Employment with a Human Face: Balancing Equity, Efficiency, and Voice.* Ithaca, NY: ILR Press.

43. R. Eisenberger, R. Huntington, S. Hutchinson, and D. Sowa. 1986. "Perceived organizational support," *Journal of Applied Psychology,* vol. 71, pp. 500–507.

44. L. Rhoades and R. Eisenberger. 2002. "Perceived organizational support: A review of literature," *Journal of Applied Psychology,* vol. 87, pp. 698–714.

45. Ibid.

46. D. G. Allen, L. M. Shore, and R. W. Griffeth. 2003. "The role of perceived organizational support and supportive human resources practices in the turnover process," *Journal of Management,* vol. 29, pp. 99–118.

47. L. Rhoades and R. Eisenberger. 2002. "Perceived organizational support: A review of literature," *Journal of Applied Psychology,* vol. 87, pp. 698–714.

48. D. W. Organ. 1988. *Organizational Citizenship Behavior: The Good Soldier Syndrome.* Massachusetts: Lexington Books.

49. C. A. Smith, D. W. Organ, and J. P. Near. 1983. "Organizational citizenship behavior: Its nature and antecedents," *Journal of Applied Psychology,* vol. 68, pp. 653–663.

50. K. Lee and N. J. Allen. 2002. "Organizational citizenship behavior and workplace deviance: The role of affect and cognitions," *Journal of Applied Psychology,* vol. 87, pp. 131–142.

51. B. P. Niehoff and R. H. Moorman. 1993. "Justice as a mediator of the relationship between methods of monitoring and organizational citizenship behavior," *Academy of Management Journal,* vol. 36, pp. 527–556.

52. M. Schnake. 1991. "Organizational citizenship: A review, proposed model, and research agenda," *Human Relations,* vol. 44, pp. 735–759.

Chapter **Three**

The Economics of Employee Benefits*

Chapter Outline

Why Do Employers Offer Benefits?
Cost Advantage
Recruiting Certain Types of Workers
Tax Incentives

Who Pays for Benefits?

Two Extensions
Government Mandates
Differences in Benefit Cost
Increases across Groups of Workers

Summary

Learning Objectives

In this chapter, you will gather information about:

1. The economic rationales for employers to offer a mixture of cash and benefits in a compensation package.
2. Why insurance is less costly for larger groups.
3. How changes in benefit costs affect employer profits and the amount of cash wages employers are willing to pay.
4. How changes in the value that workers place on their benefits package influence their choice of job and acceptable salary range.
5. The effect of government-mandated benefits on wages and profits.

---

* This chapter was prepared by Professor Darren Lubotsky, Department of Economics and Institute of Labor and Industrial Relations, University of Illinois at Urbana-Champaign, and edited for this edition by Joseph Martocchio.

Driving to your first day of work this morning, you heard a radio talk show host introduce the topic for discussion: "Why companies sponsor employee benefits, particularly given the rapidly rising costs of health care insurance." One guest reported that many politicians and business professionals have argued that the cost of employee benefits could hurt the competitiveness of U.S. companies. Quite simply, money spent on your benefits could be used to increase research and development for better-quality products or services. A more obvious point, perhaps, is that cutting expenditures on benefits would translate into higher corporate profits. In other words, the guest argued that offering employee benefits may not be economical. But, another guest indicated that there is sound economic rationale for current employee benefits practices, and went on to explain that rationale using health insurance as an illustrative case.

If health insurance and other benefit costs really do harm U.S. businesses, why do so many firms offer these benefits? Why not pay workers a higher salary and let them buy insurance on their own? Do benefit costs, in fact, reduce the profits of U.S. firms? These are the topics to be explored in this chapter.

WHY DO EMPLOYERS OFFER BENEFITS?

Most employers compensate employees with some combination of cash plus benefits such as health insurance. This combination of cash plus benefits represents the extrinsic component of total compensation, as discussed in Chapter 1. At first glance, it might seem that employees and employers would both prefer a cash-only compensation package rather than a mixture of cash and benefits. After all, employees can use cash to buy health insurance, save for retirement, or buy any other goods or services they want. This freedom would allow employees who want a generous health plan to have it, while employees who prefer a cheaper health plan could spend less on health insurance and have more money available for other goods and services. Additionally, benefits are expensive and time-consuming for employers to administer. Year-to-year changes in the costs of health insurance make benefits planning particularly difficult. It would seem, therefore, that employers also might prefer to pay all employees in cash only. So what advantages are there to employers and employees from having benefits?

Before we answer this question, it is important to clarify that the question is not meant to ask whether an employer should pay, for example, a salary of $50,000 per year plus a health plan and a retirement plan, or whether it should pay $50,000 per year without the health and retirement plans. Clearly, if an employer could recruit and retain the same workforce with both pay packages, it would prefer not to offer the costly benefits. Instead, the question is whether an employer would want to reduce the amount of cash compensation and substitute the health and retirement plans. The relevant choice for the employer might be between paying $50,000 a year plus benefits versus paying $75,000 a year and providing no benefits. Or, the choice might be between paying $50,000 a year plus a generous and expensive health plan, or paying $60,000 a year plus a less generous and cheaper health plan.

An employer might choose to include benefits in their compensation package for three primary reasons:

- A cost advantage to the employer
- Recruitment of certain types of workers
- Tax incentives

Cost Advantage

The first reason an employer may want to provide a benefit is that the employer may be able to buy the product or service at a lower cost than employees would pay if they tried to buy it on their own. Health insurance is a perfect example: Employers can generally purchase health insurance for a substantially lower premium per enrollee than the amount employees would have to pay for identical coverage if they bought the insurance on their own. A particular insurance plan might cost $1,000 per employee when purchased by an employer that employs 500 workers, but cost $2,500 if purchased by a single individual. Employees are therefore better off getting the health plan through their employer and having their cash wages reduced by any amount less than $2,500. The employer is better off by providing the health insurance to its employees and reducing their wage by anything more than $1,000. Together, this means that both the employer and the employees will be better off if the compensation package includes the health plan and salaries are decreased by an amount between $1,000 and $2,500. When the employer can buy a benefit for a lower cost than the employee could buy it, the employer is essentially acting as a buying agent for the worker. Retirement annuities and disability and life insurance are other leading examples of benefits that tend to be cheaper when purchased as part of a large group.[†]

So why does health insurance become less expensive when the size of the insurance group increases? Many products are sold with quantity discounts. Is health insurance just another example? Actually, it isn't that simple. Three primary reasons explain why insurance costs tend to fall as the insured group—also known as the insurance pool—gets larger. First, as the group gets larger, insurance becomes less

---

[†]Retirement annuities are a series of monthly or annual payments to a retiree that begin at retirement and end when the retiree dies. Employers typically pay a fixed dollar amount to a financial or insurance company, who then pays the regular annuity payments to the retiree. The "cost" of the annuity is the rate at which the fixed dollar payment is translated into the stream of future regular payments. Retirement annuities are discussed in Chapter 5. Disability and life insurance are discussed in Chapter 7.

risky to provide. Second, insurance companies need to worry less about the phenomenon of high-risk individuals driving out low-risk individuals in large insurance groups in which all members are required to buy insurance. Third, as the group gets larger, fixed administrative costs can be spread out among more people. Let's discuss these factors in turn.

As the size of the insured group gets larger, it becomes much easier for the insurance company to predict the total medical expenses for the group. That means it is less risky to provide health insurance to a larger group than to a smaller group. For example, in 2006, average total medical expenditures were $4,078 per person and by age:

- $1,510 for children aged 5 to 17
- $2,703 for adults aged 18 to 44
- $5,455 for adults aged 45 to 64
- $9,080 for adults aged 65 and older

Medical expenses also tend to be higher for women than men, and higher for whites than for minority groups.[1] Medical expenses are also naturally higher for people who have experienced medical problems in the past. Insurance companies can use these and other data, in combination with information on the characteristics of the group to be insured, to come up with an estimate of the expected medical expenses that the group will generate over the upcoming year. In very large groups, total medical expenses are likely to be close to that predicted by the age, gender, and past medical history of the group. The number of people who have particularly bad luck and have larger-than-expected medical expenses is likely to be offset by a roughly equal number of people who have smaller-than-expected medical expenses. In a small group, by contrast, there is much less certainty that the number of people with bad luck will roughly offset the number of people with good luck. That is, it is much more difficult to predict the medical expenses a small group will experience in the future.

A different way to think about this is to note that if you flipped a standard U.S. quarter four times, you would expect to get two heads and two tails, but you would not be terribly surprised if you got three heads and one tail. By contrast, if you had the energy to flip the coin 1,000 times, you should be very suspicious about the authenticity of the coin if you ended up with 750 heads and 250 tails. The more times you flip a standard coin, the more likely it is that you'll receive roughly the same number of heads as tails. In the case of health insurance, the more people in the group, the more likely that total medical expenses will be close to that predicted by the characteristics of people in the group.

The fact that total medical expenses—and hence the amount that insurance companies have to pay out to medical care providers—are more predictable for larger groups of people means that insurance companies bear less risk when they insure these larger groups. They are therefore willing to provide the insurance at a lower cost to larger groups than to smaller groups. Smaller groups, by contrast, will tend to face higher insurance costs to compensate insurance companies for the added risk they bear. Similarly, an insurance policy that covers a single individual or family will tend to be more expensive than a similar policy that covers a small group of people. Because of the riskier nature of individual and small group policies, they are more likely to be subject to what is called **medical underwriting,** a process by which employees provide information on their past medical history in a questionnaire or physical examination. Insurers use this health information to exclude coverage or to tie premiums more closely to past medical history.

The bottom line is that employers can purchase group health insurance at a better rate than individuals could purchase the same policies on their own. This gives employers and employees an incentive to have a compensation package that includes group health insurance in lieu of some cash salary. It also means that this incentive is relatively larger in big employers than in small employers, which explains in part why small employers are less likely to offer health insurance to employees.

A second motivation for employer-provided insurance is to avoid an inherent problem in insurance markets that is referred to as **adverse selection.** This is the tendency of an insurance pool to disproportionately attract "bad risks" and discourage the participation of "good risks." Suppose a health insurance company operating in a particular city does market research and concludes that the average resident has medical expenses of $5,000 per year. On this basis, the insurance company offers residents a comprehensive health insurance policy with a premium of $5,500 per year. Which residents would choose to buy this plan?

Clearly, people who think they are relatively healthy and therefore unlikely to have anywhere close to $5,000 in expenses are not going to buy this health insurance plan. On the other hand, people who think they are more likely to have high expenses are likely to buy the plan. Thus, the average medical expenses of people who buy the plan will be larger than $5,000 since only people with relatively high medical expenses will purchase the plan. The insurance company has a risk pool composed mostly of "bad risks." The result is that the insurance company can no longer afford to offer this plan for $5,500 and will have to raise its premium. This will lead the insurance pool to become even more unbalanced as some of the healthier policyholders decide the policy is too expensive given their own expected medical costs.

Adverse selection in insurance markets stems from the fact that individuals know more about their own health status than does the insurance company. One solution to this problem is for the company to gather as much information as possible about each participant's risk profile and then offer the insurance at a lower price to healthier people and at a higher price to less healthy people. This is referred to as **experience rating** and is how most automobile insurance policies work. It is also how most individual, single-family, and small group health insurance policies work.

A different solution to the adverse selection problem is for a large group of people who come together for some other purpose to buy group insurance together, with the requirement that all group members must buy into the insurance pool. A group of people who come together to build and sell television sets, provide investment advice, or teach college students, for example, are unlikely to be composed of disproportionately good or bad risks. In any event, as long as everyone in the group is required to participate in the insurance pool, the insurance company can set the premium accordingly without fear that relatively good risks will drop out.

Avoiding the adverse selection problem is one reason why employment-based insurance is so popular, especially among large and medium-sized employers. It also helps us understand why employers provide a whole range of insurance products as part of a benefits package, including disability insurance, life insurance, and retirement annuities. Indeed, avoiding the adverse selection problem is one justification for various government-provided insurance programs, such as Social Security, Medicare, and workers' compensation programs.

Finally, administering an insurance policy involves a good deal of paperwork, claims processing, and other administrative functions. Many of these functions are not much more time-consuming and expensive to perform for a large group than for a smaller group, a process referred to as **economies of scale.** Because of this, as the group gets larger, the fixed costs of these administrative tasks can be shared among a larger number of people, thereby reducing the average cost per insured person.

Recruiting Certain Types of Workers

A second reason that employers may want to offer a compensation package that includes both cash and benefits is to aid in recruiting and retaining certain types of employees, particularly when the employer managers have a difficult time observing all relevant characteristics of potential employees. In management's perfect world, job applications would contain all relevant information about a potential worker, such as his or her future productivity, work habits, career plans, commitment to the employer, and commitment to undergoing future training. Unfortunately, many important characteristics are not observed, and managers may have a difficult time eliciting such information. By offering a compensation plan that includes both cash and benefits that are more highly valued by some applicants than by others, an employer may be able to get applicants to reveal some of these characteristics themselves.

For example, suppose the ideal candidate for a particular employer is a highly motivated recent college graduate who would like to work for a few years and then go to graduate school for an MBA. Looking at the job applications received by the employer, however, it is difficult to tell which potential employees actually fit this description. How should the employer go about selecting a candidate?

One strategy is the employer could simply ask each applicant whether or not they are highly motivated and would like to go on for an MBA. But talk is cheap, which makes this strategy problematic. All the applicants will likely say they fit this description if they think it will increase their chances of getting the job. Also, potential employees may not know for sure whether they will want to go on for an MBA or may not know what the employer defines as "highly motivated." The employer needs a way to separate those applicants who are truly motivated and interested in getting the degree from everyone else.

A second strategy is the employer could offer a pay package that includes a slightly reduced salary and also the promise to pay tuition in an MBA program. (In Chapter 10, we will discuss **tuition reimbursement benefits,** which fully or partially reimburse an employee for expenses incurred for education or training.) This package would be valued relatively more by the exact employees the employer wants to recruit. Potential employees who feel there is little chance they would seek an MBA would prefer to take a job with a higher salary without the promise of tuition assistance. Offering the tuition assistance in the compensation package would induce highly motivated potential employees to reveal valuable information about themselves to the employer.

Offering particular benefits in a compensation package could also have unintended consequences for the types of employees most attracted to the employer. For example, an employer that touted its generous benefits for mental health services or substance abuse treatments may feel that it is offering a progressive benefit package. But it may also find that the types of employees who are most likely to accept a position at the employer, or most likely to stay at the employer, are those suffering from these conditions. In some cases, this may not be the outcome employer managers intended.

Tax Incentives

A third reason that employers may want to offer benefits is that the U.S. federal tax code—the Internal Revenue Code (IRC)—provides financial incentives to do so. The most important tax provision is that many benefits are not taxed as income to the employee. Suppose an employee has a 25 percent marginal tax rate. If the employer increases her pay by $1,000 in cash, she must pay $250 of that to the government, leaving her with $750 in after-tax income. By contrast, if the employer gives her a benefit that costs $1,000, she receives the full benefit and does not incur any tax burden. A different way to see the effect of taxes on benefits provision is to suppose an employee wants to buy a health insurance policy that costs $1,000. If she were to buy the policy on her own, she would have to earn $1,333.33. Of this, she would pay 25 percent, or $333.33, in taxes to the government, which would leave her with $1,000 in after-tax income needed to purchase the insurance. She would be better off receiving the plan as part of her compensation package and having her salary reduced by any amount less than $1,333.33. If her employer could buy the same policy for $1,000, the employer would also be better off by including the insurance in the compensation package and reducing the employee's wage by any amount over $1,000. Within these stated limits, the employer and employee are both better off if the insurance plan is part of the compensation package and the salary is reduced by any amount between $1,000 and $1,333.33. Retirement plans are a second example of a benefit that is partly driven by generous tax treatment. More details about tax treatment of benefits are provided in Chapter 4 and in other chapters as appropriate.

All three of the preceding motivations presuppose that employees value a particular benefit and are willing to give up something to receive it. Two important consequences of this are, first, that employers need to figure out the cash value that employees place on a particular benefit and which types of employees value the benefit more than others. Second, if employees are willing to give up something to receive a particular benefit, then the cash component of wages and the types and amounts of benefits an employer offers will be inexorably linked. This link is the subject of the next part of this chapter.

Students usually give two other answers when asked why they think employers offer benefits. The first answer is that employers are just trying to match what every other employer is doing. This probably has a lot of truth to it: A lot of businesses do a lot of things simply because everyone else is doing it. Managers may not have the time, inclination, or expertise to investigate every alternative business practice, so why not cut some corners and follow the pack on compensation practices? This argument, though, doesn't really answer the question—it just leads us to ask, Why does every other employer offer benefits? If all employers continued to follow unprofitable compensation practices, presumably new employers would enter the market to take advantage of unrealized profit opportunities. Existing employers would either follow the lead of new, more profitable employers, or eventually find themselves out of business.

The second answer is that employer managers want their employees to be healthy, so they provide health insurance, or they want their employees to be well prepared for retirement, so they offer pension plans. It is clear that most employer managers do, in fact, want their employees to be healthy, but it is not obvious that this is why employers offer health insurance. First, is directly providing health insurance or a pension the most effective way for an employer to promote these goals? Second, why would employers choose to promote these goals in their compensation policy rather than promote other worthy goals?

WHO PAYS FOR BENEFITS?

One of the biggest misconceptions about employee benefits is that employers give them as "free add-ons" in a compensation package and that employees do not give up anything to get them. The truth is that in large part, employees pay for all of their benefits in the form of a lower cash wage or salary than they would have otherwise received. An important consequence of this is that when the cost of providing a benefit increases, it is employees who pay for the increase; employers' profits are generally not affected.[2]

The degree to which an increase in benefit costs is passed along to employees in the form of lower cash wages generally depends on four factors:

- The cash value employees place on the benefit.
- The degree to which employers will increase or decrease their hiring when the market compensation level decreases or increases, and the degree to which employees will change their desire to work when the market compensation package changes.
- Whether the benefit cost increases for all employers in a market or for a particular employer.
- Whether the hiring decisions of a particular employer affect the market compensation level.

Let's begin by more precisely defining the concept of the "value that employees place on the benefit." Suppose you've just accepted a new job and your employer offers you the choice of a $75,000 annual salary plus a comprehensive fee-for-service health plan, or a $90,000 salary and no health plan. Which compensation package would you choose? Both options probably would have some takers. Those who tend to use health services more frequently, who use more expensive health services, or who are more risk averse, will tend to place a relatively higher value on the health insurance plan, and are therefore more likely to forgo the extra $15,000 in salary. On the other hand, healthier people and those willing to bear more financial risk are more likely to choose the extra salary in lieu of the health insurance. Those with access to insurance through a spouse's employer might be more willing to take the higher salary. Finally, the choice naturally would also depend on the cost of health insurance purchased from an alternative source.

What if the choice was between a $75,000 salary plus the health plan, or a $100,000 salary and no health plan? Chances are that many people who would have opted for the health insurance in the first example would now choose the higher salary instead. That is, some people would rather have the health insurance than an extra $15,000 in cash, but would also rather have $25,000 in cash than the health insurance. Put differently, those who switched from the cash-only package to the health plan package value the health insurance at some amount between $15,000 and $25,000 per year.

Some people may be uncomfortable with the concept of placing a dollar value on health insurance or on any other product. Although we aren't always conscious of it, every time we buy a product or service, we are implicitly deciding that we value the product more than (or equal to) what the merchant is charging for it. Workers make choices about which job to accept, how many days or hours to work each week, and even whether to work at all, based in part on a comparison of the value of compensation packages and the value they place on their leisure time or time spent doing unpaid work at home.

The first lesson is the greater value employees place on a benefit, the larger reduction in cash wages they will accept if the benefit is introduced into a compensation package. Suppose an employer currently offers a compensation package that only includes a cash salary of $100,000 per year, but is thinking about introducing a health plan that costs her $10,000 per year. If she simply added the health plan to the $100,000 salary, her total profits would decrease by $10,000 times the number of employees. For her to consider offering the health plan and also maintain her profit level, she'd have to reduce the salary she offers by at least $10,000.

Would she be able to recruit and retain the same workforce if she reduced the salary from $100,000 to $90,000 per year? It depends on the value that potential employees place on having the health plan. An employee who valued the plan at exactly $10,000 would be indifferent between the current compensation package of $100,000 plus no health plan, and a new package that includes a salary of $90,000 plus the new health plan. In general, though, there are bound to be some employees who value the plan at less than $10,000 per year and some who value it at more. Any employee who valued the plan at less than $10,000 per year would view this move as a cut in compensation and would likely seek employment elsewhere.

By contrast, employees who valued the health plan at more than $20,000 per year would view this as an increase in compensation. The employer could cut the salary from $100,000 to $85,000 per year and these employees would still be better off (because they gave up $15,000 per year in salary and received instead a health plan they valued at $20,000 per year). What's more, the employer's profits would rise because labor costs went down by $5,000 per employee per year. In effect, the employer is buying health insurance and providing it to employees at a lower cost than the amount employees value the benefit.

Let's think through what would happen if an employer introduced the $10,000 health plan but kept cash wages at their initial level of $100,000 per year. At the same time, other employers would either continue to pay a salary of $100,000 per year with no health benefits or would offer a lower salary and include the health benefits. One consequence is that profits would fall by $10,000 times the number of employees. The employer may try to raise the price it charges its customers, but competition from other employers with lower labor costs would certainly make it difficult to sustain this strategy. Thus, faced with reduced profits, the likelihood that this employer will go out of business is increased. In extreme situations, such as in the commercial airline industry, employees will be willing to accept significant cuts in pay and benefits to help the company remain in business.

If the employer remains in business, workers at other employers and people out of the labor force would realize that the employer was offering a significantly more generous compensation package than that offered by other employers. The employer's human resource manager would soon realize there are many more applications than there are positions. The employer would find itself in a position where it can be choosier about which employees to hire and also find that it can fill its staffing needs at a lower salary. Thus, it's unlikely the employer would continue to offer an above-market compensation package.

What would happen if the employer decided to cut wages by more than the amount employees value the health insurance package? Let's say that the employer cut salaries from $100,000 per year to $80,000 per year, but employees only value the insurance at $10,000 per year. In this case, employees would view their total compensation package as being worth $90,000, or $10,000 less than what it was previously. Some employees would decide they would prefer to work at another employer, or not work at all, rather than take a pay cut. To fill their staffing needs, the employer would have to raise its cash wage to maintain the value of the total compensation package.

A related but more common scenario is that an employer already offers a compensation package that includes both salary and benefits, and the cost of providing some benefit increases. The leading example is the steady rise in health insurance costs experienced by most U.S. employers. Suppose you are a human resource manager and your CEO tells you that your health insurance company is going to raise the rate it charges your employer for health insurance by 10 percent for the coming year. Since this rise stands to cost the company a lot of money, one option the CEO proposes is to scale back a planned salary increase for the coming year from 5 percent to 3 percent. This 2 percent savings will offset the 10 percent increase in health insurance costs. What is your reaction to this proposal?

Do you think a decline in the growth of wages will lead some employees to leave the employer? What factors are important in answering the question?

One thing to consider in this situation is the underlying reason for the rise in health insurance costs. The following are some examples:

1. The rise reflects a general improvement in medical care technology and health care quality, but also more expensive technology.
2. Legal changes allow doctors to unionize and thereby charge higher prices for the existing services they provide.
3. Health insurance costs rose by 10 percent at only this employer because the company workforce is a year older and is at an increased likelihood of contracting additional medical conditions and hence generating additional medical costs.
4. Health insurance costs rose by 10 percent at only this employer because the employer decided to lay off a significant portion of their employees, thereby reducing the size of the insured group.

These scenarios are distinguished by whether the rise in medical costs reflects something that adds to employees' valuation of the insurance (examples 1 and 3) or does not add value (examples 2 and 4); and whether health insurance costs rise for all employers (examples 1 and 2) or for just this particular employer (examples 3 and 4). Take some time to think about whether your reaction to the CEO's proposal depends on which of the four preceding explanations is the cause of the increased health insurance premium.

The conclusion we reached earlier that employees' cash wages will tend to fall whenever benefits are fully valued holds when benefit costs rise as well. That is, wages will tend to fall when health insurance cost increases derive from improved quality of care (example 1) or an increased use of care among employees (example 3). In this view, gloomy assessments of the recent increases in health care costs may have missed the point entirely. If rising health insurance premiums signal that health care is more valuable, then recent rises in health care costs are good news for employees—at least for those who use medical care.[3]

On the other hand, if increased health insurance costs are not accompanied by an increase in employees' valuation of the insurance, as in examples 2 and 4 earlier, cash wages may not be able to adjust downward. Whether or not cash wages will, in fact, fall depends on two additional factors: (1) whether health insurance costs rise for this particular employer only or for all employers in the market, and (2) the degree to which workers and employers will change their labor demand and supply when compensation costs change.

When health benefit costs rise for a single employer in a market, the employer will likely not be able to pass along the benefit costs to workers if the workers' valuation hasn't changed (or has increased, but by less than the increased benefit cost). Let's work through an example. Suppose that to hire an average-quality lawyer with 10 years of litigation experience, a law firm in New York City must offer a total compensation package worth about $100,000. An offer of less than that will likely only attract the lowest-quality lawyers, if any at all. Let's suppose the firm of Lawyers Inc. currently meets the market by offering a compensation package of $80,000 in salary and a health insurance package valued at $20,000 by the current employees. Now suppose that the employer lays off a quarter of its staff, reducing the size of the insurance pool. So the same policy now costs the employer an extra $5,000 per employee per year. Could the law firm reduce the salary level from $80,000 to $75,000?

Probably not. The increase in health insurance costs were not accompanied by any increase in employees' valuation of the insurance, so employees still value their insurance at $20,000 per year. If the market compensation level remains at $100,000, the law firm must maintain the $80,000 salary in conjunction with the insurance to meet the market and retain its current workforce.

The salient factors in the last example are that the employer must meet the market compensation level and that health insurance costs rose only at this law firm. Thus, the employer must pay the increase in costs.[4] Many commentators and business leaders mistakenly apply that conclusion to the more general scenario when health insurance costs rise for all employers. The same logic does not carry over, however. To investigate the response of wages to an economywide increase in benefit costs, let's pick up with the earlier example 2 in which health insurance costs rise because doctors' fees increase. Clearly the employees' valuation of their health insurance plan has not changed. There is a still a possibility for wages to offset the health insurance cost increase, however. The degree to which wages will fall—that is, the degree to which employees pay for the cost increase—depends on the degree to which workers will drop out of the labor market when their compensation level falls, and the degree to which employers will reduce their workforce when employment costs rise. To understand this, let's consider two relatively polar opposite cases.

In the first case, employers are relatively insensitive to changes in compensation costs, but workers are sensitive. That is, employers would go about hiring approximately the same number of people if compensation costs rose or fell by 10 percent. By contrast, if total compensation fell by 10 percent, many workers would decide they have better uses for their time (such as raising children at home, staying in school a little longer, or retiring a little earlier) and choose not to work anymore. If total compensation rose by 10 percent, some people who are not working might choose to do so.

In this situation, employers that would not generally be able to pass along higher benefit costs to their employees instead will end up paying for the benefit out of their profits. What would happen if an employer did try to pass along the benefit cost to employees? Since employees' valuation of their benefits did not change, the decrease in salary would certainly be viewed as a decrease in total compensation. Thus, some employees would likely begin looking for employment elsewhere. Workers in general would gravitate toward employers who maintained their salary base in the face of higher benefit costs. But we've assumed in this example that employers' hiring needs are relatively insensitive to compensation costs. That is, employers still need about as many workers now as they did prior to the benefit cost increase. Thus, employers that cut wages and lost employees would need to hire additional workers to replace them, which would necessitate raising their compensation level—the result being that the employer would pay the increase in benefit costs.

But what if all employers could somehow agree to pass along the higher benefit cost to employees, so workers didn't have the option of moving to higher-wage employers? Well, workers in this example always have the option of leaving the workforce altogether. So if all employers decided to cut wages, some workers would leave the market, leaving some employers understaffed. The smaller workforce would force employers to raise their wage offers to fill their staffing needs. The bottom line is that if workers are willing to leave the labor market when compensation falls, and employers have relatively inflexible staffing needs, employers will tend to pay for benefit cost increases.

In the second scenario, employees are totally insensitive to marketwide changes in compensation levels. That is, if total compensation fell by 10 percent at all employers, no workers would reduce their hours or weeks of work or drop out of the labor market in response. That's what is meant by "insensitive." Although this view of workers' behavior may sound rather extreme, there's actually quite a bit of evidence that most prime-age workers (those ages 30 to 54) behave this way, especially men. By contrast, the groups most likely to adjust their labor supply—and thus fit the previous scenario—are women with young children, the elderly, part-time workers, and young workers.

In the situation where employees are totally insensitive to changes in marketwide compensation levels, all the increase in benefit costs will be passed along to employees in the form of lower salary levels, even if employees' valuation of the benefit has not changed. An employee whose salary was reduced by the cost of the benefit might at first perceive a cut in his pay relative to what he could receive at other employers, and thus try to seek employment elsewhere. But all employers have experienced the same increase in benefit costs, and thus all employers will be seeking to cut salaries. Thus, the employee would soon find that although his salary has been cut, so have the wages at other employers. The employee's only options are to drop out of the labor market altogether or accept the lower pay, and we've ruled out the former. Exhibit 3.1 summarizes whether employers or employees will tend to pay for a benefit cost increase in various scenarios.

Most workers with employer-sponsored health insurance pay a token monthly contribution toward their health insurance premium, which is typically deducted

EXHIBIT 3.1			
Summary of the Incidence of Employee Benefit Cost Increases	**Does employees' valuation of the benefit increase?**	**Employees' valuation increases at least as much as the benefit cost increases.**	**Employees' valuation of benefit does not increase.**
	Do costs increase for all employers in the market?	**Costs increase for single employer**	**Costs increase for all employers**
	Who pays for benefit cost increases?	Employees pay for all benefit cost increases.	Employer pays for all benefit cost increases. · Employers and employees split the cost increase. Party that is least likely to adjust tends to pay more.

from each monthly paycheck. According to data from the 2006 National Compensation Survey (the latest available at the time of publication), 75 percent of private sector employees with single-person coverage and 87 percent of employees with family coverage were required to make a contribution toward their health insurance cost. The average monthly contribution was $76.05 for people with single coverage and $296.88 for people with family coverage.[5] This monthly premium is usually paid from pretax dollars and usually represents only a small fraction of the actual cost of the health insurance. Importantly, this monthly payment should not be interpreted as employees' only contribution toward their health insurance. Rather, the view advanced in this chapter is that the full cost of health insurance is paid for by employees. Part is paid for through this monthly contribution and the remainder is paid for through lower cash wages.

It may seem peculiar that employers charge employees these monthly contributions since they come from after-tax dollars. One advantage of these fees, however, is that they easily allow employers to charge different health insurance prices to people with different family sizes, or to people who choose health plans of different quality, such as a preferred provider organization (PPO) versus a health maintenance organization (HMO) (both discussed in Chapter 6). A second advantage is that employers can more easily raise these contributions when benefit costs increase, making it more evident to the worker that health costs have increased.

Business managers and human resource practitioners sometimes question whether economists' view of the relationship between cash wages and benefits is correct because, they contend, employers are rarely observed cutting wages when a new benefit is introduced or the cost of providing an existing benefit increases. In fact, such wage cuts happen much more frequently than you might think. An employer may scale back a scheduled bonus or reduce the year-to-year rate of growth of cash wages. An employer may also hire new workers at a lower wage rate than existing workers are paid. If there is relatively fast turnover, the wage decrease will quickly filter through the employer. Finally, an employer may increase employees' "contribution" toward their health insurance premium. An increase in the contribution is in effect taking compensation out of the hands of employees, which has the same effect as a reduction in cash wages. A difference is that increasing the benefit contribution helps employees realize that their wage cut results from an increase in their benefit costs, not from, for example, a decrease in the employer's profitability. For an employer with both employees who receive health insurance and those who don't, increasing the contribution may be a particularly effective way to target a wage decrease on those employees whose benefit cost was actually affected.

TWO EXTENSIONS

Government Mandates

Frequently, the federal government, or local or state governments, will pass a law that requires private employers to provide employees with a particular benefit or accommodation. For example, employers are required to meet minimum health and safety codes. The Family and Medical Leave Act requires that eligible employers provide certain employees with up to 12 weeks of unpaid leave per year (the FMLA is covered in detail in Chapter 10). This law and many others (discussed in Chapter 4 and in some other chapters) are referred to as **employer mandates** because the government mandates that employers do something they might otherwise not do. There are also **employee mandates** or **individual mandates,** which require individuals to take some action. For example, many states require that all car owners have automobile insurance. Many proposals for expanding health insurance coverage in the United States contain either employer mandates that require all employers to offer health insurance to all workers, or individual mandates that require all individuals to purchase health insurance. (These are distinct from a national health insurance program, such as that in Canada, which is a government health insurance program that covers all citizens.)

Employer managers and policymakers are naturally concerned about the effect of mandates on profits and employees' well-being. In one view, these policies improve working conditions or increase employee compensation, but are paid for by employers in the form of reduced profits. In another view, the costs of providing these benefits are passed from employers to employees, which means employees may or may not be better off, depending on how much they value the new benefits.

The framework introduced earlier for thinking about how benefits are related to cash wages can be easily extended to shed light on the impact of government mandates. Let's think through an example in which the government passed a hypothetical law that requires all employers to offer health insurance to all employees. Currently, about 53 percent of private sector firms offer health insurance and would thus already be in compliance with the hypothetical law.[6] There would not be any change in employment or compensation at these firms. For the 47 percent of employers that do not already offer health insurance, the mandate would represent an increase in employment costs. Will these employers be able to shift that cost to their employees in the form of lower wages?

The first question is whether or not employees at these companies value the health insurance. Most employees likely will place some value on the health insurance. But it is also likely that most will value it less than it costs their employers to provide it. Why? If the employees valued the insurance at more than the cost for the employer to provide it, presumably the employer would have already provided it. After all, as we discussed earlier in this chapter, employers and employees may be better off if health insurance is substituted for cash in a compensation package, provided the employer can purchase the insurance at a lower cost than that faced by employees. Thus, most of the 47 percent of employers that do not already provide insurance will find themselves in a situation where they must provide a benefit that costs more than their typical employee would be willing to pay for it themselves.

The second factor is whether the increase in employment costs occurs for all employers in the market, or for just one employer. In this case, the mandate applies to all employers in the market, so all employers are affected.

When these factors are taken together—that employment costs rise for all employers and that the rise is larger than the increase in value to employees—our previous analysis tells us that employers and workers are likely to split the cost of the benefit. Recall the earlier statement that most prime-age workers, especially men, do not adjust the amount they work in the face of changes in their compensation. In the vast majority of companies that primarily employ prime-age workers, workers will end up paying for the increase in health costs. The employment and profitability of these employers will be largely unaffected by the mandate. On the other hand, the cost of mandated health insurance will likely be split between workers and employers in companies that primarily hire younger workers, older workers, or married women with young children. Since these employers will be paying for part of the cost of the benefit, their profits may fall. They may also decide to hire fewer workers in response to the increase in employment costs. It is important to emphasize, though, that the number of employers that fall into this category is likely to be very small.

Differences in Benefit Cost Increases across Groups of Workers

Sometimes the cost of providing health insurance—or any employee benefit—only increases for a subset of workers in a company. For example, the Pregnancy Discrimination Act of 1978 requires health insurance to cover maternity costs just as it would any other health condition (see Chapter 4). Today, proposals are frequently made for health insurance carriers to be required to cover birth control pills if they cover other prescription medications. These public policies raise the cost of health insurance to younger families and women of childbearing age, while having no effect on the cost of insurance for single men or older married adults.

Our previous discussion might lead many to believe that if the cost of providing a benefit to a subset of workers increases, the cash wages of that group may fall relative to the wages of other workers who have the same employer. For example, adding maternity coverage to the health insurance plan at a particular company may lead to a reduction in the wages of women of childbearing age relative to men at the company. But is it always the case that wages can adjust within a company? If so, under what conditions will this happen?

Two reasons explain why wages may not adjust within a firm to reflect differences in health insurance costs across easily identifiable groups of workers. First, antidiscrimination laws may prevent an employer from systematically paying different wages to people of different genders, race, or other protected groups (see Chapter 4). If health insurance is more costly for women than men, employers may not be able to systematically pay women lower cash wages than men are paid. Second, employer managers may prefer a relatively flat compensation structure for people with similar jobs. This may be a compensation policy designed to keep things simple, or designed to foster a sense of equity within the company. In either case, paying different cash wages to people with higher and lower health insurance costs may violate this tenet of an employer's internal culture.

If wages did not adjust to reflect differences in benefit costs, then employers would have an incentive to hire workers who are cheaper to insure. In the earlier example, if health insurance is more costly for certain women than for men, and employers pay the same cash salary to each, then the employer can reduce its compensation costs by hiring men over women. By contrast, if wages do fall for groups who experience rising benefit costs, then employers do not have an incentive to prefer one group over the other. There is evidence that wages do, in fact, adjust for differences in benefit costs. In the mid-1970s some states passed regulations to require health insurance companies to treat maternity costs just as they would any similar medical condition, which added coverage for maternity costs to most health insurance plans in these states. This raised the cost of health insurance for women and families, especially those who might experience a pregnancy, by about 4 percent of their initial wage level. Research by Jonathan Gruber, an economist at the Massachusetts Institute of Technology, showed that the cash wages of married women ages 20 to 40 tended to fall in states that passed maternity coverage laws compared to the wages of similar women in states that did not pass such laws.[7] He also found that the wages of these women fell relative to the wages of single men ages 20 to 40 and to those of people over the age of 40 who also lived in states where maternity coverage laws were passed. In 1978, the federal government passed the Pregnancy Discrimination Act, which essentially extended the equal treatment of maternity coverage in health insurance plans to those states that had not already required it. Gruber again found that wages for married women ages 20 to 40 tended to fall in states affected by the federal law. This evidence suggests that when the costs of a benefit rise for an identifiable group of workers, those workers alone may end up paying for the cost increase. It is important to stress, though, that this finding of wage adjustments across groups may not hold in every instance where benefit costs rise for a demographically identifiable group.

Summary

This chapter explored why many employers offer a mixture of cash and benefits in compensation packages and whether workers tend to pay for benefit cost increases in the form of lower cash wages. The primary reasons why employers offer benefits are that they can purchase the benefit at a lower cost than could employees on their own, employers use benefits to attract particular types of employees, and the government gives employers a tax incentive to provide some benefits. Whether workers or employers pay for benefit cost increases depends crucially on why costs increase, whether costs increase for all employers in the market, and how willing employees and employers are able to adjust their labor supply and demand when compensation costs change.

Key Terms

medical underwriting, *53*	economies of scale, *54*	employer mandates, *63*
adverse selection, *53*	tuition reimbursement	employee mandates, *63*
experience rating, *53*	benefits, *54*	individual mandates, *63*

Discussion Questions

1. One reason employers offer benefits is that the benefit may be cheaper for the employers to provide than it would be for the employees to purchase on their own. Besides the insurance examples discussed in this chapter, what other benefits are cheaper for employers to provide than for individuals to purchase on their own? Even if a particular benefit is cheaper for an employer to provide, would that employer always want to provide it as part of a compensation package? Why or why not?

2. One reason employers might offer a particular employee benefit is to aid in recruiting certain types of workers. One example given in the text is a tuition reimbursement program to attract highly motivated employees. What other examples of benefits are you familiar with that might be used to attract a particular type of employee? Which types of employees are most attracted to these benefits?

3. Small employers are less likely than large employers to offer health insurance to their employees. One reason for this is that health insurance tends to cost more for small employers than for large employers. Explain why health insurance costs more for smaller insurance pools. What public policies are currently being proposed to remedy the disparity in health insurance coverage between small and large employers?

4. A major theme of this chapter is that employers need to know the dollar value employees place on benefits. Explain concisely why this type of information is important for employers to have. What methods do employers actually use to gauge their employees' valuation of benefit packages?

5. Explain why the impact of a benefit cost increase on employee cash wages will generally depend on whether benefit costs rose for all employers in a market or for just one employer. Give some examples of factors that would cause benefit costs to increase in all employers in a market and some that would affect only a single employer.

Endnotes

1. U.S. Agency for Healthcare Research & Quality. 2009. Medical Panel Expenditure Survey. Table 1: Total Health Services—Median and Mean Expenses per Person with Expense: United States. Online: www.meps.ahrq.gov. Accessed April 11, 2009.

2. The effect of benefit costs on cash wages, employer profits, and employment is complex. A more in-depth discussion of the economic issues surrounding employment-based health insurance can be found in Mark V. Pauly. 1999. *Health Benefits at Work: An Economic and Political Analysis of Employment-Based Health Insurance*, Ann Arbor: University of Michigan Press.

3. An excellent source for more information on the U.S. health care system and alternative reform proposals is David M. Cutler. 2004. *Your Money or Your Life: Strong Medicine for America's Health Care System*, New York: Oxford University Press.

4. An alternative is that when faced with a large increase in health insurance costs, an employer may be more likely to drop health insurance altogether and instead raise employees' salaries.

5. See "Employee Benefits in Private Industry, 2006," United States Department of Labor, Bureau of Labor Statistics. Available at www.bls.gov/ncs/ecbs/home.htm.

6. See "Employee Benefits in the United States, March 2008," United States Department of Labor, Bureau of Labor Statistics. Available at www.bls.gov.

7. See Jonathan Gruber. 1994. "The Incidence of Mandated Maternity Benefits," *The American Economic Review*, 84, no. 3, pp. 622–641.

Chapter **Four**

Regulating Employee Benefits

Learning Objectives

In this chapter, you will gather
information about:

1. The necessity of government
   regulation of employment practices,
   including benefits.

2. The National Labor Relations Act of
   1935.

3. Internal Revenue Code and its impact
   on employee benefits plans.

4. Fair Labor Standards Act of 1938 and
   its definition of compensable
   nonwork time.

5. Employee Retirement Income
   Security Act of 1974 (ERISA) and key
   amendments such as Pension
   Protection Act, COBRA, and HIPAA.

6. Federal equal opportunity
   employment laws that influence
   discretionary employee benefits
   plans.

As you review your benefits materials, you notice a veritable alphabet soup of laws—ERISA, COBRA, HIPAA—that establish and protect your rights to many of the benefits you will receive from your new employer. Then, you begin to wonder, "How is the employer regulated? How much can Congress or the courts tell an employer how to run its business, who it should hire or fire, or how it should treat its employees?"

In a nutshell, according to Bennett-Alexander and Hartman:

> The freedom to contract is crucial to freedom of the market; an employee may choose to work or not to work for a given employer, and an employer may choose to hire or not to hire a given applicant. As a result, the employment relationship is regulated in some important ways. Congress tries to avoid telling employers how to manage their employees. . . . However, Congress has passed employment-related laws when it believes that the employee is not on equal footing with the employer. For example, Congress has passed laws that require employers to pay minimum wages and to refrain from using certain criteria, such as race or gender, in arriving at specific employment decisions. These laws reflect the reality that employers stand in a position of power in the employment relationship. Legal protections granted to employees seek to make the power relationship between employer and employee one that is fair and equitable.[1]

The focus of this chapter is to introduce you to the complex set of federal regulations that shape discretionary benefits practices. A sound working knowledge of these laws is essential to effective management of employee benefits practices in companies. Exhibit 4.1 lists them. In this chapter, we look at these laws and their influence on discretionary benefits practices more closely.

Our focus in this chapter will be on the regulation of employee benefits in the private sector (for-profit companies such as Wal-Mart and not-for-profit agencies such as the American Cancer Society) rather than the public sector (municipal, county, state, and federal governments). Private sector employment accounts for approximately 85 percent of civilian employment in the United States. A complex set of public laws across the levels of government determine the regulation of benefits in the public sector, and these topics are largely outside the scope of this book. Nevertheless it is imperative to note that many states have adopted laws that seem to overlap with federal regulation. Such "duplication" is permissible only when protection or benefit under the state law

EXHIBIT 4.1
Legal and Regulatory Influences on Discretionary Benefits Practices

- The National Labor Relations Act of 1935
- The Internal Revenue Code
- The Fair Labor Standards Act of 1938
- The Employee Retirement Income Security Act of 1974 (ERISA) and noteworthy amendments:
  - The Pension Protection Act of 2006 (PPA)
  - The Consolidated Omnibus Budget Reconciliation Act of 1985 (COBRA)
  - The Health Insurance Portability and Accountability Act of 1996 (HIPAA)
- Federal Employment Equal Opportunity laws:
  - The Equal Pay Act of 1963
  - Title VII of the Civil Rights Act of 1964
  - The Age Discrimination in Employment Act of 1967
  - The Pregnancy Discrimination Act of 1978
  - The Americans with Disabilities Act of 1990
  - The Civil Rights Act of 1991
- Genetic Information Nondiscrimination Act of 2008 (GINA)

is equal to or greater than the corresponding federal law. For example, many states have minimum wage laws that set this wage higher than the current federal minimum wage.

LABOR UNIONS AND EMPLOYEE BENEFITS: THE NATIONAL LABOR RELATIONS ACT OF 1935

Congress enacted the **National Labor Relations Act of 1935 (NLRA)** to restore equality of bargaining power between employees and employers. As discussed in Chapter 1, the industrialization of the U.S. economy and the economic devastation during the Great Depression placed workers at a disadvantage; they were subject to poor pay, unsafe working conditions, and virtually no job security. Workers banded together to negotiate better terms of employment, but employers were not willing to negotiate because collective action could jeopardize their control over the terms of employment. Consequently, employees continued to experience poor working conditions, substandard wage rates, and excessive work hours.

For example, a tragedy occurred at the Triangle Shirtwaist factory located in New York City in 1911. Approximately 150 teenage girls perished when a fire broke out on the eighth floor of the building. Most were burned alive in their work areas, and others jumped out of the windows to their deaths on the sidewalks about 80 feet below. The company routinely kept the exits locked during work shifts, and a single fire escape could not support the weight of the people attempting to escape.

A strong public reaction across the country led politicians to embrace the idea that one of the responsibilities of government is to protect the welfare of workers. Ultimately, the New York Factory Investigating Commission, established to investigate the circumstances of the fire, led to the passage of New York State's Industrial Code, providing the impetus for national laws such as the NLRA to help protect the interests of workers. As you will see, the NLRA is a comprehensive law that speaks to various terms of employment, including employee benefits.

Coverage

The NLRA applies to private sector companies, except for companies whose main business is passenger or freight rail or air carrier. This act does not extend protection to agricultural workers, domestic service workers, independent contractors, or employees of the federal, state, or municipal governments. The **National Labor Relations Board (NLRB)** oversees the enforcement of the NLRA.

Relevance to Employee Benefits

Section 1 of the NLRA declares the policy of the United States to protect commerce:

> by encouraging the practice and procedure of collective bargaining and by protecting the exercise by workers of full freedom of association, self-organization, and designation of representatives of their own choosing for the purpose of negotiating the terms and conditions of employment.

Collective bargaining refers to the process in which representatives of employees (e.g., General Motors employees are represented by the United Auto Workers union) and representatives of company management negotiate the terms of employment. Under the NLRA, the possible subjects for bargaining fall into three categories: mandatory, permissive, or illegal. Specific employee benefits are included on the lists of mandatory and permissive subjects. **Mandatory bargaining subjects** are those that employers and unions must bargain on if either constituent makes proposals about them. The following employee benefits items are mandatory subjects of bargaining:

- Disability pay (supplemental to what is mandated by Social Security and the various state workers' compensation laws).
- Employer-provided health insurance.
- Paid time-off.
- Pension and retirement plans.

The NLRA strictly limits management discretion in unionized firms to establish major elements of the benefits program. For example, the NLRB held that an employer committed an unfair labor practice when it unilaterally switched insurance carriers and changed the health protection benefits provided under its collective bargaining agreement. The NLRB held that the collective bargaining agreement contemplated that the same insurance carrier would be retained while the contract was in effect and that benefits would remain as agreed upon during negotiations.[2]

Although employee health care benefits plans are mandatory subjects for bargaining, under certain circumstances the change in the identity of the plan's insurance carrier or third-party administrator is not a compulsory bargaining subject. For example, a federal appeals court ruled that an employer's unilateral change to a new insurance carrier that was substantively the same as the old carrier was lawful.[3] The employer had proposed that it unilaterally be able to change insurance carriers. The union countered by saying that change would come only after both parties agreed on the terms and conditions of the health care coverage. When neither could agree on the terms, an interim contract provision was inserted which stated that the employer could not unilaterally adopt an alternate delivery system. Subsequently, the employer changed carriers without first consulting the union. The union sued to prevent the company from switching carriers, but the court held the change of carriers was lawful for two reasons: First, the coverage under the new carrier remained substantially the same. Second, the provision restricting the unilateral adoption of an alternative delivery system, although ambiguous enough to be capable of more than one meaning, did not prevent the employer from switching insurance carriers.

Permissive bargaining subjects are those subjects on which neither the employer nor the union is obligated to bargain. The following employee benefits items fall in the permissive subjects category:

- Administration of funds for employee benefits programs.
- Retiree benefits (e.g., medical insurance).
- Workers' compensation, within the scope of state workers' compensation laws.

Illegal bargaining subjects include proposals for contract revisions that are either illegal under the NLRA or violate federal or state laws. For example, employers and labor unions may not bargain over particular standards for employee benefits plans set forth by the Employee Retirement Income Security Act of 1974 (ERISA): minimum funding standards; minimum participation standards; minimum vesting standards; benefit accrual standards; and joint, survivor, and preretirement survivor benefit requirements. We discuss these aspects of ERISA later in this chapter.

The role of labor unions goes well beyond the collective bargaining process. Increases in layoffs and plant shutdowns promote immediate cost savings for companies, but these activities threaten the bargaining power of unions. Unions are willing to accept lower pay and benefits for its members in exchange for job security. Unions were also instrumental in securing the **Worker Adjustment and Retraining Notification (WARN) Act,** which generally requires that management give at least a 60-day advance notice of a plant closing or mass layoff. An employer's failure to comply with the requirement of the WARN Act entitles employees to recover pay and benefits for the period for which notice was not given, typically up to a maximum of 60 days.

Companies with labor unions often try to avoid instituting mass layoffs whenever possible because of recall features in collective bargaining agreements. In other words, management is expected to rehire most of its laid-off workers when business conditions rebound. However, with the deep recessionary period that began in late 2007, companies are trying to make permanent cuts to their workforces for substantial labor force savings. For example, the auto sales declines in the United States are said to be the worst since the early 1980s during a deep recessionary period.

In early 2009, in response to this dire situation, Ford Motor Company announced to local union leaders that it would make buyout or early retirement offers to all its 42,000 U.S. hourly workers. These cuts are part of a series of contract concessions in a tentative agreement reached between the United Auto Workers union and Ford Motor Company's management. In addition, the union agreed to a suspension of cost-of-living pay raises and lump-sum performance bonuses in the remaining three years of the recently negotiated collective bargaining agreement.

THE INTERNAL REVENUE CODE

The **Internal Revenue Code (IRC)** is the set of regulations pertaining to taxation in the United States (e.g., sales tax, company [employer] income tax, individual [employee] income tax, and property tax). Taxes represent the main source of revenue to fund federal, state, and local government programs. The Internal Revenue Service (IRS) is the government agency that develops and implements the IRC, and levies penalties against companies and individuals who violate these penalties. Since 1916, the federal government encouraged employers to provide retirement benefits to employees with tax breaks or deductions. In other words, the government allowed employers to exclude retirement plan payments from their income subject to taxation. This "break" reduced the amount of a company's required tax payments. In general, the larger the contributions to retirement plans, the greater the reduction in the amount of taxes owed to the government.

The IRC contains multiple regulations for legally required and discretionary benefits. For example, the **Federal Insurance Contributions Act (FICA)**[4] taxes employees and employers to finance the Social Security Old-Age, Survivor, and Disability Insurance (OASDI) program. Unemployment insurance benefits are financed by federal and, sometimes, state taxes levied on employers. Federal tax is levied on employers under the **Federal Unemployment Tax Act (FUTA).**

Since the inception of the IRC, the federal government also contains incentives for employers who offer discretionary benefits and for employees as recipients of these benefits. An employee may deduct the cost of benefits from annual income, reducing tax liability. Employers may also deduct the cost of benefits from their annual income as a business or trade expense when the cost is an ordinary and necessary expense of the company's trade or business. For example, the costs of electricity for a factory and the purchase of raw materials to manufacture products are ordinary and necessary expenses. Payroll costs and benefits costs also qualify as ordinary and necessary business expenses. Without pay and benefits, companies would not be able to recruit and retain competent employees who are crucial for business operations. In addition, companies can deduct these costs only during the current tax period. So, the benefits costs incurred during 2008 may be deducted only for the 2008 tax year.

The tax deductibility of benefits costs also requires that employers meet additional requirements set forth by the Employee Retirement Income Security Act of 1974. Benefits qualify for tax deductibility when they meet nondiscrimination rules. **Nondiscrimination rules** prohibit employers from giving preferential treatment to key employees and highly compensated employees—for example, by contributing 10 percent of the annual salary to the retirement accounts of some employees, but only 5 percent to other employees. The Internal Revenue Service defines the meanings of these employee groups. The term **key employee** means any employee who at any time during the year is at least one of the following:

- A 5 percent owner of the employer.
- A 1 percent owner of the employer, having an annual compensation from the employer of more than $160,000.
- An officer of the employer having an annual compensation greater than $160,000 in 2009 (indexed for inflation in increments of $5,000 beginning in 2003).

U.S. Treasury Regulations define the term *officer* in this definition of key employees:[5]

> Generally, the term officer means an administrative executive who is in regular and continued service. The term officer implies continuity of service and excludes those employed for a special and single transaction. An employee who merely has the title of an officer but not the authority of an officer is not considered an officer for purposes of the key employee test. Similarly, an employee who does not have the title of an officer but has the authority of an officer is an officer for purposes of the key employee test. In the case of one or more employers treated as a single employer under sections 414(b), (c), or (m), whether or not an individual is an officer shall be determined based upon his responsibilities with respect to the employer or employers for which he is directly employed, and not with respect to the controlled group of corporations, employers under common control, or an affiliated service group.

A partner of a partnership will not be treated as an officer for purposes of the key employee test merely because she owns a capital or profits interest in the partnership; exercises her voting rights as a partner; and may, for limited purposes, be authorized and does in fact act as an agent of the partnership.

The Internal Revenue Service defines a **highly compensated employee** as one of the following:

- A 5 percent owner at any time during the year or preceding year.
- An employee who had compensation from the employer, for the preceding year, in excess of $110,000.
- A member of the top-paid group of employees for the preceding year (if the employer elects the application of this clause for a plan year).

THE FAIR LABOR STANDARDS ACT OF 1938

The **Fair Labor Standards Act (FLSA)** contains provisions for minimum wage, overtime pay, and child labor.

Coverage

The FLSA minimum wage provision applies to virtually all employees working for private sector employers and the federal, state, or local government agency. Employers must comply with the FLSA requirements if they are engaged in at least one of several activities:

- A federal, state, or local government agency.
- A hospital or an institution primarily engaged in the care of the sick, the aged, or the mentally ill or developmentally disabled who live on the premises.
- A preschool, elementary, or secondary school or institution of higher learning (e.g., college), or a school for mentally or physically handicapped or gifted children.
- A company or organization with an annual dollar volume of sales or receipts of at least $500,000.

This provision of the act does not apply to all employees of covered employers. The overtime pay provision applies to employees whose jobs are classified as nonexempt by the act and excludes jobs that are classified as exempt by this act. Generally, executive, administrative, learned professional, creative professional, computer workers, and outside sales employees are exempt from the FLSA overtime and minimum wage provisions. Most other jobs are nonexempt. Nonexempt jobs are subject to the FLSA overtime pay provision.

Determining whether jobs are exempt from the FLSA overtime pay provision has become even more complex since the U.S. Department of Labor introduced revised guidelines, known as the **FairPay Rules,** in August 2004. Previously, an employee was considered exempt under the FLSA overtime pay provisions if an employee earned more than the minimum wage and exercised independent judgment when working. Under the new FairPay Rules, workers earning less than $23,660 per year—or $455 per week—are guaranteed overtime protection. The U.S. Department of Labor provides extensive information regarding the new FairPay Rules, including instructional videos and a "frequently asked questions" section (www.dol.gov).

Relevance to Employee Benefits Practices

The FLSA applies to benefits practices in two ways. First, under the overtime pay provision, employees who are covered by the FLSA are entitled to pay at a rate of one and one-half times their normal hourly rate for hours worked in excess of 40 during a workweek. A workweek, which can begin on any day of the week, is seven consecutive 24-hour periods, or 168 consecutive hours. Employee benefits linked to pay, as in the case of unemployment insurance, increase correspondingly during those overtime hours.

Second, the FLSA reaches specific paid time-off practices that qualify as hours worked. The **Portal-to-Portal Act of 1947** defines the term **hours worked** as the compensable activities that precede and follow the primary work activities, including:

- The time spent on the activity was for the employee's benefit.
- The employer controlled the amount of time spent.
- The time involved is categorized as suffered and permitted, meaning that the employer knew the employee was working on incidental tasks either before or after the scheduled tour of duty. According to the U.S. Department of Labor, an employee may voluntarily continue to work at the end of regular working hours. He or she may need to finish an assigned task, prepare reports, finish

waiting on a customer, or take care of a patient in an emergency. An employee may take work home to complete in the evening or on weekends to meet a deadline. All of these are examples of hours worked under the FLSA.

- The time spent was requested by the employer.
- The time spent is an integral part of the employee's principal duties.
- The employer has a union contract with employees providing such compensation or, as a matter of custom or practice, the employer has compensated for the activities in the past.

Common examples of compensable nonwork times include nonproduction time cleanup, preparation, travel time between job locations within the scope of the regular work shift, rest periods (shorter than 20 minutes), and meal periods (at least 30 minutes in duration, during which employees are required to take their meals). For instance, time spent by state correctional officers caring for police dogs at home is compensable under the FLSA.[6] The care of dogs, including feeding, grooming, and walking, is indispensable to maintaining dogs as a critical law enforcement tool. It is part of the officers' principal activities, and it benefits the corrections department. However, the court ruled that time spent by state correction canine handlers transporting dogs between home and a correctional facility is not compensable under FLSA.

THE EMPLOYEE RETIREMENT INCOME SECURITY ACT OF 1974

The **Employee Retirement Income Security Act of 1974 (ERISA)** was established to regulate the establishment and implementation of discretionary benefits practices. These include medical (Chapter 6), life and disability insurance programs (Chapter 7), and retirement programs (Chapter 5).

Coverage

ERISA generally covers private sector employee benefits plans. The following employee benefits plans are not subject to ERISA requirements: federal, state, or local government plans, church plans, workers' compensation plans, plans maintained outside the United States for nonresident aliens, and top hat plans. **Top hat plans** are unfunded deferred compensation plans for a select group of managers or highly compensated employees. Finally, ERISA excludes plans covering only partners or sole proprietors.

ERISA is a far-reaching law. Many states enforce laws pertaining to employee benefits practices. ERISA preempts most state laws and is also a very detailed and complex law. Some law schools devote one or more entire courses to ERISA regulation. Like virtually every other law, various stakeholders, including employees, employers, and even the government, have interpreted its language differently, leading to a multitude of court rulings to help guide interpretation. Moreover, ERISA has been amended several times by specific legislation in an attempt to balance the interests of employees and employers as social norms evolved and to adjust to changing business conditions. For example, as we will discuss, the

Consolidated Omnibus Budget Reconciliation Act of 1985 permitted employees to continue to receive health insurance coverage under an employer's plan for a limited time after termination. Over the years, this law prevented interruption of health insurance benefits for millions of people (former employees and their dependents) during periods of unemployment. The Pension Protection Act of 2006 permits an employer to automatically enroll employees in its defined contribution retirement plan and to deduct a limited amount of pay to deposit into each employee's account. Prior to this law, employees had the choice to participate, but a significant number did not. Ultimately, the federal government stepped in to promote savings for retirement because of concerns that a significant number of people would not have sufficient funds to retire, especially in light of concerns about the future solvency of the federal government's Social Security retirement program (discussed in Chapter 8).

Relevance to Employee Benefits Practices

The essence of ERISA is to provide protection of employee benefits rights. Until the passage of this act in 1974, employer-sponsored pension plans were largely unregulated. The IRC, the Taft-Hartley Act of 1947, and the Federal Welfare and Pension Plans Disclosure Act of 1958 applied limited restrictions to the operation of employer-sponsored plans.

ERISA has several major objectives:[7]

- To ensure that workers and beneficiaries receive adequate information about their benefits plans.
- To set standards of conduct for those managing employee benefits plans and plan funds.
- To determine that adequate funds are being set aside to pay promised pension benefits.
- To ensure that workers receive pension benefits after they have satisfied certain minimum requirements.
- To safeguard pension benefits for workers whose pension plans are terminated.

ERISA has four broad titles and general sections contained within each title. Exhibit 4.2 displays a listing of the titles and sections. Title I specifies a variety of protections for participants and beneficiaries. Title II has the IRC provisions pertaining to the taxation of employee benefits and pension plans. Title III addresses the administration and enforcement of ERISA, including the jurisdiction of relevant federal agencies. Title IV contains terms for pension insurance programs, including the establishment of the Pension Benefit Guarantee Corporation (PBGC).

Some provisions of Titles I and II contribute several minimum standards necessary to "qualify" pension plans for favorable tax treatment. Additional regulations (e.g., U.S. Treasury rules) also contribute minimum standards for the same purpose. Failure to meet any of the minimum standards "disqualifies" pension plans for favorable tax treatment. Pension plans that meet these minimum standards are known as **qualified plans. Nonqualified plans** fail to meet at least one of the minimum standard provisions.

EXHIBIT 4.2
Summary of
ERISA Titles

Title I: Protection of Employee Rights

1. Reporting and disclosure.
2. Participation and vesting.
3. Funding.
4. Fiduciary responsibilities.
5. Administration/enforcement.
6. Continuation coverage and additional standards for group health plans.
7. Group health plan requirements.

Title II: Amendments to the Internal Revenue Code Relating to Retirement Plans

Title III: Jurisdiction, Administration, Enforcement, Joint Pension Task Force

Title IV: Plan Termination Insurance

We will cover all the main provisions of ERISA in this chapter. In Chapter 5, we will revisit the applicable ERISA Titles I and II provisions for the minimum standards necessary to establish qualified pension plans. We also will cover non-ERISA rules that complete the full set of minimum standards.

Defining Pension Plans and Welfare Plans

ERISA applies to **pension plans** and **welfare plans.*** Pension plans are any plan, fund, or program that

> (i) provides retirement income to employees, or (ii) results in a deferral of income by employees for periods extending to the termination of covered employment or beyond, regardless of the method of calculating the contributions made in the plan, the method of calculating benefits under the plan, or the method of distributing benefits from the plan.[8]

The two most commonly used pension plans in companies are defined benefit and defined contribution plans, which we discuss in great detail in Chapter 5. For the purposes of introducing ERISA, a brief definition of each is warranted because some of the ERISA provisions refer to one type versus another. A **defined benefit plan** guarantees the retirement benefits specified in the plan document. This benefit usually is expressed in terms of a monthly sum equal to a percentage of a participant's preretirement pay multiplied by the number of years he or she has worked for the employer. Although the benefit in such a plan is fixed by a formula, the level of required employer contributions fluctuates from year to year. The contribution depends on the amount necessary to make certain that the benefits promised will be available when participants and their beneficiaries are eligible to receive them. Under a **defined contribution plan,** employers and employees make annual contributions to separate accounts established for each participating employee, based on a formula contained in the plan document. The amount each participant receives in retirement depends on the performance of the selected investment vehicle

---

*We use the term *employee benefits* generally to refer to both pension and nonpension benefits practices. ERISA distinguishes between pension benefits and nonpension benefits. Welfare practices under ERISA refer to nonpension benefits.

(e.g., company stock, government bonds). Typically, formulas call for employers to contribute a given percentage of each participant's annual pay each year. Employers invest these funds on behalf of the employee in any of a number of ways, such as company stocks, diversified stock market funds, or federal government bond funds.

Another important pension term under ERISA is **multiemployer plans.** Multiemployer plans are pension plans for workers in industries where it is common to move from employer to employer where work becomes available, such as in the skilled trades (for example, carpentry), the trucking industry, and small grocery stores whose owners could not afford the costs of a retirement plan. As the name indicates, multiemployer pension plans cover workers from more than one employer compared to most pension plans that apply to workers at a single employer. Under multiemployer plans, employees continue to earn credit toward qualifying for retirement benefits no matter whether they remain with a single employer or move from one company to another that is involved in the plan.

Traditionally, multiemployer plans were established through the collective bargaining process. The IRC uses a broader definition of a multiemployer plan by relaxing the stipulation that the plan is part of a collective bargaining agreement.

ERISA defines a welfare plan as

> any plan, fund, or program which was heretofore or is hereafter established or maintained by an employer or by an employee organization, or by both, to the extent that such plan, fund, or program was established or is maintained for the purpose of providing for its participants or their beneficiaries through the purchase of insurance or otherwise, (A) medical, surgical, or hospital care or benefits, or benefits in the event of sickness, accident, disability, death, or unemployment, or vacation benefits, apprenticeship, or other training programs, or day care centers, scholarship funds, or prepaid legal services, or (B) any benefit described in section 302(c) of the Labor Management Relations Act, 1947 (other than pensions on retirement or death; and insurance to provide such pensions).[9]

Scope of Coverage for Pension Plans and Welfare Plans

Although ERISA covers both pension plans and welfare plans, most of its provisions pertain to pension plans. The protection of employee rights (Title I) addresses seven issues, which we describe next. Only two issues (1 and 4) apply to welfare plans; two additional issues (6 and 7) address group health plans exclusively.

Title I: Protection of Employee Rights

Title I contains provisions that provide employees protections for benefits rights:

1. Reporting and disclosure.
2. Minimum standards for participation and vesting.
3. Funding.
4. Fiduciary responsibilities.
5. Administration and enforcement.
6. Continuation coverage and additional standards for group health plans.
7. Group health plan portability, access, and renewability requirements.

Congress endorsed the need for this title based on four major considerations. First, Congress observed that many companies terminated pension plans after employees had accumulated several years of service. Second, many companies were forced to terminate pension plans due to insufficient funding to pay retirement benefits. Third, many companies did not provide employees information about their pension plans (e.g., the rate at which benefits accumulate over time). Fourth, the absence of federal regulations setting minimum standards for funding pension programs resulted in the financial failure of many pension plans, leaving beneficiaries without any retirement benefits. Altogether, these problems threatened employee security, particularly with regard to progressive wages and benefits.

Part 1: Reporting and Disclosure

These provisions impose three requirements on employers regarding pension plans and other employee benefits plans. First, employers must provide employees understandable and comprehensive summaries of their pension and welfare benefits plans, information about changes to these plans, and advance notification of planned termination of these plans. Second, employees are entitled to receive reports on their status in the plans, including service credits and accumulated benefits. Third, employers are required to report detailed financial and actuarial data about the plans to the U.S. Treasury Department. Companies may satisfy this reporting requirement by completing **Form 5500.** This form can be obtained from the Internal Revenue Service Web site at www.irs.gov.

Part 2: Participation and Vesting

Strict participation requirements apply to pension plans. Specifically, employees must be allowed to participate in pension plans after they have reached age 21[10] and have completed one year of service (based on 1,000 work hours).[11] These hours include all paid time for performing work and paid time-off (e.g., vacation, sick leave, holidays). The one-year requirement may be extended to two years if the company grants full vesting after two years of participation in the pension plan. In addition, companies may not exclude employees from participating in pension plans because they are too old.

Vesting refers to an employee's nonforfeitable rights to pension benefits.[12] Vesting has two aspects. First, employees are always vested in their contributions to pension plans. Second, companies must grant full vesting rights to employer contributions on one of the following two schedules. **Cliff vesting** schedules must grant employees 100 percent vesting after no more than three years from beginning participation in the retirement plan. This schedule is known as cliff vesting because leaving one's job prior to becoming vested under this schedule is tantamount to falling off a cliff because an employee loses all the accrued employer contributions. Alternatively, companies may use a gradual vesting schedule. The **six-year graduated schedule** allows workers to become 20 percent vested after two years and to vest at a rate of 20 percent each year thereafter until they are 100 percent vested after six years from beginning participation in the retirement plan. Exhibit 4.3 shows an example of the six-year graduated schedule. For example, let's assume an employer has adopted the six-year gradual vesting schedule. Also

EXHIBIT 4.3
Sample of a
Six-Year
Graduated
Vesting
Schedule
under ERISA

Years of Vesting Service	Nonforfeitable Percentage
2	20%
3	40
4	60
5	80
6	100

assume that this employer has contributed $15,000 to an employee's retirement account since she began her employment two years ago. According to the gradual vesting schedule, this employee has earned a 20 percent nonforfeitable right to the employer's contribution—that is, $3,000 = (20% × $15,000). Plans may have faster gradual schedules to 100 percent vesting in fewer than six years. The graduated schedule is preferable to employees who anticipate changing jobs frequently because they will earn the rights to keep part of the employer's contribution sooner. Moreover, employees recognize that layoffs are more common in today's volatile business environment and they stand to benefit by earning partial vesting rights sooner than earning full vesting rights at a later date. On the other hand, employers prefer the cliff vesting schedule. The use of this schedule allows employers to reclaim nonvested contributions for employees who leave before becoming vested.

Sometimes, employees experience breaks in service by terminating employment for a period, followed by reemployment.[13] Companies may choose to factor breaks in service into calculations of years of service for vesting purposes. Breaks in service are based on one-year increments. Employees have a one-year break in service when they did not work more than 500 hours during a 12-month period from the date of hire. These individuals may earn service credit for the period prior to the break if they complete at least one year of work following the service break.

However, companies are not required to take into account breaks in service if the number of consecutive one-year breaks equals or exceeds the greater of five or the aggregate number of years of service before such period.

Once employees attain full vesting rights, they cannot lose their pension benefits if they terminate employment prior to reaching retirement age. If individuals resume employment at a later date, companies must use total years of service (i.e., service prior to termination plus service following reemployment) to calculate retirement benefits.

Finally, vesting rights require provisions for survivor benefits to married employees.[14] However, married employees may waive survivor benefits with a spouse's written consent.

Part 3: Funding

ERISA imposes several funding requirements on employers. Essentially, employers must contribute sufficient annual funding for all pension benefits earned by employees. In the event of underfunding, companies must notify plan participants. Failure to comply with this funding requirement leads to excise tax penalties. These penalties are expressed as a percentage of the amount in question, and the percentage may vary based on the length of time an employer remains in violation. In the event of underfunding, employers must speed up the amortization schedule for covering liabilities. Failure to correct underfunding entitles the federal government to place liens against the employer's assets.

Part 4: Fiduciary Responsibilities

Fiduciaries are individuals who manage employee benefits plans and pension plan funds. One or more individuals may serve as fiduciaries. Examples of possible fiduciaries include the following:

- Employers.
- Insurance companies.
- Attorneys.
- Corporate directors, officers, or principal stockholders.

ERISA requires fiduciaries to use prudence in the exercise of their duties as they ensure the welfare of participants and beneficiaries while defraying reasonable plan expenses.[15] There are three additional **fiduciary responsibilities:**[16]

- Using the care, skill, and diligence that a prudent person would use under similar circumstances.
- Diversifying plan investments to minimize the risk of large losses.
- Acting according to the plan document, as long as it is consistent with ERISA.

ERISA indicates that plan assets generally are held in trust. These **trusts** are managed by trustees who are either named in the trust instrument or appointed by the plan's named fiduciary.[17] **Trustees** have exclusive authority to manage and control plan assets unless otherwise specified in the plan document.

Part 5: Administration and Enforcement

Three federal government agencies share responsibility for the administration and enforcement of ERISA provisions: the **U.S. Department of Labor,** the **Internal Revenue Service (IRS),** and the **Pension Benefit Guarantee Corporation (PBGC).** Title III of ERISA empowers the U.S. Department of Labor and the Internal Revenue Service to administer and enforce specific sections of this Act. Title IV established the PBGC.

Part 6: Continuation Coverage and Additional Standards for Group Health Plans

The **Consolidated Omnibus Budget Reconciliation Act of 1985 (COBRA)** amended ERISA by providing employees and beneficiaries the right to elect continuation coverage under group health plans if they would lose coverage due to a qualifying event. We will review COBRA and such concepts as qualifying events later in this chapter.

Part 7: Group Health Plan Portability, Access, and Renewability Requirements

The **Health Insurance Portability and Accountability Act of 1996 (HIPAA)** amended ERISA. HIPAA imposes requirements on group health and health insurance issuers relating to portability, increased access by limiting preexisting limitation rules, renewability, and health care privacy. We will review HIPAA later in this chapter.

Title II: Amendments to the Internal Revenue Code Relating to Retirement Plans

Title II amends the IRC relating to the tax treatment of pension and employee benefits plans. Benefits professionals often describe the interplay between ERISA and the IRC as the "carrot and the stick." The IRC provides the carrot, or incentive, for employers to establish employee benefits plans through favorable tax treatment. ERISA serves as the stick or deterrent to possible illegal employer treatment of benefits and pension plans by providing legal remedies to employees and beneficiaries.

Some of these amendments mirror the following Title I provisions: participation, vesting, and minimum funding standards. Additional amendments pertain to (1) nondiscrimination of coverage requirements (Chapter 5 for the treatment of employer-sponsored retirement plans); (2) contribution and benefits limits to company-sponsored retirement plans (Chapter 5); and (3) Individual Retirement Accounts and Keogh Plans for self-employed persons.

We will review the first two amendments in the designated forthcoming chapters. The third amendment falls outside the scope of company-sponsored plans.

Title III: Jurisdiction, Administration, Enforcement, Joint Pension Task Force, and Other Issues

Title III of ERISA grants power to the U.S. Department of Labor for administering and enforcing Title I of ERISA: reporting and disclosure requirements and fiduciary responsibility. The U.S. Department of Labor's **Pension and Welfare Benefits Administration,** an agency of the department, possesses responsibility for enforcing Title I. The Pension and Welfare Benefits Administration enforces ERISA by conducting investigations through its 10 regional offices and 5 district offices located in major cities throughout the country. These field offices conduct investigations to gather information and evaluate compliance with ERISA's civil law requirements, as well as criminal law provisions relating to employee benefits plans.

In April 2000, the Pension and Welfare Benefits Administration announced its **Strategic Enforcement Plan (StEP)** for enforcing Title I. The primary purpose of the StEP is to establish a general framework through which the Pension and Welfare Benefits Administration's enforcement resources may be efficiently and effectively focused to achieve the agency's policies and operational objectives.[18]

The Internal Revenue Service ensures compliance with the tax qualification requirements of the IRC. The IRS has the primary responsibility for enforcing the Title II provisions of ERISA: minimum participation, vesting, distributions, and funding rules of qualified plans. It uses a system called **Employee Plans Compliance Resolution System (EPCRS)** that encourages companies to take the initiative to correct violations.[19] Title III established various ad hoc committees to study a host of issues pertaining to ERISA. The duration of the work of these committees was relatively short, spanning approximately two years following the enactment of ERISA. For example, the **Joint Pension, Profit-Sharing, and Employee Stock Ownership Plan Task Force** examined several issues, including the means of providing for the portability of pension rights among different pension plans and the appropriate treatment under Title IV.

Title IV: Plan Termination Insurance

Title IV established the Pension Benefit Guarantee Corporation (PBGC), which is a tax-exempt, self-financed corporation created to insure defined benefit pension plans. Its operations are financed by insurance premiums set by Congress and paid for by sponsors of defined benefit plans, investment income, assets from pension plans trusteed by the PBGC, and recovery of at least some money from the companies formerly responsible for the plans. The PBGC pays monthly retirement benefits, up to a guaranteed maximum, currently to about 1,152,000 retirees in 3,860 pension plans that were terminated. It is also responsible for providing the current and future pensions for those who have not yet retired and participants in multiemployer plans receiving financial assistance. In 2008, the PBGC paid more than $4.3 billion in benefits to retirees of terminated pension plans.

PBGC currently insures about 29,000 private defined benefit pension plans covering more than 44 million American workers and retirees. Under PBGC's pension insurance programs, the administrators of these plans and the companies that sponsor the plans have a number of reporting and administrative responsibilities. These duties include paying annual pension insurance premiums and reporting significant events affecting their plans.

The PBGC's program recognizes three types of plan terminations: distress terminations, involuntary terminations, and standard terminations. Exhibit 4.4 contains a description of these termination types and the PBGC-mandated procedures for conducting them.

Defined contribution plans are not eligible to participate in this program because they do not guarantee a particular benefit at retirement. Some employer pension programs are excluded:

- Plans maintained by professional service employers with fewer than 25 active participants. Examples include sole proprietorships, partnerships, corporations, or other organizations owned by professionals for the purpose of offering professional services (e.g., medical doctors, dentists, attorneys, psychologists).
- Plans maintained by governmental entities or agencies.
- Most church plans.

EXHIBIT 4.4 Types of Pension Plan Termination

Source: www.pbgc.gov/publications/factshts/TERMFACT.HTM. Accessed March 1, 2007.

The Pension Benefit Guarantee Corporation (PBGC) recognizes three types of plan termination, with specific requirements for the termination process.

Distress Termination

A company in financial distress may voluntarily terminate a pension plan if:

- The plan administrator has issued a Notice of Intent to Terminate to affected parties, including PBGC, at least 60 days, and no more than 90 days, in advance of the proposed termination date.
- The plan administrator has issued a subsequent termination notice to PBGC, which includes data concerning the number of participants and the plan's assets and liabilities.
- PBGC has determined that the plan sponsor and each of its corporate affiliates have satisfied at least one of the following financial distress tests—though not necessarily the same test:
  - A petition has been filed seeking liquidation in bankruptcy;
  - A petition has been filed seeking reorganization in bankruptcy, and the bankruptcy court (or an appropriate state court) has determined that the company will not be able to reorganize with the plan intact and approves the plan termination;
  - It has been demonstrated that the sponsor or affiliate cannot continue in business unless the plan is terminated; or
  - It has been demonstrated that the costs of providing pension coverage have become unreasonably burdensome solely as a result of a decline in the number of employees covered by the plan.

Involuntary Termination

The law provides that PBGC may terminate a pension plan, even if a company has not filed to terminate a plan on its own initiative, if:

- The plan has not met the minimum funding requirements.
- The plan cannot pay current benefits when due.
- A lump sum payment has been made to a participant who is a substantial owner of the sponsoring company.
- The loss to PBGC is expected to increase unreasonably if the plan is not terminated.

PBGC must terminate a plan if assets are unavailable to pay benefits currently due.

Standard Termination

A plan may terminate only if plan assets are sufficient to satisfy all plan benefits and if the plan administrator has taken the following steps:

- Issued a Notice of Intent to Terminate to affected parties other than PBGC at least 60 days, and no more than 90 days, before the proposed termination date; it also must inform plan participants that PBGC's guarantee of their benefits will cease upon distribution of plan assets.
- Informed plan participants of the identity of the private insurer from whom an annuity is being purchased or the names of insurers from whom bids will be sought no later than 45 days before the distribution of plan assets.
- Sent each plan participant a notice that includes the benefit the participant has earned and data the plan used to calculate the value of the benefit.
- Submitted a termination notice to PBGC, which includes certified data on the plan's assets and liabilities as of the proposed date of distribution.
- Distributed plan assets to cover all benefit liabilities under the plan.

(continued)

EXHIBIT 4.4 (*Continued*)

Plans must provide PBGC with the names of any missing participants and either money to pay their benefits or the name of the insurer holding their annuities. Before sending money to PBGC, the plan administrator must conduct a diligent search that includes using a commercial locator service.

If assets cannot cover all benefit liabilities, the plan administrator must notify PBGC and stop the termination process. If the plan administrator does not follow proper procedures, PBGC may issue a Notice of Noncompliance that nullifies the proposed termination.

Annuity insurer selections are fiduciary decisions and must comply with fiduciary provisions of Title I of ERISA, which is enforced by the Department of Labor.

- Plans established and maintained exclusively for a business's "substantial owners" (e.g., a person who owns the entire interest in an unincorporated trade or business, or a partner who possesses more than a 10 percent financial interest).
- Plans maintained solely to comply with workers' compensation, unemployment compensation, or disability insurance laws.

Termination insurance protects against the loss of vested pension benefits when plans fail. Employers with eligible defined benefit pension plans must purchase termination insurance. Insurance premiums are set by Congress for employers according to the number of covered employees and whether a pension plan covers employees of just one company (single-employer plans) or a collective bargaining agreement maintains a pension plan to which more than one employer contributes (multiemployer plans).

In addition, the PBGC ensures a basic level of annual benefits to participants in the event that a plan terminates with insufficient assets to pay its obligations. The maximum PBGC-guaranteed annual benefit is adjusted every year.[20] For plans ended in 2009, the maximum annual benefit was $54,000 for those who retire at age 65. The amount is higher for those who retire later and lower for those who retire earlier or elect survivor benefits. The guarantee is lower for those who retire early or when there is a benefit for a survivor. The maximum benefit amount is lower for benefits commencing at ages below 65, reflecting the fact that younger retirees receive more monthly pension checks over a longer remaining lifespan. The maximum amount is higher for benefits commencing at ages above 65, reflecting the fact that older retirees receive fewer monthly pension checks over their remaining lifespan.

Further, ERISA requires the PBGC to audit a random sample of terminated single-employer plans to make certain participants have received the right amount of benefits. The PBGC also audits premium payments by reviewing premium forms and coordinating information with other agencies. On its own initiative, the PBGC developed an early warning program for large underfunded plans to identify and address potential problems. An analysis of company financial statements, government reports, and actuarial valuations assists the PBGC judgment of the possibility of future plan terminations and potentially undermining transactions.

Unfortunately, there has been a trend toward increasing defined benefit plan terminations over the past few years because of the poor economy, which has led many companies to file for bankruptcy protection. More often than not, companies that go into bankruptcy or are struggling to survive during slow economic times do not adequately fund plans. Inadequate funding could easily leave employees without promised retirement benefits in the future when they are eligible to retire. For example, the PBGC assumed responsibility in 2007 for the pensions of almost 900 current and former employees of Kaiser Aluminum & Chemical Company. The PBGC assumed the plans after a federal appeals court affirmed a lower court ruling that upheld a bankruptcy court which found that the company satisfied the legal test for terminating the plans. Retirees will continue to receive their monthly benefit checks without interruption, and other workers will receive their pensions when they are eligible to retire. The four Kaiser pension plans, which terminated as of October 10, 2006, are known as the Bellwood Plan, the Los Angeles Extrusion Plan, the Sherman Plan, and the Tulsa Plan. Together, the plans have assets of $20.1 million to cover promised benefits totaling $29.6 million, according to PBGC estimates. The agency expects to be liable for $2.7 million of the $9.5 million shortfall.

The PBGC also announced that it has become trustee of the Delta Air Lines Inc. Pilots Retirement Plan, taking over the responsibility for paying pension benefits to more than 13,000 active and retired pilots. The pension plan for pilots is underfunded by about $3 billion, with $1.7 billion in assets to cover more than $4.7 billion in benefit liabilities. Of the $3 billion in underfunding, the PBGC estimates that it will be liable for almost $920 million, making the Delta pilots plan the sixth-largest claim in the agency's 32-year history. The plan ended as of September 2, 2006, and the PBGC became trustee on December 31, 2006.

THE CONSOLIDATED OMNIBUS BUDGET RECONCILIATION ACT OF 1985

COBRA is a substantial amendment to ERISA, Title I (Part 6: Continuation Coverage and Additional Standards for Group Health Plans).

Coverage

COBRA applies to private sector companies with at least 20 employees, and state and local government agencies. However, churches and the federal government are exempt because COBRA is an amendment to ERISA, which excludes church plans and the federal government.[21]

Relevance to Group Health Plans

Companies are required to permit *qualified beneficiaries* to elect *continuation coverage* under group health plans if they would lose coverage due to a *qualifying event*. In other words, an employee or his or her dependents may continue to receive employer-sponsored health insurance for a designated period of time. To fully understand COBRA, it is necessary to know the meanings of qualifying events, qualified beneficiaries, and continuation coverage.

Qualifying events include the following:

- Death of the covered employee.
- Termination or reduction in hours of employment (other than by reason of misconduct).
- Divorce or legal separation.
- Dependent child ceasing to meet the health plan's definition of a dependent child.
- Covered employee becoming eligible for Medicare benefits under the Social Security Act.[22]

In general, a **qualified beneficiary**[23] is any individual who is a beneficiary under the group health plan:

- Spouse of the covered employee.
- Dependent child of the covered employee.

Qualified beneficiaries include the covered employees themselves when the qualifying event is termination of employment (other than by reason of misconduct) or a reduction in work hours.

The **election period** generally refers to the period that begins on or before the occurrence of the qualifying event, and it extends for at least 60 days.

Beneficiaries are responsible for paying the insurance premium. Companies are permitted to charge COBRA beneficiaries a premium for **continuation coverage** of up to 102 percent of the cost of the coverage to the plan. The 2 percent markup reflects a charge for administering COBRA. Continuation coverage must be identical to coverage offered to active employees in terms of deductibles, coinsurance, plan options, and benefit limitations. For instance, an employer pays $250 per month per employee to provide health insurance protection. A qualified beneficiary would generally pay the monthly premium plus an additional 2 percent. In this case, that amount would be

$$\$250 + (2\% \times \$250) = \$255$$

The **American Recovery and Reinvestment Act of 2009** (ARRA) provides for a 65 percent reduction in COBRA premiums for certain assistance-eligible individuals for up to 9 months. An assistance-eligible individual is a COBRA "qualified beneficiary" who meets all the following requirements:

- Is eligible for COBRA continuation coverage at any time during the period beginning September 1, 2008, and ending December 31, 2009.
- Elects COBRA coverage (when first offered or during the additional election period).
- Has a qualifying event for COBRA coverage (that is the employee's involuntary termination) during the period beginning September 1, 2008, and ending December 31, 2009.

Those who are eligible for other group health coverage (such as a spouse's plan) or Medicare are not eligible for the premium reduction. Other limitations may also apply. There is no premium reduction for periods of coverage that began prior to February 17, 2009.

The period of continuation coverage ranges between 18 and 36 months after the qualifying event, which specifies the minimum coverage period. The normal COBRA coverage continuation period is either 18 or 36 months.[24] Covered employees and qualified beneficiaries may receive continuation coverage for an 18-month period in cases where coverage is lost due to the employee's termination or reduction of hours. Qualified beneficiaries with disabilities are entitled to extended coverage for 29 months. The 29-month period applies to disabilities incurred prior to, or up to, 60 days after the qualifying event.[25] Qualified beneficiaries may receive up to 36 months of continued coverage if the qualifying event includes the covered employee's divorce or legal separation, or death. The 36-month period also applies to dependent children who reach the maximum age for coverage under an employer's plan.[26]

The standard coverage rules change with fewer than two particular circumstances. First, covered employees and qualified beneficiaries receiving 18 months of continuation coverage are entitled to receive extended continuation coverage due to divorce or the death of the covered employee following the original qualifying event. **Multiple qualifying event rules** entitle these individuals to receive up to 36 months of continuation coverage from the original qualifying event.[27]

Second, employer bankruptcy under Chapter 11 of the Federal Bankruptcy Code modifies continuation coverage rules. Retirees and their qualified beneficiaries who lose health coverage due to employer bankruptcy (within one year of this event) are entitled to receive lifetime continuation coverage. Survivors of covered retirees are entitled to receive 36 months of continuation coverage following the retiree's death.[28]

Employers may terminate continuation coverage under the following circumstances:[29]

- The employer no longer offers health plans to any employees.
- The qualified beneficiary or covered employee fails to pay premiums on a timely basis, usually within 30 days of the due date or as specified by the health plan.
- The qualified beneficiary receives coverage under another health plan, as long as termination does not violate the new health plan's preexisting conditions clause.
- The qualified beneficiary becomes entitled to Medicare benefits under the Social Security Act.
- The qualified beneficiary is no longer disabled.

THE HEALTH INSURANCE PORTABILITY AND ACCOUNTABILITY ACT OF 1996

HIPAA is a substantial amendment to ERISA, Title I (Part 7: Group Health Plan Portability, Access, and Renewability Requirements). This act contains four main provisions. The first provision is intended to guarantee that employees and their dependents that leave their employer's group health plan will have ready access to coverage under a subsequent employer's health plan, regardless of their health or claims experience. The second provision sets limits on the length of time health plans and health insurance issuers may impose preexisting conditions and identifies conditions to which no preexisting condition may apply. A preexisting health condition generally refers to a medical condition for which a diagnosis was made or treatment given prior to enrolling in a health insurance plan. The third provision counts periods of continuous coverage under another form of comprehensive health coverage toward a preexisting condition limit. In other words, time covered under a previous health insurance plan reduces the preexisting condition requirement imposed by a new health insurance company. The fourth provision protects the transfer, disclosure, and use of health care information.

Coverage

HIPAA applies to all employers offering group health plans.

Availability and Portability

HIPAA prohibits discrimination against individuals and beneficiaries based on health status and related factors. Specifically, health plans may not create rules that would limit eligibility for initial enrollment, continued eligibility for currently covered employees and beneficiaries, or require higher premiums based on any of the reasons listed in Exhibit 4.5.

Limits to Preexisting Condition Rules

Prior to HIPAA, group insurance plans excluded coverage of **preexisting conditions** for up to 12 months. HIPAA reduces **preexisting condition periods** based on credits for prior coverage under a former employer's health plan. In this context, credits refers to the period of prior creditable coverage. Companies usually base creditable coverage on an individual's participation in the following:[30]

- A group health plan, including a governmental or church plan.
- Health insurance coverage, either group or individual insurance.
- Medicare.

EXHIBIT 4.5   **Prohibited Reasons for Limiting Participation in Group Health Plans under HIPAA**

Source: 29 C.F.R. §2590.702.

- Health status.
- Medical condition, including physical and mental illness.
- Claims experience.
- Receipt of health care.
- Medical history.
- Genetic information.
- Evidence of insurability (including conditions arising out of acts of domestic violence).
- Disability.

- Medicaid.
- Military-sponsored health care.
- Public health plan.
- A medical care program of the Indian Health Service or of a tribal organization.
- A health benefits plan under paragraph 5 of the Peace Corps Act.

Renewability

HIPAA generally mandates that group health insurance issuers renew coverage. However, group health insurance issuers are not required to renew coverage under certain conditions. These include:[31]

- Nonpayment of contributions.
- Fraud or other intentional misrepresentation of material facts by the employer.
- Noncompliance with plan provisions.
- Ceasing to offer coverage to all individuals in a geographic area.
- Failure to meet the terms of an applicable collective bargaining agreement, or failure to renew a collective bargaining or other agreement authorizing contributions to the health insurance plan.

Health Care Privacy

Effective February 2003, covered health care entities must receive a patient's consent for use and disclosure of health records.[32] Covered care entities include health plans, health care clearinghouses, and those health care providers who conduct certain financial and administrative transactions (e.g., electronic billing). Also, employers may not make employment decisions based on health status unless they receive written employee consent. Before employers obtain written consent, they must fully disclose how and for what purpose the health information will be used.

THE PENSION PROTECTION ACT OF 2006

The **Pension Protection Act** is designed to strengthen protections for employees' company-sponsored retirement plans in at least two ways. The first consideration refers to defined benefit plans, and the second refers to defined contribution plans. First, this law should strengthen the financial condition of the PBGC by requiring that private sector companies that underfund their defined benefit plans pay substantially higher premiums (i.e., cost to provide insurance protection) to insure retirement benefits. After all, experience tells us there is a greater likelihood that the PBGC will have to take over highly underfunded defined benefit plans. The increase in underfunded plans poses a greater risk to the financial solvency of the PBGC. In other words, think of the PBGC as an automobile insurance company, and young drivers with automobile insurance as companies with underfunded defined benefit plans. An automobile insurance company charges higher premiums to drivers under age 25 because years of data show that young drivers are more likely to get into multiple serious accidents than older drivers. After getting into a car accident, a person files a claim to the insurance company to pay for the cost of repairs. Of course, repair costs for serious accidents will be much more expensive than for minor accidents. So, insurance companies charge higher premiums to these drivers because they are more likely to file expensive claims. Higher premiums will make it easier for insurance companies to stay financially solvent because they anticipated such claims. The Pension Protection Act law also aims to shore up the PBGC's financial condition by making it more difficult for companies to skip making premium payments. Finally, this new law raises the amount that employers can contribute to pension funding with tax advantages, creating an additional incentive to adequately fund pension plans.

Second, the Pension Protection Act makes it easier for employees to participate in employer-sponsored defined contribution plans such as 401(k) plans. Millions of workers who are eligible to participate in their employers' defined contribution plans choose not to contribute to them for a variety of reasons, but one prominent reason is that most individuals feel they do not have sufficient knowledge about how to choose investment options (e.g., a high-risk mutual fund versus a fixed-rate annuity) that will help them earn sufficient money for retirement. Also, once employees make the decision to participate in these plans and have been making regular contributions, they are not likely to stop. With these issues in mind, the Pension Protection Act enables companies to automatically enroll their employees in defined contribution plans and provides greater access to professional advice about investing for retirement. In addition, this act requires that companies give multiple investment options to allow employees to select how much risk they are willing to bear. As an aside, risky investments usually have the potential for substantial gains or losses in value. Less risky investments usually have the potential for lower gains or losses. Previously, some companies limited investment opportunities to company stock, which exposed employees to substantial investment risk.

FEDERAL EQUAL EMPLOYMENT OPPORTUNITY LAWS

Several federal **equal employment opportunity** laws prohibit illegal discrimination against various protected classes of individuals regarding all employment practices, including employee benefits. The Equal Employment Opportunity Commission (EEOC), a federal government agency, oversees the enforcement of these laws. Job applicants and employees file claims with the EEOC if they have reason to believe they were discriminated against on the basis of race, color, sex, religion, national origin, age, or disability, or believe they have been discriminated against because of opposition to a prohibited practice or participation in an equal employment opportunity matter. The EEOC provides a number of services to employers, including training sessions and policy manuals, that help them comply with the following laws:

- The Equal Pay Act of 1963.
- Title VII of the Civil Rights Act of 1964.

- The Age Discrimination in Employment Act of 1967.
- The Pregnancy Discrimination Act of 1978.
- The Americans with Disabilities Act of 1990.
- The Civil Rights Act of 1991.
- Genetic Information Nondiscrimination Act of 2008.

Coverage

The scope of coverage varies somewhat for each law. Specific coverage requirements are stated for each law.

The Equal Pay Act of 1963

The **Equal Pay Act of 1963** is an amendment to the minimum wage provisions of the FLSA. Congress enacted the Equal Pay Act of 1963 to remedy a serious problem of employment discrimination in private industry: "Many segments of American industry have been based on an ancient but outmoded belief that a man, because of his role in society, should be paid more than a woman even though his duties are the same."[33]

Coverage

The Equal Pay Act applies to the same organizations as does the FLSA.

Relevance to Employee Benefits Practices

The Equal Pay Act of 1963 is based on a simple principle. Men and women should receive equal pay for performing equal work. Specifically:

> No employer . . . shall discriminate within any establishment in which such employees are employed, between employees on the basis of sex by paying wages to employees in such establishment at a rate less than the rate at which he pays wages to employees of the opposite sex . . . for equal work on jobs the performance of which requires equal skill, effort, and responsibility, and which are performed under similar working conditions, except where such payment is made pursuant to (i) a seniority system; (ii) a merit system; (iii) a system which measures earnings by quantity or quality of production; or (iv) a differential based on any other factor other than sex.[34]

The definition of wages in the Equal Pay Act encompasses employee benefits. The Equal Employment Opportunity Commission defined wages to include all payments made to, or on behalf of, an employee as compensation for employment. Thus, employers must provide equal employee benefits to male and female employees who perform equal work, along with their beneficiaries, regardless of cost differences.

The Equal Pay Act of 1963 pertains explicitly to jobs of *equal* worth. Companies assign pay rates to jobs according to the levels of skill, effort, responsibility, and working conditions. *Skill, effort, responsibility,* and *working conditions* represent **compensable factors.** Exhibit 4.6 lists the U.S. Department of Labor's definitions of these compensable factors.

EXHIBIT 4.6 U.S. Department of Labor's Definitions of Skill, Effort, Responsibility, and Working Conditions

Source: U.S. Department of Labor, *Equal Pay for Equal Work under the Fair Labor Standards Act* (Washington, DC: U.S. Dept. of Labor, December 31, 1971).

Skill	Experience, training, education, and ability as measured by the performance requirements of a job.
Effort	Mental or physical. The amount of effort expended in the performance of the job.
Responsibility	The degree of accountability required in the performance of a job.
Working Conditions	The physical surroundings and hazards of a job, including dimensions such as inside versus outside work, heat, cold, and poor ventilation.

Title VII of the Civil Rights Act of 1964

Title VII of the Civil Rights Act of 1964 prohibits illegal discrimination against protected-class individuals in employment. The Civil Rights Act grew out of broader social unrest among members of different underrepresented minorities such as women and African Americans who spoke out against unfair treatment throughout society. Prior to Title VII, employers could legally refuse to hire highly qualified individuals simply on the basis of race, color, religion, sex, or national origin in favor of less qualified individuals who were not members of underrepresented minority groups.

Coverage

Title VII protects employees who work for all private sector employers; local, state, and federal governments; and educational institutions that employ 15 or more individuals. Title VII also applies to private and public employment agencies, labor organizations, and joint labor management committees controlling apprenticeship and training.

Relevance to Employee Benefits Practices

> It shall be an unlawful employment practice for an employer—(1) to fail or refuse to hire or to discharge any individual, or otherwise to discriminate against any individual with respect to his compensation *including employee benefits* [author's emphasis], terms, conditions, or privileges of employment, because of such individual's race, color, religion, sex, or national origin; or (2) to limit, segregate, or classify his employees or applicants for employment in any way which would deprive or tend to deprive any individual of employment opportunities or otherwise adversely affect his status as an employee, because of such individual's race, color, religion, sex, or national origin.[35]

The Age Discrimination in Employment Act of 1967 (ADEA)

The **Age Discrimination in Employment Act of 1967 (ADEA)** prohibits illegal discrimination in employment on the basis of age. The ADEA specifies that it is unlawful for an employer

(1) to fail or refuse to hire or to discharge any individual or otherwise discriminate against any individual with respect to his compensation, terms, conditions, or privileges of employment, because of such individual's age; (2) to limit, segregate or classify his employees in any way which would deprive or tend to deprive any individual of employment opportunities or otherwise adversely affect his status as an employee, because of such individual's age; or (3) to reduce the wage rate of any employee in order to comply with this Act.[36]

Coverage

ADEA applies to all private sector employers with 20 or more employees; state and local governments, with some exceptions; employment agencies serving covered employers; and labor unions with 25 or more members.

Relevance to Employee Benefits Practices

The ADEA makes specific reference to employee benefits. The ADEA also sets limits on the development and implementation of employer "early retirement" practices, which many companies use to reduce the size of the workforce. Most early retirement programs are offered to employees who are at least 55 years of age. These early retirement programs are permissible when companies offer them to employees on a voluntary basis. Forcing early retirement upon older workers represents age discrimination (*EEOC v. Chrysler*).[37]

The **Older Workers Benefit Protection Act (OWBPA)**[38]—the 1990 amendment to the ADEA—placed additional restrictions on employer benefits practices. When employers require employee contributions toward their benefits, under particular circumstances, employers can require older employees to pay more for health care insurance, disability insurance, or life insurance than younger employees because these benefits generally become more costly with age (for example, older workers may be more likely to incur serious illnesses; thus, insurance companies may charge employers higher rates to provide coverage to older than younger workers). Here are some examples:

- An older employee may not be required to pay more for the benefit *as a condition of employment*. Where the premium has increased for an older employee, the employer must offer the employee the option of withdrawing from the benefit plan altogether. The employer can alternatively offer the employee the option of reducing his/her benefit coverage in order to keep his/her premium cost the same.
- An older employee may be offered the *option* of paying—or paying more—for the benefit in order to avoid otherwise justified reductions in coverage. Where the employee does choose to pay more, s/he can be charged no more than the amount that is necessary to maintain full coverage.
- An older employee who chooses to participate in a voluntary plan *can* be required to pay more for the benefit, but only if the employee does not pay a greater percentage of his/her premium cost than younger employees do.

To illustrate the previous point, let's assume that Company A has 3,000 employees, and 25 percent (750 employees) are age 40 or older while 75 percent (2,250 employees) are age 39 or younger. Let's also assume that the annual employee contributions total $120,000 for Company A's workforce. Finally, an analysis of these contributions reveals that the older workers paid $84,000, accounting for 70 percent of these contributions (70% × $120,000). The younger workers paid $36,000, accounting for only 30 percent (30% × $120,000). The older workers paid disproportionately more than the younger workers.

- Older workers: 25 percent of the workforce paid 70 percent of the total contributions.
- Younger workers: 75 percent of the workforce paid 30 percent of the total contributions.

In addition, employers can legally reduce the coverage of older workers for benefits that may become more costly as they further age. Benefits that may meet this criterion include disability insurance, health insurance, and life insurance. The employer may reduce the coverage of these benefits *only if* the costs for providing insurance to them are significantly greater than the cost for younger workers, and not simply because they are assumed to be more expensive. When costs differ significantly, the employer may reduce the benefit for older workers only to the point where it is paying just as much per older worker (with lower coverage) as it is for younger workers (with higher coverage). This practice is referred to as the **equal benefit or equal cost principle.**

The OWBPA does not apply to the following benefits:

- Voluntary early retirement plans.
- Early retirement benefit subsidies in defined benefit pension plans.
- Payment of Social Security supplements under defined benefit pension plans.
- Minimum ages for benefit eligibility in pension plans.
- Reduced severance benefits.
- Deductions for long-term disability benefits.

The Pregnancy Discrimination Act of 1978

The **Pregnancy Discrimination Act of 1978 (PDA)** is an amendment to Title VII of the Civil Rights Act of 1964. The PDA prohibits discrimination against pregnant women in all employment practices. Congress enacted the Pregnancy Discrimination Act because various court rulings revealed that employment discrimination against pregnant women did not violate the "sex" provision of Title VII. In *Nashville Gas Co. v. Satty,*[39] the court held that excluding benefits for pregnant women from the company's disability plan did not violate Title VII. The court's decision was based on the following rationale: Both men and women who were not pregnant benefited from the company's disability plan, and there was no reason to believe that men received more benefits than women.

Coverage

The Pregnancy Discrimination Act applies to the same organizations as Title VII of the Civil Rights Act.

Relevance to Employee Benefits Practices

Employers must not treat pregnancy less favorably than other medical conditions covered under employee benefits plans. In addition, employers must treat pregnancy and childbirth the same way they treat other causes of disability. Further, the PDA protects the rights of women who take leave for pregnancy-related reasons. The protected rights include credit for previous service, accrued retirement benefits, and accumulated seniority.

The Americans with Disabilities Act of 1990

The Equal Employment Opportunity Commission ruled that employers must offer benefits to workers with disabilities on the same basis as those offered for nondisabled employees. To rectify abuses to the disabled, Congress passed the Americans with Disabilities Act (ADA) in 1990. In particular, employers are required to provide the same health insurance coverage to employees regardless of disability status. Also, an employer may not fire or refuse to hire a person with a disability or any qualified person with a family member who is disabled or dependent with a disability because the health insurance policy does not cover the disability, or because the costs of insurance coverage would increase. Finally, retirement plans cannot impose different requirements on employees with disabilities. Sometimes employers offer disability insurance for retirees. The ADA does not prohibit employers from offering less generous disability retirement benefits to the disabled than to those without disabilities.

On September 25, 2008, President George W. Bush signed the **Americans with Disabilities Act Amendments Act of 2008**, making important changes to the definition of the term *disability*. These changes make it easier for an individual seeking protection under the ADA to establish that he or she has a disability within the meaning of the ADA.

The act retains the ADA's basic definition of disability as an impairment that substantially limits one or more major life activities, a record of such an impairment, or being regarded as having such an impairment. However, it changes the way that these statutory terms should be interpreted:

- Expands the definition of "major life activities" by including two nonexhaustive lists:
- The first list includes many activities that the EEOC has recognized (e.g., walking) as well as activities that EEOC has not specifically recognized (e.g., reading, bending, and communicating).
- The second list includes major bodily functions (e.g., "functions of the immune system, normal cell growth, digestive, bowel, bladder, neurological, brain, respiratory, circulatory, endocrine, and reproductive functions").
- States that mitigating measures other than "ordinary eyeglasses or contact lenses" shall not be considered in assessing whether an individual has a disability.
- Clarifies that an impairment that is episodic or in remission is a disability if it would substantially limit a major life activity when active.

Coverage

The **Americans with Disabilities Act (ADA)** applies to the same organizations as Title VII of the Civil Rights Act.

Relevance to Employee Benefits

Lawsuits alleging ADA violations have been extremely complex, particularly regarding benefits. For example, an employee could claim under ADA that he is a qualified individual with a disability and simultaneously apply for disability benefits. These claims appear to be contradictory. On one hand, the employee is capable of working with reasonable accommodation. On the other hand, the same employee's application for disability benefits indicates otherwise.

Giles injured his back while performing his job as a machinist at General Electric (GE). Eventually, he required surgery. Following surgery and a convalescent period, Giles's surgeon gave medical clearance for him to return to work, subject to a permanent lifting restriction of 50 pounds and a "medium physical demand level." These restrictions prohibited Giles from performing his work as a machinist, which led GE to terminate his employment. Giles received company-sponsored long-term disability benefits.

After exhausting these disability benefits, Giles wanted to return to work at General Electric. He asked GE to make reasonable accommodation for his disability; such accommodation would make him a qualified individual with a disability. At the same time, Giles applied for disability benefits under the Social Security program. GE refused to make reasonable accommodation to make the necessary endorsements to support his application for Social Security benefits. Giles pursued a lawsuit claiming that GE violated the ADA, and he won the suit. General Electric appealed the decision to the U.S. Court of Appeals for the Fifth District. In *Giles v. General Electric Co.*, the appellate court upheld the lower court's decision to award Giles $590,000 for damages, front pay, and attorneys' fees.[40] The Court of Appeals reasoned that the application for Social Security benefits did not contradict Giles's claim that he could work with reasonable accommodation. These benefits would have been denied if GE had reinstated Giles.

The Civil Rights Act of 1991

Congress enacted the **Civil Rights Act of 1991** to overturn several Supreme Court rulings that limited employee rights. Perhaps most noteworthy is the reversal of *Atonio v. Wards Cove Packing Company*.[41] The Supreme Court ruled that plaintiffs (employees) must indicate which employment practices were discriminatory and demonstrate how so. Since the passage of the Civil Rights Act of 1991, employers must show that the challenged employment practice is a business necessity. **Business necessity** is a legally acceptable defense against charges of alleged discriminatory employment practices in Title VII (the Civil Rights Act of 1964) and in the 1991 act claims. Under the business necessity defense, an employer must prove that the suspect practice prevented irreparable financial damage to the company.

Coverage

The Civil Rights Act of 1991 provides coverage to the same groups protected under the Civil Rights Act of 1964. The 1991 act also extends coverage to Senate employees and political appointees of the federal government's executive branch.

Relevance to Employee Benefits Practices

Waiting periods based on seniority influence who is eligible to receive benefits. Also, as we discuss throughout this book, employers increase the level of benefits based on seniority. For example, employees earn more annual vacation days as their length of service increases. The Civil Rights Act of 1991 overturned the Supreme Court's decision in *Lorance v. AT&T Technologies*,[42] which allowed employees to challenge the use of seniority systems only within 180 days from the system's implementation date. Now, employees may file suits claiming discrimination either when the system is implemented or whenever the system negatively affects them.

For instance, let's assume that about 95 percent of Company A's workforce was male during the 1990s. In recent years, new additions to the workforce have been female, changing the workforce mix to 60 percent male and 40 percent female in 2007. Until June 30, 2008, every employee received two weeks of annual vacation. Beginning July 1, the company changed to a seniority basis for determining the number of vacation weeks per year. As a result, the male employees qualified for four or five weeks of annual vacation because they had the most seniority. Female employees qualified for one or two weeks of annual vacation because they had much less seniority, and believed that the company unfairly discriminated against them on the basis of sex. Prior to the 1991 act, female employees could challenge the new seniority system within the first 180 days of implementation—until about December 31, 2008. Since the act's passage, female employees have the right to challenge the seniority-based vacation system beyond December 31, 2008. In effect, the Court's ruling enhanced employee rights by removing time limits for alleging possible illegal discrimination.

Genetic Information Nondiscrimination Act of 2008

On May 21, 2008, Congress enacted the **Genetic Information Nondiscrimination Act of 2008 (GINA)** to protect job applicants, current and former employees, labor union members, and apprentices and trainees from discrimination based on their genetic information by making unlawful the misuse of genetic information to discriminate in health insurance and employment. GINA contains two titles, which went into effect on November 21, 2009.

Title I of GINA applies to employer-sponsored group health plans. This title generally prohibits discrimination in group premiums based on genetic information and the use of genetic information as a basis for determining eligibility or setting health insurance premiums. Title I also places limitations on genetic testing and the collection of genetic information.

Title II of GINA prohibits the use of genetic information in the employment setting, restricts the deliberate acquisition of genetic information by employers and others covered by Title II, and strictly limits such entities from disclosing genetic information. The law incorporates by reference many of the definitions, remedies, and procedures from Title VII of the Civil Rights Act of 1964 and other statutes protecting federal, state, and congressional employees from discrimination.

Coverage

Title II applies to private and state and local government employers with 15 or more employees, employment agencies, labor unions, and joint labor–management training programs. It also covers Congress and federal executive branch agencies.

Relevance to Employee Benefits

GINA was enacted because of developments in the field of genetics, the decoding of the human genome, and advances in the field of genomic medicine. Genetic tests now exist that can inform individuals whether they may be at risk for developing a specific disease or disorder. As a result, individuals possess concerns about whether they may be at risk of losing access to health coverage or employment if insurers or employers have their genetic information.

Summary

This chapter provided a discussion of the major pieces of federal legislation that influence discretionary benefits practices. The regulation of discretionary benefits practices is quite complex since a variety of forces play a role, including tax code and federal equal employment opportunity laws. Familiarity with these laws and regulations should put you on a firm footing for further exploring how discretionary benefits practices are regulated.

Key Terms

National Labor Relations Act of 1935 (NLRA), *69*
National Labor Relations Board (NLRB), *70*
mandatory bargaining subjects, *70*
permissive bargaining subjects, *71*
illegal bargaining subjects, *71*
Worker Adjustment and Retraining Notification (WARN) Act, *71*
Internal Revenue Code (IRC), *72*
Federal Insurance Contributions Act (FICA), *72*
Federal Unemployment Tax Act (FUTA), *72*
nondiscrimination rules, *72*
key employee, *73*

highly compensated employee, *73*
Fair Labor Standards Act (FLSA), *73*
FairPay Rules, *74*
Portal-to-Portal Act of 1947, *74*
hours worked, *74*
Employment Retirement Income Security Act of 1974 (ERISA), *75*
top hat plans, *75*
qualified plans, *76*
nonqualified plans, *76*
pension plans, *77*
welfare plans, *77*
defined benefit plan, *77*
defined contribution plan, *77*
multiemployer plans, *78*
Form 5500, *79*
vesting, *79*
cliff vesting, *79*

six-year gradual vesting schedule, *79*
fiduciaries, *81*
fiduciary responsibilities, *81*
trusts, *81*
trustees, *81*
U.S. Department of Labor, *81*
Internal Revenue Service (IRS), *81*
Pension Benefit Guarantee Corporation (PBGC), *81*
Consolidated Omnibus Budget Reconciliation Act of 1985 (COBRA), *81*
Health Insurance Portability and Accountability Act of 1996 (HIPAA), *82*
Pension and Welfare Benefits Administration, *82*
Strategic Enforcement Plan (StEP), *82*

Employee Plans Compliance Resolution System (EPCRS), *83*
Joint Pension, Profit-Sharing, and Employee Stock Ownership Plan Task Force, *83*
termination insurance, *85*
qualifying events, *87*
qualified beneficiary, *87*
election period, *87*
continuation coverage, *87*
American Recovery and Reinvestment Act of 2009, *87*

multiple qualifying event rules, *88*
preexisting conditions, *89*
preexisting condition periods, *89*
Pension Protection Act, *90*
equal employment opportunity, *91*
Equal Pay Act of 1963, *92*
compensable factors, *92*
Title VII of the Civil Rights Act of 1964, *93*
Age Discrimination in Employment Act of 1967 (ADEA), *93*

Older Workers Benefit Protection Act (OWBPA), *94*
equal benefit or equal cost principle, *95*
Pregnancy Discrimination Act of 1978 (PDA), *95*
Americans with Disabilities Act Amendments Act of 2008, *96*
Americans with Disabilities Act (ADA), *97*
Civil Rights Act of 1991, *97*
business necessity, *97*
Genetic Information Nondiscrimination Act of 2008 (GINA), *98*

Discussion Questions

1. Describe the difference between pension plans and welfare plans.

2. Some people argue that there is too much government intervention, while others say there is not enough. Given the presentation of laws and regulations in this chapter, do you think there is too little or too much government intervention? Explain your answer.

3. Use your familiarity with employee benefits practices to identify an area of practice that would benefit from government regulation. Describe the rationale for your answer.

4. Explain the difference between COBRA and HIPAA.

5. What is the main gist of the Pension Protection Act of 2006 and why has it been necessary?

Endnotes

1. D. D. Bennett-Alexander and L. P. Hartman. 2007. *Employment Law for Business*, 5th ed., Burr Ridge, IL: McGraw-Hill/Irwin, p. 3.

2. *Wisconsin Southern Gas Co.*, 69 L.R.R.M. 1374, 173 N.L.R.B. No. 79 (1968).

3. *UAW v. Mack Trucks Inc.*, 135 L.R.R.M. 2833 (3rd Cir. 1990).

4. 26 U.S.C. §§3101–3125.

5. I.R.C. §3121(d); Treas. Reg. §§31.3121(d)-2; 31.3121(d)-1.

6. *Andrews v. DuBois*, 888 F. Supp. 213 (D.C. Mass. 1995), 2 WH Cases 2d 1297 (1995).

7. B. J. Coleman. 1993. *Primer on Employee Retirement Income Security Act*, 4th ed., Washington, DC: Bureau of National Affairs.

8. ERISA §3(2)(A), 29 U.S.C. §§1002(2)(A).

9. ERISA §3(1), 29 U.S.C. §1002(1).

10. I.R.C. §§410(a)(1), 410(a)(4); Treas. Reg. §1.410(a)-3T(b); ERISA §202(a).

11. I.R.C. §410(a)(3), Treas. Reg. §1.410(a)-5, 29 C.F.R. §2530.200b-2(a), ERISA §202(a)(3).

12. I.R.C. §§411(a)(2), 411(a)(5); Treas. Reg. §1.411(a)-3T; ERISA §203(a).

13. I.R.C. §411(a)(6); 29 C.F.R. §2530.200b-4; ERISA §203(b)(3).

14. ERISA §205.

15. ERISA §404(a)(1)(A).

16. ERISA §404(a)(1)(B)–(D).

17. ERISA §403(a).

18. 65 Federal Register 18208 (April 6, 2000).

19. Rev. Proc. 2001-17, 2001-7 I.R.B. 589 (February 17, 2001).
20. I.R.C. §§414(b), 414(c); ERISA §§4011, 4044, 4062(b), 4068; 29 C.F.R. §4011.10; PBGC Technical Update 00-7.
21. I.R.C. §4980B(d); Treas. Regs. §54.4980B-2.
22. I.R.C. §4980B(f).
23. I.R.C. §4980B(g)(1); Treas. Regs. §54.4980B-3.
24. I.R.C. §4980B(f)(3).
25. I.R.C. §4980B(f)(2); Treas. Regs. §54.4980B-7.
26. I.R.C. §4980B(f)(2)(B)(I)(IV).
27. I.R.C. §4980B(f)(2)(B)(I)(II); Treas. Regs. §54.4980B-7.
28. I.R.C. §4980B(f)(2)(B)(I)(III).
29. I.R.C. §4980B(f)(2)(B)(ii-v); Treas. Regs. 54.4980B-7.
30. 22 U.S.C. 2504(e).
31. ERISA, Sec. 703.
32. 45 C.F.R. Parts 160 and 164.
33. S. Rep. No. 176, 88th Congress, 1st Session, 1 (1963).
34. 29 U.S.C. §206.
35. 42 U.S.C. §2000.
36. 29 U.S.C. §623.
37. *EEOC v. Chrysler Corp.*, 625 F. Supp. 1523, 45 FEP Cases 513 (N.D. Ohio 1987) 83.
38. Older Workers Benefit Protection Act of 1990, Pub. L. No. pl 101-433.
39. *Nashville Gas Co. v. Satty*, 434 U.S. 136 (1977).
40. *Giles v. General Electric Co.*, 5th Cir., No. 99-11059 (February 26, 2001).
41. *Atonio v. Wards Cove Packing Co.*, 490 U.S. 642, 49 FEP Cases 1519 (1989).
42. *Lorance v. AT&T Technologies*, 49 FEP Cases 1656 (1989).

Retirement, Health, and Life Insurance

Chapter **Five**

Employer-Sponsored Retirement Plans

Learning Objectives

In this chapter, you will gather information about:

1. Differences between qualified plans and nonqualified plans.
2. Features of defined benefit plans and defined contribution plans.
3. Specific types of defined contribution plans.
4. Various hybrid plans, especially the controversy surrounding cash balance plans.

Your new employer has informed you that you will automatically be enrolled in the company's 401(k) defined contribution retirement plan and 2 percent of your salary will be deducted from your paycheck each month. You are given the option to have more set aside from your paycheck as long as the amount doesn't exceed $16,500 (in 2009) or $22,000 if you are 50 or older. Then, you review information showing the allocation of your monthly contribution to various mutual funds, and you are encouraged to consider other mutual funds that will help you achieve having enough money to support retirement. At that moment, you remember that your parents' retirement plans are a defined benefit pension plan, which does not require any input from them. In fact, they mentioned that they know how much money they will receive from their plans each month for the rest of their lives. And you begin to wonder why your employer does not offer the same plan.

The purpose of this chapter is to review the fundamentals of company-sponsored pension plan design.* It is essential to note that individuals may receive retirement benefits from as many as three sources: First, employer-sponsored retirement plans provide employees with income after they have met a minimum retirement age and have left the company. Second, the Social Security Old-Age, Survivor, and Disability Insurance (OASDI) program, described in Chapter 8, provides government-mandated retirement income to employees who have made sufficient contributions through payroll taxes. Third, individuals may use their initiative to take advantage of tax regulations that have created such retirement programs as individual retirement accounts (IRAs) and Roth IRAs.

Companies establish retirement or pension plans following one of three design configurations: a defined benefit plan, a defined contribution plan, or hybrid plans that combine features of traditional defined benefit and defined contribution plans. For example, these configurations determine such outcomes as whether retirement income is fixed by a formula or depends on the performance of investment vehicles such as company stock, company profits, mutual funds, or bonds. With defined benefit plans, retirees receive guaranteed payments for the duration of their lives, but represent a substantial cost burden to companies that must ensure adequate funding to support retirees for longer periods based on rises in life expectancy. In Chapter 4, we described this challenge to companies and the role of the Pension Protection Act of 2006, which is supposed to help shore

---

*The terms *retirement plan* and *pension plan* are typically used interchangeably. Most often, pension programs refer to Social Security old-age benefits (Chapter 8) or company-sponsored defined benefit arrangements. Also, in this chapter, the terms *company-sponsored* and *employer-sponsored* are used interchangeably, referencing plans offered to eligible employees.

up the financial solvency of defined benefit plans in private sector companies and to automatically enroll employees in defined contribution plans. From the employee's perspective, defined contribution plans are much riskier than defined benefit plans because the amount and duration of retirement income depends mainly on the performance of investments. Many companies offer more than one plan based on these design configurations.

In addition, tax incentives encourage companies to offer pension programs. Some of the ERISA Title I and Title II provisions set the minimum standards required to "qualify" pension plans for favorable tax treatment. Failure to meet any of the minimum standard provisions "disqualifies" pension plans for favorable tax treatment. Pension plans that meet these minimum standards are known as **qualified plans. Nonqualified plans** refer to pension plans that do not meet at least one of the minimum standard provisions; typically, highly paid employees benefit from participation in nonqualified plans. We find that nonqualified plans often are a part of executive deferred compensation, which is beyond the scope of this book.

From here, we explore the minimum standards that distinguish qualified plans from nonqualified plans. Afterward, we examine the features of alternative company-sponsored pension plans, including defined benefit plans, defined contribution plans, and hybrid plans. Then, we discuss Social Security integration, a potentially controversial practice because it can substantially reduce the amount retirees receive from their qualified retirement plans.

DEFINED RETIREMENT PLANS

We learned from Chapter 4 that retirement or pension plans function by providing "retirement income to employees, or [result] in a deferral of income by employees for periods extending to the termination of covered employment or beyond, regardless of the method of calculating the contributions made in the plan, the method of calculating benefits under the plan, or the method of distributing benefits from the plan."[1]

Origins of Employer-Sponsored Retirement Benefits

According to the Employee Benefit Research Institute,[2] the first pension plan in the United States was established in 1759 to benefit widows and children of Presbyterian ministers. In 1875, the American Express Company established a formal pension plan. From that point until World War II, pension plans were adopted primarily in the railroad, banking, and public utility industries. The most significant growth occurred after the favorable tax treatment of pensions was established through the passage of the Revenue Act of 1921, and government-imposed wage increase controls during World War II in the early 1940s led companies to adopt discretionary employee benefits plans such as pensions that were excluded from those wage increase restrictions.

The current tax treatment of qualified plans continues to provide incentives both for employers to establish plans and for employees to participate in them. In general, a contribution to a qualified plan is deductible in computing the employer's or employee's taxes based on who made the contribution. Employees pay taxes only on the amount they withdraw from the plan each year. As we discussed in Chapter 4, this preferential tax treatment is contingent on the employer's compliance with the Employee Retirement Income Security Act of 1974 (ERISA).

Trends in Retirement Plan Coverage and Costs

According to the U.S. Bureau of Labor Statistics, nearly 55 percent of workers employed in the private sector participated in at least one company-sponsored retirement plan in 1992–1993.[3] Since then, the participation rate has declined slightly to approximately 50 percent in 2006,[4] which represents the latest available data at the time of publication. However, there has been a noticeable decrease in participation rates for defined benefit plans over the last 15 years. In 1992–1993, 32 percent of private sector employees participated in defined contribution plans, and slightly fewer participated in defined benefit plans.[5] In 2006, 42 percent participated in defined contribution plans, but only 20 percent participated in defined benefit plans.[6]

These trends in retirement plan participation have two important explanations.[7] First, there has been a shift in the labor force toward different occupations and industries. Specifically, there has been a relative decline in employment among full-time workers, union workers, and workers in goods-producing businesses. The decline in full-time workers and the increase in part-time workers has led to fewer opportunities for participation in company-sponsored retirement plans. Quite simply, employers often employ part-time workers to save benefits costs. The decline in union affiliation (union members or just part of the bargaining unit) also contributes to the overall trends described earlier. In 2006, nearly 90 percent of employees affiliated with unions were eligible to participate in a retirement plan, while only about half of the nonunion workers were eligible. As we discussed in Chapter 4, unions represent workers in negotiations with management over terms of employment. The inclusion of lucrative retirement plans was among the top priorities in negotiations to maintain the support of middle-aged and older workers. Finally, among employment trends, the expansion of service industries relative to somewhat stable employment in the goods-producing sector helps to explain retirement plan participation. Fewer service-oriented workers have access to defined benefit plans (19 percent versus 33 percent) though the percentage of workers with access to defined contribution plans is higher and similar in both industries (approximately 50 to 60 percent). However, actual employee participation in defined contribution plans is drastically lower in service employers than in goods-producing companies. Wages in the service-producing companies tend to be lower than in goods-producing companies. It is possible that service employees simply do not have enough money to set aside for retirement.

The second reason for changes away from participation in defined benefit plans to defined contribution plans is because defined benefit plans are quite costly to employers compared to defined contribution plans: Companies struggle to adequately fund these plans to ensure that retirees receive entitled benefits for the remainder of their lives. Also, as discussed in Chapter 4, the Pension Benefit

EXHIBIT 5.1
Characteristics
of Qualified
Pension Plans

- Participation requirements
- Coverage requirements
- Vesting rules
- Accrual rules
- Nondiscrimination rules: Testing
- Key employee and top-heavy provisions
- Minimum funding standards
- Social Security integration
- Contribution and benefit limits
- Plan distribution rules
- Qualified survivor annuities
- Qualified domestic relations orders
- Plan termination rules and procedures

Guaranty Corporation serves as the insurer by taking over pension obligations for companies that terminate their defined benefit plans because of severe financial stress. Companies with defined benefit plans pay premiums to the PBGC to insure defined benefit plans in the event of severe financial distress. The Pension Protection Act requires that companies at high risk of not meeting their pension obligations pay substantially more to insure defined benefit plans, adding to the substantial cost.

Qualified plans entitle employers and employees to substantial tax benefits. Specifically, employers and employees do not pay tax on their contributions within dollar limits that differ for defined benefit and defined contribution plans. In addition, the investment earnings of the trust in which plan assets are held are generally exempt from tax. Finally, participants or beneficiaries do not pay taxes on the value of retirement benefits until they receive distributions.

Minimum Standards for Qualified Plans

Qualified plans possess 13 fundamental characteristics. Exhibit 5.1 lists these characteristics.

Participation Requirements

Participation requirements include age[8] and service requirements[9] (ERISA, Title I, see the discussion in Chapter 4) for all plan designs. In general, employees must be allowed to participate in pension plans after they have reached age 21 and have completed one year of service (based on 1,000 work hours).

QUALIFIED PLANS

Coverage Requirements

Coverage requirements limit the freedom of employers to exclude employees. Qualified plans do not disproportionately favor highly compensated employees,[10] as discussed in Chapter 4.

Companies demonstrate whether plans meet the coverage requirement by maintaining a nondiscriminatory ratio of nonhighly compensated employees to highly compensated employees based on one of the following two tests:

- **Ratio percentage test.** Qualified plans cover a percentage of nonhighly compensated employees that is at least 70 percent of the percentage of highly compensated employees covered by the plan.
- **Average benefit test.** Qualified plans benefit a "nondiscriminatory classification" of employees and possess an "average benefit percentage" for nonhighly compensated employees that is, at a minimum, 70 percent of the average benefit percentage for highly compensated employees.[11]

Treasury regulations impose an additional participation standard for defined benefit plans. These plans must cover at least 50 employees, or 40 percent of the workforce must benefit from the plan on a day in which a company's employment is representative of its workforce.[12]

Vesting Rules

As described in Chapter 4, **vesting** refers to an employee's nonforfeitable rights to pension benefits.[13] These rights apply to defined benefit and defined contribution plans. Title I of ERISA mandates that companies grant full vesting rights to employer contributions on one of the following two schedules, as discussed in Chapter 4: **cliff vesting** and **six-year gradual vesting.**

Accrual Rules

Qualified plans are subject to minimum accrual rules based on the Internal Revenue Code (IRC) and ERISA.[14] **Accrual rules** specify the rate at which participants accumulate (or earn) benefits. Defined benefit and defined contribution plans use different accrual rules, which we discuss in subsequent sections of this chapter.

Nondiscrimination Rules: Testing

Nondiscrimination rules prohibit employers from discriminating in favor of highly compensated employees in contributions or benefits, availability of benefits, rights, or plan features.[15] Also, employers may not amend pension plans so that highly compensated employees are favored.

The nondiscrimination requirement may be fulfilled in one of two ways: safe harbors or nondiscrimination testing. *Safe harbors* refer to compliance guidelines in a law or regulation. Pension plans that meet safe harbor conditions automatically fulfill the nondiscrimination requirement based on particular design features. Failure to reach safe harbors requires passing at least one of two **nondiscrimination tests.** Safe harbors and nondiscrimination tests differ between defined benefit and defined contribution plans. We will review the safe harbors and nondiscrimination tests for these plans in subsequent sections of this chapter.

Top-Heavy Provisions

Qualified plans must include **top-heavy provisions** pertaining to minimum benefits accrual and vesting rights. Plans are said to be top-heavy if the **accrued benefits** (i.e., the benefit amount that a participant has earned under the plan's terms at a specified time) or account balances for *key employees* exceed 60 percent of the accrued benefits or account balances for all employees.[16]

Top-heavy provisions ensure minimum benefits or contributions for individuals who are not key employees.[17] For defined benefit plans, each nonkey employee must receive an accrued benefit of a designated percentage multiplied by the employee's average compensation. The percentage is the lesser of 2 percent times the participant's number of years of service with the employer, or 20 percent. For instance, an employee with four years of service and an average annual compensation of $75,000 would be entitled to a minimum benefit of $6,000. That is, $6,000 = (4 years × 0.02% × $75,000 average annual compensation).

For defined contribution plans, employers must make minimum contributions to nonkey employee accounts equal to the lesser of 3 percent of annual compensation or the highest contribution credited to key employee accounts.

Minimum Funding Standards

Minimum funding standards ensure that employers contribute the minimum amount of money necessary to provide employees and beneficiaries promised benefits. As we will see, the standards differ between defined benefit and defined contribution plans.

Social Security Integration

Social Security integration, also known as **permitted disparity rules,** allows employers to explicitly take into account Social Security retirement benefits when determining company-sponsored pension benefits.[18] Subject to established limits, qualified plans may reduce company-sponsored benefits based on the benefits owed under the Social Security program.

Benefit and Contribution Limits

Benefit limits refer to the maximum annual amount an employee may receive from a qualified defined benefit plan during retirement. Contribution limits apply to defined contribution plans. Employers are limited in the amount they may contribute to an employee's defined contribution plan each year. The *Economic Growth and Tax Relief Reconciliation Act of 2001* amended Section 415, mandating increases in these limits effective after December 31, 2001, and indexing them each year for inflation to keep retirement savings from falling behind increases in the cost of goods and services, thereby making retirees less dependent on Social Security retirement benefits (Chapter 8). The limits were set to expire after the year 2009, but the *Pension Protection Act of 2006* made the limits permanent. We review these limits in our respective discussions of defined benefit and defined contribution plans.

Allowable Tax Deductions for Employers

Employers may take tax deductions for contributions to employee retirement plans based on three conditions. First, as you have read, retirement plans must be qualified. Second, an employer must make contributions before the due date for its federal income tax return for that year. For example, an employer received a tax deduction on contributions for the year 2008 when the contributions were made before April 15, 2009. Third, deductible contributions are based on designated amounts set forth by the Internal Revenue Code (as subsequently amended by the Economic Growth and Tax Relief Reconciliation Act of 2001 and the Pension Protection Act of 2006).

Plan Distribution Rules

Distribution refers to the payment of vested benefits to participants or beneficiaries. Three events may initiate a mandatory distribution of benefits:

> These three events are the participant's termination of service with the employer, the 10th anniversary of the year the participant commenced participation in the plan, and the participant's attainment of the earlier of age 65 or the normal retirement age* specified in the plan. Qualified plans must provide that, unless the participant otherwise elects, the payment of benefits under the plan will commence no later than 60 days after the end of the plan year in which the last of these three events occurs.[19]

Distributions are payable in one of three forms. **Lump sum distributions** are single payments of benefits. In defined contribution plans, lump sum distributions equal the vested amount (the sum of all employee and vested employer contributions, and interest on this sum). In defined benefit plans, lump sum distributions equal the equivalent of the vested accrued benefit.

A second form of distribution is the annuity. **Annuities** represent a series of payments for the life of the participant and beneficiary. Annuity contracts are usually purchased from insurance companies, which make payments according to the contract. The inherent risk of defined contribution plans has given rise to income annuities. **Income annuities** distribute income to retirees based on retirement savings paid to insurance companies in exchange for guaranteed monthly checks for life.

A third form of distribution is a series of periodic payments paid from a trust fund containing the participant's retirement benefits. In defined contribution plans, the payments are made over a specified period of time, not to exceed the life expectancy of the participant or beneficiary. In defined benefit plans, the payments may come directly from a trust fund.

Qualified Survivor Annuities

Qualified plans must provide spouses of covered employees a **qualified joint and survivor annuity (QJSA)** or a **qualified preretirement survivor annuity (QPSA)**.[20]

A QJSA is an annuity for the life of the participant with a survivor annuity for the participant's spouse. A qualified preretirement survivor annuity (QPSA) provides payments for the life of the participant's surviving spouse if the participant dies before he or she has begun to receive retirement benefits. These benefits may

---

*The *normal retirement age* is the lowest age specified in a pension plan. Upon attaining this age, an employee gains the right to retire without the consent of the employer and to receive benefits based on length of service at the full rate specified in the pension plan.

be waived by written voluntary consent of the participant's spouse. QPSA amounts must be no less than the QJSA amounts.

Qualified Domestic Relations Orders

Qualified plans recognize **qualified domestic relations orders (QDROs).** State domestic courts may issue QDROs that permit a retirement plan to divide a participant's benefits in the event of divorce. Dividing a participant's benefits without a QDRO is a violation of ERISA and the IRC.[21] Without a QDRO, divorced spouses would be ineligible to receive retirement benefits under the participant's plan.[22]

QDROs stipulate the extent to which a former spouse is eligible to receive QJSAs (qualified joint and survivor annuities) and QPSAs (qualified preretirement survivor annuities). For example, if a QDRO stipulates that a former spouse will be treated as the current spouse for all of a participant's benefits, then the former spouse will receive the QJSA or the QPSA unless that former spouse waives the right to the benefits. On the other hand, if a QDRO provides that a former spouse will be treated as the current spouse for benefits that accrued prior to divorce, then the former spouse would be treated as the current spouse only for those accrued benefits.[23]

Plan Termination Rules and Procedures

Plan termination rules and procedures apply only to defined benefit plans. As discussed in Chapter 4, three types of plan terminations exist: standard termination, distress termination, and involuntary termination. Qualified plans must follow strict guidelines for plan terminations, including sufficient notification to plan participants, notification to the Pension Benefit Guarantee Corporation, and the distribution of vested benefits to participants and beneficiaries in a reasonable amount of time.

DEFINED BENEFIT PLANS

Defined benefit plans guarantee retirement benefits specified in the plan document. This benefit usually is expressed in terms of a monthly sum equal to a percentage of a participant's preretirement pay multiplied by the number of years he or she has worked for the employer. This monthly payment, or annuity, is usually paid to the retiree until death. While the benefit in these plans is fixed by a formula, the level of required employer contributions fluctuates from year to year. The level depends on the amount necessary to make certain that benefits promised will be available when participants and beneficiaries are eligible to receive them and on expectations of life expectancy. As life expectancy increases, it has become necessary for defined benefit plan sponsors to increase contributions.

Benefit Formulas

Companies usually choose between two types of benefit formulas: flat benefit formulas and unit benefit formulas. The key factor distinguishing these two types of formulas is whether employees' years of service are considered. Years of service are a factor in unit benefit formulas, but not in flat benefit formulas. The Internal

Revenue Service recognizes both formulas as appropriate calculation methods in employer-sponsored plans.

When companies introduce a defined benefit plan into an established workforce, they must decide whether to reward future performance only, or recognize past service as well. In the former case, all employees, regardless of service, are treated as new employees from the standpoint of benefits allocation.

Flat Benefit Formulas

Flat benefit formulas designate either a flat dollar amount per employee (flat amount formula) or a dollar amount based on an employee's compensation (flat percentage formula). Annual benefits are usually expressed as a percentage of final average wage or salary. The period used to calculate final average wage or salary usually equals the average amount based on the last three or four years of service.

Let's assume that in 2008 when Robert plans to retire, his final average salary in the three-year period preceding retirement was $100,000 (based on $99,000 in 2008, $100,000 in 2009, and $101,000 in 2010). In this example, $100,000 = ($99,000 + $100,000 + $101,000)/3 years.

Also assume that the plan's designated percentage is 60 percent. Robert's annual retirement income equals $60,000 ($100,000 average annual income × 60%).

Flat benefit formulas often lead to resentment among employees because length of service is not a consideration. Longer-service employees expect to receive a higher percentage of final average salary during retirement than employees who retire with substantially less service. There are two possible explanations for this expectation. First, longer-service employees feel they have earned the right to receive a higher percentage. They argue that the combination of more years enabled them to contribute more productively to the company than employees with substantially fewer years of service. Second, the company should owe them a larger percentage in recognition of their loyalty and commitment to the company over a longer period.

Unit Benefit Formulas

Unit benefit formulas recognize length of service. Typically, employers decide to contribute a specified dollar amount for each year worked by an employee. Alternatively, they may choose to contribute a specified percentage amount for years of service.

Annual benefits are usually based on age, years of service, and final average wages or salary. Retirement plans based on unit benefit formulas specify annual retirement benefits as a percentage of final average salary. Exhibit 5.2 illustrates these percentages for one retirement plan based on age and years of service. Looking at this exhibit, let's assume Mary retires at age 59 with 25 years of service.

Also, let's assume her final average salary is $52,500. Mary multiplies $52,500 by the annual percentage of 43.43 percent. Her annual benefit is thus $22,800.75 ($52,500 × 43.43%).

Nondiscrimination Rules: Testing

Defined benefit plans must meet several uniformity criteria as well as one additional safe harbor criterion based on particular characteristics of the plan. Uniformity refers to consistent treatment based on such factors as a benefits

EXHIBIT 5.2
Annual Retirement Benefits Based on a Unit Benefit Formula

Years of Service	Age						
	62	60+	59	58	57	56	55
5	8.35						
6	10.02						
7	11.69						
8	—	13.36	12.56	11.76	10.96	10.15	9.35
9	—	15.03	14.13	13.23	12.32	11.42	10.52
10	—	16.70	15.70	14.70	13.69	12.69	11.69
11	—	18.60	17.48	16.37	15.25	14.14	13.02
12	—	20.50	19.27	18.04	16.81	15.58	14.35
13	—	22.40	21.06	19.71	18.37	17.02	15.68
14	—	24.30	22.84	21.38	19.93	18.47	17.01
15	—	26.20	24.63	23.06	21.48	19.91	18.34
16	—	28.10	26.41	24.73	23.04	21.36	19.67
17	—	30.00	28.20	26.40	24.60	22.80	21.00
18	—	31.90	29.99	28.07	26.16	24.24	22.33
19	—	33.80	31.77	29.74	27.72	25.69	23.66
20	—	35.70	33.56	31.42	29.27	27.13	24.99
21	—	37.80	35.53	33.26	31.00	28.73	26.46
22	—	39.90	37.51	35.11	32.72	30.32	27.93
23	—	42.00	39.48	36.96	34.44	31.93	29.40
24	—	44.10	41.45	38.81	36.16	33.52	30.87
25	—	46.20	43.43	40.66	37.88	35.11	32.34
26	—	48.30	45.40	42.50	39.61	36.71	33.81
27	—	50.40	47.38	44.35	41.33	38.30	35.28
28	—	52.50	49.35	46.20	43.05	39.90	36.75
29	—	54.60	51.32	48.05	44.77	41.50	38.22
30	—	56.70	53.30	49.90	46.49	43.09	39.69
31	—	59.00	55.46	51.92	48.38	44.84	41.30
32	—	61.30	57.62	53.94	50.27	46.59	42.91
33	—	63.60	59.78	55.97	52.15	48.34	44.52
34	—	65.90	61.95	57.99	54.04	40.08	46.13
35	—	68.20	68.20	68.20	68.20	68.20	68.20
36	—	70.50	70.50	70.50	70.50	70.50	70.50
37	—	72.80	72.80	72.80	72.80	72.80	72.80
38	—	75.10	75.00	75.00	75.00	75.00	75.00
39	—	77.40	75.00	75.00	75.00	75.00	75.00
40	—	79.70	75.00	75.00	75.00	75.00	75.00
41+	—	80.00	75.00	75.00	75.00	75.00	75.00

formula. Exhibit 5.3 describes the uniformity requirements issued by the U.S. Treasury Department. Failure to satisfy safe harbor criteria requires explicit testing for nondiscrimination.

Accrual Rules

Accumulated benefit obligation refers to the present value of benefits based on a designated date. Actuaries determine a defined benefit plan's accumulated benefit

EXHIBIT 5.3 **Safe Harbors for Defined Benefit Plans**

Source: Treas. Regs. §1.401(a)(4)-3(b)(2).

A defined benefit plan must be "uniform" to meet the safe harbor requirements:

Uniform Normal Retirement Benefit

The same benefit formula must apply to all employees in the plan. The formula must provide all employees with an annual benefit payable in the same form, commencing at the same uniform normal retirement age. The annual benefit must be the same percentage of average annual compensation or the same dollar amount for all employees in the plan who will have the same number of years of service at normal retirement age. The annual benefit must equal the employee's accrued benefit at normal retirement age and must be the normal retirement benefit under the plan.

Uniform Postnormal Retirement Benefits

With respect to an employee with a given number of years of service at any age after normal retirement age, the annual benefit commencing at the employee's age must be the same percentage of average annual compensation or the same dollar amount that would be payable commencing at normal retirement age to an employee who had that same number of years of service at normal retirement age.

Uniform Subsidies

Each subsidized optional form of benefit under the plan must be available to essentially all employees in the plan. In determining whether a subsidized optional form of benefit is available, the same criteria apply that are used for determining whether an optional form of benefit is currently available to a group of employees in the plan. An optional form of benefit is considered subsidized if the normalized optional form of benefit is larger than the normalized normal retirement benefit under the plan.

Uniform Vesting and Service Crediting

All employees in the plan must be subject to the same vesting schedule and the same definition of years of service for all purposes under the plan. For the purposes of crediting service, only service with the employer (or a predecessor employer) may be taken into account.

No Employee Contributions

The plan is not a contributory defined benefit plan. Special rules apply to contributory defined benefit plans.

Period of Accrual

Each employee's benefit must be accrued over the same years of service that are taken into account in applying the benefit formula under the plan to that employee. Any year in which the employee benefits under the plan is included as a year of service in which a benefit accrues.

---

obligation by making assumptions about the return on investment of assets and characteristics of the participants and their beneficiaries, including expected length of service and life expectancies.

The Internal Revenue Service has established criteria to judge whether an employer's defined benefit plan meets its accumulated benefit obligation. These criteria discourage employers from engaging in a practice known as **backloading.** Backloading occurs whenever benefits accrue at a substantially higher rate during the years close to an employee's eligibility to earn retirement benefits. Fulfillment of at least one of these criteria ensures that benefits accrue regularly throughout employee participation in defined benefit plans.

One of the following three criteria must be met: the three percent rule, the 133⅓ percent rule, or the fractional rule.

The Three Percent Rule

Under the **three percent rule,** a participant's accrued benefit cannot be less than 3 percent of the normal retirement benefit, assuming the participant began participation at the earliest possible age under the plan, and she or he remained employed without interruption until age 65 or the plan's designated normal retirement age. For instance, Margaret recently retired at age 62 from Company A. She joined the company 41 years earlier at age 21 and immediately began participation in the employer-sponsored defined benefit plan. Company A's defined benefit plan awards an annual benefit equal to 70 percent of the four-year average highest salary. Margaret's four-year average annual salary was $50,000 upon retirement, yielding an annual retirement benefit of $35,000 ($50,000 × 70%). Under the three percent rule, Margaret's accrued benefit must be no less than $1,050 ($35,000 × 3%).

The 133⅓ Percent Rule

Under the **133⅓ percent rule,** the annual accrual rate cannot exceed 133⅓ percent of the rate of accrual for any prior year. For example, a company's retirement plan specifies the following annual accrual rates: 1.15 of compensation for the first 10 years, 1.40 for the next 10 years, and 1.88 for the years thereafter. This plan violates the 133⅓ percent rule because the 1.88 annual accrual rate exceeds 133⅓ percent of the lowest prior annual accrual rate (1.53—that is, 1.15% of compensation × 133⅓).

Fractional Rule

The **fractional rule** applies to participants who terminate their employment prior to reaching normal retirement age. This rule stipulates that benefit accrual upon termination be proportional to the normal retirement benefits. Said another way, this method compares an employee's plan participation to the total years she or he would have participated in the plan upon reaching the normal retirement age. For example, let's assume the annual annuity a person would have earned at the normal retirement age is $20,000. Let's also assume that her years of service at full retirement age would have been 30 years, but she terminated her employment at 20 years of service. Based on the fractional rule, the annual annuity is $13,333 [$20,000 × (20 years/30 years)]. Paying an annual retirement benefit less than $13,333 would be a violation of the fractional rule.

Minimum Funding Standards

As we discussed in Chapter 4, ERISA imposes strict funding requirements on qualified plans. Under defined benefit plans, employers make an annual contribution that is sufficiently large to ensure that promised benefits will be available to retirees. As previously noted, actuaries periodically review several kinds of information to determine a sufficient funding level: life expectancies of employees and their designated beneficiaries, projected compensation levels, and the likelihood of employees terminating their employment before they have earned benefits. ERISA imposes the reporting of actuarial information to the Internal Revenue Service, which in turn submits these data to the U.S. Department of Labor. The Department of Labor reviews the data to ensure compliance with ERISA regulations.

Benefit Limits and Tax Deductions

The IRC sets a maximum annual benefit for defined benefit plans that is equal to the lesser of $195,000 in 2009, or 100 percent of the highest average compensation for three consecutive years.[24] The limit is indexed for inflation in $5,000 increments each year beginning after 2006.[25]

DEFINED CONTRIBUTION PLANS

Under **defined contribution plans,** employers and employees make annual contributions to separate accounts established for each participating employee, based on a formula contained in the plan document. Typically, formulas call for employers to contribute a given percentage of each participant's compensation annually. Employers invest these funds on behalf of the employee, choosing from a variety of investment vehicles such as company stocks, diversified stock market funds, or federal government bond funds. Employees may be given a choice of investment vehicles based on the guidelines established by the employer. Defined contribution plans specify rules for the amount of annual contributions. Unlike defined benefit plans, these plans do not guarantee particular benefit amounts. Participants bear the risk of possible investment gain or loss. Benefit amounts depend upon several factors, including the contribution amounts, the performance of investments, and forfeitures transferred to participant accounts. **Forfeitures** come from the accounts of employees who terminated their employment prior to earning vesting rights.

Companies may choose to offer one or more specific types of defined contribution plans. Common examples of defined contribution plans include profit-sharing plans, stock bonus plans, and employee stock ownership plans. We will review each of these plans later in the chapter.

Individual Accounts

Defined contribution plans contain accounts for each employee into which contributions are made, losses are debited, or gains are credited. Contributions to each employee's account come from four possible sources. The first, employer contributions, is expressed as a percentage of an employee's wage or salary. In the case of profit-sharing plans, company profits are usually the basis for employer contributions. The second, employee contributions, is usually expressed as a percentage of the employee's wage or salary. The third, forfeitures, comes from the accounts of employees who terminated their employment prior to earning vesting rights. The fourth contribution source is return on investments. In the case of negative returns (or loss), the corresponding amount is debited from employees' accounts.

Investments of Contributions

ERISA requires that a named **fiduciary** manage investments in defined contribution plans. Fiduciaries are individuals who manage employee benefit plans and pension

EXHIBIT 5.4   Conditions Relieving Fiduciary of Responsibility with Employee Participation in Investments

Source: I.R.C. §404(c).

- Participants have the opportunity to choose from at least three diversified investment alternatives. Each investment has different degrees of risk.
- Participants have the opportunity to change their investment allocations at least once each three months. If market volatility is high, this opportunity must be made available more frequently.
- Participants must be given sufficient information to make informed investment decisions.

funds. Also, fiduciaries possess discretion in managing the assets of the plan, offering investment advice to employee participants, and administering the plan. Ultimately, fiduciaries are responsible for minimizing the risk of loss of assets.[26]

Fiduciaries possess the authority to delegate investment responsibility to an investment manager. Under the supervision of the fiduciary, investment managers select investments based on a comparison of the risk and return potential of various investment options. Investment managers may invest assets in a variety of investment vehicles, including equities, government bonds, cash, insurance, and real estate. Usually, investment managers invest assets in more than one type of investment vehicle to balance risk and return potential.

Employee Participation in Investments

Some companies may allow plan participants to choose the investment of funds in their individual accounts. Subject to certain conditions described in Exhibit 5.4, employee participation does not constitute fiduciary responsibility. Also, designated fiduciaries cannot be held liable for the investment choices of employees.

Nondiscrimination Rules: Testing

Defined contribution plans must meet one of two safe harbor conditions: a uniform allocation formula, or a uniform points allocation formula in the case of profit-sharing or money purchase plans.[27] Defined contribution plans satisfy the nondiscrimination rules when they offer a uniform allocation formula to each employee based on a percentage of compensation, dollar amount of allocation, or the same dollar amount for each uniform unit of service.

Profit-sharing and money purchase plans satisfy the nondiscrimination rules based on a uniform points allocation formula. This formula defines each employee's allocation for the plan year as the product of the total of all amounts taken into account. Eligible amounts include employer contributions and forfeitures allocated to an employee's account. Points for a plan year equal the sum of the employee's points for age, service, and units of plan-year compensation for the plan year. Under a uniform points allocation formula, each employee must receive the same number of points for each year of age, each year of service, and each unit of plan-year compensation.

Failure to satisfy safe harbor criteria requires explicit testing for nondiscrimination.

Accrual Rules

The accrued benefit equals the balance in an individual's account.[28] Companies must not reduce contribution amounts based on age. Also, they may not set maximum age limits for discontinuing contributions.

Minimum Funding Standards

The minimum funding standard for defined contribution plans is less complex than for defined benefit plans. This standard is met when contributions to the individual accounts of plan participants meet the minimum amounts as specified by the plan.[29]

Contribution Limits and Tax Deductions

Employer contributions to defined contribution plans represent one factor in annual additions. **Annual addition** refers to the annual maximum allowable contribution to a participant's account in a defined contribution plan. The annual addition includes employer contributions, employee contributions, and forfeitures allocated to the participant's account.[30] In 2009, annual additions were limited to the lesser of $49,000 or 100 percent of the participant's compensation.[31]

The amount of an employer's annual deductible contribution to a participant's account depends on the type of defined contribution plan.[32] The Economic Growth and Tax Reconciliation Act of 2001 raised the allowable contribution amounts in effect before January 1, 2002. In 2005, the maximum contribution to a profit-sharing, stock bonus, or employee stock ownership plan was 25 percent of the compensation paid or accrued to participants in the plan. Section 401(k), 403(b), and 457 plans have contribution limits of $16,500 in 2009. The limit is indexed for inflation in $500 increments beginning in the year 2007.

TYPES OF DEFINED CONTRIBUTION PLANS

A variety of defined contribution plans are available. These include Section 401(k) plans, profit sharing, stock bonus plans, employee stock ownership plans, savings incentive match plans for employees (SIMPLEs), Section 403(b) tax-deferred annuities, and Section 457 plans. We will review each of these plans in turn.

Section 401(k) Plans

Section 401(k) plans are retirement plans named after the section of the Internal Revenue Code that created them. These plans, also known as cash or deferred arrangements (CODAs), permit employees to defer part of their compensation to the trust of a qualified defined contribution plan. Only private sector or tax-exempt employers are eligible to sponsor 401(k) plans.

Section 401(k) plans offer three noteworthy tax benefits. First, employees do not pay income taxes on their contributions to the plan until they withdraw funds. Second, employers deduct their contributions to the plan from taxable income. Third, investment gains are not taxed until participants receive payments. Section 401(k) specifies that a 401(k) plan is any arrangement with five specific characteristics:

- Must be a part of a qualified profit-sharing or stock bonus plan, a pre-ERISA money purchase plan, or a rural electric cooperative plan.
- Permits eligible employees to choose to defer part of their compensation (regular wages, salaries, or bonus) to one of the arrangements specified in the previous statement. Deferral of regular salary or wages is known as a salary reduction agreement.
- Limits the amount of annual elective deferrals as described previously.
- Restricts distributions. Money may not be distributed to the employee or beneficiary before the earliest of the employee's death, disability, separation from service, termination of the plan, or sale of the subsidiary or division employing the employee. Profit-sharing or stock bonus plan distributions also are permitted upon hardship or after attainment of age 59. Premature withdrawals are subject to a 10 percent penalty.
- Complies with nondiscrimination rules to prevent highly compensated employees from receiving disproportionately higher benefits.

Profit-Sharing Plans

Companies set up **profit-sharing plans** to distribute money to employees. Companies start by establishing a **profit-sharing pool**—that is, the money earmarked for distribution to employees. Companies may also choose to fund profit-sharing plans based on gross sales revenue or some basis other than profits. Companies may also take a tax deduction for their contributions, not to exceed 25 percent of the plan participants' compensation.[33] As described in the previous section, a qualified profit-sharing plan may be the basis for a company's 401(k) plan.

Employer Contributions

Companies determine the pool of profit-sharing money by application of a formula every year or based on the discretion of their boards of directors. One of three common formulas establish employer contributions. A **fixed first-dollar-of-profits formula** uses a specific percentage of either pretax or after-tax annual profits (alternatively, gross sales or some other basis) contingent upon the successful attainment of a company goal. For instance, a company might establish that the profit-sharing fund will equal 1 percent of corporate profits. Second, other companies use a **graduated first-dollar-of-profits formula** instead of a fixed percentage. For example, a company may choose to share 2 percent of the first $10 million of profits and 3 percent of the profits in excess of that level. Third, **profitability threshold formulas** fund profit-sharing pools only if profits exceed a predetermined minimum level but fall below some established maximum level. Companies establish minimums to guarantee a return to shareholders before they distribute profits to employees. They establish maximums because they attribute any profits beyond this level to factors other than employee productivity or creativity such as technological innovation.

Company boards of directors may use their discretion when setting contributions. This approach is somewhat risky: The Internal Revenue Service requires that employer contributions to qualified profit-sharing plans be substantial and made on a recurring basis.[34] Failure to meet this criterion may require 100 percent vesting rights to all plan participants, regardless of tenure in the plan.

Allocation Formulas

After management selects a funding formula for the profit-sharing pool, they must consider how to distribute pool money among employees. Under a qualified defined contribution plan, the chosen allocation formula must not discriminate in favor of highly compensated employees. Usually, companies make distributions in one of three ways—equal payments to all employees, proportional payments to employees based on annual salary, and proportional payments to employees based on their contribution to profits. **Equal payments** to all employees reflect a belief that all employees should share equally in the company's gains to promote cooperation among employees. However, employee contributions to profits probably vary. Accordingly, most employers divide the profit-sharing pool among employees based on a differential basis. Companies may disburse profits based on **proportional payments to employees based on their annual salary.** Presumably, higher-paying jobs indicate the greatest potential to influence a company's competitive position. Still, another approach is to disburse profits as **proportional payments to employees based on their contribution to profits.** Some companies measure employee contributions to profits based on job performance. However, this approach is not very feasible because it is difficult to isolate each employee's contributions to profits.

Stock Bonus Plans

As described earlier, a **stock bonus plan** may be the basis for a company's 401(k) plan. Qualified stock bonus plans and qualified profit-sharing plans are similar because both plans invest in company securities. These plans are also similar regarding nondiscrimination requirements and the deductibility of employer contributions. However, stock bonus plans reward employees with company stock (i.e., equity shares in the company). Benefits are usually paid in shares of company stock. Participants of stock bonus plans possess the right to vote as shareholders. Voting rights differ based on whether company stock is traded in public stock exchanges.[35] In the case of publicly traded stock, plan participants may vote on all issues.

Employee Stock Option Plans (ESOPs)

Employee stock option plans (ESOPs) may be the basis for a company's 401(k) plan, and these plans invest in company securities, making them similar to profit-sharing plans and stock bonus plans. ESOPs and profit-sharing plans differ because ESOPs usually make distributions in company stock rather than cash. ESOPs are essentially stock bonus plans that use borrowed funds to purchase stock.

ESOPs are either nonleveraged or leveraged plans.[36] In the case of **nonleveraged ESOPs,** the company contributes stock or cash to buy stock. The stock is then allocated to the accounts of participants. Nonleveraged plans are stock bonus plans. In the case of **leveraged ESOPs,** the plan administrator borrows money from a financial institution to purchase company stock. The company may use the borrowed money for different purposes, including financing of existing debt, estate planning, or financing an acquisition or divestiture. Over time, the company makes principal and interest payments to the ESOP to repay the loan. The stock purchased with the loan is placed in a suspense account until amounts equal to the employer's contributions are allocated to the individual accounts of participants.

Savings Incentive Match Plans for Employees (SIMPLEs)

Congress enacted a law in 1996 that established **savings incentive match plans for employees (SIMPLEs)** working in small companies.[37] For the purpose of this plan, small companies employing 100 or fewer employees whose preceding year's compensation totaled at least $5,000 and who do not maintain another employer-sponsored retirement plan, are eligible.

Companies may establish SIMPLEs as either individual retirement accounts (IRAs) or as 401(k) plans. We will review SIMPLEs as 401(k) plans in this chapter. As a qualified plan, SIMPLEs must meet nondiscrimination and vesting requirements under ERISA. In addition, employees may contribute up to $11,500 in 2009. The annual limit is indexed for inflation in $500 increments.

Section 403(b) Tax-Deferred Annuity Plans

Section 403(b) of the IRC established **tax-deferred annuity (TDA)** programs. A TDA represents a type of retirement plan for employees of public educational institutions (e.g., state colleges and universities) or private tax-exempt organizations (e.g., charitable organizations, state-supported hospitals).[38] Congress enacted Section 403(b) because such organizations may not have sufficient resources to provide a qualified retirement plan. TDAs are not qualified plans under ERISA.

Under TDAs, contributions come mainly from either employers or employees. Employees make contributions through salary reduction agreements with their employers. A less common method is direct employee contributions outside salary reduction agreements. TDAs may be the only retirement program offered in these organizations, or these plans may supplement other employer-sponsored pension programs, usually defined benefit plans. Private tax-exempt organizations may offer both 401(k) and 403(b) plans, but public organizations are prohibited from offering 401(k) plans.

Three common methods for funding TDAs include annuity contracts, custodial agreements, and life insurance. Eligible annuity contracts may take different forms. Annuities may be individual or group contracts, and these may be fixed dollar or variable annuities. Also, eligible annuities must be nontransferable. In other words, annuity contracts may not be sold, signed, or pledged as security for collateral. Custodial accounts permit investments in mutual funds.

TDAs possess features similar to 401(k) plans. First, earnings on contributions are also tax-deferred until distributed. Second, the tax code restricts when distributions may be taken and under what conditions. These stipulations are the same as those found in 401(k) plans, except participants may not roll over assets into

EXHIBIT 5.5 Characteristics of Defined Benefit and Defined Contribution Plans

Source: U.S. Department of Labor (2006). *What You Should Know About Your Retirement Plan.* Online: www.dol.gov/ebsa. Accessed April 26, 2009.

	Defined Benefit Plan	Defined Contribution Plan
Employer Contributions and/or Matching Contributions	Employer funded. Federal rules set amounts that employers must contribute to plans in an effort to ensure that plans have enough money to pay benefits when due. There are penalties for failing to meet these requirements.	There is no requirement that the employer contribute, except in the SIMPLE 401(k) and Safe Harbor 401(k), money purchase plans, and SIMPLE IRA and SEP plans. The employer may choose to match a portion of the employee's contributions or to contribute without employee contributions. In some plans, employer contributions may be in the form of employer stock.
Employee Contributions	Generally, employees do not contribute to these plans.	Many plans require the employee to contribute for an account to be established.
Managing the Investment	Plan officials manage the investment, and the employer is responsible for ensuring that the amount it has put in the plan plus investment earnings will be enough to pay the promised benefit.	The employee often is responsible for managing the investment of his or her account, choosing from investment options offered by the plan. In some plans, plan officials are responsible for investing all the plan's assets.
Amount of Benefits Paid Upon Retirement	A promised benefit is based on a formula in the plan, often using a combination of the employee's age, years worked for the employer, and/or salary.	The benefit depends on contributions made by the employee and/or the employer, performance of the account's investments, and fees charged to the account.
Type of Retirement Benefit Payments	Traditionally, these plans pay the retiree monthly annuity payments that continue for life. Plans may offer other payment options.	The retiree may transfer the account balance into an individual retirement account (IRA) from which the retiree withdraws money, or may receive it as a lump sum payment. Some plans also offer monthly payments through an annuity.
Guarantee of Benefits	The federal government, through the Pension Benefit Guaranty Corporation (PBGC), guarantees some amount of benefits.	No federal guarantee of benefits.
Leaving the Company Before Retirement Age	If an employee leaves after vesting in a benefit but before the plan's retirement age, the benefit generally stays with the plan until the employee files a claim for it at retirement. Some defined benefit plans offer early retirement options.	The employee may transfer the account balance to an individual retirement account (IRA) or, in some cases, another employer plan, where it can continue to grow based on investment earnings. The employee also may take the balance out of the plan, but will owe taxes and possibly penalties, thus reducing retirement income. Plans may cash out small accounts.

any qualified plan. TDA participants may roll over a TDA distribution to another TDA or an Individual Retirement Account (IRA).[39]

Section 457 Plans

Section 457 plans, named after the section of the Internal Revenue Code that created them, are nonqualified retirement plans for government employees. Until 2002, Section 457 plans were less generous than either 401(k) or 403(b) plans because maximum annual contributions were substantially lower [$7,000 versus $10,000 for 401(k) or 403(b) plans in 2001]. Now 457 plans have the same limits as 401(k) or 403(b) plans. However, unlike 401(k) and 403(b) plans, only employees may contribute to 457 plans.

Exhibit 5.5 summarizes selected differences between defined benefit and defined contribution plans.

HYBRID PLANS

Hybrid plans combine features of traditional defined benefit and defined contribution plans. We will discuss four common hybrid plans in turn: (1) cash balance plans and pension equity plans, (2) target benefit plans, (3) money purchase plans, and (4) age-weighted profit-sharing plans.

Many employers have set aside traditional defined benefit pension plans for hybrid plans: Numerous accounts describe defined benefit plans as **"golden handcuffs,"** providing generous (golden) retirement income to workers who remain with the same employer (the handcuffs) throughout their work life. Such plans, which often base benefits on earnings in a worker's last years with the company, may provide lower benefits for those employees who work in multiple jobs throughout their lifetimes.

In January 2007, all employees had worked for their current employer for an average of 3.7 years; those aged 35 to 44 had worked for their current employer an average of 4.9 years and those aged 55 to 64 had worked for their current employer an average of 9.3 years. These data suggest workers may be accumulating retirement benefits from several jobs; employers have attempted to deal with these changing needs by seeking alternative approaches to providing retirement income.

The different career plans of the younger generations have led many employers to conclude that their retirement plans were not beneficial to these younger, more mobile workers. This was not conducive to attracting potentially valuable employees that could help increase efficiency.[40]

Cash Balance Plans and Pension Equity Plans

Internal Revenue Service guidelines define **cash balance plans** as "defined benefit plans that define benefits for each employee by reference to the amount of the employee's hypothetical account balance."[41] **Pension equity plans** are similar to cash balance plans, except, as described shortly, for how benefits are calculated. Cash balance plans are a relatively new phenomenon compared to traditional defined benefit and defined contribution plans. Many companies have chosen to convert their defined benefit plans to cash balance plans for two key reasons. First, cash balance plans are less costly to employers than defined benefit plans. Second, cash balance plans pay out benefits in a single lump sum payment instead of a series of monthly payments, typically for the remainder of the retiree's life. Calculating benefits as a lump sum increases the portability of pension benefits from company to company. That is, employees who have achieved full vesting may roll over the lump accumulated in a cash balance plan to their new employer's qualified retirement plan. Thus, companies are in a better position to recruit more mobile workers. Under a traditional defined benefit plan, an employee who leaves employment prior to qualifying for a retirement annuity (again, monthly payments for the rest of one's life) will forfeit the annuity.

Benefit Formulas

Companies establish individual accounts for employees as in defined contribution plans. They may choose from several methods of crediting contributions to cash balance plans. The most common approaches include a fixed percentage of earnings and percentages that vary by age, length of service, or earnings.

Participants receive credits expressed as a percentage of annual pay, and these credits earn interest at a designated rate. The interest rate credit is guaranteed instead of fluctuating with the performance of the investments. In addition, the amounts stated in these individual accounts are strictly hypothetical because the employer contributes money to the plan as a whole, covering all employees.

Complex federal rules require that employers have sufficient assets to cover the amounts expressed in every employee's hypothetical account. In defined contribution plans, on the other hand, the account balance is equal to actual assets held in trust for the participant, and the interest rate fluctuates with the performance of the investments.

Under a cash balance plan, for example, an employer may choose to credit 5 percent of each employee's annual earnings, and these credited amounts grow based on a preestablished interest rate of 7 percent. Typically, employers establish annual interest credits where the employee receives interest credits on December 31 of each year. Interest is credited on the benefit amount credited on January 1 of the same year, as well as on all benefit and interest credits accumulated during earlier years.

Let's assume an employee earns $100,000 per year in 2007 and in 2008. Also assume that the value of his cash balance account is $22,000 at the end of 2006. This figure represents the sum of all benefit and interest credits earned through the year 2006. On January 1, 2007, the employer would credit $5,000 ($100,000 annual earnings × 5% annual benefit credit rate) to the employee's account. That is, on January 1, 2007, the account total would equal $27,000 ($22,000 balance as of December 31, 2006 + $5,000). On December 31, 2006, the employer would credit the account with $1,890, which represents 7 percent (the annual interest rate) on the $27,000 balance on January 1, 2007. That is, on December 31, 2007, the account total would equal $28,890 ($27,000 balance on January 1, 2007 + $1,890 interest credited on December 31, 2007). Continuing with the cycle, the account balance would be $33,890 on January 1, 2008, based on the addition of a benefit credit equaling 5 percent of the employee's $100,000 annual earnings for 2008.

Pension equity plans credit employees' accounts with points based on years of service. The points are often expressed as a percentage of pay. When an employee terminates employment or retires, the benefit is calculated as the product of the employee's average pay (average of one's pay over a career) and the total number of points earned. The benefit is expressed as an account balance, much like the benefit of a cash balance plan.

Years of Service	Percentage of Pay
Less than 5	2%
5 to 9	4
10 to 14	6
15 to 19	8
20 and above	10

Controversy Surrounding Cash Balance Plans

Two controversies have emerged. The first issue centers on favorable treatment of younger workers and unfavorable treatment of older employees. The second issue is based on the practice of converting traditional defined benefit plans to cash balance plans. We will review each of these in turn.

Age-Related Treatment   Cash balance plans are said to provide favorable treatment to younger workers and to workers who switch employers from time to time. These plans do not define benefits as a percentage of final or career average pay or as a flat dollar amount per year of service, which is the case for defined benefit plans. Defined benefit plans provide more favorable treatment to older employees because benefits accrue on an age-related basis, permitting older employees to earn benefits more quickly than younger workers. Cash balance plans, on the other hand, award annual pay-related credits, much as defined contribution plans, with the contributions appreciating each year based on a specified interest rate.

The U.S. General Accounting Office (GAO) compared the rates of retirement benefit accrual in defined benefit plans and cash balance plans under a variety of assumptions. It concluded that cash balance plan accrual favors younger employees.[42] For example, a 25-year-old employee who is assumed to participate in a cash balance plan until retirement at age 65 accrues an incremental annuity benefit of about $1,660 at age 26 but earns a smaller incremental benefit of about $630 at age 65. Under a defined benefit plan, this same individual earns an incremental annuity benefit of $310 at age 26 but earns a higher incremental annuity benefit of about $2,440 at age 65.

The difference in accrual patterns between these plan types has led some people to question whether cash balance plans illegally discriminate on the basis of age. According to the GAO:

> Cash balance proponents define the accrued benefit as the employee's hypothetical account balance. Under this definition, cash balance plans generate a level rate of accrual for all employees regardless of age and therefore do not appear to raise

issues of disparate treatment of employees based on age. Critics state that cash balance plans, as defined benefit plans under the law, must express an employee's accrued benefit as an annual benefit beginning at normal retirement age or the actuarial equivalent to a deferred annuity.[43] When cash balance plans are viewed in this way, the amount of the actuarially determined benefit is a function of the participant's age and decreases as the participant ages. Therefore, critics argue, cash balance plans violate the prohibition on age discrimination. Federal agencies are considering the issue of whether cash balance plans violate age discrimination statutes. Participants have filed a number of court cases alleging that cash balance plans are age discriminatory but no definitive decision has been reached.[44]

Converting Defined Benefit Plans to Cash Balance Plans As we discussed earlier, retirement benefits accrue at a decreasing rate in cash balance plans in contrast to an increasing rate in defined benefit plans. Converting from defined benefit plans to cash balance plans may result in older workers receiving smaller benefits. The GAO compared lump sum distributions for a traditional defined benefit plan with lump sum distributions for a cash balance plan following conversion at various ages at separation from employment.[45] Exhibit 5.6 shows the increasing disparity in lump sum distributions for older workers after a conversion from a defined benefit plan to a cash balance plan.

Further consideration reveals that cash balance plans tend to produce the lowest annuity at retirement for the employee who was oldest at conversion. For example, the GAO study modeled benefits from a basic cash balance

EXHIBIT 5.6 Lump Sum Distributions from a Traditional Final Average Pay Formula and a Cash Balance Formula after Conversion

Source: U.S. General Accounting Office, *Private Pensions: Implications of Conversions to Cash Balance Plans,* GAO/HEHS-00-185 (Washington, DC: General Accounting Office, 2000), pp. 22–23.

Age at Separation	Final Average Pay Formula*	Cash Balance Formula†
30	$ 2,476	$ 2,476
35	7,849	13,699
40	18,684	30,358
45	39,618	54,510
50	79,096	88,926
53	117,686	116,000
55	152,611	137,322
60	288,878	204,673
65	544,153	297,625

Notes: Results are based on baseline scenario assumptions for a 30-year-old worker at conversion and show several possible ages when the worker might leave the firm. The 30-year-old worker was assigned a tenure and income value at conversion that corresponds to the worker's age. Lump sum distributions paid from the traditional formula are calculated on the basis of annuity values that the formula would have produced had no conversion occurred and in accordance with IRC 417(e) regulations. Lump sum values are comparable at given ages but are not comparable across years.
* Based on normal retirement age annuity.
† Nominal account balance.

formula for a 35-, 45-, and 55-year-old employee with equal salary and tenure at conversion.[46]

At retirement the 55-year-old employee would receive an annual annuity of $6,900 from the cash balance plan, the 45-year-old employee would receive $12,600 per year, and the 35-year-old employee about $24,000 a year. These monetary values simply represent the expected magnitude of differences.

Another problem with conversion is known as "wearaway." According to the U.S. Department of Labor, **wearaway** is said to occur when the formula in a defined benefits plan is changed to a cash balance formula. Oftentimes, when the defined benefit plan formula is changed to a cash balance plan formula, the benefit earned under the defined benefit plan formula may exceed the amount determined to be the benefit under the cash balance plan formula. When this situation arises, an employee may not earn additional benefits until the benefit under the cash balance plan formula exceeds the benefit amount under the defined benefit plan formula. There are legal requirements that have to be satisfied with respect to benefit accruals, including prohibition against age discrimination. "Wearaway" is one of the issues being closely studied by the Equal Employment Opportunity Commission, the Internal Revenue Service, and the U.S. Department of Labor.

Not all employees experience wearaway following the conversion of their defined benefit plan to a cash balance plan. The GAO study indicated that the wearaway period at conversion is longer for older employees, and in addition, found that the wearaway period is increasingly longer the older the workers are at conversion. Wearaway has two causes. First, companies may create wearaway by setting a participant's hypothetical balance under the cash balance plan lower than the present value of accrued benefits under the traditional defined benefit plan. Currently, no regulations exist for setting opening hypothetical balances. Second, wearaway may occur because of changes in the federally mandated discount rate for determining lump sum distributions from defined benefit plans. The value of lump sum distributions increases when the discount rate falls, while the value of distributions decreases when the discount rate increases.

Indeed, a variety of recent court rulings proved mixed on the issue about whether cash balance plans discriminate on the basis of age. Some courts recently concluded that these plans do not violate the Age Discrimination in Employment Act. In *Easton v. Onan Corp.*, a federal district judge ruled that pension age discrimination prohibitions do not apply to employees younger than normal retirement age.[47] The provisions were set to ensure that employees who chose to work past the normal retirement age continue to accrue pension benefits. In *Dan C. Tootle v. ARINC Inc.*, the judge ruled that a "sensible approach" to determine whether cash balance plans are discriminatory is to use a test from ERISA for defined contribution plans.[48]

Specifically, plans are not discriminatory as long as employer contributions are not reduced by age.

However, in *Cooper v. The IBM Personal Pension Plan*,[49] a U.S. District Court judge in southern Illinois ruled in 2003 that IBM Corporation's cash balance plan discriminated against IBM's older employees because the benefit credit provided to older employees purchased a much smaller benefit than the same benefit provided to a younger employee. The judge in the IBM case relied on ERISA-based discrimination tests for defined benefit plans, as described earlier in the chapter.

Since then, language in the Pension Protection Act of 2006 tries to resolve the misunderstanding over wearaway provisions. This act makes it illegal for employers to use wearaway provisions when converting a defined benefit plan to a cash balance plan. As a result, cash balance plan provisions must credit a participant with his or her accrued benefit under the old formula plus full credit for years of service after the adoption of the cash balance formula. The Pension Protection Act also allows employers to create new cash balance plans—or to convert existing defined benefit plans to a cash balance design—with much less fear of litigation.

Shortly after the Pension Protection Act was signed into law in August 2006, judges from the U.S. Seventh Circuit Court revisited the 2003 ruling in *Cooper v. The IBM Personal Pension Plan*. They reversed the 2003 ruling, concluding that the IBM Personal Pension Plan did not discriminate against employees on the basis of age. Older workers at IBM maintained that "someone who leaves IBM at age 50, after 20 years of service, will have a larger annual benefit at 65 than someone whose 20 years of service conclude with retirement at age 65. The former receives 15 years' more interest than the latter." Judges in the 2006 review indicated that nothing in the ERISA language legislates against "the fact that younger workers have (statistically) more time left before retirement, and thus a greater opportunity to earn interest on each year's retirement savings. Treating the time value of money as a form of discrimination is not sensible."[50]

Most recently, Cooper made a request to the U.S. Supreme Court to hear this case in the hopes of overturning the Seventh Circuit Court's ruling. The U.S. Supreme Court declined to review the 2006 court decision in *Cooper v. The IBM Personal Pension Plan*. In 2007, Cooper appealed the Seventh Circuit Court's decision. The court refused to rehear the case.

Target Benefit Plans

As a hybrid plan, **target benefit plans** combine features of defined benefit and defined contribution plans. Target benefit plans calculate benefits in a fashion similar to defined benefit plans based on formulas that use income and years of service. However, target benefit plans are fundamentally defined contribution plans because the benefit amount at retirement may be more or less than the targeted benefit amount based on the investment performance of the plan assets. "Targeted" benefit is based on the assumption that the actual return on plan assets equals the expected return.

Consistent with defined contribution plans, target benefit plan participants have individual accounts. Employers use actuarial calculations of the annual contribution amount that would be necessary to fully fund the retirement benefit at a participant's normal retirement age. These contributions are invested on behalf of the participant. In a defined benefit plan, employers would modify the annual contribution amount according to the performance of the investments to ensure benefit amounts at retirement. In a target benefit plan, employers do not adjust their contributions. As a result, retirement benefits may be more or less than projected.

Target benefit plans at first glance appear to violate ERISA's nondiscrimination rules because employers contribute greater amounts on behalf of more highly paid employees (usually older employees) than lower-paid employees (usually younger employees). For the moment, let's assume that older workers are more highly paid than younger workers. The Internal Revenue Service cross-testing rules[51] permit age-based contributions in target benefit plans and age-weighted profit-sharing plans under the following conditions: Lower contributions are permissible for lower-paid (younger) employees because the contributions are projected over a longer period than for higher-paid (older) employees. In the end, plans with age-based contributions are not discriminatory if projected benefits are comparable regardless of age.

Target benefit plans tend to be less expensive than either defined benefit or defined contribution plans. Under a defined benefit plan, employers are required to increase contribution amounts to compensate for shortfalls caused by poor investment performance. Employers do not make adjustments to their annual contributions in target benefit plans. Under a defined contribution plan, the annual contributions of employers are usually based on a fixed percentage of each employee's income regardless of age. Actuarially determined contributions in target benefit plans mean that larger contributions are made for older workers whose possible length of service is shorter than younger employees. The costs of target benefit plans in companies with predominantly younger workforces may be less than the costs of defined contribution plans.

Money Purchase Plans

Money purchase plans are defined contribution plans because the benefit is based on the account balance—that is, the employer contributions plus the returns on investment of employer contributions—at retirement. However, these plans possess the funding requirements of defined benefit plans. Employers must make annual contributions according to the designated formula for the plan. These contributions are not tied to company performance indicators such as profits or stock price. Failure to make these contributions will result in excise tax penalties.[52]

Age-Weighted Profit-Sharing Plans

As a hybrid plan, **age-weighted profit-sharing plans** combine features of defined benefit and defined contribution plans. Fundamentally, these plans are defined contribution plans because benefit amounts fluctuate according to the performance of investments of plan assets. In this regard, age-weighted profit-sharing plans are like the deferred profit-sharing plans we discussed earlier. Consideration of age makes these plans similar to defined benefit plans. Employers contribute disproportionately more to the accounts of older employees based on a projected hypothetical benefit at normal retirement age. The idea is to fund all employee accounts sufficiently well so that each employee would likely achieve a similar hypothetical retirement benefit.

Summary   This chapter reviewed the fundamental concepts of company-sponsored retirement plans. Companies must follow a set of strict guidelines in designing and implementing pension plans to qualify for favorable tax treatment. We also reviewed the main features of defined benefit, defined contribution, and hybrid plans.

Key Terms

qualified plans, *107*
nonqualified plans, *107*
coverage requirements, *109*
ratio percentage test, *110*
average benefit test, *110*
vesting, *110*
cliff vesting, *110*
six-year gradual vesting, *110*
accrual rules, *110*
nondiscrimination tests, *110*
top-heavy provisions, *110*
accrued benefits, *110*
minimum funding standards, *111*
Social Security integration, *111*
permitted disparity rules, *111*
distribution, *112*
lump sum distributions, *112*
annuities, *112*
income annuities, *112*
qualified joint and survivor annuity (QJSA), *112*
qualified preretirement survivor annuity (QPSA), *112*

qualified domestic relations orders (QDROs), *113*
plan termination rules, *113*
defined benefit plans, *113*
flat benefit formulas, *114*
unit benefit formulas, *114*
accumulated benefit obligation, *115*
backloading, *116*
three percent rule, *117*
$133\frac{1}{3}$ percent rule, *117*
fractional rule, *117*
defined contribution plans, *118*
forfeitures, *118*
fiduciary, *118*
annual addition, *120*
Section 401(k) plans, *120*
profit-sharing plans, *121*
profit-sharing pool, *121*
fixed first-dollar-of-profits formula, *121*
graduated first-dollar-of-profits formula, *121*
profitability threshold formulas, *121*

equal payments, *122*
proportional payments to employees based on their annual salary, *122*
proportional payments to employees based on their contribution to profits, *122*
stock bonus plan, *122*
employee stock option plans (ESOPs), *122*
nonleveraged ESOPs, *122*
leveraged ESOPs, *123*
savings incentive match plans for employees (SIMPLEs), *123*
tax-deferred annuity (TDA), *123*
Section 457 plans, *125*
hybrid plans, *125*
golden handcuffs, *125*
cash balance plans, *125*
pension equity plans, *125*
wearaway, *129*
target benefit plans, *130*
money purchase plans, *131*
age-weighted profit-sharing plans, *131*

Discussion Questions

1. Describe three criteria used to qualify pension plans for preferential tax treatment.
2. Are employees more likely to favor defined contribution plans over defined benefit plans? How about employers? Explain your answer.
3. Summarize the controversial issues regarding cash balance plans.
4. Explain why mobile employees might prefer cash balance plans over defined benefit plans.

Endnotes

1. ERISA §3(2)(A), 29 U.S.C. §1002(2)(A).
2. Employee Benefits Research Institute. 1997. Pension Plans (Chapter 4) in *Fundamentals of Employee Benefits Programs*. Washington, D.C. Employee Benefits Research Institute.

3. S. L. Costo. 2006. "Trends in retirement plan coverage over the last decade," *Monthly Labor Review,* February, 58–64.

4. Ibid.; U.S. Department of Labor. August 2006. *National Compensation Survey: Employee Benefits in Private Industry in the United States, March 2006* (Summary 06-05). Online at www.bls.gov/ecthome.htm. Accessed March 5, 2007.

5. S. L. Costo. "Trends in retirement plan coverage over the last decade."

6. U.S. Department of Labor. *National Compensation Survey.*

7. S. L. Costo. "Trends in retirement plan coverage over the last decade"; W. J. Wiatrowski. 2004. "Medical and retirement plan coverage: Exploring the decline in recent years," *Monthly Labor Review,* August, 29–36.

8. Internal Revenue Code (hereafter cited I.R.C.) §§410(a)(1), 410(a)(4); Treas. Reg. §1.410(a)-3T(b); ERISA §202(a).

9. I.R.C. §410(a)(3), Treas. Reg. §1.410(a)-5, 29 C.F.R. §2530.200b-2(a), ERISA §202(a)(3).

10. I.R.C. §414(q).

11. I.R.C. §410(b); Treas. Regs. §§1.410(b)-2, 1.410(b)-4, 1.410(a)(4)–11(g)(2).

12. I.R.C. §401(a)(26), Treas. Reg. §1.401(a)(26)–2(a).

13. I.R.C. §§411(a)(2), 411(a)(5); Treas. Reg. §1.411(a)-3T; ERISA §203(a).

14. I.R.C. §§411(a)(7), 411(b); ERISA §§204, 3(23); Treas. Reg. §1.411(b)-1.

15. I.R.C. §401(a)(4).

16. I.R.C. §416(g)(1).

17. I.R.C. §416; Treas. Reg. §1.416-1.

18. I.R.C. §§401(a)(5)(C), 401(l).

19. ABA Section of Labor and Employment Law. 2000. *Employee Benefits Law,* 2nd ed., Washington, DC: Bureau of National Affairs, pp. 252–53.

20. I.R.C. §§401(a), 417(b), 417(c); ERISA §205; Treas. Regs. §§1.401(a)-11, 1.401(a)-20.

21. ERISA §206(d)(1), I.R.C. §401(a)(13).

22. I.R.C. §§401(a)(13), 414(p); ERISA §206(d).

23. Treas. Regs. §§1.401(a)–13(g)(4)(i).

24. I.R.C. §415(b).

25. I.R.C. §404(a)(1)(A)(i)–(iii).

26. I.R.C. §404(a)(1)(C).

27. Treas. Regs. §1.401(a)(4)-2(b).

28. I.R.C. §411(a)(7)(A)(ii); ERISA §204(b)(2).

29. Prop. Treas. Reg. §§1.412(b)-1(a).

30. I.R.C. §415(c)(2); Treas. Reg. §1.415-6(b)(1).

31. I.R.C. §415(c).

32. I.R.C. §§404(a)(3), 402(g).

33. I.R.C. §404(a)(3).

34. Treas. Reg. §1.401-1(b)(2).

35. I.R.C. §404(a)(3).

36. I.R.C. §§401(a), 4975(e)(7)–(8).

37. I.R.C. §408.

38. I.R.C. §§501(c)(3); 501(a).

39. I.R.C. §§401(a)(9); 401(a)(31); 403(b)(10).

40. L. B. Green. October 29, 2003. *What Is a Pension Equity Plan? Compensation and Working Conditions Online.* Online at http://bls.gov/opub/cwc/cm20031016ar01p1.htm. Accessed July 29, 2004.

41. 26 Code of Federal Regulations §§1.401(a)(4)-8(c)(3)(I).

42. U.S. Department of Labor, Bureau of Labor Statistics. September 23, 2003. "Questions and answers on cash balance plans," *Compensation and Working Conditions Online.* Online at www.bls.gov/opub/cwc/print/cm20030917ar01p.htm. Accessed July 29, 2004.

43. 26 U.S.C. §411(a)(7).

44. U.S. General Accounting Office. September 2000. *Private Pensions: Implications of Conversions to Cash Balance Plans* (GAO/HEHS-00-185). Washington, DC: GAO.

45. U.S. General Accounting Office. *Private Pensions.*

46. Ibid.

47. *Eaton v. Onan Corp.*, 2000 WL 1459801 (S.D. Ind. 2000).

48. *Dan C. Tootle v. ARINC Inc.*, U.S. District Court for the District of Maryland, No. CCB-03-1086.

49. *Cooper v. The IBM Personal Pension Plan,* Civil No. 99-829-GPM (S.D. Ill. July 31, 2003).

50. *Cooper v. The IBM Personal Pension Plan*, Civil No. 05-3588, U.S. District Court of Appeals for the Seventh Circuit, August 7, 2006.

51. ERISA §401(a)(4); I.R.C. §1.401(a)(4)–(8).

52. I.R.C. §412(h).

Chapter **Six**

Employer-Sponsored Health Insurance Programs

Learning Objectives

In this chapter, you will gather information about:

1. Health insurance concepts.
2. Origins of employer-sponsored health insurance programs.
3. Federal and state laws influencing employer-sponsored health insurance practices.
4. Differences between fee-for-service plans and managed care plans.
5. Rationale behind consumer-driven health care plans.
6. Disincentives to offering health care benefits to retirees.

So, now, you have a better understanding of your retirement plan and are ready to consider the various options available to provide you with health insurance. Unfortunately, all the different acronyms involved have quickly turned it into a befuddling alphabet soup—POS, HMO, PPO, FSA. "Yikes!" you exclaim. As you read about these options, you learn that each plan has its own set of coinsurance rates and deductibles. Now, you are really confused!

DEFINING AND EXPLORING HEALTH INSURANCE PROGRAMS

Health insurance covers the costs of a variety of services that promote sound physical and mental health, including physical examinations, diagnostic testing, surgery, hospitalization, psychotherapy, dental treatments, and corrective prescription lenses for vision deficiencies. Employers usually enter into a contractual relationship with one or more insurance companies to provide health-related services for their employees and, if specified, employees' dependents. The contractual relationship, or **insurance policy,** specifies the amount of money the insurance company will pay for particular services such as physical examinations. Employers pay insurance companies a negotiated amount, or **premium,** to establish and maintain insurance policies. The term *insured* refers to employees covered by the insurance policy.

Companies can choose from three broad classes of health insurance programs in the United States, including *fee-for-service plans, managed care plans,* and *point-of-service plans,* the latter of which combines features of fee-for-service and managed care plans. An emerging class of health insurance programs is based on *consumer-driven health care,* where employees play a greater role in decisions on their health care, have better access to information to make informed decisions, and share more in the costs. We discuss these types of plans later in this chapter.

It is also important to mention that health care in the United States is classified as a **multiple-payer system.** In a multiple-payer system, more than one party is responsible for covering the cost of health care, including the government, employers, labor unions, employees, or individuals not currently employed (e.g., retirees, the unemployed, and employees whose employer does not pay for health care coverage). As we will discuss shortly, a variety of forces have contributed to the existence of a multiple-payer health care system in the United States. A multiple-payer system stands in contrast to a **single-payer system** in which the government regulates the health care system and uses taxpayer dollars to fund health care, as in Canada and some other countries. Single-payer systems are often referred to as **universal health care systems** because the government ensures that all its citizens have access to quality health care regardless of their ability to pay. These approaches to health care coverage have been at the heart of political and social debate for years. The debate has taken front stage since President

Barack Obama was elected in 2008 to serve as President of the United States. On the table is talk of adopting a universal health care approach, which would essentially shift the responsibility for providing health care coverage from the employer to the federal or state governments. We take up the issues that lie at the heart of this debate in Chapter 11.

Origins of Health Insurance Benefits

The predecessor to company-sponsored insurance benefits appeared in the late 1800s for mining and railroad workers. Those companies hired doctors to provide medical services to employees. The hazardous work of railroad workers, miners, and employees in other industrial businesses led to frequent illnesses and injuries, employee absences from work, and costly disruptions to these businesses. In those days, working-class employees could not readily afford to pay for medical services, so employers quickly recognized that bearing such costs would help maintain a more productive workforce.

The Great Depression of the 1930s gave rise to employer-sponsored health insurance programs. Widespread unemployment made it impossible for most individuals to afford health care. During this period, Congress proposed the Social Security Act of 1935 to address many of the social maladies caused by the adverse economic conditions, incorporating health insurance programs. However, President Franklin D. Roosevelt opposed the inclusion of health coverage under the Social Security Act. Health insurance did not become part of the Social Security Act until an amendment to the act in 1965 established the Medicare program.

The government's choice not to offer health care benefits created opportunities for private sector companies to meet the public's need. In the 1930s, hospitals controlled nonprofit companies that inspired today's Blue Cross and Blue Shield plans. At the time, Blue Cross plans allowed individuals to make monthly payments to cover the expense of possible future hospitalization. For-profit companies also formed to provide health care coverage, creating fee-for-service plans.

In the 1940s, local medical associations created nonprofit Blue Shield plans, which were prepayment plans for physician services. Also, the federal government imposed wage freezes during World War II, which did not extend to employee benefit plans. Many employers began offering health care benefits to help compete for and retain the best employees, particularly during the labor shortage when U.S. troops were overseas fighting in the war. Also, employers recognized that they could promote productivity with healthier workforces. Without the assistance of employer-sponsored health insurance, employees could not afford to pay for medical services on their own. Many companies sought ways to promote productivity and morale through the implementation of welfare practices. In Chapter 1, we defined welfare practices as "anything for the comfort and improvement, intellectual or social, of the employees, over and above wages paid, which is not a necessity of the industry nor required by law."[1] Health insurance programs were among these practices.

Many companies discontinued health insurance benefits soon after the government lifted the wage freeze. The withdrawal of these and other benefits created discontent among employees, who viewed benefits as an entitlement. Legal battles ensued based on the claim that health protection was a fundamental right. In unionized companies, health insurance benefits became a mandatory subject of collective bargaining.

The 1950s were relatively uneventful years regarding employee benefits. In the 1960s the federal government amended the Social Security Act. Titles XVIII and XIX of the act established the Medicare and Medicaid programs, respectively (see Chapter 7). These public programs provided access to health care services for a wide segment of the U.S. population in a relatively short period. The demand for health care services rose quickly relative to the supply of health care providers, prompting inflation in the price of health care services.

Congress enacted the Employee Retirement Income Security Act of 1974 to protect employee interests (see Chapter 3). By providing financial incentives to companies, subject to becoming federally qualified, the **Health Maintenance Organization Act of 1973 (HMO Act)** promoted the use of health maintenance organizations. We discuss the HMO Act later in the chapter.

Since the 1970s, substantial emphasis has been placed on managing costs, and consideration has been given to providing coverage to the uninsured (e.g., the failed national health care proposal under former President Bill Clinton). Some factors have eroded health insurance practices in companies. Unionized companies set the standards for employee benefits practices. In the 1980s, unions made concessions on wages and benefits in exchange for promises of greater job security. Also, the decline in the manufacturing or goods-producing sector (e.g., automobiles, steel, mining), which was traditionally highly unionized, gave way to the typically nonunion service and information sectors of the economy (e.g., health care industry, retail trade, and high-technology companies, such as software development). Further, foreign competition created pressures, forcing U.S. companies to reduce costs. For example, many U.S. manufacturers moved operations to foreign countries with cheaper labor and fewer legal protections for employees (e.g., People's Republic of China, India). Notwithstanding these pressures, health insurance still is the mainstay of employee benefits programs in companies.

Health Insurance Coverage and Costs

Both employees and employers place a great deal of significance on company-sponsored health insurance benefits. Of course, company-sponsored programs provide employees with the means to afford expensive health care services. Companies stand to gain from sponsoring these benefits in at least two ways, as we noted before. First, a healthier workforce should experience a lower incidence of sickness absenteeism. By keeping absenteeism in check, a company's overall productivity and product or service quality should be higher. Second, health insurance offerings should help the recruitment and retention of employees. Not surprisingly, a large percentage of companies include health insurance programs as a feature of employee benefits programs, extending coverage to substantial numbers of employees and their dependents. At the same time, the rampant rise in health care prices is putting substantial pressure on cost-conscious companies.

At the time of this book's publication, the most recent comprehensive national data indicate that 71 percent of all private sector employees had access to at least one employer-sponsored health insurance program in 2008.[2] Employees' access to health insurance programs varies by their company's size, industry group, and union presence. A higher percentage of employees in larger companies had access to employer-sponsored health insurance than employees in smaller companies.

This is also the case for employees in goods-producing companies compared to service-providing companies, and for union employees compared to nonunion employees. Exhibit 6.1 illustrates these facts in greater detail.

Health insurance premiums are quite high, often amounting to as much as one-third of annual benefits costs. In March 2006 (the most recent data available at the time of publication), the average monthly health insurance premium was $266.50 per employee for single coverage.[3] **Single coverage** extends benefits only to the covered employee. Family coverage is substantially higher, averaging $617.18 per employee.[4] **Family coverage** offers benefits to the covered employee and his or her family members as defined by the plan (usually the spouse and children). Since the 1980s, many insurance plans have extended family coverage to unmarried heterosexual or homosexual domestic partnerships. Domestic partnership is established by providing evidence of living together, financial interdependence, and joint responsibility for each other's welfare.

Many private sector companies require employees to contribute a portion of health insurance premiums because of their considerable cost.[5] In 2008, employee contributions represented a relatively small percentage of the health insurance premiums. Employees with single coverage contributed nearly 17 percent, and those with family coverage contributed nearly 29 percent.

Health insurance premiums are likely to increase based on the trend in prices for medical services. For example, the prices for medical care services overall have increased more than 300 percent since 1982 (compared to a 115 percent increase for all goods and services purchased by consumers during the same period).

The substantially higher rate increases for medical services may be explained by several factors:

- Longer life expectancies.
- Aging baby-boom-era individuals, who place higher demands on health care.
- Advances in medical research that add diagnostic tests and treatments, such as substantially more effective (and expensive) treatments to save low-birth-weight babies.
- A general tendency for the health profession and family members to treat death as unnatural rather than as a natural ending to life, leading to higher expenditures to prolong the lives of the terminally ill.

There is no reason to expect that health care costs will decrease in the foreseeable future. Continuing medical research, more advanced diagnostic tools, and higher demand due to the aging population and the desire for better treatment will contribute to higher costs.

EXHIBIT 6.1 Medical Care Benefits: Access, Participation, and Take-up Rates (All workers = 100 percent)

Source: U.S. Bureau of Labor Statistics. *Employee Benefits in the United States, March 2008* (Summary 08-1122).

Characteristics	Civilian*			Private Industry			State and Local Government		
	Access	Participation	Take-up Rate[†]	Access	Participation	Take-up Rate	Access	Participation	Take-up Rate
All workers	74	56	76	71	53	75	87	73	83
Worker Characteristics									
Management, professional, and related	87	70	80	86	68	79	90	74	83
Management, business, and financial	94	78	83	94	77	82	—	—	—
Professional and related	84	67	79	82	64	78	89	73	82
Teachers	83	67	80	—	—	—	88	73	83
Primary, secondary, and special education school teachers	91	73	80	—	—	—	95	78	83
Registered nurses	76	59	77	—	—	—	93	72	77
Service	52	35	67	46	29	62	80	67	83
Protective service	—	—	—	—	—	—	89	76	86
Sales and office	73	53	73	71	51	72	88	75	84
Sales and related	63	43	67	63	42	67	—	—	—
Office and administrative support	78	60	76	77	57	75	89	75	84
Natural resources, construction, and maintenance	78	64	81	77	62	81	94	80	86
Construction, extraction, farming, fishing, and forestry	73	59	81	71	57	81	—	—	—
Installation, maintenance, and repair	84	69	82	83	68	81	—	—	—
Production, transportation, and material moving	78	61	79	78	61	78	82	70	85
Production	83	67	81	82	67	81	—	—	—
Transportation and material moving	74	56	76	73	55	75	—	—	—

(continued)

(continued)

Full time	88	68	78	85	65	76	98	83	84
Part time	25	15	60	24	14	60	28	18	65
Union	91	79	86	88	79	89	95	79	83
Nonunion	70	52	74	69	50	73	81	67	83
Average wage within the following percentiles:‡									
Less than 10	25	13	52	25	13	51	52	39	76
10 to under 25	51	31	61	48	28	59	81	67	82
25 to under 50	79	58	74	77	55	72	91	77	85
50 to under 75	86	70	81	84	67	79	94	80	85
75 to under 90	90	75	83	88	72	83	97	80	83
90 or greater	92	76	82	91	75	82	97	81	84

Establishment Characteristics

Goods-producing industries	85	69	82	85	69	82	—	—	—
Service-providing industries	71	53	75	68	49	73	87	73	83
Education and health services	80	60	75	74	51	69	88	72	81
Educational services	86	69	81	76	58	77	88	72	82
Elementary and secondary schools	88	70	80	—	—	—	89	72	81
Junior colleges, colleges, and universities	87	72	83	90	73	81	86	72	84
Health care and social assistance	75	52	69	74	50	68	91	71	78
Hospitals	88	67	76	—	—	—	94	70	75
Public administration	88	76	86	—	—	—	88	76	86
1 to 99 workers	60	44	73	60	43	72	74	63	85
1 to 49 workers	56	41	72	56	40	72	68	58	86
50 to 99 workers	71	52	74	70	51	73	83	70	84
100 workers or more	85	67	79	84	65	77	89	74	83
100 to 499 workers	81	61	76	80	60	74	84	72	85
500 workers or more	89	72	81	88	71	81	91	75	82

EXHIBIT 6.1 Medical Care Benefits: Access, Participation, and Take-up Rates (All workers = 100 percent)   (*Continued*)

Characteristics	Civilian*			Private Industry			State and Local Government		
	Access	Participation	Take-up Rate†	Access	Participation	Take-up Rate	Access	Participation	Take-up Rate
Geographic Areas									
New England	70	51	72	68	48	71	85	68	80
Middle Atlantic	74	58	78	72	55	76	85	77	90
East North Central	72	55	76	71	54	75	80	63	78
West North Central	72	56	78	69	54	77	83	66	80
South Atlantic	76	57	75	73	53	73	90	75	83
East South Central	78	61	78	75	57	77	93	75	81
West South Central	70	52	74	66	47	71	90	76	84
Mountain	72	53	73	70	49	71	87	72	83
Pacific	75	61	81	72	58	80	90	77	86

*Includes workers in the private nonfarm economy except those in private households, and workers in the public sector, except the federal government. See Technical Note for further explanation.
†The take-up rate is an estimate of the percentage of workers with access to a plan who participate in the plan, rounded for presentation. See Technical Note for more details.
‡The percentile groupings are based on the average wage for each occupation surveyed, which may include workers both above and below the threshold. The percentile values are based on the estimates published in the "National Compensation Survey: Occupational Earnings in the United States, 2007." See Technical Note for more details.
NOTE: Dash indicates no workers in this category or data did not meet publication criteria.

Individual versus Group Insurance Coverage

Companies offer employees coverage under health insurance programs on either an individual policy or group policy basis. **Individual coverage** extends insurance protection to a named employee* and possibly to his or her dependents, including the spouse and children. The insurance provider (indemnity plan through an insurance company, a health maintenance organization, a preferred provider organization, or a point-of-service plan) issues separate policies to every covered individual and conducts transactions directly with them. These transactions include the collection of premiums and the settlement of claims for benefits from the insured. Under individual plans, insurance providers require that prospective participants furnish evidence of health status based on a medical examination. Insurance providers use mortality tables and morbidity tables to decide whether to offer insurance and, if so, the terms and premium amount. This decision-making process is known as **underwriting. Mortality tables,** created by actuaries, indicate yearly probabilities of death based on such factors as age and sex. **Morbidity tables,** also created by actuaries, express annual probabilities of the occurrence of health problems. In general, insurance companies set insurance rates higher as the probability of death or the occurrence of health problems increases.

Group coverage extends coverage to a group of employees and their dependents under a single master contract. Insurance providers issue master contracts to employers, professional associations, labor unions, and trust funds established to provide health insurance to designated people. These entities are known as **group policyholders.** The underwriting process is somewhat different for group policies. Group policies generally do not exclude any group member based on health status. Instead, they focus mainly on establishing the premium for the master contract, usually expressed on an annual basis. Insurance providers use experience ratings issued by actuaries to set premiums. **Experience ratings** specify the incidence, type, and financial cost of insurance claims for groups (i.e., everyone as a whole covered under a group plan). Experience ratings hold employers (and other group entities described earlier) financially accountable for past claims, establishing the basis for charging different premiums.

Earlier, we referred to a variety of group policyholders including employers and trusts. Exhibit 6.2 describes the categories of group plans based on the type of policyholder.

REGULATION OF HEALTH INSURANCE PROGRAMS

A variety of federal and state laws affect employer and insurer practices, respectively. Every state has regulations pertaining to health insurance programs.

Federal Regulation

The main federal laws influencing employer-sponsored health insurance programs include the Health Maintenance Organization Act of 1973, the Employee

---

*We will also use the terms *covered individual, insured,* and *participant* interchangeably.

EXHIBIT 6.2
Types of
Group Plans

- *Single-employer arrangements.* An employer arranges for group coverage of all employees under one policy.
- *Pooled coverage.* An employer pools money with other employers to provide coverage for its employees under one policy. Oftentimes, employers in the same industry with similar workforces use pooled arrangements. Employer contributions are based on a percent of payroll, cents per hour, or dollar amount per worker per week or per month.
- *Multiple employer welfare arrangements.* This arrangement offers health insurance and other benefits to the employees of two or more unaffiliated employers, except for any arrangement established or maintained by a collective bargaining agreement.
- *Multiple employer trusts.* This arrangement is made for employers with relatively small workforces. A single master trust holds each employer's contributions, and insurance premiums are paid from the trust.
- *Voluntary employee beneficiary associations.* This arrangement permits tax-deductible contributions to a trust to fund health care benefits or other types of employee benefits. The return on investment of contributions is also tax-free.
- *Collective bargaining agreements.* A labor union can negotiate the terms of health insurance coverage for its members and members of the bargaining unit with employers.

Retirement Income Security Act of 1974, and the Americans with Disabilities Act of 1990. Tax regulations issued by the Internal Revenue Service may influence employer-sponsored health insurance practices.

The Health Maintenance Organization Act of 1973

Health maintenance organizations (HMOs) are regulated at both federal and state levels. At the federal level, HMOs are governed by the *Health Maintenance Organization Act of 1973 (HMO Act),*[6] amended in 1988, to encourage employers to include HMOs as a choice in their benefits programs. Congress enacted the HMO Act based on the idea that HMOs are a viable option of financing and delivering health care. Companies must offer HMOs if they are subject to the minimum wage provisions of the Fair Labor Standards Act (Chapter 4). The act spurred the growth of HMOs by making development funds available to qualifying HMOs and imposing a dual choice requirement on employers that sponsored health benefits programs. Qualified HMOs provide basic and supplemental health services that follow the U.S. Department of Health and Human Services guidelines, and demonstrate sound finances to minimize the likelihood of insolvency. Under the dual choice requirement, employers with at least 25 employees had to offer at least one HMO as an alternative to a fee-for-service plan when an HMO formally offered its services to an employer's workforce.

The dual choice requirement was eliminated in 1995 to allow HMOs and other types of health care programs to compete on a more equal footing in two ways. First, employers now can negotiate rates based on the expected experience of their employee population. That is, the premium amount varies by the likelihood that employees will use HMO services. Oftentimes, HMOs and employers review recent usage of HMO services to predict future usage. Employers whose employees tend to use HMO services more extensively pay higher premiums than employers whose employees tend to use HMO services less extensively.

Second, the HMO Act promotes more equal competition because employers may not financially discriminate against employees choosing an HMO option. In other words, companies must make the same percentage contribution toward an HMO's premium as they do to provide other health insurance plans. Suppose, for example, that an employer has paid 75 percent of the premiums for traditional indemnity plans. Previously, this employer paid only 40 percent of the premiums to provide HMO coverage. Contributing less is no longer acceptable. This employer now must pay at least 75 percent of the HMO premium to remain in compliance with the HMO Act.

The Employee Retirement Income Security Act of 1974 (ERISA)

In Chapter 4, we discussed that ERISA heavily governs the operation of pension plans and welfare plans. The definition of welfare plans encompasses medical, surgical, or hospital care or benefits, or benefits in the event of sickness.[7] Four parts of Title I (protection of employee rights) apply to welfare plans:

- Reporting and disclosure.
- Fiduciary responsibilities.
- Continuation coverage.
- Additional standards for group health plans, and group health plan portability, access, and renewability requirements.

The latter two provisions are amendments to ERISA since its passage in 1974. The *Consolidated Omnibus Budget Reconciliation Act of 1985* established continuation coverage and additional standards for group health plans. The *Health Insurance Portability and Accountability Act of 1996* created standards for group health plan portability, access, and renewability requirements. Chapter 4 includes a discussion of these ERISA provisions.

An additional amendment to ERISA, the **Women's Health and Cancer Rights Act of 1998,**[8] requires group health plans to provide medical and surgical benefits for mastectomies. Medical and surgical benefits must cover surgical reconstruction of either breast for a symmetrical appearance.

As we know, ERISA protects the rights of employees in retirement and welfare benefit plans. However, a recent Supreme Court decision imposes limits on patients' rights to sue HMOs for malpractice or negligence in particular circumstances. The Court reasoned that states with patient protection laws exceeded their authority by enacting laws that interfere with ERISA's exclusive remedy in private sector employee benefit matters.

The Americans with Disabilities Act of 1990

The *Americans with Disabilities Act of 1990 (ADA)*[9] prohibits illegal discrimination in employment practices on the basis of disability. The U.S. Equal Employment Opportunity Commission (EEOC), the government entity that oversees the administration and enforcement of the ADA, ruled that employers are required to provide the same health insurance coverage to employees regardless of disability status. Meanwhile,

> Congress recognized . . . that some types of benefit plans rest on an assessment of the risks and costs associated with various health conditions in accordance with accepted principles of risk assessment. As a result, the ADA permits employers to make disability-based distinctions in employee benefit plans where the distinctions are based on sound actuarial principles or are related to actual or reasonably anticipated experience.[10]

The EEOC requires employers to justify disability-based distinctions in health plans. Companies can justify disability-based distinctions with two justifications: by demonstrating that the health plan is bona fide, and that the plan is not a subterfuge to evade the purposes of the ADA. Exhibit 6.3 contains an elaboration of the bona fide plan and subterfuge justifications.

The EEOC applies different standards for disability-based treatment between physical health conditions and mental health conditions. Specifically:

> The Commission has also taken the position that it is not necessarily a disability-based distinction if an employer's health insurance plan provides unequal benefits for mental conditions compared to physical conditions. This is because, in the context of health insurance, the term "mental conditions" covers, for example, not only impairments like schizophrenia and major depression—which likely would be disabilities under the ADA—but also counseling for grief, self-esteem, or marital problems, which are not impairments and so are not ADA disabilities.
>
> As a result, a distinction in a health insurance plan's coverage of expenses for treatment of physical, as compared with mental, conditions (a) constitutes a broad distinction that covers a multitude of dissimilar conditions, and (b) limits both individuals with and those without disabilities. Such distinctions in health insurance plans thus will not generally violate the ADA.[11]

Tax Regulations

The Internal Revenue Code (Chapter 4) allows companies to take deductions for providing health insurance coverage. The rules differ according to whether health insurance plans are self-funded. We discuss this distinction in more detail later in this chapter. For now, **self-funding** or self-funded plans pay benefits directly from an employer's assets. Companies may take tax deductions for the amount of money they contribute toward health insurance premiums for non-self-funded plans subject to the following restrictions: Employers do not give preferential treatment to highly compensated employees regarding the level of benefits received, unless based solely on employees' compensation or years of service.

State Regulation

A variety of state laws regulate health insurance company practices. As we discuss later, employers may contract with health insurers—that is, companies offering fee-for-service plans or a managed care arrangement. Alternatively, employers may choose self-funding as a basis to provide health care benefits to employees. State regulation of health benefits does not influence self-funded plans.

EXHIBIT 6.3   Justifications for Disability-Based Distinctions

Source: U.S. Equal Employment Opportunity Commission. October 3, 2000. *EEOC Compliance Manual.* Washington, DC. Online at www.eeoc.gov/docs/benefits.html. Justifications for Disability-Based Distinctions. Accessed April 19, 2009.

Bona Fide Plans

Under the first prong of the defense, an employer must demonstrate that its plan is either a bona fide insured plan that is not inconsistent with state law, or a bona fide self-insured plan. To be bona fide, a plan must exist and pay benefits; in addition, the terms of the plan must have been accurately communicated to eligible employees. To determine whether a plan meets this standard, investigators typically need simply obtain a copy of the employer's plan documents and confirm that benefits have in fact been paid.

Subterfuge

The term *subterfuge* refers to disability-based disparate treatment in an employee benefit plan that is not justified by the risks or costs associated with the disability—that is, to disability-based distinctions that are not "based on sound actuarial principles or related to actual or reasonably anticipated experience." Whether a provision of a benefit plan is a subterfuge must be determined on a case-by-case basis. There are several ways that an employer can prove that a disability-based distinction in a benefit plan is not a subterfuge. Among possible justifications are the following:

- The employer may prove that it has not engaged in the disability-based disparate treatment alleged.
- The employer may prove that the disability-based disparate treatment is justified by legitimate actuarial data, or by actual or reasonably anticipated experience, and that conditions with comparable actuarial data and/or experience are treated the same way.
- Actuarial data will measure both the likelihood that the employer will incur insurance costs related to the disability and the magnitude of those costs as they arise. Thus, employers must show that the reduction in coverage for the disability or disabilities is required to account for an increased possibility that the benefit will be claimed or that the amounts required for coverage will be higher. Employers may not, however, rely on actuarial data that is outdated or that is based on myths, fears, stereotypes, or assumptions about the disability at issue.
- Even where employers can produce actuarial data that demonstrates that the risks and costs of treatment of a condition justify differential treatment of it, employers must also show that they have treated other conditions that pose the same risks and costs the same way. If there is evidence that an employer has treated other conditions differently from the disability at issue, the employer has discriminated by singling out a particular disability for disadvantageous treatment. Investigators should find cause.

Every state has laws regulating health insurers' practices. State laws mandating health benefits require that insurance companies include certain health benefits in insurance policies offered or make particular optional health benefits available upon request. Overall, these laws address four areas of responsibility:

- Extending coverage to particular services, treatments, or health conditions (e.g., substance abuse treatment).
- Reimbursing recognized health care providers for health care services.
- Individuals who must be covered by health insurance policies (e.g., adopted children).
- Length of time coverage must be available to employees terminating employment.

Laws vary from state to state. Every state includes a department that oversees insurance regulations. These data are available to the public upon request. Also, the **National Association of Insurance Commissioners (NAIC),**[12] a nonprofit organization, addresses issues concerning the supervision of insurance within each state (www.naic.org).

FEE-FOR-SERVICE PLANS

Three long-standing forms of health insurance programs include fee-for-service plans, managed care plans, and point-of-service plans. Larger employers commonly offer employees one or more types of health insurance programs. We discuss each of these in turn.

Fee-for-service plans provide protection against health care expenses in the form of a cash benefit paid to the insured or directly to the health care provider after the employee has received health care services. These plans pay benefits on a reimbursement basis. Three types of eligible health expenses are hospital expenses, surgical expenses, and physician charges. Under fee-for-service plans, policyholders (employees) may generally select any licensed physician, surgeon, or medical facility for treatment, and the insurer reimburses the policyholders after medical services are rendered.

Two types of fee-for-service plans are available. The first type, **indemnity plans,** is based on a contract between the employer and an insurance company. The contract specifies the expenses covered and the rate. The second type, **self-funded plans,** operates in the same fashion as indemnity plans.

The main difference between insurance plans offered by independent insurance companies and self-funded insurance plans centers on how benefits provided to policyholders are financed. When companies elect indemnity plans, they establish a contract with an independent insurance company. Insurance companies pay benefits from their financial reserves, which are based on the premiums companies and employees pay to receive insurance. Companies may instead choose to self-fund employee insurance. Such companies pay benefits directly from their own assets, either current cash flow or funds set aside in advance for potential future claims. The decision to self-fund is based on financial considerations. Self-funding makes sense when a company's financial burden of covering employee medical expenses is less than the cost to subscribe to an insurance company for coverage. By not paying premiums in advance to an independent carrier, a company retains these funds for current cash flow.

Types of Medical Expense Benefits

Fee-for-service plans provide three types of medical benefits under a specified policy: hospital expense benefits, surgical expense benefits, and physician expense benefits. Sometimes, companies select major medical plans to provide comprehensive medical coverage instead of limiting coverage to the three specific kinds just noted, or to supplement these specific benefits.

Hospitalization Benefits

Hospitalization benefits defray expenses associated with treatment in hospitals. Fee-for-service plans distinguish between inpatient benefits and outpatient benefits.

Inpatient benefits cover expenses associated with overnight hospital stays, while **outpatient benefits** cover expenses for treatments in hospitals not requiring overnight stays. Fee-for-service plans also describe the extent of coverage based on a schedule of benefits, usually expressed as the daily amount of the hospital stay.

Inpatient benefits fall into two categories: room and board, and other related benefits. Room and board benefits defray the costs of overnight hospital stays, including the room fee and related expenses. Typical related expenses are nursing care and meals. Fee-for-service plans usually specify coverage for a designated number of days per hospital stay. The second category, other related benefits, defrays a variety of costs associated with hospital stays. These costs include physician-ordered services (e.g., consultation with a physical therapist), pharmaceutical products, laboratory services (e.g., analysis of blood samples), X-rays, and the use of operating rooms.

Outpatient benefits apply to treatments and related expenses not associated with overnight hospital stays. Three types of outpatient benefits include emergency room treatment, preadmission testing, and surgery. Emergency room treatment applies to the sudden onset of serious illness or the occurrence of accidents. As the name implies, preadmission testing takes place within a few days prior to hospital admission for surgical procedures. The goal is to determine whether a patient possesses a medical condition that could place him or her at risk for complications or death from surgery (e.g., an abnormal heart rhythm). Outpatient benefits also cover surgical procedures not requiring overnight stays. Increasingly, medical advancements enable treatment of serious health conditions that avoids close monitoring by doctors and nurses for a period of days following surgery.

Surgical Benefits

Surgical expense benefits pay for medically necessary surgical procedures but usually not for elective surgeries such as cosmetic surgery. Generally, fee-for-service plans pay expenses according to a schedule of **usual, customary, and reasonable charges.** The usual, customary, and reasonable charge is defined as not more than the physician's usual charge, within the customary range of fees charged in the locality, and reasonable based on the medical circumstances. Whenever actual surgical expenses exceed the usual, customary, and reasonable level, the patient must pay the difference. Finally, such policies cover a physician's charges for services rendered in the hospital on an inpatient or outpatient basis, as well as office visits.

Physician Benefits

Physician benefits defray the costs of physician fees associated with hospital stays or office visits. In extenuating circumstances, fee-for-service plans provide coverage for home visits. Extenuating circumstances usually refer to instances when travel to a medical facility would jeopardize a patient's life.

Features of Fee-for-Service Plans

Fee-for-service plans contain a variety of stipulations designed to control costs and to limit a covered individual's financial liability. Common fee-for-service stipulations include deductibles, coinsurance, out-of-pocket maximums, preexisting condition clauses, preadmission certification, second surgical opinions, and maximum benefits limits.

Deductible

A common feature of fee-for-service plans is the **deductible.** Over a designated period, employees must pay for services (i.e., meet a deductible) before insurance benefits become active. The deductible amount is modest, usually a fixed amount ranging anywhere between $100 and $500, depending on the plan. Alternatively, deductible amounts may depend on annual earnings, either expressed as a fixed amount for a range of earnings or as a percentage of income. Fee-for-service plans usually apply separate deductible amounts for each type of coverage (i.e., hospitalization, surgical, and physician expenses). In other words, insured individuals must pay a specified amount for hospitalization, surgical, and physician expenses, respectively. Exhibit 6.4 illustrates deductibles based on annual salary. The deductible feature applies to a designated period, usually a one-year period that corresponds with the calendar year or the company's benefit plan year (see Chapter 11).

Coinsurance

Insurance plans feature coinsurance, which becomes relevant after the insured pays the annual deductible. **Coinsurance** refers to the percentage of covered expenses paid by the insured. Most indemnity plans stipulate 20 percent coinsurance. This means that the plan will pay 80 percent of covered expenses while the policyholder is responsible for the difference—in this case, 20 percent.

Coinsurance amounts vary according to the type of expense. Most commonly, insurance plans apply no coinsurance for diagnostic testing and 20 percent for other medical services. Many insurance plans provide benefits for mental health services. Coinsurance rates for these services tend to be the highest, usually 50 percent.

EXHIBIT 6.4
Plan Year Deductibles

The benefits described in this summary represent the major areas of coverage. The plan year is July 1 through June 30 of the following year.		
Plan year deductible	The plan year deductible is indexed to salary for employees. See the following table for current plan year information.	
Additional deductibles	Each emergency room visit $200 Non-PPO hospital admission $200 Transplant deductible $100	

Employee's Annual Salary (Based on each employee's annual salary as of April 1)	Member Plan Year Deductible	Family Plan Year Deductible Cap
$52,700 or less	$250	$300
$52,701–$66,000	$350	$400
$66,001 or more	$450	$550
Retiree/annuitant/survivor	$250	$300
Dependents	$200	NA

Out-of-Pocket Maximum

As discussed earlier, health care costs are on the rise. Despite generous coinsurance rates, the expense amounts for which individuals are responsible can be staggering. Oftentimes, these amounts are beyond the financial means of most individuals. Thus, most plans specify the maximum amount a policyholder must pay per calendar year or plan year, known as the **out-of-pocket maximum** provision.

The purpose of the out-of-pocket maximum provision is to protect individuals from catastrophic medical expenses or expenses associated with recurring episodes of the same illness. Out-of-pocket maximums are usually stated as a fixed dollar amount and apply to expenses beyond the deductible amount. Unmarried individuals often have an annual out-of-pocket maximum of $1,000, and family out-of-pocket maximums are as high as $3,500. For example, an insurance plan specifies a $200 deductible. An unmarried person is responsible for the first $200 of expenses plus additional expenses up to $800 per year—that is, the out-of-pocket maximum—for a total of $1,000.

Exhibit 6.5 shows an example of an out-of-pocket maximum as well as coinsurance rates and deductible amounts for specific services.

Preexisting Condition Clauses

A **preexisting condition** is a condition for which medical advice, diagnosis, care, or treatment was received or recommended during a designated period preceding the beginning of coverage and for which coverage is excluded. The designated period for preexisting conditions usually spans between three months and one year. Insurance companies impose preexisting conditions to limit their liabilities for serious medical conditions that predate an individual's coverage. As discussed in Chapter 4, the Health Insurance Portability and Accountability Act of 1996

EXHIBIT 6.5
Deductibles
and Out-of-
Pocket
Maximums

General Deductibles: $1,250 per Individual; $2,500 per Family per Plan Year
Professional and physician coinsurance (20%)
Physician network, where available (10%)
PPO inpatient coinsurance (10%)
Transplant deductible ($100)
Transplant inpatient and outpatient coinsurance (20%)
Standard hospital coinsurance (20%)
Standard hospital admission deductible ($200)
All emergency room deductibles ($200)
Emergency room coinsurance (20%)

The Following Do Not Apply toward Out-of-Pocket Maximums:

- Prescription drug benefits or copayments.
- Mental health substance abuse benefits, coinsurance, or copayments.
- Notification penalties.
- Ineligible charges (amounts over usual and customary and charges for noncovered services).

places restrictions on the use of preexisting condition clauses based on credits for prior coverage under a former employer's health plan.

Preadmission Certification

Many insurance plans require **preadmission certification** of medical necessity for hospitalization. Specifically, physicians must receive approval from a registered nurse or medical doctor employed by an insurance company before admitting patients to the hospital on a nonemergency basis—that is, when a patient's life is not in imminent danger. Insurance company doctors and nurses judge whether hospitalization or alternative care is necessary. In addition, they determine the length of stay appropriate for the medical condition. Precertification requirements reserve the right for insurance companies not to pay for unauthorized admissions or hospital stays that extend beyond the approved period.

Second Surgical Opinions

Second surgical opinions reduce unnecessary surgical procedures (and costs) by encouraging an individual to seek an independent opinion from another doctor. Following a recommendation of surgery from a physician, many individuals are inclined to seek an independent opinion to avoid the risks associated with surgery. With second surgical opinion provisions, insurance companies cover the cost of this consultation. Some insurance companies require second surgical opinions before authorizing surgery, while others offer second surgical opinion consultations as an option to each individual.

Maximum Benefit Limits

Insurance companies specify **maximum benefit limits,** expressed as a dollar amount over the course of one year or over an insured's lifetime. In many cases, insurance policies specify both annual maximums and lifetime maximums. They may also choose not to set any dollar limit to benefits. Setting annual maximums provides insurance companies with greater control over total cost expenditures. A maximum lifetime benefits provision protects employers from the costs of long-term or catastrophic claims and repeating incidences of illness.

Major Medical Insurance Plans: Supplemental and Comprehensive

Employers may choose to include major medical insurance plans as a supplement to the hospitalization, surgical, and physician expense benefits, or in place of those plans. Supplemental major medical plans act as a backup to basic insurance by covering expenses that exceed maximum benefit limits. Alternatively, these plans extend coverage to services not included in the regular fee-for-service plans. These services include prescription drugs, medical equipment and appliances, private duty nursing, and ambulance service. Supplemental plans possess the same features as regular fee-for-service plans, including deductibles, coinsurance, and out-of-pocket maximums.

 Comprehensive major medical plans replace traditional fee-for-service plans by extending coverage to a broader array of services (similar to supplemental plans). Unlike traditional plans, comprehensive plans usually apply a single deductible for all covered services. Many companies have moved toward comprehensive major medical plans because a single plan helps reduce possible duplication of coverage by different insurers offering specialized insurance.

MANAGED CARE PLANS

Managed care plans emphasize cost control by limiting an employee's choice of doctors and hospitals. Three common forms of managed care include *health maintenance organizations (HMOs)*, *preferred provider organizations (PPOs)*, and *point-of-service (POS)* plans.

Health Maintenance Organizations

HMOs are sometimes described as providing **prepaid medical services** because fixed periodic enrollment fees cover HMO members for all medically necessary services only if the services are delivered or approved by the HMO. HMOs generally provide inpatient and outpatient care as well as services from physicians, surgeons, and other health care professionals. Most medical services are either fully covered or, in the case of some HMOs, participants are required to make nominal **copayments.** Copayments represent nominal payments an individual makes as a condition of receiving services. HMOs express copayments as fixed amounts for different services such as office visits, prescription drugs, and emergency room treatment. Common copayment amounts vary between $15 and $25 for each doctor's office visit, and $10 to $50 per prescription drug. We address the reason for the wide variation in prescription drug copayment amounts later in this chapter.

Types of Health Maintenance Organizations

HMOs differ based on where service is rendered, how medical care is delivered, and how contractual relationships between medical providers and the HMOs are structured.

Prepaid Group Practice Model

Prepaid group practices provide medical care for a set amount. Group HMOs typically operate around the clock with phone coverage for emergencies or emergency room treatment. Prepaid group practices may take one of three specific forms.

Staff model HMOs own the medical facilities, and these organizations employ medical and support staff on these premises. These practices compensate physicians on a salary basis. Staff physicians treat only members of their HMO. Occasionally, staff model HMOs establish contracts with specialists to provide services not covered by staff members. Contract physicians are compensated according to a capped fee schedule. This means that the HMO establishes the amount it will reimburse physicians for each procedure (we discuss capped fee schedules in more detail later in this chapter). If contract physicians charge more than the fee set by the HMO, then they must bill the difference to the patients. For example, an HMO sets a cap of $40 for an annual physical examination. If the physician charges $55 for the annual examination, then the physician bills the HMO for $40 and the patient for the remaining $15.

Group model HMOs primarily use contracts with established practices of physicians that cover multiple specialties. Unlike staff model HMOs, group model HMOs do not directly employ physicians. These HMOs compensate physicians according to a preestablished schedule of fees for each service or on a capitation basis by setting monthly amounts per patient. We discuss capitation in more detail later in this chapter.

Network model HMOs and group model HMOs are similar except for one feature. **Network model HMOs** contract with two or more independent practices of physicians. These HMOs usually compensate physicians according to a capped fee schedule.

Individual Practice Associations

Individual practice associations (IPAs) are partnerships of independent physicians, health professionals, and group practices. IPAs charge lower fees to designated populations of employees (e.g., Company A's workforce) than fees charged to others. Physicians who participate in this type of HMO practice out of their own facilities and continue to see HMO enrollees and patients who are not HMO enrollees.

Features of Health Maintenance Organizations

HMO plans share several features in common with fee-for-service plans, including out-of-pocket maximums, preexisting condition clauses, preadmission certification, second surgical opinions, and maximum benefits limits. HMOs differ from fee-for-service plans in three important ways. First, HMOs offer prepaid services while fee-for-service plans operate on a reimbursement basis. Second, HMOs include the use of primary care physicians as a cost-control measure. Third, coinsurance rates are generally lower in HMO plans than in fee-for-service plans. Exhibit 6.6 illustrates the features of an HMO.

Primary Care Physicians

HMOs designate some of their physicians, usually general or family practitioners, as primary care physicians. HMOs assign each member to a primary care physician or require each member to choose one. **Primary care physicians** determine when patients need the care of specialists. HMOs use primary care physicians to control costs by significantly reducing the number of unnecessary visits to specialists. As primary care physicians, doctors perform several duties. Exhibit 6.7 lists the major duties of primary care physicians.

Copayments

The most common HMO copayments apply to physician office visits, hospital admissions, prescription drugs, and emergency room services. Office visits are nominal amounts, usually $10 to $15 per visit. Hospital admissions and emergency room services are higher, ranging between $50 and $150 for each occurrence. Mental health services and substance abuse treatment require copayments as well. Inpatient services require copayments that are similar in amount to those for hospital admissions for medical treatment. However, copayments for outpatient services (e.g., psychotherapy, consultation with a psychiatrist, or treatment at a substance abuse facility) are generally expressed as a fixed percentage of the fee for each visit or treatment. HMOs usually charge a copayment ranging between 15 and 25 percent.

EXHIBIT 6.6
HMO
Benefits

HMO Plan Design	
Plan year maximum benefit	Unlimited
Lifetime maximum benefit	Unlimited
Hospital Services	
Inpatient hospitalization	100% after $150 copayment per admission
Alcohol and substance abuse* *(maximum number of days determined by the plan)*	100% after $150 copayment per admission
Psychiatric admission* *(maximum number of days determined by the plan)*	100% after $150 copayment per admission
Outpatient surgery	100%
Diagnostic lab and X-ray	100%
Emergency room hospital services	100% after $200 or 50% copayment, whichever is less
Professional and Other Services	
Physician visits	100%, $15 copayment may apply *(including physical exams & immunizations)*
Well baby care	100%
Psychiatric care* *(maximum number of days determined by the plan)*	100% after $20 or 20% copayment per visit
Alcohol and substance abuse care* *(maximum number of days determined by the plan)*	100% after $20 or 20% copayment per visit
Prescription drugs	$12 copayment, generic incentive and formulary restrictions may apply. Formulary is subject to change during the plan year.
Durable medical equipment	80%

*HMOs determine the maximum number of inpatient days and outpatient visits for psychiatric and alcohol/substance abuse treatment. Each plan must provide for a minimum of 10 inpatient days and 20 outpatient visits per plan year. These are in addition to detoxification benefits, which include diagnosis and treatment of medical complications.
Some HMOs may provide benefit limitations on a calendar year.

EXHIBIT 6.7
Role of
Primary Care
Physicians

- Make an initial diagnosis and evaluation of the patient's condition.
- Identify applicable treatment protocols and practice guidelines.
- Decide whether treatment is warranted; if warranted, specify the treatment.
- Approve referrals to medical specialists.
- Evaluate patient's health following treatment.

PREFERRED PROVIDER ORGANIZATIONS

Under a **preferred provider organization (PPO),** a select group of health care providers agrees to furnish health care services to a given population at a higher level of reimbursement than under fee-for-service plans. Physicians qualify as preferred providers by meeting quality standards, agreeing to follow cost-containment procedures implemented by the PPO, and accepting the PPO's reimbursement structure. In return, the employer, insurance company, or third-party administrator helps guarantee provider physicians minimum patient loads by furnishing employees with financial incentives to use the preferred providers. Exhibit 6.8 summarizes the main features of a PPO plan.

The **exclusive provider organization (EPO)** is a variation of PPOs. EPOs operate similarly to PPOs, but these systems differ in a significant way: EPOs do not offer reimbursement for services provided outside the established network. That is, EPOs are more restrictive than PPO plans. Exceptions to this rule include medical emergencies or the need for a medical specialty not contained in the provider network.

Features of Preferred Provider Organizations

PPO plans include features that resemble fee-for-service plans or HMO plans. Features most similar to fee-for-service plans are out-of-pocket maximums and coinsurance, and those most similar to HMOs include the use of nominal copayments. Preexisting condition clauses, preadmission certification, second surgical opinions, and maximum benefits limits are similar to those in fee-for-service and HMO plans. PPOs contain deductible and coinsurance provisions that differ somewhat from other plans.

Deductibles

PPOs include deductible features. The structure and amount of deductibles under PPO plans most closely resemble practices commonly used in fee-for-service plans. Unlike fee-for-service plans, PPOs often apply different deductible amounts for services rendered within and outside the approved network. Higher deductibles are set for services rendered by non-network providers to discourage participants from using services outside the network.

Coinsurance

Coinsurance is a feature of PPO plans, and its structure is most similar to fee-for-service plans. PPOs calculate coinsurance as a percentage of fees for covered services. PPOs also use two sets of coinsurance payments: The first set applies to services rendered within the network of care providers; the second to services rendered outside the network. Coinsurance rates for network services are substantially lower than for non-network services. Coinsurance rates for network services range between 10 and 20 percent. Non-network coinsurance rates run between 60 and 80 percent.

EXHIBIT 6.8 PPO Plan Coverage

Inpatient Hospital Services	
Preferred provider organization hospital	90% after annual plan deductible. No admission deductible.
Non-preferred provider organization hospital	$300 per admission deductible. The plan pays 65% after annual plan deductible if member voluntarily chooses to use a non-PPO, or voluntarily travels in excess of 25 miles when a PPO hospital is available within the same travel distance. Coverage will be at 80% after annual plan deductible if a PPO hospital within 25 miles of a member's residence is not medically qualified to perform the required services, if no PPO exists within 25 miles of the member's residence, or if a member utilizes a non-PPO for emergency services.
Outpatient Services	
Lab/X-ray	100% of usual and customary (U&C) after annual plan deductible.
Approved durable medical equipment and prosthetics	80% of U&C after annual plan deductible. Contact the plan administrator for approval prior to obtaining items.
Facility charges	90% after annual plan deductible for PPOs and licensed, free-standing surgical facilities. (Note: Outpatient facility charges will be covered at 65% after annual plan deductible if member voluntarily chooses to use a non-PPO, or voluntarily travels in excess of 25 miles when a PPO hospital is available within the same travel distance. Coverage will be at 80% after annual plan deductible if a PPO hospital within 25 miles of a member's residence is not medically qualified to perform the required services, if no PPO exists within 25 miles of the member's residence, or if a member utilizes a non-PPO for emergency services.)
Professional and Other Services	
Physician and surgeon services	80% of U&C after annual plan deductible for inpatient, outpatient, and office visits.
Preventive services	Well baby care (through age 6), pap smears (includes office visit), mammograms, prostate screening, routine adult physicals and school health exams (grades 5 and 9) are covered per the applicable coverages listed in the Benefits Handbook. No deductibles apply.
Physician Network	
Physician and surgeon services (where available)	90% of billed charges. U&C charges do not apply.

POINT-OF-SERVICE PLANS

A **point-of-service (POS) plan** combines features of fee-for-service systems and health maintenance organizations. Employees pay a nominal copayment for each visit to a designated network of physicians. In this regard, POS plans are similar to HMOs. Unlike HMOs, however, employees possess the option to receive care

EXHIBIT 6.9 POS Benefits

POS Plan Design	In-Network Benefit	Out-of-Network Benefit
Plan year maximum benefit	Unlimited	Unlimited
Lifetime maximum benefit	Unlimited	Unlimited
Annual out-of-pocket maximum	Individual $300 Family $600	Individual $1,500 Family $3,500
Annual plan deductible	Individual $0 Family $0	Individual $300 Family $600
POS Services Covered		
Inpatient hospitalizations	100% after $250 copayment	80% of covered charges after $300 copayment
Psychiatric admission (*maximum of 30 visits per calendar year*)	100% after $200 copayment	No out-of-network benefit, covered in-network only
Inpatient alcohol and/or substance abuse treatment (*maximum of 30 visits per calendar year*)	100% after $150 copayment	No out-of-network benefit, covered in-network only
Emergency room services	100% after $100 copayment per occurrence	80% after lesser of $200 copayment or 50% of usual and customary (U&C)
Outpatient surgeries	100%	80% of U&C after plan deductible
Diagnostic lab and X-ray	100%	80% of U&C after plan deductible
Physician visits	100% after $10 copayment	80% of U&C after plan deductible
Preventive services (*including immunizations*)	100% after $10 copayment	No out-of-network benefit, covered in-network only
Well baby care	100% after $10 copayment	No out-of-network benefit, covered in-network only
Outpatient psychiatric (*maximum of 30 visits per calendar year*)	100% after $10 copayment	No out-of-network benefit, covered in-network only
Outpatient substance abuse (*maximum of 20 visits per calendar year*)	100% after $10 copayment	No out-of-network benefit, covered in-network only
Prescription drugs (*generic incentive and formulary restrictions may apply. Formulary is subject to change during the plan year.*)	Generic: $12 copayment Brand: $17 copayment Nonformulary: $35 copayment	Emergency drugs only. In-network copayment applies
Durable medical equipment	100%	80% of U&C after plan deductible

from health care providers outside the designated network of physicians, but they pay somewhat more for this choice. This choice feature is common to fee-for-service plans. Exhibit 6.9 describes the features of a POS plan.

SPECIALIZED INSURANCE BENEFITS

Oftentimes, employers use separate insurance plans to provide specific kinds of benefits. Benefits professionals refer to these plans as **carve-out plans.** Carve-out plans are set up to cover dental care, vision care, prescription drugs, mental health

EXHIBIT 6.10
Typical
Benefits of
Dental
Insurance
Plans

- Diagnostics
- Endodontics (e.g., nerve of a tooth)
- Maxillofacial surgery (e.g., surgery of upper jaw and face)
- Oral surgery (e.g., removal of impacted wisdom teeth)
- Orthodontics (e.g., straightening teeth)
- Palliative
- Periodontics (e.g., treats tissue and bone disease)
- Preventive (e.g., removal of plaque)
- Restorative

and substance abuse care, and maternity care. Usually, specialty HMOs or PPOs manage carve-out plans based on the expectation that single-specialty practices may control costs more effectively than multispecialty organizations.

Dental Insurance

Dental insurance benefits may cover routine preventative procedures (e.g., cleanings once every six months) and necessary procedures to promote the health of teeth and gums. Most dental programs do not include procedures for cosmetic improvements. Exhibit 6.10 lists services and procedures commonly covered by dental insurance plans. Employers have several options from which to choose for providing dental benefits, including fee-for-service plans and various managed care systems.

Dental insurance benefits are becoming more common. In 1970, only 15 percent of the American population received dental insurance as part of their benefits packages.[13] Nowadays, nearly half of the benefits packages of working Americans includes dental insurance. Dental insurance benefits encourage preventative treatment. Common wisdom indicates that prevention is far less costly than necessary procedures to remedy serious problems (e.g., gum disease). Dental care is essential to people at all ages, particularly young children and older adults because both groups are particularly prone to cavities.[14]

Types of Dental Plans

Three main types of dental plans are available: dental fee-for-service, dental service corporations, and dental maintenance organizations. Dental service corporations and dental maintenance organizations represent managed care options. Increasingly, companies are choosing to offer employees managed care options because of the anticipated cost savings.

Dental fee-for-service plans possess features similar to medical fee-for-service plans. These plans specify covered dental services based on a usual, customary, and reasonable charge. Dental fee-for-service plans also include deductibles (similar in amount to medical plans), coinsurance, and maximum benefits. Coinsurance rates often vary between 20 and 40 percent of usual, customary, and reasonable charges after the insured pays the deductible. Dental fee-for-service plans usually set limits to the dollar amount of benefits over a subscriber's lifetime. These limits generally vary by procedure.

Dental service corporations are nonprofit organizations that are owned and administered by state dental associations. Like HMOs, dental service corporations offer prepaid benefits and require copayments, usually equal to 20 to 30 percent of fees. The basis for reimbursement is either usual, customary, and reasonable fees or a negotiated schedule of fees for specific dental treatments and procedures. It is not uncommon for fees to exceed the amounts dental service corporations are willing to pay. In this case, patients pay the difference, but this excess amount does not count toward annual deductibles. Unlike HMOs, dental service corporations allow participants to receive benefits from a list of approved dentists.

Dental maintenance organizations, or **dental HMOs,** are most similar to HMOs for medical care. Dental HMOs provide prepaid dental services. Participants are required to seek treatment from an approved provider, and they pay a nominal copayment. Sometimes, managed care providers offer members a choice between a dentist within the network of approved providers and a dentist outside the network. In this case, the level of prepaid benefits is significantly less for non-network dentists, creating an incentive for members to seek treatment from an approved provider.

Vision Insurance

Vision insurance plans usually cover eye examinations, lenses, frames, and the fitting of glasses. Similar to dental protection, vision insurance benefits may be delivered through indemnity plans or managed care arrangements. All forms of delivery limit the frequency and types of services. Typically, benefits are limited to eye examinations, basic prescription lenses, and frames once every one to two years. Vision plan benefits are relatively limited because they exclude coverage of specialty prescription eyeglass lenses (e.g., sunglasses, lightweight plastic lenses, and photosensitive lenses), and these plans restrict the coverage amount for frames. These plans generally do not cover any of the costs of contact lenses unless a vision care provider deems their usage a medical necessity.

Prescription Drug Benefits

Prescription drug plans cover the costs of drugs. These plans apply exclusively to drugs that state or federal laws require to be dispensed by licensed pharmacists. Prescription drugs dispensed to individuals during hospitalization or treatment in long-term care facilities are not covered by prescription drug plans. Insurers specify which prescription drugs are covered, how much they will pay, and the basis for paying for drugs.

Currently, three kinds of prescription drug programs are available to companies that choose to provide these benefits to employees. The first, **medical reimbursement plans,** reimburse employees for some or all of the cost of prescription drugs. These programs are usually associated with self-funded or independent indemnity plans. Similar to indemnity plans, medical reimbursement plans pay benefits after an employee has met an annual deductible for the plan. After meeting the deductible, these plans offer coinsurance, usually 80 percent of the prescription drug cost, and the participant pays the difference. Maximum annual and lifetime benefits amounts vary based on the provisions set forth in the plan.

The second kind of plan, often referred to as a **prescription card program,** operates similarly to managed care programs because it offers prepaid benefits with nominal copayments. The name arose from the common practice of pharmacies requiring the presentation of an identification card. Prescription card programs limit benefits to prescriptions filled at participating pharmacies, similar to managed care arrangements for medical treatment. Copayment amounts vary from $5 to $50 per prescription. The amount depends upon whether the prescriptions meet criteria set by the plan, including the use of generic alternatives and the categorization of prescription drugs on formularies. **Formularies** are lists of drugs proven to be clinically appropriate and cost effective. Participants pay lower copayments for prescription drugs that meet the established criteria. Prescription card programs may be associated with an independent insurer or as part of an established HMO.

The third type of plan, a **mail-order prescription drug program,** dispenses expensive medications used to treat chronic health conditions such as HIV infection or neurological disorders like Parkinson's disease. Health insurers specify whether participants must receive prescription drugs through mail-order programs or locally approved pharmacies. Cost is the driving factor for this decision. Mail-order programs offer a cost advantage because they purchase medications at discounted prices in large volumes. A single mail-order program supplies medication to participants of many health insurance plans nationwide. Local pharmacies do not enjoy this advantage because their patronage is much smaller and is limited to people who live in close proximity.

The costs of these prescription drug plans vary. Reimbursement plans tend to be most expensive because pharmacies charge full retail price. Also, reimbursement plans entail substantial administrative costs because an administrator evaluates each claim, applies deductibles, and prepares an explanation of benefits. The prescription card and mail-order programs are usually less expensive because insurance companies have negotiated lower prices in exchange for providing a significant volume of individuals who will need prescription medications. In addition, costs are lower because participants make copayments when they order prescriptions and then the pharmacy bills the insurance company on a set interval for all the prescriptions filled during this period (e.g., every week or two weeks).

Increasingly, many prescription drug plans contain two cost-control features: formularies and multiple tiers. Many plans establish formularies to manage costs. The basis for setting formularies varies from plan to plan. For example, some plans prescribe drugs that are therapeutically equivalent to more expensive drugs and use lower levels of coinsurance or copayments to encourage usage. Other plans are more restrictive by limiting coverage only to a specified set of prescription drugs.

Multiple tiers specify copayment amounts an individual will pay for a specific prescription. Usually, multitier prescription drug programs specify three tiers, from least copayment amount to highest copayment amount: generic ($10 to $20 per prescription), formulary brand name medication ($25 to $40 per prescription), and nonformulary brand name medication ($40 to full price per prescription). The idea behind multiple-tier prescription plans is that employees will choose less expensive and equally effective alternatives to nonformulary medications. For example, bupropion hydrochloride (used to relieve symptoms of clinical depression or to aid in smoking cessation) may be obtained as a generic of the brand name *Wellbutrin,* manufactured by GlaxoSmithKline.

Presumably, multitier prescription plans should save employers considerable costs while also providing effective treatments based on less expensive alternative prescription medication. However, a recent study suggests that attaining the intended goals of multitier prescription plans may be more challenging.

A study by Medco Health Solutions Inc. and Harvard Medical School, published in the December 2003 *New England Journal of Medicine,* examined how a move to a three-tier plan affects drug spending and utilization. The article also provided information for health plan providers who are considering increasing member cost sharing as a strategy for reducing their drug spending.

The study found that for two employers who implemented multitier plan designs, this change led a significant proportion of patients who were on brand-name drugs (with the highest copayment) to choose more cost-effective alternatives. Depending on the particular drug class, at least 18 percent, and as many as 49 percent of plan members switched to lower-cost medication. However, the survey also found that an aggressive approach to plan changes can have the unintended result of causing some patients to stop taking their medications altogether.

Mental Health and Substance Abuse

Approximately 25 percent of Americans experience some form of mental illness such as clinical depression at least once during their lifetimes. Psychiatrists define mental disorder as "a behavioral or psychological syndrome or pattern . . . associated with present distress (a painful symptom) or disability (impairment in one or more important areas of functioning) or with a significantly increased risk of suffering death, pain, disability, or an important loss of freedom."[15] Nearly 20 percent develop a substance abuse problem. As a result, insurance plans provide mental health and substance abuse benefits designed to cover treatment of mental illness and chemical dependence on alcohol and legal and illegal drugs. Delivery methods include fee-for-service plans and managed care options. As we discuss in Chapter 10, employee assistance programs (EAPs) represent a portal to taking advantage of employer-sponsored mental health and substance abuse treatment options. EAPs help employees cope with personal problems that may impair their personal lives or job performance. Examples of these problems are alcohol or drug abuse, domestic violence, the emotional impact of AIDS and other diseases, clinical depression, and eating disorders. EAPs also assist employers in helping troubled employees identify and solve problems that may be interfering with their job or personal life.

Features of Mental Health and Substance Abuse Plans

Mental health and substance abuse plans cover the costs of a variety of treatments, including prescription psychiatric drugs (e.g., antidepressant medication), psychological testing, inpatient hospital care, and outpatient care (individual or group therapy).

Mental health benefits amounts vary by the type of disorder. Psychiatrists and psychologists rely on the *Diagnostic and Statistical Manual of Mental Disorders (DSM-IV)* to diagnose mental disorders based on symptoms, and both fee-for-service and managed care plans rely on the *DSM-IV* to authorize payment of benefits. As discussed earlier, HMOs usually charge a copayment ranging between 15 and 25 percent.

From the employee's perspective, coinsurance and maximum benefits amounts are generally less generous than general health plans in three ways. First, coinsurance amounts for mental health and substance abuse benefits, expressed as a percentage of treatment cost for both indemnity and managed care plans, range between 40 and 50 percent. Second, mental health and substance abuse plans limit the annual number of outpatient visits or days of inpatient care. Third, annual and lifetime maximum benefits were set significantly lower—for example, $1,500 and $10,000, respectively. However, the **Mental Health Parity Act,** described in the next section, mandated increases in annual lifetime limits for mental health plans.[16]

Regulation of Mental Health and Substance Abuse Plans

Various federal and state laws apply to the operation of mental health and substance abuse plans. At the federal level, the Mental Health Parity Act established parity requirements for mental health plans offered in conjunction with a group health plan that contains medical and surgical benefits. **Parity requirements** prohibit setting lower annual or lifetime maximums for mental health and substance abuse benefits than for medical and surgical benefits. This act contains a sunset clause that discontinued parity requirements for mental health benefits rendered on or after September 30, 2001. It has been temporarily extended seven different times. President George Bush enacted the most recent extension to December 21, 2009.[17] Actions to permanently extend this sunset clause have not been successful due in large part to Congress's focus on the weakened economy and the outcry of Republicans who maintain that the costs of parity would be burdensome to employers.

State laws also play a role in mental health and substance abuse plans. The specific provisions vary from state to state, but, in general, state laws specify minimum standards for coverage, including the minimum number of days of inpatient treatment and the minimum number of outpatient counseling sessions.

Maternity Care

Maternity care benefits cover all or a portion of the costs during pregnancy and for a short period after giving birth. Most maternity care benefits apply to physicians' fees, laboratory work (e.g., blood work, amniocentesis), and hospitalization during and following the time of delivery. Federal and state laws influence maternity care benefits. Federal law does not require that employers provide maternity care benefits. However, some federal laws do influence how companies design and implement maternity care benefits. As we discuss shortly, some state laws mandate the inclusion of maternity care benefits in employee benefits plans.

At the federal level, the Pregnancy Discrimination Act of 1978 (Chapter 4) prohibits employers from treating pregnancy less favorably than other medical conditions covered under employee benefits plans. In addition, employers must treat pregnancy and childbirth the same way they treat other causes of disability. The **Family and Medical Leave Act of 1993** entitles most male and female employees of private sector companies (with 50 or more employees) and government organizations up to 12 unpaid workweeks of leave during any 12-month period because of the birth of their child (and other family-related reasons that we discuss in Chapter 10). The **Newborns' and Mothers' Health Protection Act of 1996**[18] sets minimum standards for the length of hospital stays for mothers and newborn children; it prohibits employers and all insurers (independent and self-funded indemnity plans as well as managed care plans) from using financial incentives to shorten hospital stays. At the state level, some states require that employers offer maternity care benefits to employees if other health care benefits are provided. These mandates exclude employers offering health benefits through self-funded plans.

CONSUMER-DRIVEN HEALTH CARE

Managed care plans became popular alternatives to fee-for-service plans mainly to help employers and insurance companies more effectively manage the costs of health care. As discussed, managed care plans by design imposed substantial restrictions on an employee's ability to make choices about whom they could receive medical treatment from, the gatekeeper role of primary care physicians, and the level of benefits they could receive based on designated in- and non-network providers.

Despite the cost control objectives of managed care, health care costs have continued to rise dramatically over the years while also restricting employee choice. **Consumer-driven health care** refers to the objective of helping companies maintain control over costs while also enabling employees to make greater choices about health care. This approach may enable employers to lower the cost of insurance premiums by selecting plans with higher employee deductibles. The most popular consumer-driven approaches are flexible spending accounts and health reimbursement accounts. These accounts provide employees with resources to pay for medical and related expenses not covered by higher deductible insurance plans at substantially lower costs to employers.

Flexible spending accounts permit employees to pay for specified health care costs that are not covered by an employer's insurance plan. Prior to each plan year, employees elect the amount of pay they wish to allocate to this kind of plan. Employers then use these moneys to reimburse employees for expenses incurred during the plan year that qualify for repayment.

Qualifying expenses include an individual's out-of-pocket costs for medical treatments, products, or services related to a mental or physical defect or disease, along with certain associated costs, such as health insurance deductibles or transportation to get medical care. However, health, life, or long-term care insurance premiums paid for by an employer or through an employee's pretax salary reductions generally do not qualify for reimbursement under a health FSA. Other exclusions include medical expenses reimbursed through health insurance plans and the costs of purely cosmetic procedures that enhance appearance but are not related to treating a disease or defect. Over-the-counter products are qualified expenses if they are used to diagnose, treat, alleviate, or prevent a disease or ailment, such as blood sugar monitoring kits for diabetic patients or crutches and bandages for someone with a serious leg injury.

A significant advantage to employees is the ability to make contributions to their FSAs on a pretax basis; however, a noteworthy drawback is the "use it or lose it" provision of FSAs. FSAs require employees to estimate the amount of money they think they will need for eligible medical expenses. Of course, it is difficult to predict many medical needs and to estimate the costs of anticipated medical needs. Employees lose contributions to their FSAs when they overestimate the cost of medical needs because employers neither allow employees to carry balances nor do employers reimburse employees for balances remaining at the end of the year.

Employers bear some risk from offering FSAs to employees. The maximum amount of expenses an employee can be reimbursed for under a dependent care FSA is $5,000 annually ($2,500 for a married taxpayer filing separately). Although there is no statutory limit on the amount of reimbursement employees can receive under a medical FSA, employers usually set a maximum limit—say, $3,000—to protect themselves against major losses under the **risk-of-loss rules** or **uniform coverage requirement.** Under this requirement, employers are obligated to make the full amount of benefits and coverage elected under an FSA plan available to employees from the first day the plan becomes effective, regardless of how much money an employee has actually contributed.

Let's assume an employee plans to contribute $1,500 per year to her employer's FSA plan, based on monthly contributions of $125. In this case, $125 per month equals the $1,500 total annual contribution divided by 12 months per year. Continuing with this example, we assume that this employee has a minor illness after making only three monthly contributions to the account ($375), and the medical and prescription costs to treat this minor illness are $1,275. The employer must allow this employee to withdraw $1,275 even though she has contributed only $375 thus far. This situation places demands on employer cash resources. Also, if this employee were to leave the company after this three-month period, the employer would have paid $900 out of its own funds toward this employee's treatment (that is, $1,275 for the treatment cost, less $375, this employee's contribution to the FSA).

Alternatively, employers may establish **health reimbursement accounts (HRAs).** The purpose of HRAs and FSAs are similar with two important differences. First, only employers may make the contributions to each employee's HRA, whereas employees fund FSAs with pretax contributions deducted from their pay. Second, HRAs permit employees to carry over unused account balances from year to year, whereas employees forfeit unused FSA account balances present at the end of the year.

The idea of consumer-driven health care received substantially greater attention than ever before because of the Bush Administration (President George W. Bush) and the Republican-led Congress, who favored greater employee involvement in their medical care and reducing the cost burden for companies to help maintain competitiveness in the global market. The **Medicare Prescription Drug, Improvement and Modernization Act of 2003**[19] added section 223 to the IRC, effective January 1, 2004, to permit eligible individuals to establish **health savings accounts (HSAs)** to help employees pay for medical expenses. In 2009, an employer, an employee, or both, may contribute as much as $3,000 annually for unmarried employees without dependent children or as much as $5,950 for married or unmarried employees with dependent children. Employers may require employees to contribute toward these limits. Employee contributions would be withheld from an employee's pay on a pre-tax basis. Employers offer HSAs along with a high-deductible insurance policy, established for employees. **High-deductible health insurance plans** require substantial deductibles and low out-of-pocket maximums. For individual coverage, the minimum annual deductible was $1,150 with maximum out-of-pocket limits at or below $5,800 in 2009. For family coverage, the deductible was $2,300 with maximum out-of-pocket limits at or below $11,600.

HSAs offer four main advantages to employees relative to FSAs and HRAs. First, HSAs are portable, which means that the employee owns the account balance after the employment relationship ends. Second, HSAs are subject to inflation-adjusted funding limits. In 2009, total contributions from both an employer or employee to an individual's HSA cannot exceed the high-deductible health plan's annual deductible or $3,000 for individual coverage ($5,950 in the case of family coverage), whichever is less. An additional $1,000 may be contributed for employees who are at least 55 years old, but not yet eligible for Medicare. Third, employees may receive medical services from doctors, hospitals, and other health care providers of their choice and they may choose the type of medical services they purchase, including such items as long-term care, eye care, and prescription drugs. FSAs and HRAs substantially limit employee choice. Fourth, HSA assets must be held in trust and cannot be subject to forfeiture. That is, any unspent balances in the HSA can be rolled over annually and accumulate tax-free until the participant's death. FSAs and HRAs have no legal vesting requirement, which means employees do not possess the right to claim unused balances when they terminate employment.

A Watson Wyatt survey of large U.S. employers revealed that about half of these companies offer employees a consumer-driven health plan, and the percentage is likely to increase by approximately 10 percent in 2010.[20] Employers are concerned that employees will not seek preventative or necessary care because of the cost. There could be underlying health problems in the early stages that do not affect how one feels. However, if preventative care is avoided, health issues that could have been easily treated could become serious, leading to short- or long-term disability. Ultimately, the cost of disability insurance will increase, adding to the heavy cost burden of employee benefits plans.

RETIREE HEALTH CARE BENEFITS

Since the early 1980s, companies have encountered a strong financial disincentive to provide health insurance benefits to retired employees for three reasons. First, the substantial increases in health care costs and costs of medical insurance have created a tremendous financial strain on companies that choose to offer them. As noted earlier in this chapter, the cost of medical services has increased more than 300 percent since the early 1980s. The financial pressure on companies intensifies with coverage of retirees because older individuals are more likely to need expensive prescription medication and are more likely to require hospitalization because of serious health problems than younger individuals. Of course, the lasting effects of a sharp economic slowdown since the year 2000, particularly since late 2007, intensified global competition, and higher energy costs have made it more difficult for companies to support full workforces. As a result, many employees have experienced small pay increases relative to increases in the cost of living, reductions in benefits offerings, higher contributions for their benefits such as health insurance coverage, and layoffs.

Second, changes in company accounting practices have made offering health care benefits to retirees less appealing. The **Financial Accounting Standards Board (FASB),** a nonprofit company responsible for improving standards of financial accounting and reporting in companies, implemented FASB 106 in 1990 and FASB 158 in 2005. **FASB 106** is a rule that changed the method of how companies recognize the costs of nonpension retirement benefits, including health insurance, on financial balance sheets. This rule effectively reduces the amount of a company's net profit amount listed on the balance sheet. The Board's view is that benefits such as health care coverage establish an exchange between the employer and the employee. In exchange for the current services provided by the employee, the employer promises to provide, in addition to current wages and other benefits, health and welfare benefits after the employee retires. In other words, postretirement benefits are part of an employee's compensation for services rendered. Since payment is deferred, the benefits are a type of deferred compensation. The employer's obligation for that compensation is incurred as employees render the services necessary to earn their postretirement benefits.

In 2003, FASB instituted **FASB 132,** which requires that companies disclose substantial information about the economic value and costs of retiree health care programs. The Board maintains that health care benefits are probably as significant to current employees and retirees as are defined benefit plans. Other FASB rules require clear disclosure of economic resources and obligations related to defined benefit plans. Thus, FASB 132 requires similar disclosure. As a result, companies without sufficient current assets to maintain retiree health care programs are less likely to continue offering these benefits. At the time this book went to print, FASB was entertaining a variety of other accounting rules related to retiree health care and other postretirement employee benefits (OPEB).

For example, FASB established 132(R)a titled *Employers' Disclosures about Postretirement Benefit Plan Assets.* The Board decided to amend FASB Statement No. 132 (revised 2003), *Employers' Disclosures about Pensions and Other Postretirement Benefits,* to include additional reporting requirements:

1. The entity's objective in disclosing information about plan assets, which is to provide users of financial statements with an understanding of:

    a. The major categories of assets held in an employer's plan(s).

    b. How management makes investment allocation decisions, including the factors that are pertinent to an investor's understanding of investment policies or strategies.

    c. Significant concentrations of risk within plan assets.

2. A list of examples of detailed categories of plan assets that would include a category for investment funds (for example, mutual funds, hedge funds, and commingled funds).

3. A requirement that an entity disclose the significant investment strategies for investment funds as major categories of plan assets.[21]

Further updates may be found on the FASB Web site (www.fasb.org), based on a search for "OPEB."

Third, companies, particularly those with defined benefit retirement plans, are less likely to offer retiree health care benefits. As we discussed in Chapter 5, the federal government, through the Employee Retirement Income Security Act, the recent Pension Protection Act, and the Pension Benefit Guaranty Corporation, requires that employers adequately fund their defined benefits pension plan. Currently, there are no such regulations to shore up other postretirement benefits, like health care. Labor unions and employees are most dissatisfied with these trends because they stand to lose the most. The U.S. auto industry recently has been the stage for cuts in postretirement employee benefits. The dire financial trouble of U.S. automakers is well known, and many factors have been cited as the sources of their problems, including the relatively higher prices of vehicles relative to competing foreign automakers that have substantial market share in the United States. Management has resorted to desperate measures to control costs such as multiple large reductions in the workforce in hopes of instituting competitive pricing. Other measures are likely to include management resistance to maintain the generous level of retiree health care during future labor contract negotiations with the United Auto Workers.

For example, Ford Motor Company negotiated a tentative agreement with the United Auto Workers (UAW) to pay $6.6 billion in obligations to the union's health care trust fund in Ford Motor stock. The deal was struck with Ford ahead of similar current negotiations with General Motors and Chrysler. While it is common in some European countries for union officials to have board seats, it is practically unheard of in the United States. Daimler-Benz, Volkswagen, and BMW have a representative of organized labor on their supervisory boards. Until the recent dire financial crisis experienced by U.S. automakers, the idea that the UAW would possess power on their corporate boards of directors was unthinkable.

In 2007, Ford, GM, and Chrysler entered into agreements with the UAW to reduce billions of dollars in future health care obligations from their balance sheets. The changes are estimated to have reduced the companies' liabilities for retiree health care by 50 percent. In return, the automakers promised to make huge lump sum payments into the trusts to cover much of the retirees' plans. Ford, for instance, paid $2.7 billion into the union's Voluntary Employment Benefits Association (VEBA) in 2009 but still owes a total of $13.2 billion to the VEBA over the next few years. GM is expected to make a payment of about $7 billion in 2010 and owes the UAW a total of about $22 billion.

In sum, nowadays, there is the sobering realization that the soaring costs of retiree health care benefits may be pushing some companies to the financial limit. Current forces may lead companies to stand down from such offerings in the future.

Summary

This chapter reviewed the fundamental concepts of company-sponsored health insurance plans, starting with basic definitions and a perusal of the level of health insurance coverage and costs in the United States. We also reviewed the government regulation of health plans, distinguishing between federal and state laws. Further, we studied a variety of health plans such as fee-for-service plans and managed care plans and discussed how these plans differ in cost control features. Finally, we discussed FASB 106 and 132, which have created a disincentive to companies that offer health care benefits to retirees, and the mounting pressures companies face to meet these obligations.

Key Terms

health insurance, *136*
insurance policy, *136*
premium, *136*
multiple-payer system, *136*
single-payer system, *136*
universal health care systems, *136*
Health Maintenance Organization Act of 1973 (HMO Act), *138*
single coverage, *139*
family coverage, *139*
individual coverage, *143*
underwriting, *143*
mortality tables, *143*
morbidity tables, *143*
group coverage, *143*
group policyholders, *143*
experience ratings, *143*
Women's Health and Cancer Rights Act of 1998, *145*
self-funding, *146*
National Association of Insurance Commissioners (NAIC), *148*
fee-for-service plans, *148*
indemnity plans, *148*
self-funded plans, *148*
hospitalization benefits, *148*
inpatient benefits, *149*
outpatient benefits, *149*
usual, customary, and reasonable charges, *149*
deductible, *150*
coinsurance, *150*
out-of-pocket maximum, *151*

preexisting condition, *151*
preadmission certification, *152*
second surgical opinions, *152*
maximum benefit limits, *152*
comprehensive major medical plans, *152*
managed care plans, *153*
prepaid medical services, *153*
copayments, *153*
prepaid group practices, *153*
staff model HMOs, *153*
group model HMOs, *154*
network model HMOs, *154*
individual practice associations (IPAs), *154*
primary care physicians, *154*
preferred provider organization (PPO), *156*
exclusive provider organization (EPO), *156*
point-of-service (POS) plan, *157*
carve-out plans, *158*
dental insurance, *159*
dental fee-for-service plans, *159*
dental service corporations, *160*
dental maintenance organizations, *160*
dental HMOs, *160*
vision insurance, *160*
prescription drug plans, *160*

medical reimbursement plans, *160*
prescription card program, *161*
formularies, *161*
mail-order prescription drug program, *161*
multiple tiers, *161*
Mental Health Parity Act, *163*
parity requirements, *163*
Family and Medical Leave Act of 1993, *164*
Newborns' and Mothers' Health Protection Act of 1996, *164*
consumer-driven health care, *164*
flexible spending accounts, *164*
risk-of-loss rules (alternatively, uniform coverage requirement), *165*
health reimbursement accounts (HRAs), *165*
Medicare Prescription Drug, Improvement, and Modernization Act of 2003, *165*
health savings accounts (HSAs), *165*
high-deductible health insurance plans, *166*
Financial Accounting Standards Board (FASB), *167*
FASB 106, *167*
FASB 132, *167*

Discussion Questions

1. Discuss the basic concept of insurance. How does this concept apply to health care?
2. Compare the main objectives of the federal and state regulation of employer-sponsored health insurance practices.
3. What is the most influential event in the history of employer-sponsored health care benefits? Explain why.
4. Describe the principles of fee-for-service plans and managed care plans. What are the similarities and differences?
5. Discuss some of the choices an employer may make to help control health care costs.

Endnotes

1. U.S. Bureau of Labor Statistics. 1919. "Welfare work for employees in industrial establishments in the United States," *Bulletin #250*, pp. 119–23.
2. U.S. Bureau of Labor Statistics. August 2008. *National Compensation Survey: Employee Benefits in the United States, March 2008* (BLS 08-1122). Online at www.bls.gov. Accessed April 19, 2009.
3. U.S. Bureau of Labor Statistics. 2006. *Employee Benefits in Private Industry, 2006* (06-1482). Online at www.bls.gov. Accessed April 19, 2009.
4. Ibid.
5. U.S. Bureau of Labor Statistics. August 2008. *National Compensation Survey: Employee Benefits in the United States, March 2008* (BLS 08-1122). Online at www.bls.gov. Accessed April 19, 2009.
6. 42 U.S.C. 300e to 330e-17.
7. ERISA §3(1), 29 U.S.C. §1002(1).
8. Added to the Omnibus Consolidated Emergency Supplemental Act on October 21, 1998, Public Law No. 105-277.
9. 42 U.S.C. §12101.
10. U.S. Equal Employment Opportunity Commission. October 3, 2000. *EEOC Compliance Manual.* Washington, DC: EEOC. Online at www.eeoc.gov/docs/benefits.html#IV. Justifications for Disability-Based Distinctions. Accessed July 26, 2004.
11. Ibid.
12. National Association of Insurance Commissioners. Online at www.naics.org. Accessed March 1, 2007.
13. Delta Dental Association. 1999–2000. *Survey: Facts & Figures on the Dental Benefits Market, 1999/2000 Update.* Oak Brook, IL: Delta Dental Plans Association.
14. U.S. Centers for Disease Control and Prevention. 2007. *Oral Health: Preventing Cavities, Gum Disease, and Tooth Loss.* Online at www.cdc.gov/nccdphp/publications/aag/oh.htm. Accessed April 19, 2009.
15. American Psychiatric Association. 1994. *Diagnostic and Statistical Manual of Mental Disorders (DSM-IV).* Washington, DC: American Psychiatric Association.
16. Mental Health Parity Act, Public Law No. 104-204, August 2, 1996.
17. Mental Health Parity Act, Public Law No. 110-460, December 23, 2008.
18. 42 U.S.C. §300gg-(4)-(51).
19. Public Law. No. 108-173.
20. Watson Wyatt. (2009). www.watsonwyatt.com. Accessed April 19, 2009.
21. Financial Accounting Standards Board (2008). *Employers' Disclosures about Postretirement Benefit Plan Assets.* Online at www.fasb.org. Accessed April 19, 2009.

Employer-Sponsored Disability Insurance and Life Insurance

Learning Objectives

In this chapter, you will gather information about:

1. Disability and life insurance concepts.
2. Origins of disability and life insurance programs.
3. Differences between short- and long-term disabilities.
4. A variety of different types of life insurance—term, universal life, and accidental death and dismemberment.

You breathe a sigh of relief when you learn that your new employer provides disability insurance. Sure, most people do not expect to become disabled, particularly younger persons. But you recall the difficulties some of your childhood friends' families experienced when one or both parents became disabled and could not work for several months or at all. Disabilities of any kind can be devastating to workers and their dependents. The emotional and physical trauma of disability can be overwhelming. In most cases, disability comes with financial devastation: Temporary and permanent disabilities prevent workers from engaging in any gainful employment. Virtually none of these disabled workers or their families possess the financial resources to support themselves for more than a very brief period. Following the death of a worker, dependent family members also find themselves in a financially uncertain situation. Without disability or life insurance programs, families once holding their own—making monthly mortgage payments, car payments, and supporting their children—now find themselves without the means necessary to meet their obligations.

In this chapter, we will explore two types of insurance benefits that provide financial support for disabled or deceased workers and their family members: disability insurance and life insurance. Disability insurance is offered at the discretion of employers to protect for work- and nonwork-related injuries or illnesses. As we will discuss in Chapter 8, two public insurance programs also provide disability protection—the OASDI program established by the Social Security Act and state compulsory disability laws (workers' compensation). The second type we discuss in this chapter, life insurance, focuses almost exclusively on protecting dependents of deceased workers. Employers extend life insurance to employees on a discretionary basis. The two public programs just mentioned also include life insurance protection.

DISABILITY INSURANCE

Disability insurance replaces income for employees who become unable to work on a regular basis because of an illness or injury. Employer-sponsored disability insurance is more encompassing than workers' compensation because its benefits generally apply to work- and nonwork-related illness or injury, whereas workers' compensation insurance applies only to work-related illness or injury. Unfortunately, employees need this kind of protection. At all working ages, the probability of being disabled for at least 90 consecutive days is much greater than the chance of dying while performing one's job; one of every three employees will have a disability that lasts at least 90 days.[1]

Much as they do for company-sponsored health insurance plans, employers usually enter into a contractual relationship with one or more insurance companies to provide disability benefits for their employees and, if specified, their dependents. The contractual relationship, or **insurance policy,** specifies the amount of money it will pay for particular disabilities. Employers pay insurance companies a negotiated amount, or **premium,** to establish and maintain insurance policies. The term *insured* refers to an employee covered by the insurance policy.

Employer-sponsored or group disability insurance typically takes two forms. The first, **short-term disability insurance,** provides benefits for limited periods of time, usually less than six months. The second, **long-term disability insurance,** provides benefits for extended periods of time anywhere between six months and life. Disability criteria differ between short- and long-term plans. Short-term plans usually consider disability as an inability to perform any and every duty of one's (the disabled person's) occupation. Long-term plans use a more stringent definition, typically specifying an inability to engage in any occupation for which the individual is qualified by reason of training, education, or experience. We elaborate on these definitions in our discussion of short-term and long-term disability plans.

Both short- and long-term disability plans may duplicate public disability benefits mandated by the Social Security Act and state workers' compensation laws (both topics are discussed in Chapter 8). These employer-sponsored plans generally supplement legally required benefits. Employer-sponsored plans do not replace disability benefits mandated by law.

Sick leave policies (Chapter 9) are separate from disability leave policies. Sick leave policies compensate employees when absent due to occasional minor illness or injury such as the stomach flu or sprained ankle. In addition, employers pay sick leave benefits from regular payroll. In contrast, employers provide disability benefits from disability insurance policies or self-insurance.

Origins of Disability Insurance

Instances of company-sponsored and individual disability insurance appeared in the 1800s as the United States shifted from an agrarian economy to an industrialized economy. The agrarian economy was largely based on self-employment and the employment of family members. The industrialized economy, in contrast, mainly entailed ownership of manufacturing facilities that employed scores of workers. Many workers became seriously ill or injured while performing their jobs due to the absence of health and safety regulations. The Occupational Safety and Health Act (OSHA) was passed in the early 1970s. In the 1800s and early 1900s, the seriously injured and ill workers were left with virtually no recourse because social insurance programs to protect injured and ill workers were nonexistent. After the introduction of social insurance programs (including workers' compensation and Social Security in the 1910s and 1930s, respectively), private disability insurance was still necessary because the government programs were not designed to provide complete income replacement as the result of illness or injury.

Prior to the 1960s, there were three forms of relatively primitive employer-sponsored insurance that emerged. First, employers created **establishment funds** to provide minimal cash payments to workers who became occupationally ill or injured. Second, insurance companies sold individual disability insurance policies to workers. Third, greater awareness following state workers' compensation laws in the early 20th century led employers to purchase group disability insurance policies. The initial forms of disability insurance were primitive because they paid lump sum benefits following the occurrence of disability, and the amounts were generally the same regardless of age or the severity of illness or injury. This approach left the youngest and more seriously disabled workers with insufficient funds to help cover their lost income over longer periods of time than the oldest and least seriously ill or injured disabled workers.

During the 1960s, insurance companies began to manage liability more effectively, by offering benefits on an income replacement basis to avoid the previously noted shortcomings of earlier disability insurance approaches.

Short-Term Disability Insurance Programs

Short-term disability plans classify **short-term disability** as an inability to perform the duties of one's regular job. Manifestations of short-term disability include the following temporary (short-term) conditions:

- Recovery from injuries.
- Recovery from surgery.
- Treatment of an illness requiring any hospitalization.
- Pregnancy—the Pregnancy Discrimination Act of 1978 mandates that employers treat pregnancy and childbirth the same way they treat other causes of disability (Chapter 3).

Most short-term disability plans pay employees 50 to 66.67 percent of their pretax salary on a monthly or weekly basis; some pay as much as 100 percent. Short-term disability plans pay benefits for a limited period, usually no more than six months (26 weeks). Many companies set a monthly maximum benefit amount, which could be less for highly paid employees. For example, a company pays employees 66.67 percent, subject to a monthly maximum benefit totaling $5,000. Let's assume an employee's annual income equals $130,000 ($10,833 per month). Without the cap, he or she would earn $7,225 a month (0.667 × $10,833). The cap results in a monthly loss of income totaling $2,225 ($7,225 – $5,000).

Three additional features of short-term disability plans include:

- Preexisting condition clause.
- Waiting periods: Preeligibility period and elimination period.
- Exclusion provision for designated health conditions.

Similar to health insurance plans, a **preexisting condition** is a mental or physical disability for which medical advice, diagnosis, care, or treatment was received during a designated period preceding the beginning of disability insurance coverage. The designated period usually is any time prior to employment and enrollment in a company's disability insurance plan. Insurance companies impose exclusions for preexisting conditions to limit their liabilities for disabilities that predate an individual's coverage.

Two waiting periods include the preeligibility period and an elimination period. The **preeligibility period** spans from the initial date of hire to the time of eligibility for coverage in a disability insurance program. Once the preeligibility period has expired, an **elimination period** refers to the minimum amount of time an employee must wait after becoming disabled before disability insurance payments begin. Employees are responsible for paying a limited amount to cover the costs of treating illness or injury. Employers prefer disability insurance policies with longer elimination periods because the premiums (costs to purchase insurance coverage) are lower. Insurance companies charge less for policies with longer elimination periods because longer periods reduce the amount the company will have to pay in claims. The most common elimination period for short-term disability plans is three months, but it can range anywhere between one month and a year.

Short-term disability plans often contain exclusion provisions. **Exclusion provisions** list the particular health conditions that are ineligible for coverage. Disabilities that result from self-inflicted injuries are almost always excluded. Short-term disability plans often exclude most mental illnesses or disabilities due to chemical dependencies (for example, addictions to alcohol or illegal drugs). Employers support addicted workers through separate programs known as employee assistance programs (see Chapter 10).

Long-Term Disability Insurance Programs

Long-term disability insurance carriers use a two-stage definition for long-term disability. At the first stage, **long-term disability** refers to illnesses or accidents that prevent an employee from performing his or her "own occupation" over a designated period. The term *own occupation* refers to education, training, or experience necessary to perform work in one's occupation such as a pipefitter or crane operator. After the designated period elapses, the second stage definition adds the phrase "inability to perform work in any occupation or paid employment." The second-stage definition is consistent with the concept of total disability in workers' compensation programs.

Traditionally, long-term disability plans covered only total disabilities. More recently, many long-term disability insurance carriers have also added partial disabilities for the following reason. Including partial disabilities results in cost savings to insurance companies because, in most cases, totally disabled individuals avoid paid employment since they would forfeit future disability benefits. With the **partial disabilities inclusion,** insurance companies cover a portion of income loss associated with paid part-time employment while the disabled works on a part-time basis in any job. For example, long-term disability plans become effective when part-time employment falls below a designated level expressed as a percentage of income (adjusted for cost-of-living increases) prior to the qualifying event—for example, below 75 or 80 percent.

Maximum benefits usually equal 50 to 70 percent of monthly pretax salary, subject to a maximum dollar amount. Similar to short-term plans, the maximum benefit may be as high as $5,000 per month. Generally, long-term benefits are subject to an elimination period of anywhere between six months and one year, and usually become active only after an employee's sick leave and short-term disability benefits have been exhausted. Payments of long-term disability benefits continue until retirement or for a specified number of months. Payments generally equal a fixed percentage of predisability earnings subject to a maximum amount as previously noted.

Funding Disability Insurance Programs

Employers may fund short- and long-term disability programs in three ways. First, employers may use an independent insurance company to provide disability benefits. Similar to health insurance programs, companies pay premiums to one or more insurance companies to insure against the costs of disabilities. Second, employers may support disability benefits through partial self-funding. This option applies mainly to long-term disability insurance programs. Under partial self-funding, employers pay claims from their assets invested in a trust fund for a limited period (e.g., two or three years) or up to a maximum dollar amount. Also, employers purchase stop-loss insurance from an independent insurance company to cover the claims that exceed the self-funding limits. Third, full self-funding arrangements may provide all disability benefits from company assets. Self-funded plans may be handled internally or through a third-party claims management company. When handled in this fashion, full self-funded plans are described as administrative services only (ASO) plans.

Employers should factor two considerations into their decisions to partially or fully self-fund disability insurance plans. First, the size of the employee group helps employers predict the probability of disability occurrences. Statistically, larger employee groups enable more accurate predictions than smaller groups. Predictions of tolerable disability events support partial or full self-funding. Second, estimating exposure or liability for disability claims is essential. Exposure refers to the anticipated amount of annual disability claims under partial and full self-funding. Employers consider their tolerance for risk and pursue either partial or full self-funding.

Employee and Employer Tax Obligations

Taxation of employees and employers is specified in the Internal Revenue Service Code for accident and health insurance plans. Employers typically exclude their contributions to disability insurance programs as a normal ordinary and necessary business expense. Both FICA[2] and FUTA[3] recognize payments to disabled employees or their beneficiaries as taxable wages for six calendar months following the last date of service.

Another important issue regarding taxation focuses on who is responsible for withholding FICA and FUTA taxes and making payments of these taxes to the federal government. In some cases, the employer has this responsibility. In other instances, an entity other than the employer has the responsibility for withholding and paying FICA and FUTA taxes based on their liability for losses: these are third-party payers or agents for employers. The distinguishing factor between third-party payers and agents rests on who assumes the responsibility for covering losses.

Independent insurance companies qualify as third-party payers because they bear the risk of loss. For taxation purposes, insurance companies are the employer because they render the disability payments to disabled employees and their dependents. As a result, independent insurance companies are responsible for withholding and paying both FICA and FUTA taxes.

Agents for employers administer an employer's disability program, and could be a payroll service, accounting firm, or the employer's internal payroll department. Technically, they do not bear the risk of loss because of their administration-only role. The employer is responsible for withholding and paying FICA and FUTA taxes. One exception applies. The agreement established between the employer and an external agency (i.e., accounting firm or payroll service) may specify who is responsible for FICA taxes.

Relationships between Company-Sponsored Disability Plans and Benefits Laws

Four benefits laws influence the design and implementation of company-sponsored disability plans:

- The Age Discrimination in Employment Act of 1967.
- The Americans with Disabilities Act of 1990.
- The Employee Retirement Income Security Act of 1974.
- State workers' compensation and Social Security disability regulations.

The Age Discrimination in Employment Act (ADEA) of 1967

The **Older Workers Benefit Protection Act (OWBPA),** the 1990 amendment to the ADEA, generally bans the termination of an employee's long-term disability benefits for active employees based on age.[4] The OWBPA applies the **equal benefit** or **equal cost principle.** Specifically, employers must offer benefits to older workers that are equal to or more generous than the benefits given to younger workers with one exception.

Employers may reduce the level and duration of any benefit when the cost for older workers is prohibitively high.[5] However, employers may not use costs to legally exclude workers disabled at an older age for long-term disability benefits when workers disabled at a younger age receive these benefits.[6] An ADEA safe harbor* allows employers to reduce the duration of long-term disability benefits as long as the level of benefits is the same for all workers with the same disability:[7]

- Occurrence of disability at or below age 60. Employers may terminate benefits at age 65.
- Occurrence of disability after age 60. Employers may terminate benefits as early as five years following disablement.

Safe harbors refer to compliance guidelines in a law or regulation.

That is, an employer may choose to lessen the amount of time disabled *older* employees may receive long-term disability benefits as long as all employees (regardless of age) with the same disability are subject to the shorter time. For example, it is legally permissible to shorten the time frame for Ms. Johnson, a disabled employee who lost her leg at age 66, from the standard ten-year benefits payment period to five years, as long as her employer consistently applies the shorter benefit payment period to all employees at any age who lost a leg.

The Americans with Disabilities Act of 1990

The **Americans with Disabilities Act** prohibits discriminatory employment practices against qualified individuals with disabilities. A **qualified individual with a disability** is a person who possesses the necessary skills, experience, education, and other job-related requirements and, regardless of reasonable accommodation, can perform the essential functions of the job. Two federal courts, the Sixth and Seventh Circuits, maintain that recipients of long-term disability benefits are not qualified individuals with the rights to raise ADA claims.[8]

In addition, the U.S. Equal Employment Opportunity Commission (EEOC), the government entity that oversees the administration and enforcement of the ADA, ruled that employers may lawfully offer different benefits under disability retirement plans. According to the EEOC, disability retirement plans "provide lifetime income for an employee unable to work because of illness or injury, without regard to the employee's age."[9] For example, it is permissible not to provide cost-of-living adjustments for disability benefits. It is also acceptable to include offset provisions in disability plans that reduce disability benefits to compensate for other insured income benefits. Employers violate the ADA when they do not extend coverage to qualified individuals with disabilities or they provide less favorable treatment. Examples of unfavorable treatment include exclusion of eligible qualified employees from participation in disability retirement plans and requiring a longer preeligibility period for qualified individuals with disabilities than for nondisabled employees.

The Employee Retirement Income Security Act of 1974

The Employee Retirement Income Security Act (ERISA) of 1974 regulates the establishment and implementation of company-sponsored benefits practices. These include the following plans:

- Disability insurance
- Health insurance
- Life insurance
- Pensions

Most titles of ERISA apply to pension and health insurance plans. Only Titles I, II, and III apply to nonpension benefits. (Discussions in Chapter 4 describe pension plan features in detail.) Title I specifies a variety of protections for participants and beneficiaries and contains provisions that provide employees protections for benefits rights: reporting and disclosure, fiduciary responsibilities, and administration and enforcement. Title II has the IRC provisions pertaining to the taxation of employee benefits and pension plans. Title III addresses the administration and enforcement of ERISA, including the jurisdiction of relevant federal agencies.

State Workers' Compensation and Social Security Disability Regulations

Employees may receive long-term disability benefits from public disability programs (Social Security disability and workers' compensation) and company-sponsored programs. Company-sponsored insurance plans may include an offset provision.

Offset provisions reduce company-sponsored disability benefits by subtracting a particular percentage of the amount an employee is eligible to receive from workers' compensation or Social Security. Offset provisions limit the total disability benefits amount an individual receives. Without offset provisions, an employee stands to earn as much or more than their income prior to becoming disabled. The goal of all disability programs is to provide some income replacement, not total or excess income replacement.

LIFE INSURANCE

Employer-sponsored **life insurance** protects family members by paying a specified amount to an employee's beneficiaries upon the employee's death. Most policies pay some multiple of the employee's salary—for instance, benefits paid at twice the employee's annual salary. Employees usually have the option of purchasing additional coverage. Frequently, employer-sponsored life insurance plans also include accidental death and dismemberment claims, which pay additional benefits if death was the result of an accident or if the insured incurred the accidental loss of a limb.

Individuals can subscribe to life insurance on an individual basis by purchasing policies from independent insurance agents or representatives of insurance companies. Alternatively, they can subscribe to group life insurance through their employers, which has clear benefits for them and their employers. Group plans allow all participants covered by the policy to benefit from coverage while employers assume the burden of financing the plan either partly or entirely. Also, group policies permit a larger set of employees to participate in a plan at a lower per employee cost than if each employee purchased life insurance on an individual basis.

Origins of Life Insurance

Many of the social forces that gave rise to Social Security survivors' insurance (Chapter 8), workers' compensation, and private disability insurance apply to the advent of private life insurance. In sum, the major factors include the era of industrialization in the United States, government-imposed wage freezes during World War II, and favorable tax treatment for employers and employees.

Coverage and Costs of Life Insurance

In 2008, approximately 75 percent of full-time employees and 17 percent of part-time employees received employer-sponsored life insurance.[10]

Types of Life Insurance Programs

Three kinds of life insurance plans are available: term life insurance, whole life insurance, and universal life insurance. **Term life insurance,** the most common type offered by companies, provides protection to employees' beneficiaries only during a limited period based on a specified number of years (for example, 5 years) subject to a maximum age (usually 65 or 70). After that, the insurance automatically expires. Neither the employee nor his or her beneficiaries receives any benefit upon expiration of the plan. For example, if an employee chooses not to continue participation in a term life insurance plan after several years, she will not receive any benefits such as a cash payment, nor will her beneficiaries. To continue coverage under a term life plan, an employee must renew the policy and make premium payments as long as she is younger than the maximum allowed age for coverage.

Whole life insurance pays an amount to the designated beneficiaries of the deceased employee, but unlike term policies, whole life plans do not terminate until payment is made to beneficiaries. As a result, whole life insurance policies are substantially more expensive than term life insurance, making the whole life insurance approach an uncommon feature of employer-sponsored insurance programs. From the employee's or beneficiary's perspective, whole life insurance policies combine insurance protection with a savings feature (or cash accumulation plan) because a portion of the money paid to meet the policy's premium will be available in the future plus interest earned on this amount. Fixed annual interest rates of 2 or 3 percent are fairly common (which is substantially higher than the interest rates applied to money in a savings account held in a bank or credit union).

Universal life insurance provides protection to employees' beneficiaries based on the insurance feature of term life insurance and a more flexible savings or cash accumulation plan than that found in whole life insurance plans. Our focus will be on employer-sponsored group term life insurance and universal life insurance.

Group Term Life Insurance

Offering term life insurance to a group of employees does not constitute a group term life insurance plan. This designation generally rests on providing term life insurance to at least 10 full-time employees who are members of a group of employees. This minimum coverage rule has two major exceptions. Exhibit 7.1 lists them.

Employers may offer group term life insurance on a contributory or noncontributory basis. Under **contributory plans,** employees pay the entire insurance premium or they share the cost with their employer. Under **noncontributory plans,** the employer pays the entire premium for coverage within designated limits (e.g., twice an employee's annual salary). Most group term life insurance is offered on a noncontributory basis mainly because the employer receives substantially higher tax benefits with noncontributory than with contributory plans.

Term life insurance plans must meet four criteria for classification as a group term plan. Meeting all four criteria makes a group term plan eligible for favorable tax treatment under Internal Revenue Code Section 79. Exhibit 7.2 lists these four criteria.

EXHIBIT 7.1
Exceptions for Minimum Group Term Life Insurance Coverage

Source: I.R.C. §79, 7701(a)(20); Treas. Regs. §1.79-1.

A group may include fewer than 10 full-time employees if:

First, the insurance is provided to all full-time employees, including full-time employees who show evidence of insurability when required. Employees must receive insurance coverage as a percentage of compensation or on coverage brackets set by the insurance company. Insurance companies may reduce benefits for full-time employees with some limitations to evidence of insurability.

Second, the insurance is provided under a common plan to the employees of two or more unrelated employers. In addition, the insurance is restricted to, but mandatory for, all employees who belong to, or are represented by, a union or other employee representative. Finally, evidence of insurability does not affect an employee's eligibility for insurance or the amount of insurance provided to that employee.

Note: These exceptions do not include (1) employees ineligible for insurance because of a waiting period, (2) part-time employees who work fewer than 20 hours a week or five months a year, or (3) employees age 65 or older.

Section 79 of the Internal Revenue Code specifies that the cost of employer-provided group term life insurance qualifies as a tax-free benefit to an employee, with some exceptions.[11] We discuss taxation of group term life insurance in the next section of this chapter. Section 79 includes the following five criteria, which are described in Exhibit 7.3, to determine tax qualification:

- General rule for tax benefits of group term life insurance.
- Exceptions to the general rule that imposes taxation.
- Determination of cost of insurance.
- Nondiscrimination requirements—**nondiscrimination rules** prohibit employers from discriminating in favor of highly compensated employees in contributions or benefits, availability of benefits, rights, or plan features.
- Employee includes former employee for Internal Revenue Service Code, Section 79.

EXHIBIT 7.2
Criteria for Exempting Group Term Life Insurance for Taxation

Source: U.S. Treasury Department Regulations §1.79-1(a).

- It provides a general death benefit that is excludable from gross income under Internal Revenue Code, Section 101(a).
- It is provided to a group of employees.
- It is provided under a policy carried directly or indirectly by the employer.
- The amount of insurance provided to each employee is computed under a formula that precludes individual selection. This formula must be based on factors such as age, years of service, compensation, or position. This condition may be satisfied even if the amount of insurance provided is determined under a limited number of alternative schedules that are based on the amount each employee elects to contribute. However, the amount of insurance provided under each schedule must be computed under a formula that precludes individual selection.

EXHIBIT 7.3 **Internal Revenue Code Section 79: Group Term Life Insurance Purchased for Employees**

79(a) General Rule

There shall be included in the gross income of an employee for the taxable year an amount equal to the cost of group term life insurance on his life provided for part or all of such year under a policy (or policies) carried directly or indirectly by his employer (or employers); but only to the extent that such cost exceeds the sum of—

79(a)(1) the cost of $50,000 of such insurance, and

79(a)(2) the amount (if any) paid by the employee toward the purchase of such insurance.

79(b) Exceptions

Subsection (a) shall not apply to—

79(b)(1) the cost of group term life insurance on the life of an individual which is provided under a policy carried directly or indirectly by an employer after such individual has terminated his employment with such employer and is disabled (within the meaning of section 72(m)(7)),

79(b)(2) the cost of any portion of the group term life insurance on the life of an employee provided during part or all of the taxable year of the employee under which—

79(b)(2)(A) the employer is directly or indirectly the beneficiary, or 79(b)(2)(B) a person described in section 170(c) is the sole beneficiary, for the entire period during such taxable year for which the employee receives such insurance, and 79(b)(3) the cost of any group term life insurance which is provided under a contract to which section 72(m)(3) applies.

79(c) Determination of Cost of Insurance

For purposes of this section and section 6052, the cost of group term insurance on the life of an employee provided during any period shall be determined on the basis of uniform premiums (computed on the basis of five-year age brackets) prescribed by regulations by the Secretary.

79(d) Nondiscrimination Requirements

79(d)(1) In general, in the case of a discriminatory group term life insurance plan—

79(d)(1)(A) subsection (a)(1) shall not apply with respect to any key employee, and 79(d)(1)(B) the cost of group term life insurance on the life of any key employee shall be the greater of—

79(d)(1)(B)(i) such cost determined without regard to subsection (c), or 79(d)(1)(B)(ii) such cost determined with regard to subsection (c).

79(d)(2) Discriminatory Group Term Life Insurance Plan

For purposes of this subsection, the term "discriminatory group term life insurance plan" means any plan of an employer for providing group term life insurance unless—

79(d)(2)(A) the plan does not discriminate in favor of key employees as to eligibility to participate, and 79(d)(2)(B) the type and amount of benefits available under the plan do not discriminate in favor of participants who are key employees.

79(d)(3) Nondiscriminatory Eligibility Classification

79(d)(3)(A) In general, a plan does not meet the requirements of subparagraph (A) of paragraph (2) unless—

79(d)(3)(A)(i) such plan benefits 70 percent or more of all employees of the employer, 79(d)(3)(A)(ii) at least 85 percent of all employees who are participants under the plan are not key employees, 79(d)(3)(A)(iii) such plan benefits such employees as qualify under a classification set up by the employer and found by the Secretary not to be discriminatory in favor of key employees, or 79(d)(3)(A)(iv) in the case of a plan which is a part of a cafeteria plan, the requirements of section 125 are met.

(continued)

EXHIBIT 7.3   (*Continued*)

79(d)(3)(B) Exclusion of Certain Employees
For purposes of subparagraph (A), there may be excluded from consideration—
79(d)(3)(B)(i) employees who have not completed 3 years of service; 79(d)(3)(B)(ii) part-time or seasonal employees; 79(d)(3)(B)(iii) employees not included in the plan who are included in a unit of employees covered by an agreement between employee representatives and one or more employers which the Secretary finds to be a collective bargaining agreement, if the benefits provided under the plan were the subject of good faith bargaining between such employee representatives and such employer or employers; and 79(d)(3)(B)(iv) employees who are nonresident aliens and who receive no earned income (within the meaning of section 911(d)(2)) from the employer which constitutes income from sources within the United States (within the meaning of section 861(a)(3)).

79(d)(4) Nondiscriminatory Benefits
A plan does not meet the requirements of paragraph (2)(B) unless all benefits available to participants who are key employees are available to all other participants.

79(d)(5) Special Rule
A plan shall not fail to meet the requirements of paragraph (2)(B) merely because the amount of life insurance on behalf of the employees under the plan bears a uniform relationship to the total compensation or the basic or regular rate of compensation of such employees.

79(d)(6) Key Employee Defined
For purposes of this subsection, the term "key employee" has the meaning given to such term by paragraph (1) of section 416(i). Such term also includes any former employee if such employee when he retired or separated from service was a key employee.

79(d)(7) Exemption for Church Plans
79(d)(7)(A) In general, this subsection shall not apply to a church plan maintained for church employees. 79(d)(7)(B) Definitions: For purposes of subparagraph (A), the term "church plan" and "church employee" have the meaning given such terms by paragraphs (1) and (3)(B) of section 414(e), respectively, except that—79(d)(7)(B)(i) section 414(e) shall be applied by substituting "section 501(c)(3)" for "section 501" each place it appears, and 79(d)(7)(B)(ii) the term "church employee" shall not include an employee of—79(d)(7)(B)(ii)(I) an organization described in section 170(b)(1)(A)(ii) above the secondary school level (other than a school for religious training), 79(d)(7)(B)(ii)(II) an organization described in section 170(b)(1)(A)(iii), and 79(d)(7)(B)(ii)(III) an organization described in section 501(c)(3), the basis of the exemption for which is substantially similar to the basis for exemption of an organization described in subclause (II).

79(d)(8) Treatment of Former Employees
To the extent provided in regulations, this subsection shall be applied separately with respect to former employees.

79(e) Employee Includes Former Employee
For purposes of this section, the term "employee" includes a former employee.

Tax Treatment of Group Term Life Insurance

Employers may deduct the paid premium amount as an ordinary and necessary business expense for noncontributory plans and their contributions to contributory plans of group term life policies. There is one exception: The beneficiary of the policy must be someone other than the employer. Employers may not deduct the paid premiums whenever they list themselves as the primary or secondary beneficiary.

These rules apply regardless of whether employers meet the tax qualification criteria for employees stated in Internal Revenue Service Code, Section 79.

Employees must pay taxes on an employer's contributions to group term life insurance programs except for (1) the first $50,000 of coverage when it meets the criteria for tax qualification contained in Section 79, and (2) the employer is the beneficiary under the group term life insurance policy.

The first statement contains three exceptions that permit employees to exclude group term life insurance coverage in excess of $50,000.

1. An employee's voluntary employment termination for a disability that may lead to incapacitation for an indefinite period or death.

2. An employee voluntarily naming the employer as the primary or secondary beneficiary or a tax-exempt charity as the sole beneficiary.

3. An employee receives group term life insurance coverage when purchased under a qualified pension, profit-sharing, stock bonus, or annuity plan, and the insurance benefits are payable to a participant or his or her beneficiary.[12]

A point of clarification is in order. Employers' costs for the purposes of Section 79 do not refer to the actual annual premium amounts. Rather, employers' costs are based on a regulation established by the U.S. Code in a table titled "Uniform Premiums for $1,000 of Group Term Life Insurance Protection."[13] It expresses the monthly cost for group term life insurance based on sex and age (five-year brackets). Exhibit 7.4 contains the Uniform Premiums table for age only.

The cost amounts listed in the current version of this table represent mortality experience for group term life insurance subscribers between 1985 and 1989. Insurance providers use mortality tables to decide whether to offer insurance and, if so, the terms and premium amount. This decision-making process is known as **underwriting. Mortality tables** indicate yearly probabilities of death based on factors such as age and sex established by the Society of Actuaries. The Uniform Table combines probabilities for men and women. The values in the current Uniform Table were adjusted to reflect lower rates of mortality between 1988 and 2000.

EXHIBIT 7.4
Uniform Premiums for $1,000 of Group Term Life Insurance Protection

Source: Table I, Treas. Regs. §1.79-3(d)(2).

Five-Year Age Bracket	Cost per $1,000 of Protection for One Month
Under 25	$0.05
25 to 29	0.06
30 to 34	0.08
35 to 39	0.09
40 to 44	0.10
45 to 49	0.15
50 to 54	0.23
55 to 59	0.43
60 to 64	0.66
65 to 69	1.27
70 and above	2.06

Universal Life Insurance

As previously noted, universal life insurance combines features of term life insurance and whole life insurance. Universal life insurance was created to provide more flexibility than whole life insurance by allowing the policyowner to shift money between the insurance and savings components of the policy. The insurance company initially breaks down the premium into insurance and savings. The policyowner may make adjustments to the amounts of the premium that are directed to insurance and savings. For example, if the savings portion is earning a low return, it can be used instead of external funds to pay the premiums. Also, unlike whole life insurance, universal life policies permit the cash value of investments to grow at a variable rate that is tied to market rates. As a result, the premium, benefits, and payment schedules will change.

Accidental Death and Dismemberment Insurance

Accidental death and dismemberment insurance (AD&D) covers death or dismemberment as a result of an accident. Dismemberment refers to the loss of two limbs or the complete loss of sight (i.e., blindness). Compared to life insurance, AD&D generally does not pay survivor benefits in the case of death by illness. AD&D premiums are generally lower than life insurance because the incidence of death by accident is lower than death by natural causes.

At one time, AD&D protection was provided as an extra provision in a company's group life insurance program. However, as more and more workplaces contain fewer hazards with the decline of the manufacturing and mining business sectors, but heavily emphasize safety training where relevant, accidental death at work has become less of a concern. Also, as the cost of providing mandatory workers' compensation coverage has risen substantially over the years, companies have found that including AD&D coverage was becoming cost prohibitive. In many workplaces, companies offer voluntary AD&D coverage, which means that employees who wish to have this coverage may pay the premium under the company's group contract. In addition, most companies shy away from AD&D because an employee older than age 40 is more likely to die from natural causes than from an accident. This statistic is important considering that a large proportion of the workplace is older than age 40.[14] Companies are more inclined to spend their benefits dollars on health insurance, or increase contributions to 401(k) retirement accounts, because most employees stand to benefit more from health insurance and retirement plans than AD&D coverage. Nevertheless, many companies do include AD&D coverage to employees on a voluntary basis. Offering voluntary AD&D coverage to employees has been a reasonable compromise between balancing employers' costs and the limitations of workers' compensation insurance in some states that pay relatively small benefits for accidental death or dismemberment.

Summary

This chapter reviewed the fundamental concepts of employer-sponsored disability and life insurance programs. The social maladies of the late 19th and early 20th centuries gave rise to these protection programs. These programs, along with the Social Security disability insurance program and workers' compensation program (Chapter 8) provide the backup to workers and their dependents for work- and nonwork-related injuries, illnesses, or death. The programs examined in this chapter interface with a variety of tax regulations and employment laws. Managing the risks and liabilities represents a significant challenge to insurers and employer sponsors.

Key Terms

insurance policy, 173
premium, 173
short-term disability insurance, 173
long-term disability insurance, 173
establishment funds, 174
short-term disability, 174
preexisting condition, 174
preeligibility period, 175
elimination period, 175
exclusion provisions, 175
long-term disability, 175

partial disabilities inclusion, 175
Older Workers Benefit Protection Act (OWBPA), 177
equal benefit principle, 177
equal cost principle, 177
Americans with Disabilities Act, 178
qualified individual with a disability, 178
offset provisions, 179
life insurance, 179
term life insurance, 180

whole life insurance, 180
universal life insurance, 180
contributory plans, 180
noncontributory plans, 180
nondiscrimination rules, 181
underwriting, 184
mortality tables, 184
accidental death and dismemberment insurance (AD&D), 185

Discussion Questions

1. Discuss the basic concept of insurance. How does this concept apply to disabilities and life?
2. Compare the main objectives of state regulation of workers' compensation programs and employer-sponsored disability and life insurance plans.
3. What benefits do companies receive when they provide disability and survivor benefits for nonwork-related occurrences?

Endnotes

1. Society of Actuaries. 2006. *Experience Studies in Individual Disability.* Online at www.soa.org. Accessed April 5, 2009.
2. 26 U.S.C. §§3101–3125.
3. I.R.C. §3121(d); Treas. Reg. §§31.3121(d)-2; 31.3121(d)-1.
4. I.R.C. §104(a)(3).
5. 29 C.F.R. §1625.10(f)(1)(ii).
6. 29 C.F.R. §1625.10(f)(1)(ii).
7. *Parker v. Metropolitan Life Insurance Company,* 99 F.3d 181, 20 2033, rev., 121 F.3d 1006, 21 EB Cases 1369 (6th Cir. 1997) (en banc); *EEOC v. CAN Insurance Companies,* 96 F.3d 1039, 20 EB Cases 1949 (7th Cir. 1996); *Esfahani v. Medical College of Pennsylvania,* 919 F. Supplement 832, *Agster v. Furnival/State Machine Company,* 4 AD Cases 1614 (E.D. PA 1995).
8. U.S. Equal Employment Opportunity Commission. June 8, 2000. *Interpretive Guidance on Title I of ADA,* 29 C.F.R. §1630. Online at www.eeoc.gov/policy/regs/1630-mitigating-qanda.html. April 4, 2009; Equal Employment Opportunity Commission. January 27, 1992. *Technical Assistance Manual on Title I of ADA.* Online at www.eeoc.gov. Accessed July 26, 2001.

9. Bureau of Labor Statistics. 1999. *Employee Benefits in Medium and Large Private Establishments, 1997.* Washington, DC: U.S. Government Printing Office.

10. U.S. Department of Labor. 2008. *Employee Benefits in the United States—March 2008.* (USDOL 08-1122). Washington, DC: U.S. Department of Labor.

11. I.R.C. §§79; 170(c).

12. Originally established in 31 Fed. Reg. 9199, July 6, 1966; first revision in 48 FR 54595 on December 6, 1983; second revision in 64 FR 2164 on January 13, 1999.

13. I.R.C. §79; Treas. Regs. §1.79-1; §1.79-3(d)(2).

14. Anonymous. 2007. *Basics of AD&D Insurance.* Online at www.insurance.com. Accessed April 11, 2009.

Government-Mandated Social Security and Workers' Compensation Programs

Learning Objectives

In this chapter, you will gather information about:

1. Basic Social Security programs affecting employment: OASDI, Medicare, and unemployment insurance.

2. Administration and funding of Social Security programs.

3. Structure of Social Security program benefits.

4. The reasoning behind workers' compensation insurance.

5. Types of workers' compensation claims.

During the company benefits orientation, the speaker tells you that some of your benefits—retirement, disability insurance, life insurance, accidental death and dismemberment insurance—are offered through both government-mandated programs and at the discretion of your employer. Immediately, you wonder why there is an apparent duplication of some benefits, particularly given the high cost of employee benefits. The speaker goes on to explain the rationale for these programs and the details of each.

*The U.S. government established Social Security and workers' compensation insurance programs because of the social problems associated with chronic unemployment due to severely depressed economic conditions and devastating financial consequences for families whose primary wage earners could no longer work due to a serious work-related illness or injury. Also, the government recognized that most employees did not earn enough money to pay for medical services nor could most employees save enough money from their wages to support their retirement, and that most employees did not receive retirement benefits from their employers. Various Social Security and workers' compensation insurance programs were established by the U.S. government to contribute to the attainment of the social good. In the employment context, the **social good** refers to a booming economy, low levels of unemployment, progressive wages and benefits, and safe and healthful working conditions. Progressive wages and benefits help to promote the social good by enabling citizens to actively participate as consumers in the economy.*

ORIGINS OF SOCIAL SECURITY AND WORKERS' COMPENSATION PROGRAMS

Income discontinuity caused by the Great Depression led to the Social Security Act as a means to protect families from financial devastation in the event of unemployment. During the **Great Depression** of the 1930s, scores of businesses failed and masses of employees became chronically unemployed. Employers shifted their focus from maximizing profits to simply staying in business. Overall, ensuring the financial solvency of employees during periods of temporary unemployment and following work-related injuries promoted the well-being of the economy and contributed to the ability of some companies to remain in business. Specifically, these subsistence payments contributed to the viability of the economy by providing temporarily unemployed or injured individuals with the means to contribute to economic activity by making purchases that resulted in a demand for products and services.

The Social Security Act of 1935 also addressed retirement income and the health and welfare of employees and their families. Most employees could not afford to meet their basic financial obligations on a daily basis. Undoubtedly, most employees could not afford to retire because they were unable to save sufficient funds to support themselves in retirement. Further, the poor financial situations of employees prevented them from affording medical treatment for themselves and their families.

Work-related injuries and diseases became rampant in the late 19th and early 20th centuries. In large part, there were no laws that required employers to ensure the health and safety of employees during the early years of industrialization of the U.S. economy. Seriously injured and ill workers were left with virtually no recourse because social insurance programs to protect injured and ill workers were nonexistent. The limited avenues for recourse entailed lawsuits against the employer for negligence. However, common law doctrines of the period made it difficult for employees to prevail. As a result, these workers faced impoverishment.

Workers' compensation insurance came into existence during the early decades of the 20th century, when industrial accidents were very common and workers suffered from occupational illnesses at alarming rates.[1] State governments, rather than the federal government, were responsible for creating workers' compensation programs. At the time, the U.S. Supreme Court interpreted the Constitution to preclude federal legislation of private sector employers. The first constitutionally acceptable workers' compensation law was enacted in 1911. By 1920, all but six states had instituted workers' compensation laws. State workers' compensation laws are based on the principle of liability without fault—that is, an employer is absolutely liable for providing benefits to employees for occupational disabilities or injuries that result, regardless of fault.[2] Another key principle of workers' compensation laws is that employers should assume the costs of occupational injuries and accidents. Presumably, these expenses represent costs of production that employers are able to recoup by setting higher prices.

INTRODUCTION TO THE SOCIAL SECURITY PROGRAMS

The Social Security Act of 1935 and subsequent amendments to the act established four public social insurance programs:

- Old-Age, Survivor, and Disability Insurance (OASDI)
- Medicare
- Unemployment insurance
- Supplemental Security Income benefits

The economic devastation of the Great Depression era prompted the federal government into action because most people used up any life savings to survive, and opportunities for gainful employment were scarce. The passage of the act set up two programs: a federal system of income benefits for retired workers, and a system of unemployment insurance administered by the federal government and state governments. Amendments to the Social Security Act in 1965 established the disability insurance program and the Medicare program. The term **Old-Age, Survivor, and Disability Insurance (OASDI)** refers to the programs that provide retirement income, income to the survivors of deceased workers, and income to disabled workers and their family members. The **Medicare** program serves nearly all U.S. citizens of at least age 65, or disabled Social Security beneficiaries, by providing insurance coverage for hospitalization, convalescent care, and major doctor bills.

In this chapter, we review the fundamentals of OASDI, and Medicare and unemployment insurance as employee benefits, financed through the federal government's taxation of employers and employees. We also review practices employers follow when reporting Social Security taxes to the federal government. We do not review the supplemental security income (SSI) program because it is unrelated to employee benefits programs. The SSI program, financed through general tax revenues, provides income payments to elderly (age 65 or older) or disabled people with low incomes.

Employers Required to Participate in Social Security Programs

Coverage rules differ somewhat for OASDI and Medicare programs, and the unemployment insurance programs, respectively.

OASDI and Medicare

Virtually all U.S. workers are eligible for protections under the OASDI and Medicare programs except for three exempt classes. First, civilian employees of the federal government and railroad employees with at least 10 years of service are exempt from the retirement program; however, these individuals are not exempt from the Medicare program. Second, employees of state and local governments who are already covered under other retirement plans are exempt from Social Security retirement contributions unless these government organizations choose to participate in this program. Third, children under age 21 who work for a parent are exempt, except children age 18 or older who work in their parent's business.

Millions of Americans receive Social Security OASDI and Medicare benefits every year. In 2008, more than 50 million Americans were expected to receive over $53 billion in Social Security benefits.[3]

The prevalence of Social Security benefits among various groups of individuals and the importance of the benefits to them is staggering:[4]

- Social Security is the major source of income for most of the elderly.
- Social Security provides more than just retirement benefits.
- An estimated 162 million workers, 94 percent of all workers, are covered under Social Security.

Exhibit 8.1 details the scope of these facts about Social Security.

EXHIBIT 8.1   **Basic Social Security Fact Sheet**

Source: The Future of Social Security (Web Version 2009). Online at www.socialsecurity.gov. Accessed April 25, 2009.

Social Security Must Change to Meet Future Challenges

Social Security has been a basic part of American life for over 70 years. It provides a base of economic security in today's society through a valuable package of retirement, disability and survivors insurance.

About 164 million workers are earning Social Security protection, and about 50 million people receive retirement, survivors and disability benefits from Social Security.

The Social Security system is designed so that there is a link between how much workers and their employers pay into the system over their working years and how much they will get in benefits. Basically, high-wage earners receive a higher benefit payment than low-wage earners. However, the benefit "formula" is set up so that lower wage earners will get a higher percentage of their pre-retirement earnings.

Social Security has been changed over time to meet the needs of the American people. It will need to change again to meet future challenges.

Strengthening Social Security to meet changing needs is important to you . . . to your parents and grandparents . . . to your children and grandchildren. In the upcoming national debate on Social Security reform, it is important that you understand the issues presented in this booklet about the system's long-range future.

Social Security Has Made an Enormous Difference in the Lives of Older Americans

Social Security provides older Americans with a dependable monthly income with automatic increases tied to increases in the cost of living.

Workers can retire as early as age 62 and get reduced Social Security benefits. Or they can wait until full retirement age and receive full benefits. The full retirement age is increasing gradually. It will reach 67 for people born after 1959.

More than 9-in-10 retirees now get Social Security benefit payments each month. For two-thirds of the elderly, Social Security is their major source of income. For a third of the elderly, Social Security is virtually their only income.

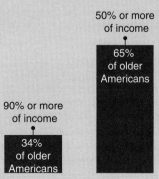

SOCIAL SECURITY IS THE MAJOR SOURCE OF INCOME FOR MOST OLDER AMERICANS

50% or more of income — 65% of older Americans

90% or more of income — 34% of older Americans

Social Security Is More Than a Retirement Program

Social Security also is "America's Family Protection Plan." Younger workers and their families receive valuable disability and survivors insurance protection. In fact, about 1-in-3 Social Security beneficiaries is not a retiree.

(continued)

EXHIBIT 8.1 Basic Social Security Fact Sheet *(Continued)*

Almost nine million workers and family members get disability benefits, and about $6\frac{1}{2}$ million people get monthly survivors benefits. These benefits can make a significant difference. For example, a 35-year-old worker with expected lifetime average earnings of $40,000 a year and who has a spouse and children could get about $1,890 a month from Social Security if he or she became disabled. If that same worker were to die, his or her family could receive about $2,480 a month from Social Security in survivors benefits.

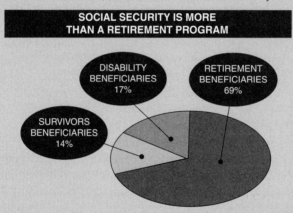

Social Security Provides a Foundation on Which to Build Retirement Security

A comfortable retirement rests on a three-legged financial stool—Social Security, pensions, and savings.

Today, about half of all workers are covered under an employer-sponsored pension, and many people are not saving as much as they should. While Social Security replaces about 40 percent of the average worker's pre-retirement earnings, most financial advisors say that you will need 70 percent or more of pre-retirement earnings to live comfortably. Even with a pension, you will still need to save. If you will not have a private pension, you will need to save more—and start saving sooner.

Each year, we mail a *Social Security Statement* to workers age 25 and older. This *Statement* shows your earnings history and also gives estimates of your retirement, survivors and disability benefits provided by Social Security. You should use this *Statement* to help you with your future financial planning.

Changing Demographics Are Driving Need for Changes in Social Security

The main reason for Social Security's long-range financing problem is demographics. We are living longer and healthier lives than ever before. When the Social Security program was created in 1935, a 65-year-old American had an average life expectancy of about $12\frac{1}{2}$ more years; today, it is 18 years and rising.

EXHIBIT 8.1   **Basic Social Security Fact Sheet**   (*Continued*)

In addition, more than 80 million "baby boomers" started retiring this year, and in about 30 years, there will be twice as many older Americans as there are today. At the same time, the number of workers paying into Social Security per beneficiary will drop from 3.3 today to about 2.1 in 2034.

These demographic changes will severely strain Social Security financing.

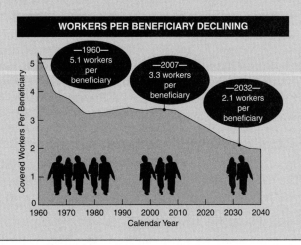

Unemployment Insurance

State unemployment insurance programs provide benefits to millions of unemployed individuals every year. The number of monthly initial claims is noteworthy, exceeding more than one million. A worker files an initial claim at the beginning of an unemployment spell. Wide variation in the number of monthly claims has occurred, often increasing with major economic recessions as currently experienced during the preparation of this revision or large-scale layoffs by major employers such as in U.S. automobile manufacturers (Chrysler, Ford Motor Company, and General Motors), also evident at the time of publication.

Unemployed individuals usually collect unemployment insurance benefits for several weeks. Since 1972, the average duration of benefits has ranged between 12 and 18 weeks. The average duration refers to the mean number of weeks for which unemployment insurance claimants collect benefits under regular state programs. The deep economic recession, which began in late 2007, and the subsequent loss of millions of jobs, left most of the millions of newly unemployed unable to secure work within the scope of state unemployment insurance programs. As a result, Congress approved the **Emergency Unemployment Insurance (EUC) Program** in June 2008 in the **Supplemental Appropriations Act of 2008.**[5] The EUC program provided 13 additional weeks of federally funded unemployment insurance benefits to the unemployed who had exhausted all state unemployment insurance benefits for which they were eligible. As the economic recession deepened, particularly in several states such as Michigan, it became apparent to the federal government that the EUC program extensions were not sufficient to bridge the lengthening gap between employment. In response, Congress enacted the **Unemployment Compensation Act of 2008**[6] on November 21, 2008. This law expanded the EUC benefits to 20 weeks nationwide (from 13 weeks), and it provided for 13 more weeks of EUC (for a total of 33 weeks) to individuals who reside in states with high unemployment rates.

In 2009, significant temporary enhancements were made to the unemployment insurance program under the **American Recovery and Reinvestment Act of 2009** (ARRA, passed on February 16) in addition to the extended benefits approved in 2008. There were two enhancements. First, the temporary Federal Additional Compensation program will provide a $25 weekly increase in unemployment compensation pay for eligible workers. It is important to note that states fund the unemployment insurance program, but this enhancement was funded entirely by the federal government. Second, the ARRA extended the EUC program, which was set to expire on August 27, 2009, to December 31, 2009.

Administration of Social Security Programs

Federal agencies possess primary responsibilities for OASDI and Medicare programs. The federal government and states share the responsibility for the administration of the unemployment insurance programs in each state.

OASDI and Medicare Administration

Two federal agencies primarily oversee Social Security programs: the **Social Security Administration** and the **Centers for Medicare & Medicaid Services.** The Social Security Administration (SSA) "administers the federal retirement, survivors, and disability insurance programs, as well as the program of supplemental security income (SSI) for the aged, blind, and disabled, and performs certain functions with respect to the black lung benefits program. SSA also directs the aid to the aged, blind, and disabled in Guam, Puerto Rico, and the Virgin Islands."[7]

Unemployment Insurance Administration

Titles III and IX of the Social Security Act authorized the federal government to grant money to states to administer unemployment compensation, and established a federal unemployment insurance trust fund. The Federal Unemployment Tax Act authorized the collection of both federal and state payroll taxes from employers and specified how these funds were to be used. The federal share of these taxes covers the cost of administering the unemployment insurance and employment service programs. The state share of these taxes may be used only for benefit costs. Each state sets its own rules and oversees program administration. State laws vary regarding eligibility for benefits, the amount of benefits, and the number of weeks during which they may be paid.

At the federal level, the **Employment and Training Administration** in the U.S. Department of Labor oversees unemployment insurance programs. The Employment and Training Administration strives "to contribute to the more efficient and effective functioning of the U.S. labor market by providing high-quality job training, employment, labor market information, and income maintenance services primarily through state and local workforce development systems."[8]

Employment security agencies in state labor departments or independent agencies or commissions oversee the administration of unemployment insurance programs at the state level. Each state maintains records, collects taxes, determines the eligibility of individuals for benefits, processes claims, and disburses unemployment benefits.

Social Security Numbers

Originally, the Social Security Act authorized the creation of a record-keeping system to keep track of employees' wages for determining the amount of employee benefits under the original OASDI and unemployment insurance programs. This authorization led to the creation of the nine-digit **Social Security number system** in the late 1930s.

Over the years, government regulation established mandatory and permissible uses of Social Security numbers within and outside the employment context. Nowadays, the Social Security Administration issues Social Security numbers to U.S. citizens, foreign students, and resident aliens for a variety of reasons.

OLD-AGE, SURVIVOR, AND DISABILITY INSURANCE (OASDI)

OASDI contains two additional benefits that were established by amendments to the Social Security Act following its enactment in 1935. Besides providing retirement income, the amendments include survivors' insurance (1939) and disability insurance (1965). The phrase "old-age" refers to retirement income benefits.

Qualifying for OASDI Benefits

Earlier, we indicated that employees from a wide variety of employers are eligible to receive Social Security program benefits. The Social Security Administration uses a system of **Social Security credits** to determine whether eligible individuals qualify for OASDI and Medicare benefits. Employees accumulate credits based on their payment of Social Security taxes that employers withhold from earnings.

Employees earn one Social Security credit for a specified earnings amount. The designated earnings amount increases every year based on the increase in average earnings in the United States. In 2009, an employee earned one credit for each $1,090 of earnings, subject to a maximum of four credits per calendar year. Credits accumulate over the course of employment. In general, an employee must earn at least 40 credits to be eligible to receive retirement benefits (fewer than this amount for a disabled individual). Earned benefits are recognized on an individual's Social Security record. Employees do not forfeit credits when they change jobs or become unemployed.

The number of credits required to qualify for benefits depends on a person's age and the particular Social Security benefit. We review these criteria in our discussion of each Social Security program.

Determining Benefit Amounts

The Social Security Administration pays monthly benefits to recipients of the OASDI program. The primary insurance amount equals the monthly benefit amount paid to a retired worker at full retirement age or to a disabled worker. As we discuss later, survivor benefit amounts depend on several additional criteria. A person's **average indexed monthly earnings (AIME)** determine the initial **primary insurance amount (PIA). Automatic cost-of-living adjustments (COLAs)** are applied to guard against inflation. The formulas used to determine OASDI benefits are complex. Chapter 7 of the *Social Security Handbook*,[9] published by the Social Security Administration, provides a detailed description of these procedures.

Average Indexed Monthly Earnings

Average indexed monthly earnings (AIME) represent a person's earnings prior to age 62, disability, or death, adjusted for changes in the person's earnings over the course of his or her employment, and changes in average wages in the economy over the same period. The Social Security Administration uses the AIME to ensure that the proportion of benefits to past earnings is about the same for all OASDI recipients. In other words, using AIME to determine the primary insurance amount (PIA) helps ensure that every beneficiary will have the same proportion of discontinued income (due to retirement, disability, or death) replaced by OASDI benefits.

Automatic Cost-of-Living Adjustments

The Social Security Administration increases annual benefits each December to account for changes in the cost of living based on the Consumer Price Index. Effective January 2009, the annual increase in Social Security benefits was 5.8 percent. The **Consumer Price Index (CPI)** is the most commonly used method for tracking changes in the costs of goods and services throughout the United States. According to the U.S. Bureau of Labor Statistics (BLS):

> The CPI reflects spending patterns for each of two population groups: all urban consumers and urban wage earners and clerical workers. The all urban consumers group represents about 87 percent of the total U.S. population. It is based on the expenditures of almost all residents of urban or metropolitan areas, including professionals, the self-employed, the poor, the unemployed, and retired persons, as well as urban wage earners and clerical workers. Not included in the CPI are the spending patterns of persons living in rural nonmetropolitan areas, farm families, and persons in the Armed Forces.[10]

Old-Age Benefits

The Social Security Administration uses several criteria to determine an individual's eligibility for retirement benefits, and formulas to calculate monthly benefits.

Eligibility Criteria

The number of credits needed to participate in the old-age program depends on the year of birth. Everyone born in 1929 or later needs 40 credits. Individuals born prior to 1929 require fewer credits. Individuals become **fully insured** for life when they achieve the minimum number of credits.

Year of Birth	Credits Needed
1929 or later	40
1928	39
1927	38
1926	37
1925	36
1924	35

Once an individual has become fully insured, he or she must meet an age criterion before receiving retirement benefits. Individuals may begin receiving retirement benefits as early as age 62, but their benefits will be permanently reduced prior to reaching **full retirement age.** Benefits are reduced to account for the longer period over which benefits will be paid. The year of birth determines full retirement age for the purposes of these benefits. Fully insured individuals born prior to 1938 meet the full retirement age criterion at age 65. Congress increased the full retirement age for people born in 1938 or later because of higher life expectancies of 65-year-old individuals—12.7 years beyond age 65 in 1940, 18.4 years in 2003.[11] The age for collecting full Social Security retirement benefits is gradually increasing from 65 to 67 over a 22-year period ending in 2022. Exhibit 8.2 shows the changes in full retirement age based on year of birth and the reduction in benefits received before full retirement age.

For example, Mary was born in 1941, which means she will be entitled to full Social Security retirement benefits when she turns 65 years and 8 months (full retirement age). She has decided to retire at age 62, making her eligible to receive

EXHIBIT 8.2
Social Security Full Retirement and Reductions by Age

Source: Social Security Full Retirement and Reductions by Age. Online at www.socialsecurity. gov. Accessed April 25, 2009.

No matter what your full retirement age is, you may start receiving benefits as early as age 62; the earliest a person can start receiving Social Security retirement benefits will remain at age 62.

Year of Birth*	Full Retirement Age	Total % Reduction
1937 or earlier	65	20.00
1938	65 and 2 months	20.83
1939	65 and 4 months	21.67
1940	65 and 6 months	22.50
1941	65 and 8 months	23.33
1942	65 and 10 months	24.17
1943–1954	66	25.00
1955	66 and 2 months	25.84
1956	66 and 4 months	26.66
1957	66 and 6 months	27.50
1958	66 and 8 months	28.33
1959	66 and 10 months	29.17
1960 and later	67	30.00

*Persons born on January 1 of any year should refer to the previous year.

reduced Social Security retirement benefits. Let's assume her annual Social Security retirement benefit will be $15,000 at full retirement age. At age 62, Mary falls three years and eight months short of full retirement age. As a result, her benefits will be reduced by 22.50 percent until full retirement age. Look carefully at Exhibit 8.2. The instructions direct individuals to select the "total percentage reduction" that corresponds to the year before birth. In Mary's case, she selected the total percentage reduction for 1940, the year before her birth in 1941. If this reduction did not apply, Mary would have earned $55,005 until full retirement age—that is, ($15,000 × 3 years) + ($15,000 × 0.667 year). The amount by which Mary's benefit will be reduced is $12,375 (i.e., $55,005 × 22.50%), yielding an annual benefit of $42,680 (i.e., $55,005 − $12,375).

The retirement program contains incentives to encourage individuals to delay their retirement after reaching full retirement age. The Social Security Administration increases retirement benefits by a designated percent for each month worked beyond full retirement until age 70, subject to a maximum percentage increase. The percentage increase depends upon the year of birth. Exhibit 8.3 lists the monthly and annual increases based on year of birth.

For instance, Exhibit 8.2 shows that the full retirement age for individuals born in 1937 or earlier is 65 years. John, born in 1937, turned age 65 in 2002. Let's assume that John would earn an annual benefit of $13,200 at full retirement age. However, John decides to postpone his retirement an additional three years. Exhibit 8.3 shows that individuals born in 1937 may increase their annual benefits by 6.5 percent for each year beyond full retirement age. John's annual benefits will be substantially greater because he will work until age 68. Specifically, John's annual benefit will be about $15,945 when he retires—that is:

$$\$13{,}200 + [(\$13{,}200 \times 6.5\%) + (\$14{,}058 \times 6.5\%) + (\$14{,}972 \times 6.5\%)]$$

Family members may be eligible to receive monthly benefits in addition to the benefits paid to retirees. Eligible family members include the retiree's:

- Wife or husband age 62 or older.
- Wife or husband under age 62, if she or he is taking care of children under age 16 or is disabled.
- Former wife or husband age 62 or older.
- Children up to age 18, ages 18–19 if full-time students through the 12th grade, or disabled children at any age.

When the Social Security Act was passed in the 1930s, it was based on the common model of the single-earner family—a married couple with or without children. Only one of the adults, typically the husband, worked. The OASDI benefits program was designed to compensate spouses who stayed at home to raise a family and who were financially dependent on the working spouse. Under this traditional model, the stay-at-home spouse did not have any income from employment or retirement income. Nowadays, both spouses in a married couple work, each earning their own Social Security retirement benefit, as well as possible additional income from an employer-sponsored retirement plan. To fulfill the original goal of the OASDI program, an offset provision was established to

EXHIBIT 8.3
Delayed
Retirement
Credits

Source:
www.socialsecurity.
gov. Accessed
April 25, 2009.

The Social Security Amendments of 1983 (H.R. 1900, Public Law 98-21) contained two provisions which may have an impact on when an individual decides to retire. The two provisions are an increase in the retirement age that first affected individuals retiring in 2000 and an increase in the delayed retirement credit for those who work beyond full retirement age.

Delayed Retirement Credits

- Social Security benefits are increased (by a certain percentage depending on a person's date of birth) if retirement is delayed beyond full retirement age.
- The benefit increase stops when a person reaches age 70, even if they continue to delay taking benefits.

Increase for Delayed Retirement		
Year of Birth	Yearly Rate of Increase (%)	Monthly Rate of Increase (%)
1930	4.5%	3/8 of 1%
1931–1932	5.0	5/12 of 1
1933–1934	5.5	11/24 of 1
1935–1936	6.0	1/2 of 1
1937–1938	6.5	13/24 of 1
1939–1940	7.0	7/12 of 1
1941–1942	7.5	5/8 of 1
1943 or later	8.0	2/3 of 1

- **Background**
  - A provision allowing for a 1 percent credit a year for delaying retirement past age 65, up to age 70, was first enacted as part of the 1972 Amendments. It was increased to 3 percent a year in the 1977 Amendments.
  - The 1983 Amendments phased in an increase in the percentage, based on a person's date of birth, and lowered the age at which the increase no longer applied to 70 (to correspond to the age of 70 at which the earnings test no longer applies).

The earliest a person can start receiving Social Security retirement benefits will remain age 62.

- **Social Security benefits are reduced for each month a person receives benefits before full retirement age.**
  - For persons whose full retirement age is 65, a retirement benefit is reduced by 5/9 of 1 percent for each month of benefits prior to full retirement age.
- **As the age for collecting full Social Security benefits increases, persons who retire at age 62 will see a greater reduction in their Social Security benefits.**
  - For persons whose full retirement age is age 65 and 2 months or later, a retirement benefit will be reduced by 5/9 of 1 percent for each month up to the first 36 months of benefits before full retirement age, plus 5/12 of 1 percent for each month of benefits in excess of 36 prior to full retirement age.

- **Examples:**
  1. Social Security benefits are reduced by 20 percent for a person who retires at 62 whose full retirement age is 65 (born 1937 or earlier).
  2. Social Security benefits will be reduced by 20 5/6 percent for a person whose full retirement age is 65 and 2 months (retires at 62 in 2000).

(continued)

EXHIBIT 8.3
Delayed
Retirement
Credits
(*Continued*)

3. Social Security benefits will be reduced by 25 percent for a person who retires at 62 whose full retirement age is 66 (born 1943–1954).
4. Social Security benefits will be reduced by 30 percent for a person who retires at 62 whose full retirement age is 67 (born in 1960 or later).

- **Background**
  - The Social Security Amendments of 1956 lowered the minimum age for retirement benefits to 62 for women.
  - The Social Security Amendments of 1961 extended the early retirement provision to men.

The New *Social Security Statement:*

- Tells a person their full retirement age and
- Provides a retirement benefit estimate for age 62, full retirement age, and age 70.
  - The age 62 benefit estimate incorporates the reduction for early retirement.
  - The age 70 benefit estimate incorporates delayed retirement credits.

ensure that a working spouse did not receive two Social Security retirement payments. The amount of Social Security income a surviving spouse receives is reduced dollar for dollar by the amount of his or her own Social Security retirement benefit.

Retirement Benefit Amount Determination

Earlier we reviewed the formulas to determine retirement benefits. In general, a person's retirement benefit equals the entire primary insurance amount (PIA). Exhibit 8.4 shows an example of how the Social Security Administration calculates PIAs. Family benefits usually equal 50 percent of the PIA.

Survivor Benefits

The Social Security Administration pays benefits to eligible family members of a deceased worker.

Eligibility

In general, a worker needs to have accumulated at least 40 credits to qualify family members for survivor benefits. Family members include:

- Nondisabled widow or widower at the full retirement age or older.
- Disabled widow or widower as young as age 50.
- Nondisabled widow or widower at any age if she or he takes care of the worker's children under age 16 or disabled children at any age.
- Divorced spouse as young as age 60.
- Unmarried children under 18, or up to age 19 if attending elementary or secondary school on a full-time basis.
- Disabled children at any age if disability began before age 22 and the parent was unmarried at the time.
- Stepchildren, grandchildren, or adopted children (in most cases).
- Dependent parents at age 62 or older.

EXHIBIT 8.4   **Calculating the Primary Insurance Amount (PIA)**

Source: Social Security Administration, *Primary Insurance Amount*. Online at www.ssa.gov. Accessed April 25, 2009.

The "primary insurance amount" (PIA) is the benefit (before rounding down to next lower whole dollar) a person would receive if he/she elects to begin receiving retirement benefits at his/her normal retirement age. At this age, the benefit is neither reduced for early retirement nor increased for delayed retirement.

PIA formula bend points	The PIA is the sum of three separate percentages of portions of average indexed monthly earnings. The portions depend on the *year* in which a worker attains age 62, becomes disabled before age 62, or dies before attaining age 62.
	For 2009, these portions are the first $744, the amount between $680 and $4,483, and the amount over $4,100. These dollar amounts are the "bend points" of the 2007 PIA formula. See table showing bend points for years beginning with 1979 (table also includes bend points in maximum family benefit formula).
PIA formula	For an individual who first becomes eligible for old-age insurance benefits or disability insurance benefits in 2009, or who dies in 2009 before becoming eligible for benefits, his/her PIA will be the sum of:

(a) 90 percent of the first $744 of his/her average indexed monthly earnings, plus

(b) 32 percent of his/her average indexed monthly earnings over $744 and through $4,483, plus

(c) 15 percent of his/her average indexed monthly earnings over $4,483.

We round this amount to the next lower multiple of $0.10 if it is not already a multiple of $0.10.

Determination of the PIA bend points for 2009

Amounts in formula	**Average wage indices**		**Bend points for 1979**	
	For 1977:	9,779.44	First:	$180
	For 2007:	40,405.48	Second:	$1,085
Computation of bend points for 2009	*First bend point* $180 times $40,405.48 divided by $9,779.44 equals $743.70, which rounds to $744.		*Second bend point* $1,085 times $40,405.48 divided by $9,779.44 equals $4,482.87, which rounds to $4,483.	

Survivor Benefit Amount Determination

Survivor benefits are usually less than a worker's PIA. The Social Security Administration pays monthly survivor benefits at a level ranging from 71.5 to 75 percent of the PIA, depending upon the survivor's status. In addition, the Social Security Administration pays a lump sum benefit to the surviving spouse, subject to two criteria. First, the worker must have earned at least 6 credits of the last 13 calendar quarters just before death. Second, the surviving spouse must have lived with the worker at the time of death. Surviving children receive this benefit if there is no eligible spouse.

Disability Benefits

The Social Security Administration pays benefits to seriously disabled workers and family members. In particular, Social Security pays only for total disability. Disability under Social Security is based on a person's inability to perform work done before becoming disabled and is unable to adjust to other work because of a medical condition. Also, the disability must last or be expected to last for at least one year or to result in death. As we will see later in this chapter, Social Security program rules assume that working families have access to other resources to provide support during periods of short-term disabilities, including workers' compensation, short-term disability insurance (from a private insurance company), and personal savings and investments.

Eligibility

Disability benefits are available to disabled workers who are unable to work as a result of a serious medical or mental impairment that lasts at least 12 months. Seriously disabled workers are eligible to receive disability benefits as long as they meet two criteria. First, the worker must have accumulated at least 40 credits. Second, the worker must have earned at least 20 credits of the last 40 calendar quarters in the last 10 years ending with the year of disablement. Disability benefits are subject to a waiting period of up to six months. More lenient rules apply to blind individuals and younger workers. Blind workers only need 40 credits.

Younger workers need fewer quarters of coverage because they have fewer years to accumulate quarters of coverage. Workers younger than age 23 qualify with 6 credits earned in the three-year period ending when becoming disabled. Workers ages 24 to 31 may qualify with credit for working half the time between age 21 and becoming disabled. For example, becoming disabled at age 29 requires credit for four years of employment (equivalent to 16 credits based on earning 4 credits per year) since the eight-year period beginning at age 21. The following table shows the required number of credits to qualify for benefits based on the age at which an individual becomes disabled.

Disabled at Age	Credits Needed
31–43	20
44	22
46	24
48	26
50	28
52	30
54	32
56	34
58	36
60	38
62 or older	40

Family members, as defined in the earlier section on retirement benefits, are also eligible to receive disability payments.

Disability Benefit Amount Determination

Disability benefits equal the full primary insurance amount. Disability payments to eligible family members usually equal half of the PIA.

MEDICARE

The Medicare program serves nearly all U.S. citizens age 65 or older by providing insurance coverage for hospitalization, convalescent care, and major doctor bills. The Medicare program includes five separate features:

- *Medicare Part A*—Hospital insurance.
- *Medicare Part B*—Medical insurance.
- *Medigap*—Voluntary supplemental insurance to pay for services not covered in Parts A and B.
- *Medicare Part C: Medicare Advantage*—Choices in health care providers, such as through HMOs and PPOs (Chapter 6).
- *Medicare Part D: Medicare Prescription Drug Benefit*—Prescription drug coverage.

Most individuals who are eligible to receive protection under Medicare may choose to receive coverage in one of two ways shown in Exhibit 8.5. As this exhibit shows, a person may receive coverage under the original Medicare plan or Medicare Advantage plans.

In a nutshell, the original Medicare plan is a fee-for-service plan that is managed by the federal government. As we discussed in Chapter 6, fee-for-service plans include many health care services, medical supplies, and certain prescription drugs. Participants in fee-for-service plans possess the choice to receive care from virtually any licensed health care provider or facility. On the other hand, Medicare Advantage plans include a variety of insurance options, including health maintenance organizations, preferred provider organizations, Medicare special needs plans, and Medicare medical savings account (MSA) plans. Medicare Advantage plans are run by private companies subject to strict regulations specified in the Medicare program. Restrictions pertain to pricing of the different plans. We will review the key features of these plans in subsequent sections of this chapter.

Eligibility Criteria for Medicare Benefits

Individuals age 65 or older who have earned at least 40 credits are eligible to receive Medicare benefits. Medicare coverage automatically extends to spouses of eligible individuals. Family members with disabilities are eligible to receive Medicare benefits. Younger individuals qualify for Medicare protection if seriously disabled for at least 24 months or suffering from permanent kidney failure requiring dialysis or a transplant. Meeting at least one of these criteria provides Part A coverage without paying a premium. Having fewer than 40 credits requires that an individual pay a monthly premium to receive coverage. In 2009, the monthly Part A premium was $443.

Part A coverage automatically qualifies an individual to enroll in Part B coverage for a monthly premium. Starting in 2009, the monthly premium amount is based on

EXHIBIT 8.5
Medicare
Basics

Source:
www.medicare.gov.

Original Medicare Plan		**OR**	Medicare Advantage Plans like HMOs and PPOs
Part A (Hospital)	**Part B (Medical)**		**Called "Part C," this option combines your Part A (Hospital) and Part B (Medical)**
Medicare provides this coverage. Part B is optional. You have your choice of doctors. Your costs may be higher than in Medicare Advantage plans.			Private insurance companies approved by Medicare provide this coverage. Generally, you must see doctors in the plan. Your costs may be lower than in the original Medicare plan, and you may get extra benefits.

+   +

Part D (Prescription Drug Coverage)	**Part D (Prescription Drug Coverage)**
You can choose this coverage. Private companies approved by Medicare run these plans. Plans cover different drugs. Medically necessary drugs must be covered.	Most Part C plans cover prescription drugs. If they don't, you may be able to choose this coverage. Plans cover different drugs. Medically necessary drugs must be covered.

+

Medigap (Medicare Supplemental Insurance)
You can choose to buy this private coverage (or an employer/union may offer similar coverage) to fill in gaps in Part A and Part B coverage. Costs vary by policy and company.

annual income and the premium amounts will be revised annually. In 2009, monthly Part B premiums ranged from $96.40 to $308.30 depending on income.

The Health Care Financing Administration set aside the period January 1 through March 31 as the initial enrollment period to elect Medicare Parts A through C, including Medigap. The initial enrollment period for Medicare Part D is three months before one's 65th birthday. Subsequently, individuals who initially selected either Medicare Part C or Part D may switch service providers annually from November 15 through December 31.

Cost penalties can be levied for individuals who elect the original Medicare program but do not subscribe to Medicare Part B before the end of the initial enrollment period. Typically, enrolling in Part B coverage after the first eligible general enrollment period increases the monthly premium by 10 percent for each 12-month period an eligible individual was not enrolled. This rule has a major exception, however. Eligible individuals do not have to choose Part B during the initial enrollment period if they are either currently employed and receiving coverage under an employer's plan or receiving coverage under a spouse's health plan. These individuals may subscribe to the special enrollment period by electing Part B coverage within eight months of terminating coverage from either plan. An enrollment penalty can be imposed on individuals who do not enroll in a Medicare Part D plan when first eligible and who do not possess prescription drug coverage for at least 63 days.

Medicare Part A Coverage

This compulsory hospitalization insurance covers both inpatient and outpatient hospital care and services. Examples of Part A coverage include:

- Inpatient hospital care in a semiprivate room, meals, general nursing, and other hospital supplies and services.
- Home health services limited to reasonable and essential part-time or intermittent skilled nursing care and home health aide services, and physical therapy, occupational therapy, and speech-language therapy ordered by a doctor.
- Hospice care for people with a terminal illness (i.e., an illness that is expected to lead to death within six months), including pharmaceutical products for symptom control and pain relief, medical and support services from a Medicare-approved hospice provider, and other services not otherwise covered by Medicare (e.g., grief counseling).
- Skilled nursing facility care, including semiprivate room, meals, skilled nursing and rehabilitative services, and supplies for up to 100 days per year. An example of skilled care is physical therapy after a stroke or serious accident.
- Pints of blood administered during a Medicare-approved stay in a hospital or skilled nursing facility.

Medicare Part B Coverage

This voluntary supplementary medical insurance helps pay for medical services not covered by Part A, such as doctors' services, outpatient care, clinical laboratory services (e.g., blood tests, urinalysis), and some preventative health services (e.g., cardiovascular screenings, bone mass measurement). Part B also provides ambulance services to a hospital or skilled nursing facility when transportation in any other vehicle would endanger a person's health.

This voluntary supplementary medical insurance is structured similarly to indemnity medical insurance, which we discussed in Chapter 6. Part B typically covers 80 percent of medical services and supplies after the enrolled individual pays an annual deductible for services furnished under this plan. As we discussed in Chapter 6, the **deductible** is the amount an individual pays for services before insurance benefits become active.

Medigap Insurance

Medigap insurance supplements Part A and Part B coverage, and is available to Medicare recipients in most states from private insurance companies for an extra fee. Most Medigap plans help cover the costs of coinsurance, copayments, and deductibles. Federal and state laws limit the sale of these plans to up to 12 different standardized choices that vary in terms of the level of protection. For example,

EXHIBIT 8.6   **A Brief Look at Medigap Plans**

Source: www.medicare.gov.

Medigap Benefits	Medigap Plans A through L											
	A	B	C	D	E	F*	G	H	I	J*	K	L
Medicare Part A Coinsurance and Medigap Coverage for Hospital Benefits	✓	✓	✓	✓	✓	✓	✓	✓	✓	✓	✓	✓
Medicare Part B Coinsurance or Copayment	✓	✓	✓	✓	✓	✓	✓	✓	✓	✓	50%	75%
Blood (first three pints)	✓	✓	✓	✓	✓	✓	✓	✓	✓	✓	50%	75%
Hospice Care Coinsurance or Copayment											50%	75%
Skilled Nursing Facility Care Coinsurance			✓	✓	✓	✓	✓	✓	✓	✓	50%	75%
Medicare Part A Deductible		✓	✓	✓	✓	✓	✓	✓	✓	✓		
Medicare Part B Deductible			✓			✓				✓		
Medicare Part B Excess Charges						✓			✓	✓		
Foreign Travel Emergency (up to plan limits)			✓	✓	✓	✓	✓	✓	✓	✓		
At-Home Recovery (up to plan limits)				✓			✓		✓	✓		
Preventive Care Coinsurance (included in the Part B coinsurance)	✓	✓	✓	✓	✓	✓	✓	✓	✓	✓	✓	✓
Preventive Care not Covered by Medicare (up to $120)					✓					✓		
2007 out-of-pocket limit ➡											$4,140**	$2,070**

*Medigap Plans F and J also offer a high-deductible option. You must pay the first $1,860 (deductible in 2007) in Medigap-covered costs before the Medigap policy pays anything. You must also pay a separate deductible for foreign travel emergency ($250 per year).

**After you meet your out-of-pocket yearly limit and your $131 yearly Part B deductible, the plan pays 100% of covered services for the rest of the calendar year.

some policies cover costs not covered by the original Medicare plan. Exhibit 8.6 charts the features of these Medigap choices.

Some insurers offer Medicare Select plans. **Medicare Select plans** are Medigap policies that present lower premiums in exchange for limiting the choice of health care providers. Three states—Massachusetts, Minnesota, and Wisconsin—do not subscribe to this system for offering Medigap insurance. Separate rules apply in these states.

Medicare Part C: Medicare Advantage

The Balanced Budget Act of 1997 established Medicare Choice—renamed to **Medicare Advantage** in 2004, a third Medicare program, as an alternative to the original program (Parts A and B). The Medicare Advantage program, informally referred to as Part C, provides beneficiaries the opportunity to receive health care from a variety of options, including private fee-for-service plans, managed care plans, or medical savings accounts. **Fee-for-service plans** provide protection against health care expenses in the form of cash benefits paid to the insured or directly to the health care provider after receiving health care services. These plans pay benefits on a reimbursement basis. Medicare Parts A and B are based on fee-for-service arrangements. **Managed care plans** often pay a higher level of benefits if health care is received from approved providers. Beginning in 2006, participants gained access to a wider variety of health providers. The Medicare Advantage program also allows beneficiaries to switch health plans during an annual open enrollment period each November.

Medicare Prescription Drug Benefit

The passage of the *Medicare Prescription Drug, Improvement, and Modernization Act of 2003* (also known as the *Medicare Modernization Act of 2003* for short) instituted a prescription drug benefit for Medicare program participants. Commonly referred to as Part D, the drug benefit was first offered in 2006. As noted in the following, Medicare covers 75 percent of prescription drug costs after a calendar year deductible of $295, up to $2,700. After that, expenditures up to $4,350 are not covered by Medicare. All costs are out-of-pocket. This coverage gap is known as the "donut hole" because Medicare contributes to the payment of approved prescription medications for amounts outside the $2,700 to $4,350 range less the annual deductible. Finally, Medicare covers 95 percent of the cost of prescriptions for each dollar spent in excess of $4,350 during the calendar year. The dollar amounts were valid in 2009 and are subject to change from year to year.

Total Spent on Medication during Calendar Year	Out-of-Pocket Cost	Portion Covered by Medicare
$0—$295	Deductible is out-of-pocket	No Medicare coverage of costs
$295—$2,700	25% out-of-pocket	75% covered by Medicare
$2,700—4,350	All costs are out-of-pocket	No Medicare coverage of costs
Over $4,350	5% out-of-pocket	95% covered by Medicare

The passage of this act has relevance for employers that offer a group health insurance plan that covers retirees who are eligible for Medicare. The Medicare Modernization Act provides for a federal tax-exempt subsidy to employers who sponsor drug benefits that are at least as generous as the standard Part D benefit.

Medicare as the Primary or Secondary Payer

Individuals possessing Medicare coverage may also simultaneously receive health insurance benefits from another health insurance plan, including an employer's group health plan, a retiree health insurance plan sponsored by a former employer, or an employed spouse's group health plan. An important question arises regarding which plan—Medicare or the other health plan—pays benefits first. Medicare serves as the primary payer for covered individuals and eligible family members under the following circumstances:

- An individual possesses retiree health insurance from a former employer.
- An individual possesses health insurance coverage from an employer's group health plan or an employed spouse's group health plan if the employer has fewer than 20 employees.
- An individual receives health insurance coverage through continuation provisions specified in COBRA, the Consolidated Omnibus Budget Reconciliation Act of 1985 (see Chapter 4).

Medicare serves as the secondary payer for covered individuals and eligible family members under the following circumstances:

If the other coverage is from an employer or union group health plan, these rules apply:

- If retired, Medicare pays first.
- If coverage is based on the individual's or a family member's current employment, who pays first depends on your age, the size of the employer, and whether the individual has Medicare based on age, disability, or end-stage renal failure:
  - If under age 65 and disabled, the employer plan pays first if the employer has 100 or more employees.
  - If over age 65 and still working, the employer plan pays first if the employer has 20 or more employees.
- If the individual has Medicare because of end-stage renal failure, in all cases the other plan pays first for the first 30 months following enrollment in Medicare.

The following types of coverage always pay first:

- No-fault insurance (including automobile insurance)
- Liability (including automobile insurance)
- Black lung benefits
- Workers' compensation

FINANCING OASDI AND MEDICARE PROGRAMS

Funding for OASDI and Medicare programs requires equal employer and employee contributions under the **Federal Insurance Contributions Act (FICA).**[12] FICA requires that employers pay a tax based on its payroll; employees contribute a tax based on earnings, which is withheld from each pay check. The **Self-Employment Contributions Act (SECA)**[13] requires that self-employed individuals contribute to the OASDI and Medicare programs, but at a different tax rate. In either case, the tax rate is subject to an increase each year to sufficiently fund OASDI programs. Since 1990, FICA required employers and employees to contribute 7.65 percent each. Self-employed individuals generally doubled that amount, or 15.3 percent in 2009. This tax amount is apportioned between OASDI and Medicare programs, as we will discuss next.

OASDI Programs

The largest share of the FICA tax funds OASDI programs. In 2009, 6.20 percent of the contributions of employers and employees were set aside. Self-employed individuals contributed 12.40 percent. OASDI taxes are subject to a **taxable wage base.** Taxable wage bases limit the amount of annual wages or payroll cost per employee subject to taxation. The taxable wage base may also increase over time to account for increases in the cost of living. In 2009, the taxable wage base was $106,800 for everyone. Annual wages, payroll costs per employee, and self-employed earnings above this level were not taxed.

Medicare Programs

The **Medicare tax,** or **hospital insurance tax,** supports the Medicare Part A program. Since 1990, employers, employees, and self-employed individuals contribute 1.45 percent. Self-employed individuals contribute double the amount, or 2.9 percent. The Medicare tax is not subject to a taxable wage base. All payroll amounts and wages are taxed.

According to the Social Security Administration, many people believe that the Social Security taxes they pay are held in interest-bearing accounts set aside by the federal government to meet their own future retirement income needs. To the contrary, the Social Security system represents a pay-as-you-go retirement system. In other words, Social Security taxes paid by today's workers and their employers are used to pay the benefits for today's retirees and other beneficiaries.

The Social Security Board of Trustees announced in its annual report for fiscal year 2008 that the long-range projections of the Social Security trust fund indicate that the Social Security trust fund is currently taking in more money than it pays out in retirement benefits.[14] Under the new projections, in the year 2019 payments made to retirement beneficiaries will begin to exceed the amount of money added to the funds based on FICA taxes. In addition, by the year 2041, retirement funds in the Social Security trust funds will be depleted. Finally, current projections indicate that only 78 percent of the benefits needed to pay retirees in the programs will be paid based on the expected inflow of FICA taxes from current employees. Over time, the balance in the trust fund will decrease until 2041 with an expected rapid decline after the year 2021.

For years, the viability of the Social Security programs has been the subject of heated debates between Democrats and Republicans across the country with no satisfactory solution. The Republican Bush administration diverted more than $10 billion from the Social Security trust fund to pay for general government expenses. The Democrats criticized the Republican administration for putting the security of current and prospective Social Security benefits at risk. Now, debates have arisen about whether the federal government is obligated to guarantee future benefits or simply promise benefits when economic conditions permit them.

On May 2, 2001, President George W. Bush announced the establishment of a bipartisan, 16-member commission "to study and report . . . specific recommendations to preserve Social Security for seniors while building wealth for younger Americans." Six principles guide this commission's work:[15]

- Modernization must not change Social Security benefits for retirees or near-retirees.
- The entire Social Security surplus must be dedicated only to Social Security.
- Social Security payroll taxes must not be increased.
- The government must not invest Social Security funds in the stock market.
- Modernization must preserve Social Security's disability and survivors' insurance programs.
- Modernization must include individually controlled, voluntary personal retirement accounts, which will augment Social Security.

Politicians have debated the merits and drawbacks of various solutions to shore up the Social Security system. Under President George W. Bush's administration, the focus was to encourage tax credits for individuals who save for retirement and to encourage more savings through employer-sponsored retirement plans. The Pension Protection Act of 2006 led to an increase in the number of people participating in their employer-sponsored defined contribution plans by giving employers the authority to automatically enroll new employees in the plan. The Democrats have called for increasing the tax under the Federal Income Contributions Act to bolster the trust fund; however, it has been met with strong opposition by business leaders, particularly small businesses that usually possess smaller profit margins.

UNEMPLOYMENT INSURANCE

The national federal-state unemployment insurance program provides weekly income to individuals who become unemployed through no fault of their own. Each state administers its own program and develops guidelines within parameters set by the federal government. States pay into a central unemployment tax fund administered by the federal government, which then invests these payments and disburses funds to the states as needed.

Eligibility Criteria for Unemployment Insurance Benefits

Individuals must meet several criteria to qualify for unemployment benefits. Unemployment itself does not necessarily qualify an individual for these benefits, although these criteria vary somewhat by state. In general, unemployed workers must meet several eligibility criteria, including:

- Limited voluntary employment, and involuntary unemployment except for disqualifying causes.
- Minimum earnings and employment requirements.
- A waiting period in most states.
- A capacity to work and an availability for work.
- Actively seeking suitable work.

Limited Voluntary Employment and Involuntary Unemployment

Workers who become unemployed through no fault of their own are eligible to receive unemployment insurance. Specifically, voluntary termination usually disqualifies workers from receiving unemployment insurance benefits unless they choose to quit their jobs for reasonable cause. *Reasonable cause* refers to the creation of working conditions that cannot be tolerated by any sensible person. Involuntary termination does not guarantee eligibility for benefits; most states stipulate disqualifying events. These include termination for misconduct, refusal of suitable work, and participation in some labor disputes. Some states will pay benefits for participation in labor disputes that result from a lockout by the employer or if the employer violates either the terms of a contract or labor laws. Additional disqualifying events include regular breaks between school terms for educators and deliberate misrepresentation used to receive benefits.

Minimum Earnings and Employment Requirements

Individuals applying for unemployment insurance benefits must have been employed for a minimum period of time, referred to as the **base period.** Most states define the base period as the first four of the last five completed calendar quarters immediately preceding a claim for benefits. In addition, most states require sufficient previous earnings, typically $1,090 during the last four quarter periods combined.

Waiting Period

Most states impose a **waiting period,** usually one week following submission of a claim, prior to paying benefits. States impose waiting periods for a variety of reasons, including time needed to process claims. Other states use waiting periods to limit total costs. Aggregating a week's worth of benefits over the total number of eligible individuals adds up to substantial amounts.

Capacity to Work and Availability for Work

Unemployed workers must be mentally and physically capable of performing work. Availability for work refers to a person's willingness and readiness to work. Think of the former requirement as ability, and the latter as motivation.

Actively Seeking Suitable Work

Unemployed workers must demonstrate that they are actively seeking work. The requirements vary by state. Usually, going on job interviews provides sufficient evidence. The term **suitable work** contains two elements. First, suitable work refers to jobs that require skills, knowledge, and ability similar to a person's customary work. Second, suitable work offers employment terms and conditions that do not violate relevant laws (e.g., violation of the minimum wage requirement of the Fair Labor Standards Act of 1938).

Unemployment Insurance Benefit Amounts

Individuals who meet the eligibility criteria receive weekly benefits. Because the federal government places no limits on a maximum allowable amount, the benefit amount varies widely from state to state. Most states calculate the weekly benefits as a specified fraction of an employee's average wages during the highest calendar quarter of the base period.

The majority of states pay regular unemployment benefits for a maximum of 26 weeks. A 1970 amendment to the Social Security Act established a permanent program of extended unemployment benefits, usually for an additional 13 weeks, to be paid by the federal government. The extended program in any state is triggered when the state's unemployment exceeds a predetermined level. As discussed earlier, the economic recession that began in late 2007 has led to additional measures from the federal government to offer further benefits for extended periods—as many as 21 extra weeks beyond the permanent program. Besides this statutory requirement for extended benefits is another program offering extended **supplemental unemployment benefits (SUB).** The SUB is most common in industries where employment conditions are cyclical, such as in the steel industry. Virtually all SUB benefits are part of collective bargaining agreements. Unemployment insurance benefits information for each of the 50 states and U.S. territories, including Puerto Rico and the Virgin Islands, may be obtained from the U.S. Department of Labor Web site (www.workforcesecurity.doleta.gov). Most unemployment insurance programs provide benefits that amount to 50 to 67 percent of previous earnings. States use one of three methods to calculate **weekly benefit amounts (WBAs):**

- A fraction of the highest wages for a calendar quarter earned during the base period.
- A percentage of the average weekly wage earned during the base period.
- A percentage of annual wages.

The calculation of WBAs excludes some income, including holidays, vacation, back pay, workers' compensation income, or retirement income.

Financing Unemployment Insurance Benefits

Unemployment insurance benefits are financed by federal and, sometimes, state taxes levied on employers. Federal tax is levied on employers under the *Federal Unemployment Tax Act (FUTA).*[16] Currently, only three states—Alaska, New Jersey, and Pennsylvania—require employee contributions. Employer contributions amount to 6.2 percent of the first $7,000 earned by each employee (i.e., the taxable wage base). FUTA specifies $7,000 as the minimum allowable taxable wage base. Relatively few states' taxable wage bases are as low as the FUTA-specified minimum (e.g., Florida, Indiana, and South Carolina). States typically set the taxable wage base according to the average wage level. In 2009, states' taxable wage bases ranged from $7,000 (in multiple states, including Arizona, Florida, Mississippi, Tennessee, and South Carolina) to $35,700 in Washington.

The federal government deposits 5.4 percent to the Federal Unemployment Trust Fund, which is administered by the Treasury Department. The Treasury Department invests this money in government securities, crediting the principal amount contributed by each state and investment income to an account. The federal government retains 0.8 percent to cover administrative costs and to maintain a reserve to bail out states with very low balances in their accounts.

States also impose taxes on employers to fund their unemployment insurance programs. An employer's actual tax burden varies according to an **experience rating** system. Every state applies different tax rates to companies, subject to statutory minimum and maximum rates. Each company's tax rate depends upon its prior experience with unemployment. Accordingly, a company that lays off a large percentage of employees will have a higher tax rate than a company that lays off relatively few or none of its employees. This experience rating system implies that a company can manage its unemployment tax burden.

STATE COMPULSORY DISABILITY LAWS (WORKERS' COMPENSATION)

State compulsory disability laws created **workers' compensation** programs. Workers' compensation insurance programs, run by the states individually, are designed to cover expenses incurred in employee work-related accidents or injuries. Six basic objectives underlie workers' compensation:[17]

- To provide sure, prompt, and reasonable income and medical benefits to work-accident victims, or income benefits to their dependents, regardless of fault.
- To provide a single remedy and reduce court delays, costs, and workloads arising out of personal injury litigation.
- To relieve public and private charities of financial drains.
- To eliminate payment of fees to lawyers and witnesses, as well as time-consuming trials and appeals.
- To encourage maximum employer interest in safety and rehabilitation through appropriate experience-rating mechanisms.
- To promote frank study of causes of accidents (rather than concealment of fault), reducing preventable accidents and human suffering.

The National Commission on State Workmen's Compensation Laws specified six primary obligations of state workers' compensation programs. This commission has established these obligations to ensure prompt and just remedy for workers injured on the job.[18] Exhibit 8.7 lists these obligations.

Workers' compensation differs from Social Security disability insurance and Medicare in important ways. Workers' compensation pays for

- Medical care for work-related injuries beginning immediately after the injury occurs.
- Temporary disability benefits after a waiting period of three to seven days.
- Permanent partial and permanent total disability benefits to workers who have lasting consequences of disabilities caused on the job.

EXHIBIT 8.7
Primary Obligations of State Workers' Compensation Programs

Source: J. V. Nackley. 1987. *Primer on Workers' Compensation.* Washington, DC: Bureau of National Affairs.

1. Take initiative in administering the law.
2. Continually review program performance and be willing to change procedures and to request the state legislature to make needed amendments.
3. Advise workers of their rights and obligations and assure that they receive the benefits to which they are entitled.
4. Apprise employers and insurance carriers of their rights and obligations; inform other parties in the delivery system, such as health care providers, of their obligations and privileges.
5. Assist in voluntary and informal resolution of disputes that are consistent with law.
6. Adjudicate claims that cannot be resolved voluntarily.

- In most states, rehabilitation and training benefits for those unable to return to preinjury careers.
- Benefits to survivors of workers who die of work-related causes.

Social Security, in contrast, pays benefits

- To workers with long-term disabilities from any cause, but only when the disabilities preclude work.
- For rehabilitation services.
- For survivor benefits to families of deceased workers.

Social Security begins after a five-month waiting period, and Medicare begins 29 months after the onset of medically verified inability to work.

Coverage of Workers' Compensation Programs

Employers must fund workers' compensation programs according to state guidelines. Participation in workers' compensation programs is compulsory in all states except for of Texas, where employers are not required to provide workers' compensation insurance. Compulsory laws require every employer to accept the state workers' compensation regulations. Elective laws permit employers the option of accepting or rejecting state workers' compensation regulations. Rejecting these laws causes employers to lose the common law defense of contributory negligence. Contributory negligence refers to,

> in law, behavior that contributes to one's own injury or loss and fails to meet the standard of prudence that one should observe for one's own good. Contributory negligence of the plaintiff is frequently pleaded in defense to a charge of negligence. Historically the doctrine grew out of distrust of juries, which have usually been more sympathetic to plaintiffs in personal injury lawsuits. The policy of not apportioning liability between parties to lawsuits (that is, charging each with some fraction of the blame) also encouraged the doctrine.[19]

Maritime workers within U.S. borders and federal civilian employees are covered by their own workers' compensation programs. The maritime workers' compensation program is mandated by the **Longshore and Harborworkers' Compensation Act,**[20] and federal civilian employees receive workers' compensation protection under the **Federal Employees' Compensation Act.**[21] Thus, workers' compensation laws cover virtually all employees in the United States, except for domestic workers, some agricultural workers, and workers in small businesses with fewer than a dozen regular employees.[22]

Virtually all workers covered by state unemployment insurance programs also receive coverage under workers' compensation programs.[23] As discussed in Chapter 4, the *Federal Unemployment Tax Act (FUTA)*[24] mandates employers' contributions to fund state unemployment insurance programs. FUTA also specifies two criteria to determine whether employers must participate in state unemployment insurance programs: the 1-in-20 test and the wage test. Employers must meet at least one of these tests; most do. Employees must also pass four legal tests before receiving benefits: (1) personal injury that results from (2) an accident

(3) arising out of employment that (4) occurs during the course of employment. For these tests, a personal injury pertains to physical damage rather than mental disorders. An accident generally refers to a single traumatic experience instead of injuries that develop over a long period. Arising out of employment stipulates that an injury must be the direct result of performing one's job. During the course of employment generally limits eligible injuries to those that occur when performing one's job during work hours.

Recently, questions have arisen over whether telecommuting employees injured at home may make workers' compensation claims.

Cost of Workers' Compensation Insurance

In December 2008, employers generally paid $0.46 per private sector employee for each hour worked to provide workers' compensation protection.[25] The hourly amount was substantially higher for workers in goods-producing industries at $0.84, and substantially lower for employees in service-providing industries at $0.36. Although these amounts represent no more than 3 percent of the total compensation costs (that is, the total cost of wages, salary, and all employer-sponsored benefits), the annual costs for employees in goods-producing industries is quite high. For example, let's assume a goods-producing company employs 5,000 workers. Based on a 2,000-hour work year for each employee, the cost to provide workers' compensation insurance totals $8.4 million (5,000 employees × 2,000 annual work hours each × $0.84 per hour for each employee). The cost of workers' compensation varies widely from state to state.

Workers' Compensation Claims

Employees can make three kinds of claims for workers' compensation benefits. The first, an **injury claim,** is usually defined as a claim for a disability that has resulted from an accident during the course of fulfilling work duties, such as a fall, injury from equipment use, or physical strain from heavy lifting. Employees who work long hours at computer keyboards or assembly lines, performing the same task over and over again, frequently complain of numbness in the fingers and neck as well as severe wrist pain. This type of injury is known as repetitive strain injury. A Bureau of Labor Statistics survey indicates that repetitive strain injuries represent a substantial amount of all nonfatal occupational injuries.[26]

The second kind of claim, an **occupational disease claim,** results from a disability caused by an ailment associated with a particular industrial trade or process. For example, black lung, a chronic respiratory disease, is a common ailment among coal miners. In older office buildings, lung disease from prolonged exposure to asbestos is another kind of ailment. Generally, the following occupational diseases are covered under workers' compensation programs:

- Pneumoconioses, which are associated with exposure to dusts.
- Silicosis from exposure to silica.
- Asbestosis.
- Radiation illness.

The third, a **death claim,** asks for compensation for a death that occurs in the course of employment or is caused by compensable injuries or occupational diseases. The particular injuries and illnesses covered by workers' compensation programs vary from state to state.

Workers file claims to the state commission charged with administering the workers' compensation program. The names of these agencies vary by state. Examples include bureaus of workers' compensation and industrial accident boards. Typically, one state agency oversees the administration of the program and disburses benefits to the individuals whose claims have been deemed meritorious. Another agency within the state, such as the board of workers' compensation appeal, resolves conflicts like claim denials that may arise when claimants are dissatisfied.

In recent years, workers' compensation claims have risen dramatically in both the number of claims and claims' amounts. For example, the increase in prevalence of repetitive strain injuries resulting from the use of keyboards has contributed to this trend. In December 2008, workers' compensation cost nearly 21 percent of all legally required benefits for all civilian employees.[27]

Types and Amounts of Workers' Compensation Benefits

Depending upon the claim, workers' compensation laws specify four kinds of benefits: unlimited medical care, disability income, death benefits, and rehabilitation services.

Unlimited Medical Care

The first, medical benefits, are usually provided without regard to the amount or time over which the benefits will be paid. Medical fee schedules in most states specify the maximum amount paid for particular medical procedures.

Disability Income

The second kind of benefit, disability income, compensates individuals whose work-related accident or illness has at least partially limited their ability to perform the regular duties of their jobs. Benefit amounts depend on the nature of the disability. Workers' compensation programs recognize four types of disabilities: (1) temporary total, (2) permanent total, (3) temporary partial, and (4) permanent partial.

Temporary total disabilities preclude individuals from performing meaningful work for a limited period. Individuals with temporary total disabilities eventually make full recoveries. **Permanent total disabilities** prevent individuals from ever performing any work. Individuals with **temporary partial disabilities** may perform limited amounts of work until making a full recovery. **Permanent partial disabilities** limit the kind of work an individual performs on an enduring basis.

Permanent partial disabilities fall into one of two categories: Workers' compensation programs list specific **scheduled injuries** that involve the loss of a member of the body including an arm, leg, finger, hand, or eye. **Nonscheduled injuries** refer to general injuries of the body that make working difficult or impossible. Examples of nonscheduled injuries include back or head damage.

The amount of disability income varies by state and the type of disability. For either temporary or permanent total disabilities, employees usually receive two-thirds of their average weekly wage for a predetermined period prior to the incident leading to disability. Three noteworthy exceptions are in Alaska, Iowa, and Michigan, which pay 80 percent of spendable earnings. Most states limit the duration of benefits for all temporary disabilities, with somewhat longer periods for temporary total disabilities than for temporary partial disabilities. Payments for permanent total disabilities extend for the life of an injured person. In some cases, states publish a maximum number of weeks or specify a payment period for the duration of the temporary disability. Maximum allowable scheduled injury awards vary considerably from state to state and by the particular loss (e.g., an eye, arm). Most states calculate actual scheduled benefits as the product of the specified number of weeks of benefits and the weekly benefit amount based on pretax earnings at the time of the injury.

States rely on one of three approaches to pay benefits for permanent partial disabilities of the unscheduled type: (1) impairment approach, (2) wage-loss approach, and (3) loss of wage-earning capacity.

The **impairment approach** bases benefit amounts on the physical or mental loss associated with an injury to a bodily function. This approach does not account for loss of future earnings because it ignores the physical and mental capacities necessary to perform the essential functions of one's job. For instance, the impairment approach designates the same benefit for the loss of an arm to college professors and concert pianists. Clearly, the loss of an arm will prevent a pianist from performing, but it should have little impact on a college professor's job to lecture students about employee benefits topics.

The **wage-loss approach** bases benefits on the actual loss of earnings that results directly from nonscheduled injuries. Application of this approach requires monitoring of an individual's income following an injury. The objective is to replace a part or all of the earnings loss due to the injury. Issues of fairness do arise. For example, the wage-loss approach does not provide any compensation for nonscheduled injuries when wages remain the same or increase. Also, calculating wage loss is not always straightforward: It is entirely possible that wage loss may actually be coincidental to an injury, with poor economic conditions or faltering company performance as the true causes.

The **loss of wage earning capacity approach** factors in two important issues that are likely to affect an injured worker's ability to compete for employment: human capital (e.g., work experience, age, and education) and the type of permanent impairment. This approach has the potential to control costs because it recognizes the importance of human capital variables. Many injured workers may have the necessary education and work experience to perform different jobs without any compromise in earnings. However, this approach is the most subjective method for determining nonscheduled benefit amounts. As a result, injured workers often require an attorney to represent their best interests.

Death Benefits

Third, **death benefits** are awarded in two forms: burial allowances and survivors' benefits. Burial allowances reflect a fixed amount, varying by state. Maximum burial allowances range from about $3,000 to about $15,000. Survivors' benefits are paid to the spouses of deceased employees and to any dependent children. The amounts vary widely by state, based on different criteria. For example, assuming no dependent children, the minimum allowable weekly payment to a spouse could be as little as $20 to as much as $500. States usually limit the duration of spousal benefits to a designated number of weeks or until remarriage, whichever comes first. Benefits for children typically equal two-thirds of the deceased parent's wages each year until a designated maximum age. The maximum age increases for children in college.

Rehabilitative Services

The fourth benefit, **rehabilitative services,** covers physical and vocational rehabilitation. Rehabilitative services are available in all states. Claims for this benefit must usually be made within six months to two years after the accident. In most states, the employer picks up the tab for physical and vocational rehabilitation. A minority of state governments pick up the tab for physical and vocational rehabilitation.

Employers' Rights under Workers' Compensation Programs

Participation in workers' compensation programs and compliance with applicable regulations protect employers from **torts**[*] initiated by injured workers based on the no-fault principles of these programs. However, there are four possible exceptions to immunity from legal action:

1. An employer's intentional acts.
2. Lawsuits alleging employer retaliation for filing a workers' compensation claim.
3. Lawsuits against noncomplying employers.
4. Lawsuits relating to "dual capacity" relationships.

An Employer's Intentional Acts

Most state courts consider intentional actions to harm employees as reasonable cause for holding an employer liable. Two kinds of lawsuits allege an employer's intentional acts to harm employees. The first, **deliberate and knowing torts,** entails an employer's deliberate and knowing intent to harm at least one employee. The second, **violations of an affirmative duty,** takes place when an employer fails to reveal the exposure of one or more workers to harmful substances, or the employer does not disclose a medical condition typically caused by exposure. In particular, failure to notify violates an employer's affirmative duty when the illness is either correctable at the point of discovery or its progress may be stopped by removing employees from further exposure.

Retaliation against Workers Who Filed Workers' Compensation Claims

In most states, employees possess the right to sue employers who retaliate against them for either filing a workers' compensation claim or pursuing their rights

---

[*] Tort laws offer remedies to individuals harmed by the unreasonable actions of others. Tort claims usually involve state law and are based on the legal premise that individuals are liable for the consequences of their conduct if it results in injury to others. Tort laws involve civil suits, which are actions brought to protect an individual's private rights.

established in workers' compensation programs. Retaliation usually entails an adverse effect upon a worker's status (e.g., a demotion or pay cut) or termination of a worker's employment. Employees may initiate these lawsuits by claiming retaliatory action. Employers then possess the burden of proof to establish their actions as a legally sanctioned business necessity.

Employer Noncompliance

Workers' compensation laws oblige employers to comply with applicable state laws. Employers begin to fulfill their obligations by purchasing insurance from state funds, private insurance carriers, or through self-insurance. Failure to carry workers' compensation insurance may lead to one or more consequences:

- Lost immunity, making violators susceptible to common-law charges (of contributory negligence or other torts).
- Monetary penalties, including fines and payment of unpaid premiums.
- Criminal penalties.
- Liability for the full cost of workers' compensation claims.

Most states recognize two acceptable alternatives for employees to receive remedy. First, they gain the right to initiate legal action against noncompliant employers as just described. Second, most states extend workers' compensation protection to employees regardless of an employer's compliance status.

Dual Capacity

Dual capacity is a legal doctrine that applies to the relationship between employers and employees. Specifically, a company may fulfill a role for an employee that is completely different from its role as employer. Even though an employer meets its obligations under workers' compensation laws, it may be susceptible to common-law actions. An employer's immunity does not protect it from common-law actions by employees when the company also serves a dual capacity that confers duties unrelated to, and independent of, those imposed upon it as an employer. A Supreme Court of Pennsylvania decision offers a clear illustration of the dual capacity doctrine:

> A hospital employee who became ill while performing his job received injuries during medical treatment of the illness (by the same hospital). The hospital's role as an employer was completely unrelated to its role as a medical services provider. The court ruled that Presbyterian University Hospital fulfilled a dual capacity role as an employer and provider of medical treatment to this employee. Specifically, the court concluded that the employee's injuries were sustained because of its role as medical services provider rather than as employer—(a) the purpose of the emergency room visit was to treat the illness, (b) the immediate purpose of seeking treatment was personal, and (c) the hospital billed the employee's insurance carrier for the treatment as it would have for any patient. As a result, this employee gained the right to sue the hospital for injuries sustained during treatment because an X-ray table harness broke, causing the employee to fall onto the floor and sustain injuries.[28]

Becoming injured while using an employer's product to perform work is another instance of dual capacity. For instance, a door-to-door salesperson for

Company X, a manufacturer of vacuum cleaners, becomes injured while demonstrating the use of her employer's products. A defective vacuum cleaner exploded during the demonstration, causing serious burns and the loss of her left eye. The salesperson is eligible to file a workers' compensation claim because she was injured while performing her job. She may also have the right to initiate a products liability lawsuit as the user of her employer's defective product.

Typical Employers' Defenses When Employees Challenge Immunity

As discussed earlier, employers maintain immunity from worker-initiated legal action when they are in full compliance with workers' compensation regulations. Employers lose immunity when they fail to comply. Most state courts of law usually recognize four acceptable defenses against employee lawsuits for premeditated acts. Premeditation excludes an employee's unwarrantable ignorance, bad judgment, or dishonesty. Employer defenses rely on an assertion that the causes of injuries or illnesses were unrelated to work-related activities.

- Preexisting conditions (illnesses or injuries that occurred prior to participation in an employer's workers' compensation program, except for work-related illnesses or injuries that worsen the preexisting conditions).
- Employee negligence (e.g., injuries sustained due to noncompliance with clearly communicated safety procedures).
- Employee misconduct (e.g., injuries sustained from acts of aggression against other employees).
- Safety violations by the employee.

In general, employers must continue to provide workers' compensation payments even if an employee is discharged because she or he willfully violates work rules in the course of employment after sustaining an injury. For example, a Maine appeals court required that the employer restore workers' compensation payments notwithstanding an employee's intentional dishonesty:

> An injured employee began to receive workers' compensation payments for a work-related incident that led to the loss of three fingers and serious injuries to a hand, an arm, and a shoulder. After returning to work on a light-duty basis, this employee misrepresented his use of a paid sick day. In actuality, the employer learned that he missed work to participate in a golf tournament. The employer discharged this employee and terminated his workers' compensation benefits because he willfully misused the paid time-off for illness. Ultimately, the court based its decision on the irrelevance of the employee's dishonesty to the negative impact of the injuries on earnings capacity.[29]

Financing Workers' Compensation Programs

Workers' compensation laws specify the permissible methods of funding. Employers generally subscribe to workers' compensation insurance through private carriers, or in some instances, through state funds. A third funding option, self-insurance, requires companies to deposit a surety bond, enabling them to pay their own workers' claims directly.[30] Many employers select self-insurance when available because it gives them greater discretion in administering their own risks. Nevertheless, self-insured companies must pay their workers the same benefits paid by state funds or private insurance carriers.

In most states, the insurance commissioner sets the maximum allowable workers' compensation insurance premium rates for private insurance carriers. Rates are based on each $100 of payroll. Increasingly, some states permit insurance carriers to set rates on a competitive basis.

States rely on ratemaking service organizations to set initial rates. **Ratemaking service organizations** collect data on workplace accidents and put together rating manuals. **Rating manuals** specify insurance rates based on classifications of businesses. A few states possess independent rating organizations. The remainder consults with the National Council on Compensation Insurance, a for-profit company located in Boca Raton, Florida; this organization prepares three separate manuals for state insurance agencies. Independent rating bureaus used by a few states compile manuals that correspond to the National Council's manuals.

Second-injury funds represent an important funding element of workers' compensation programs. These funds cover a portion or all of the costs of a current workers' compensation claim associated with preexisting conditions from a work-related injury during prior employment elsewhere. For instance, a current employee sustained a work-related injury to his knee while employed by Company A. A year later, he sustains a secondary injury to the same knee while working for Company B. From Company B's perspective, the injury sustained in Company A is a preexisting condition. In many cases, the cost of the second disability is compounded by the first injury (i.e., the preexisting condition). Second-injury funds cover the extra costs of the current injury due to the first injury in Company A. Coverage of preexisting conditions creates benefits for employers and qualified individuals with disabilities. Employers should be less reluctant to hire a qualified individual with a disability. Qualified individuals should have fewer barriers to employment due to the cost concerns of employers about preexisting conditions.

Employer and Employee Tax Obligations

In general, employees do not pay any income taxes on the amount of workers' compensation benefits.[31] Similarly, survivors of deceased workers do not pay any taxes on death benefits.[32] However, three circumstances may require payment of taxes. First, employees pay taxes on their workers' compensation benefits when they return to work for light duty. Second, workers' compensation benefits are taxable when they offset (reduce) Social Security Old-Age, Survivor, and Disability Insurance (OASDI) benefits. Third, employees pay taxes on workers' compensation benefits when they do not directly result from work-related illness or injury.[*]

Employers, typically, do not pay taxes on workers' compensation benefits, with one main exception: Workers' compensation benefits for non-work-related illnesses

---

[*] Workers' compensation benefits for non-work-related illnesses or injuries is inconsistent with the objectives of worker's compensation programs. However, an Internal Revenue Service ruling (Rev. Rul. 72—191, 1972—1 CB 45) classifies these benefits as part of state workers' compensation programs.

or injuries. For this circumstance, the Federal Insurance Contributions Act (FICA)[33] and the Federal Unemployment Tax Act (FUTA)[34] apply. FICA requires that an employer pay a tax based on its payroll; employees contribute a tax based on earnings, which is withheld from each paycheck. FUTA requires that employers contribute 6.2 percent of the taxable wage base, currently $7,000.

Relationship between Workers' Compensation and Benefits Laws

Workers' compensation laws may modify some of the provisions under the Family and Medical Leave Act (Chapter 9) and the Consolidated Omnibus Budget Reconciliation Act of 1985 (Chapter 4). The **Family and Medical Leave Act (FMLA)** provides employees job protection in cases of family or medical emergency. The basic thrust of the act is guaranteed leave, and a key element of that guarantee is the right of the employee to return either to the position he or she left when the leave began or to an equivalent position with the same benefits, pay, and other terms and conditions of employment. Companies must permit qualified beneficiaries to elect continuation coverage under group health plans if they would lose coverage due to a qualifying event. A **qualified beneficiary**[35] refers to any individual who is a beneficiary under the group health plan, such as the (1) spouse of the covered employee or (2) dependent child of the covered employee. Qualified beneficiaries include covered employees themselves when the qualifying event is termination of employment (other than by reason of misconduct) or a reduction in work hours. Exhibit 8.8 lists the qualifying events.[36]

These modifications depend on an employer's definition of "eligible employee" for company-sponsored health insurance. Typically, employees maintain eligibility while actively employed for a specified minimum number of weekly hours, are on approved leave of absence, or until termination of employment. Companies may not refuse an employee's request for FMLA leave to cover absences for work-related illness or injury. Also, employers may not force an employee to terminate FMLA leave for light-duty work. As previously noted, the FMLA allows employees to receive company-sponsored health insurance coverage on the same terms and conditions as for active employees.

Employees are eligible to receive continued health care coverage during and following a non-FMLA-approved leave of absence for a work-related illness or injury. During a non-FMLA-approved leave, employers may specify the time limit

EXHIBIT 8.8 **Qualifying** **Events**	• Death of the covered employee. • Termination or reduction in hours of employment (other than by reason of misconduct). • Divorce or legal separation. • Dependent child ceasing to meet the health plan's definition of a dependent child. • Covered employee becomes eligible for Medicare benefits under the Social Security Act.

after which employees are no longer eligible for health insurance coverage. Employees then become eligible for the standard COBRA continuation coverage period. However, the period of COBRA continuation coverage may be extended by law if an employee is eligible for FMLA leave. Employees then become eligible for COBRA continuation coverage as soon as they complete their FMLA leave.

Summary

This chapter reviewed the fundamental concepts of Social Security and workers' compensation programs. The social maladies of the late 19th and early 20th centuries gave rise to these protection programs. The programs examined in this chapter interface with a variety of tax regulations and employment laws.

Key Terms

social good, *190*
income discontinuity, *190*
Great Depression, *190*
Old-Age, Survivor, and Disability Insurance (OASDI), *192*
Medicare, *192*
Emergency Unemployment Insurance (EUC), *195*
Supplemental Appropriations Act of 2008, *195*
Unemployment Compensation Act of 2008, *196*
American Recovery and Reinvestment Act of 2009, *196*
Social Security Administration, *196*
Centers for Medicare & Medicaid Services, *196*
Employment and Training Administration, *196*
Social Security number system, *197*
Social Security credits, *197*
average indexed monthly earnings (AIME), *198*
primary insurance amount (PIA), *198*
automatic cost-of-living adjustments (COLAs), *198*

Consumer Price Index (CPI), *198*
fully insured, *198*
full retirement age, *199*
deductible, *207*
Medigap, *207*
Medicare Select plans, *208*
Medicare Advantage, *208*
fee-for-service plans, *208*
managed care plans, *208*
Federal Insurance Contributions Act (FICA), *210*
Self-Employment Contributions Act (SECA), *210*
taxable wage base, *210*
Medicare tax, *211*
hospital insurance tax, *211*
base period, *213*
waiting period, *213*
suitable work, *213*
supplemental unemployment benefit (SUB), *214*
weekly benefit amounts (WBAs), *214*
experience rating, *214*
state compulsory disability laws, *215*
workers' compensation, *215*
Longshore and Harborworkers' Compensation Act, *216*

Federal Employees' Compensation Act, *216*
injury claim, *217*
occupational disease claim, *217*
death claim, *218*
temporary total disabilities, *218*
permanent total disabilities, *218*
temporary partial disabilities, *218*
permanent partial disabilities, *218*
scheduled injuries, *218*
nonscheduled injuries, *218*
impairment approach, *219*
wage-loss approach, *219*
loss of wage earning capacity approach, *219*
death benefits, *219*
rehabilitative services, *220*
torts, *220*
deliberate and knowing torts, *220*
violations of an affirmative duty, *220*
dual capacity, *221*
ratemaking service organizations, *223*
rating manuals, *223*
second-injury funds, *223*
Family and Medical Leave Act (FMLA), *224*
qualified beneficiary, *224*

Discussion Questions

1. Discuss the basic concept of social insurance as provided by Social Security programs.
2. Describe the differences between FICA and FUTA.
3. Would you modify any of the eligibility criteria currently used to qualify the unemployed for unemployment insurance benefits? Explain why.
4. List and describe the types of claims in state workers' compensation programs. How much redundancy is there with employer-sponsored private insurance? Explain your answer.
5. Under what circumstances should employees be ineligible for public or private disability and life benefits? Discuss the rationale for your answer. Are the expenses associated with providing public and private programs serving the best interests of society?

Endnotes

1. F. R. Dulles and M. Dubofsky. 1993. *Labor in America: A History*. Arlington Heights, IL: Harlan Davidson.
2. U.S. Chamber of Commerce. 2007. *2007 Analysis of Workers' Compensation Laws*. Washington, DC: U.S. Chamber of Commerce.
3. U.S. Social Security Administration. 2009. Fact Sheet on the Old-Age, Survivors, and Disability Insurance Program. Online at www.ssa.gov. Accessed February 16, 2007.
4. Ibid.
5. P.L. 110-252.
6. P.L. 110-449.
7. *U.S. Social Security Administration Organization Manual*. Chapter S: Social Security Administration. Online at www.ssa.gov/org/ssaorg.htm. Accessed January 30, 2007.
8. U.S. Department of Labor. *ETA Mission, Values, Strategies, and Goals*. Online at www.doleta.gov/etainfo/mission.cfm. Accessed February 16, 2007.
9. U.S. Social Security Administration. 2009. *Social Security Handbook*. Online at www.socialsecurity.gov. Accessed April 25, 2009.
10. U.S. Bureau of Labor Statistics. *Consumer Price Index Frequently Asked Questions*. Online at www.bls.gov/cpifaq.htm. Accessed April 25, 2009.
11. U.S. Social Security Administration. 2009. *Social Security Program History*. Online at www.ssa.gov/pressoffice/history/. Accessed April 25, 2009. U.S. Census Bureau. *Statistical Abstracts of the United States* (126th ed.). Online at www.census.gov/compendia/statab/vital_statistics/life_expectancy/. Accessed February 16, 2007.
12. 26 U.S.C. §§3101–3125.
13. 26 U.S.C. §§1401–1403.
14. Social Security Commission. 2009. "The future of Social Security." Online at www.socialsecurity.gov. April 25, 2009.
15. Social Security Administration. 2001. "President Bush establishes new Social Security commission." Excerpts from the news release. Online at www.ssa.gov/pressoffice/ssacommission.htm.
16. I.R.C. §3121(d); Treas. Reg. §§31.3121(d)-2; 31.3121(d)-1.
17. U.S. Chamber of Commerce. 2007. *2007 Analysis of Workers' Compensation Laws*. Washington, DC: U.S. Chamber of Commerce.
18. J. V. Nackley. 1987. *Primer on Workers' Compensation*. Washington, DC: Bureau of National Affairs.
19. "Contributory negligence." Online at www.britannica.com. Accessed August 16, 2004.

20. 33 U.S.C. §§901–950.

21. 5 U.S.C. §§8101–8193.

22. U.S. Chamber of Commerce. 2007. *2007 Analysis of Workers' Compensation Laws.* Washington, DC: U.S. Chamber of Commerce.

23. D. Mont, J. F. Burton, Jr., and V. Reno. 2000. *Workers' Compensation: Benefits, Coverage, and Costs, 1997–1998: New Estimates.* Washington, DC: National Academy of Social Insurance.

24. I.R.C. §3121(d); Treas. Reg. §§31.3121(d)-2; 31.3121(d)-1.

25. U.S. Bureau of Labor Statistics. 2009. *Employer Costs for Employee Compensation—December 2008* (USDL 09-0247). Online at www.bls.gov. Accessed April 25, 2009.

26. U.S. Bureau of Labor Statistics. 2008. *Nonfatal Occupational Injuries and Illnesses Requiring Time Away from Work, 2007.* USDL 08-1716. Online at www.bls.gov. Accessed April 25, 2009.

27. U.S. Bureau of Labor Statistics. 2009. *Employer Costs for Employee Compensation—December 2008* (USDL 09-0247). Online at www.bls.gov. Accessed April 25, 2009.

28. *Tatrai v. Presbyterian University Hospital,* 439 A.2d 1162 (PA 1982).

29. *Cousins v. Georgia-Pacific Corp.,* 599 A.2d 73 (ME 1991).

30. Nackley, *Primer on Workers' Compensation.*

31. I.R.C. §104(a).

32. Treas. Reg. §1.104-1(b).

33. 26 U.S.C. §§3101–3125.

34. I.R.C. §3121(d); Treas. Reg. §§31.3121(d)-2; 31.3121(d)-1.

35. I.R.C. §4980B(g)(1); Treas. Regs. §54.4980B-3.

36. I.R.C. §4980B(f).

Part **Three**

Services

Chapter **Nine**

Paid Time-Off and Flexible Work Schedules

Chapter Outline

Learning Objectives

In this chapter, you will gather information about:

1. Various types of paid time-off practices.

2. Design elements of paid time-off practices.

3. Federal and state regulation of paid time-off practices.

4. Leave under the Family and Medical Leave Act of 1993.

5. Various types of flexible work schedules.

Whoa, you think. There's a lot to learn about your company benefits plan and you have done well in learning about them. Now you feel like you're ready for a vacation and you've barely started your new job! Well, perfect timing. Employers offer a variety of time-off with pay opportunities for employees, including vacation and flexible work schedules. In some cases, paid time-off is required by law. In either event, paid time-off is designed to give employees the opportunity to pursue leisure activities, balance work and family demands, meet civic duties, and continue their education.

In this chapter, we will learn additional reasons why companies offer paid time-off benefits and flexible work schedules.

DEFINING AND EXPLORING PAID TIME-OFF PROGRAMS

Paid time-off policies compensate employees when they are not performing their primary work duties. Private sector U.S. companies offer most paid time-off benefits to employees working in the United States or its territories on a discretionary basis without government intervention. These discretionary paid time-off programs include holidays, vacation, sick leave, personal days, integrated paid time-off policies, and bereavement or funeral leave. Federal or state laws play a role in other discretionary practices, including jury duty leave, military leave, and non-production time. The Family and Medical Leave Act of 1993 requires companies to grant extended leaves of absence to address family and medical circumstances. U.S. companies with operations in foreign countries typically offer the same set of paid time-off benefits in addition to others geared toward helping those employees and their accompanying family members stay in touch with family and friends in the United States and to benefit from additional rest and relaxation. As we discuss later, U.S. companies are obligated to follow the laws of foreign countries pertaining to mandatory paid time-off.

Companies offer most paid time-off as a matter of custom, particularly paid holidays. In unionized settings, paid time-off provisions are specified within the collective bargaining agreement. The paid time-off practices that are most typically found in unionized settings are jury duty, funeral leave, military leave, cleanup, preparation, travel time, rest period, and lunch period.

Both employees and employers place a lot of significance on paid time-off benefits. These benefits provide employees the opportunity to balance work and nonwork interests and demands. Companies stand to gain from sponsoring these benefits. Employees may legitimately take time-off from scheduled work without incurring loss of pay and benefits, which should help reduce unapproved or unscheduled absenteeism from work. By keeping scheduled absenteeism in check, overall productivity and product or service quality should be higher. Also, these benefits contribute toward positive employee attitudes and commitment to the company, particularly for employees with longer lengths of service. As we discuss

EXHIBIT 9.1 Percent of Workers with Access to Selected Leave Benefits, by Worker Characteristics, Private Industry, National Compensation Survey, March 2008

Source: Bureau of Labor Statistics. 2008. *Employee Benefits in the United States, March 2008* (USDOL 08-1122). Online at www.bls.gov. Accessed April 11, 2009.

Characteristics	Leave Benefits (All workers = 100 percent)						Family Leave*	
	Paid Holidays	Paid Vacations	Paid Personal Leave	Paid Funeral Leave	Paid Jury Duty Leave	Paid Military Leave	Paid	Unpaid
All workers	77	78	37	69	71	48	8	83
Worker characteristics								
Management, professional, and related	89	87	55	86	88	66	15	90
Management, business, and financial	96	96	54	89	92	68	16	92
Professional and related	86	84	55	84	86	65	14	89
Service	52	61	26	49	55	34	5	78
Sales and office	81	80	39	73	75	50	8	85
Sales and related	72	72	34	66	70	45	6	83
Office and administrative support	88	86	42	78	79	53	10	85
Natural resources, construction, and maintenance	76	76	26	56	56	38	6	76
Construction, extraction, farming, fishing, and forestry	62	63	18	41	42	29	4	70
Installation, maintenance, and repair	93	91	35	75	73	50	8	82
Production, transportation, and material moving	85	83	32	69	71	46	4	84
Production	92	90	32	73	75	52	5	85
Transportation and material moving	78	76	31	65	68	40	4	82
Full time	89	90	42	77	79	54	9	86
Part time	40	39	21	42	48	30	4	73
Union	85	84	47	82	83	56	7	90
Nonunion	76	77	36	67	70	47	8	83

*The sum of paid and unpaid family leave may exceed 100 percent because some workers have access to both types of plans.

233

shortly, the length of paid time-off such as vacation can increase substantially with length of service.

According to the U.S. Bureau of Labor Statistics, paid leave for workers in the private and public sectors (state and local government) is as follows[1]:

It is common for U.S. employers to offer paid leave to their workers in forms such as holidays, vacations, sick leave, and personal leave. Employers typically incur substantial costs in doing so. As of early 2008, state and local government workers averaged 11 holidays per year while workers in private-sector establishments averaged 8 days. Paid-leave costs were higher for government employers than for employers in private industry, both in number of dollars and as a percentage of total compensation. In March 2008, the average cost per hour worked for paid leave in the public sector was $3.12, which accounted for 8.2 percent of total compensation. The cost per hour in the private sector was $1.80, which accounted for 6.7 percent of total compensation.

Paid holidays were available to 77 percent of private-industry workers as of March 2008, and paid vacation leave was available to 78 percent of the workers (see Exhibit 9.1). Sixty-eight percent of state and local government workers received paid holidays, and 60 percent received paid vacation leave. Government workers' access to paid holidays and vacation leave was lower than that of their private-sector counterparts, primarily because workers in education occupations typically work 9 or 10 months per year and many do not receive paid holidays. For example, 29 percent of public-sector primary, secondary, and special education schoolteachers received paid holidays and only 9 percent received paid vacation leave. Compared with access to holidays and vacation leave, access to sick leave was less frequent in private industry than in government employment. Vacation leave was the most costly of the paid-leave benefits, with a cost of 92 cents in private industry and $1.08 in state and local government. The cost of holidays was 59 cents in private industry and $1.02 in state and local government. Sick leave averaged 22 cents in private industry and 78 cents in state and local government, while personal leave averaged 6 cents in private industry and 23 cents in state and local government.

Private-industry occupations that pay higher compensation incur higher paid-leave costs. For example, the average worker in management, professional, and related occupations, in which total compensation averaged $47.55, received $3.96 in paid-leave benefits; this was equal to 8.3 percent of total compensation. In contrast, service workers, who averaged $13.27 in total compensation, received 58 cents in paid-leave benefits, or 4.4 percent of total compensation.

PAID TIME-OFF PRACTICES

In this chapter, we review the following paid time-off practices:

- Holidays
- Vacation
- Sick leave
- Personal leave
- Integrated paid time-off policies

- Bereavement or funeral leave
- Jury duty and witness duty leaves
- Military leave
- Nonproduction time
- On-call time
- Sabbatical leave
- Volunteerism

Holidays

Private sector employers usually follow holiday time-off practices for federal government employees. Federal law establishes 12 public holidays with pay for federal government employees (Exhibit 9.2).[2] Most federal government employees work five days a week—Monday through Friday. When holidays fall on a weekend day, employees receive a day off during the workweek to observe the holiday. Federal government employees receive the Friday preceding an official holiday that falls on Saturday, and the Monday following an official holiday that falls on Sunday as observed holidays. Every state has laws that recognize holidays as paid time-off for its employees. Some states include additional paid holidays such as time-off on public election days. Most private sector employers choose not to recognize state-specific public holidays, such as Pulaski Day in Illinois.

Some companies add one or two floating holidays to the list of regularly scheduled holidays. **Floating holidays** allow employees to take paid time-off to observe any holiday not included on the employer's list of recognized paid holidays. Oftentimes, companies do not limit floating holidays to federal or state holidays. Employees may use floating holidays to extend the allotted number of paid vacation days or sick leave.

EXHIBIT 9.2 **United States Office of Personnel Management: Federal Holidays**	

Source: U.S. Office of Personnel Management. *2011 Federal Holidays.* Online at www.opm.gov/fedhol/. Accessed April 11, 2009.

Friday, December 31, 2010*	New Year's Day
Monday, January 17	Birthday of Martin Luther King, Jr.
Monday, February 21†	Washington's Birthday
Monday, May 30	Memorial Day
Monday, July 4	Independence Day
Monday, September 5	Labor Day
Monday, October 10	Columbus Day
Friday, November 11	Veterans Day
Thursday, November 24	Thanksgiving Day
Monday, December 26‡	Christmas Day

*January 1, 2011 (the legal public holiday for New Year's Day), falls on a Saturday. For most federal employees, Friday, December 31, 2010, will be treated as a holiday for pay and leave purposes.

†This holiday is designated as "Washington's Birthday," the law that specifies holidays for federal employees. Though other institutions such as state and local governments and private businesses may use other names, it is our policy to always refer to holidays by the names designated in the law.

‡December 25, 2011 (the legal public holiday for Christmas Day), falls on a Sunday. For most federal employees, Monday, December 26, will be treated as a holiday for pay and leave purposes.

Companies must pay attention to the treatment of religious holidays that, except for Christmas, are not included on any list of federal or state public holidays. Title VII of the Civil Rights Act prohibits illegal discrimination in employment practices on the basis of sex, religion, color, race, and national origin. The Equal Employment Opportunity Commission (EEOC) established guidelines that encourage companies to honor employee wishes to observe religious holidays, unless doing so would cause undue hardship to both the company and some employees.[3] From the EEOC's perspective, undue hardship addresses two issues: the cost of accommodation (e.g., cost of temporary replacements) and denial of the rights of other employees to benefits under a bona fide seniority system. The EEOC guidelines do not require companies to pay employees when they take time-off to observe religious holidays. Nevertheless, it is imperative that companies treat the observance of religious holidays uniformly as paid or unpaid time-off. Employees who feel they are being discriminated against on religious grounds may file a complaint at the nearest EEOC field office (www.eeoc.gov/offices.html).

It is not uncommon for holidays to occur when some employees are on scheduled vacation leave or absent because of illness. Companies must decide whether to count such instances of paid holidays as a paid vacation day or sickness day. Most often, companies choose to recognize a holiday that overlaps with paid vacation or illness as a holiday rather than as a charge against an employee's allotted paid vacation or sick leave.

Some companies extend paid time-off for holidays by granting one or two days preceding or following the holiday. The most widespread practice is to extend the Thursday Thanksgiving holiday by adding the next Friday and to recognize Christmas Eve as a paid holiday. Companies that operate on a Monday-through-Friday workweek schedule may designate Thursday or Friday as paid time-off when the holiday occurs on Wednesday.

Vacation

Companies grant vacation days solely on a discretionary basis to employees. As a discretionary benefit, vacation days may be viewed as a reward. Does paying employees for rest and relaxation seem like a good investment? Increasingly, researchers believe so. An emerging sentiment is that companies provide employees additional days off with pay given the benefits of rest and relaxation to health and long-term productivity. After all, many European countries have laws that require substantially more paid time-off for vacation than the typical 5 to 10 workdays offered by most companies in the United States.

Vacation policies entail five important considerations.

- Eligibility for vacation leave.
- Single or multiple vacation policies for different occupational groups.
- Rules for determining the amount of available vacation time per year.
- Avoiding conflicts between vacation time and pressing work deadlines.
- Handling unused vacation time at the end of the year.

First, who is eligible to receive vacation benefits? Employees generally become eligible for vacation benefits after fulfilling a minimum seniority requirement ranging anywhere between six months and one year of full-time employment. Companies may exclude part-time employees from receiving vacation benefits. Part-time employees who earn vacation benefits earn fewer days than full-time employees.

Second, companies must decide whether to set up a single vacation policy for all employees or separate ones for different employee groups. The choice to use separate policies usually provides more vacation benefits to managerial, professional, and executive-level employees to recognize the presumed higher direct impact of these employees on company performance.

Third, vacation policies specify rules for the allotment of vacation days per calendar or fiscal year. Some companies allot the same number of vacation days per employee each calendar or fiscal year. Most often, companies recognize employee seniority as the basis for allotment. Companies may indicate a particular number of annual vacation days per range of annual seniority, for example:

Employment	Vacation Earned
Less than one year	Ineligible for vacation benefits
1–5 years	5 days
6–9 years	10 days
10–19 years	15 days

Companies may also choose to increase vacation benefits by a smaller increment for each additional year of employment, for instance:

Employment	Vacation Earned
Less than one year	Ineligible for vacation benefits
One year but less than two	5 days
Two years but less than three	6 days
Three years but less than four	7 days

And so forth.

Alternatively, companies may opt to determine vacation benefits according to the number of hours worked. Usually, this approach applies to nonexempt workers as designated by the overtime pay provision of the Fair Labor Standards Act of 1938 (FLSA). Generally, administrative, professional, and executive employees are **exempt** from the FLSA overtime and minimum wage provisions. Most other jobs are *nonexempt*. **Nonexempt jobs** are subject to the FLSA overtime pay provision. There often has been controversy regarding who is actually eligible for FLSA overtime pay, in part based on the amount of an individual's earnings. In Chapter 4, we discussed the *FairPay* rules and some of the complexity in determining eligibility for overtime pay.

The following is an example of a vacation policy for nonexempt employees:

Years of Service	Hours of Vacation Earned per Biweekly Pay Period	Maximum Hours Earned per Year
Less than one year	Ineligible for vacation benefits	
1–4	4.00	104 hours or 13 days
5–9	4.62	120 hours or 15 days
10–14	5.52	144 hours or 18 days
15–19	6.46	168 hours or 21 days
20 or more	7.04	184 hours or 23 days

A fourth vacation policy provision addresses the basis for scheduling employee vacations to avoid creating temporary staffing shortages. Most often, employees must place a request for approval with supervisors or department managers. The request should indicate the start date and return-to-work date. When two or more employees request the same or substantially overlapping vacation periods, supervisors decide who may take vacation, usually giving priority to employees with greater seniority.

Fifth, vacation policies should specify carryover and cashout provisions. **Carryover provisions** permit employees to take unused vacation time awarded for a calendar or fiscal year during a subsequent calendar or fiscal year. Alternatively, vacation policies may require that employees take allotted vacation days during the designated year, forfeiting any unused vacation days for that period. Many employees refer to this choice as a **"use it or lose it" provision.** Policies that prohibit carryover may include a cashout provision. **Cashout provisions** pay employees an amount equal to the unused vacation days based on regular daily earnings.

Vacation benefits are subject to taxation when employees take vacation time. Employees pay federal and applicable state and municipal income taxes on vacation pay. Employers pay taxes under the Federal Income Contributions Act (FICA) and Federal Unemployment Tax Act (FUTA), both discussed in Chapter 8. Employers may also deduct vacation payments as business expenses. Vacation benefits are not subject to reporting requirements of the Employee Retirement Income Security Act (ERISA) of 1974, with one exception: vacation trusts of multiemployer welfare plans. In general, multiemployer plans are benefits plans to which more than one employer is required to contribute based on a collective bargaining agreement.

Most employers have instituted vacation policies without making exceptions to save costs such as not permitting employees to take time-off with pay. However, a more extreme practice has emerged that is characterized by employers desperate to make deeper cost savings during severe economic downturns. Increasingly, employers are shutting down operations for up to several weeks per year—often requiring employees to use paid vacation days or imposing mandatory time-off without pay during shutdown periods. Until recently, such mandatory leaves were used sporadically over the past several decades at workplaces as diverse as factories and software manufacturers during slowing demand. Employees' response to mandatory leaves is far less negative than anticipated when employers educate them that such forced leaves reduce the likelihood of permanent layoffs.

Sick Leave

Companies offer **sick leave** benefits to compensate employees for a specified number of days absent due to personal illness. Sick leave policies are separate from disability leave policies (Chapter 7) because they are designed to compensate employees when absent because of occasional minor illness or injury. Sometimes, these policies permit employees to take time-off with pay to care for an ill child, spouse, or parent within the limits of allotted days. Although beneficial to employees, sick leave plans can be disruptive and financially threatening to employers, particularly during challenging economic times when companies are desperate to accomplish more work at the lowest possible costs. For example, the U.S. Department of Labor cited American Airlines' management for improperly docking the pay of two absent pilots even though they provided the necessary medical documentation required by company policy.

Certification of illness is an important feature of sick leave policies. Some companies require that employees provide evidence of illness—for example, a note from a physician—to qualify for payment, while others do not require any certification. The decision to require medical certification often rests on the incidence of unscheduled absenteeism among members of the workforce. For the purposes of this discussion, unscheduled absences occur when an employee does not report to work at the scheduled time for the entire shift. Illness is perhaps the most socially acceptable reason for an unscheduled absence. Employees are probably more likely to attribute unscheduled absences to illness than to other reasons (e.g., a day at the beach). Unscheduled absences can easily impair productivity and push up costs. Companies that experience problems with unscheduled absences may require certification from a recognized health professional rather than rely on the employee's self-reported reason. Alternatively, a company may grant a relatively limited number of paid sick days and additional approved sick days without pay. Presumably, employees will be less willing to use sick days for other purposes when pay is at risk.

Personal Leave

Personal leave policies grant paid time-off for virtually any reason. Companies may choose to limit the scope of personal leave policies by specifying acceptable reasons. These policies usually apply to short-term leaves for personal reasons. Common uses of personal leave include the proverbial mental health day that allows employees the opportunity to "recharge their batteries"; for example, employees may spend a day at the beach, catch up on personal errands, or simply relax at home. Alternatively, employees may use personal leave to extend a vacation period or sick leave. Companies allot a fixed number of personal days each year to all full-time employees, or they award this benefit based on employee seniority. Annual allotments may range from 1 to 10 days. Similar to vacation and sick leave, carryover and cashout provisions apply. Pay for personal leave is subject to taxation. The Internal Revenue Service treats personal leave pay as regular income, subject to federal and state income tax. Employers deduct the amount of pay for personal leave as a business expense, and they deduct FICA and FUTA taxes.

Integrated Paid Time-Off Policies or Paid Time-Off Banks

Some employers combine holiday, vacation, sick leave, and personal leave policies into a single paid time-off policy. These **integrated paid time-off policies** or **paid time-off banks** do not distinguish among reasons for absence as specific policies do. The idea is to provide individuals the freedom to schedule time-off without justifying the reasons. Presumably, this freedom should substantially reduce the incidence of unscheduled absences that can be disruptive to the workplace because these policies require advance notice unless sudden illness is the cause (e.g., you went to sleep one evening feeling fine and then woke up the next morning on a scheduled work day with the stomach flu). Integrated paid time-off policies have become an increasingly popular alternative to separate holiday, vacation, sick leave, and personal leave plans because they are more effective in controlling unscheduled absenteeism than other types of absence control policies.[4] Also, integrated policies relieve the administrative burden of managing separate plans and the necessity to process medical certifications in the case of sick leave policies.

Paid time-off banks do not incorporate all types of time-off with pay. Bereavement or funeral leave is a stand-alone policy because the death of a friend or relative is typically an unanticipated event beyond an employee's control. Also, integrating funeral leave into paid time-off banks would likely create dissatisfaction among workers because it would signal that grieving for a deceased friend or relative is equivalent to a casual day off. Jury duty and witness leave, military leave, and nonproduction time are influenced by law, and nonproduction time is negotiated as part of a collective bargaining agreement. Sabbatical leaves are also not included in paid time-off banks because these are extended leaves provided as a reward to valued, long-service employees.

Effective paid time-off bank policies slowly increase the number of days an employee may use for time-off. For example, an employee may accumulate as many as 12 paid days off at the rate of one day per month during the first year of employment. That number may increase to 16 paid days off at the rate of 1.25 days per month during the second through fifth years of employment, respectively. Patterns such as this may extend to longer service lengths. Companies structure paid time-off banks in this fashion to reward longer-service employees who have proven their worth to the company.

Effective paid time-off bank policies include a carryover provision rather than a use-it-or-lose-it provision. Carryover policies limit the likely flood of absences that would occur toward the end of the year because employees do not feel compelled as if they were to lose a valuable unused benefit. In this case, this benefit is time-off with pay.

Companies may further curtail unscheduled time-off by compensating an employee at rates lower than full pay. For example, a company may choose to provide 90 percent of pay for each day an employee is absent. In this scenario, an employee is assuming some of the responsibility for unscheduled absences.

Bereavement or Funeral Leave

Bereavement leave or **funeral leave** provides paid time-off for employees, usually following the death of a relative. A bereavement policy specifies the relatives whose death qualifies employees for leave. Some policies are more liberal because they include unmarried domestic partners and friends. Companies grant a limited number of days off with pay for each death, ranging anywhere between one and five days. Some companies designate allowable amounts depending on the relationship between the employee and the deceased, offering longer periods for immediate relatives (e.g., a parent or spouse) and shorter periods for less immediate relatives (e.g., a cousin) or friends. The Internal Revenue Service treats pay for bereavement leave as regular income, subject to federal and state income tax. Employers deduct the amount of pay for bereavement leave as a business expense, and they deduct FICA and FUTA taxes.

Jury Duty and Witness Duty Leaves

Most employers choose to pay employees while serving on a jury or as a witness in a court of law. **Jury duty** leave policies are guided by federal and state law; **witness duty** policies are guided by state law in only about half of all states. At the federal level, the **Jury Systems Improvement Act of 1978** recognizes that participation on a jury in federal court is a protected right of an individual. Employers can neither prohibit employees from exercising this right nor treat employees who exercise this right less favorably. Unfavorable treatment includes intimidation of employees with threats of discharge or actual termination for participating on juries. Violations of this law come with penalties ranging from civil penalties of up to $1,000 per violation per employee to payment of lost wages and reinstatement with credit for lost seniority.

State laws regarding jury participation in state courts are similar to federal laws applicable to jury participation in federal courts. In general, these laws prohibit employers from treating employees who serve on state court juries unfavorably. Violations can lead to monetary fines. Unlike federal law, some states (e.g., New Jersey and Tennessee) mandate that employers compensate employees for the duration of jury duty. Montana is currently the only state without jury participation laws.

The Fair Labor Standards Act prohibits employers from reducing the salaries of exempt-status employees while participating on a jury, with two exceptions. The government pays jurors a nominal amount for participation. The first exception allows employers to reduce salary only by the government's payment amount for jury duty that lasts less than one regular workweek. The second exception applies to jury participation lasting one week or more. Employers may reduce pay only for each full workweek in which an exempt-status employee does not perform any work.

Taxation of pay for jury duty is somewhat complex. The Internal Revenue Service classifies government payments for jury duty as taxable income, requiring employees to pay applicable taxes. The duty of employers pertaining to FICA and FUTA withholdings for regular pay depends on the following conditions:

- Employers reduce regular earnings by the amount paid for jury participation by the government. In this case, employers withhold FICA and FUTA taxes on the difference between regular pay and the sum paid by the government for jury participation. Employers treat the amount of this difference as a regular business expense eligible for tax deduction.

- Employers pay regular wage or salary and they allow employees to keep the government's payment for jury participation. In this case, employers withhold FICA and FUTA taxes on both payments.
- For jury duty lasting less than one full workweek, employers pay regular wage or salary in exchange for jury payments. In this case, employees deduct the amount of jury payment from gross income. Employers withhold FICA and FUTA taxes on the wage or salary payments made during this period. However, this rule does not apply if the absence is for one or more full workweeks during which the employee performs no work.

Witness duty laws are currently limited to 20 states plus Puerto Rico and the District of Columbia. These laws usually specify the criteria of witness status (e.g., victim of a crime, subpoena by a court of law), provisions regarding prohibition of employer retaliation, the employee's duty to provide reasonable notice, and penalties for companies in violation.

Military Leave

Military leave policy is guided by federal and state laws, focusing on an employer's obligation to reemploy previously employed individuals following the completion of military service. At the federal level, the **Uniformed Services Employment and Reemployment Rights Act of 1994 (USERRA)**[5] extends reemployment rights to persons who have been absent from a position of employment because of service in the uniformed services on a voluntary or involuntary basis, including active duty, inactive duty training, full-time National Guard duty, and time for a fitness-for-duty examination. Time limits for returning to work following military service depend on the duration of military service. For example, for military service ranging between 1 and 30 days, an individual must report to his or her employer by the beginning of the first regularly scheduled workday that falls at least eight hours after the end of the calendar day. These time limits apply to returns from fitness examinations.

Employers may not discriminate or retaliate against a past or present member of the uniformed service who has applied for membership in the uniformed service or is obligated to serve in the uniformed service. USERRA offers protection against denial of initial employment, reemployment, retention in employment, promotion, or any benefit of employment because of this status. For example, protected individuals possess the right to elect to continue their existing employer-based health plan coverage for them and their dependents for up to 24 months while in the military. When reemployed following the completion of military service, employers are required to reinstate covered employees in the health plan, generally without any waiting periods or preexisting condition exclusions. Exceptions to this rule apply to service-connected illnesses or injuries.

Nonproduction Time

In general, **nonproduction time** refers to a variety of possible uses of time related to, but not in actual performance of, the main job duties, or it can refer to periods of nonwork time during a work shift. Nonproduction time related to the performance of job duties includes cleanup, preparation, and travel between job locations. Nonwork time during a work shift includes rest periods or "breaks" and periods to eat a meal.

The Fair Labor Standards Act of 1938 contains provisions about compensating employees for nonproduction time. Employees must be paid for time devoted to principal work activities—that is, performing the tasks and duties described in their job descriptions. In addition, employers must compensate employees for duties and activities that are indispensable to performing principal activities. Such duties and tasks include preparatory and concluding activities, regardless of whether these activities occur outside the regular work shift. Typical examples of compensable nonproduction time include time for:

- Cleanup.
- Preparation.
- Travel time between job locations within the scope of the regular work shift.
- Rest periods shorter than 20 minutes.
- Meal periods at least 30 minutes in duration when employees must take their lunch at their workstation.

On-Call Time

According to the U.S. Department of Labor, employers must compensate nonexempt employees for on-call time. **On-call time** requires spending time on or close to the employer's premises so that employees cannot use the time effectively for their own purposes. Virtually every employer can demand that nonexempt employees be available on an as-needed basis. For example, medical technologists and nursing staff members must be available to report to work for scheduled hours outside normal shifts when there are major medical emergencies at hospital facilities. Also, companies may place some of their maintenance staff on call to respond to major emergencies such as chemical spills or the breakdown of assembly lines during off-hours.

Nonexempt employees subject to on-call time must be compensated according to the minimum wage provisions of the Fair Labor Standards Act of 1938 (FLSA, see Chapter 4). Employers may require that exempt-status employees fulfill on-call time. However, the FLSA does not require that employers offer additional compensation for time while on call.

The concept of on-call time appears to be relatively straightforward. In practice, a multitude of court cases have focused on the on-call time policies of many employers to determine whether nonexempt employees should be compensated. Naturally, employers tend to resist compensating employees for on-call time, particularly when employees do not ultimately report to work during this period.

For instance, in *Owens v. Local No. 169,* a federal appeals court judge ruled that the time pulp mill mechanics spent on call was not compensable under FLSA since the on-call policy of the employer, while giving on-call employees the option of wearing a beeper, did not significantly restrict them from engaging in personal activities. Under the employer's policy, the mechanics were not required to remain at home or respond to specific calls. They only had to accept a "fair share" of calls, averaging six calls a year. Indeed, employees engaged in extensive personal activities during their on-call time. Therefore, the court held that the mechanics were not entitled to compensation for their on-call time.[6]

Sabbatical Leave

Sabbatical leave practices are common in college and university settings and apply most often to faculty members. Sabbatical leaves are paid time-off for professional activities such as a research project or curriculum development. Universities grant sabbatical leaves to faculty members who meet minimum service requirements (usually three years of full-time service) with partial or full pay for up to an entire academic year. The service requirement is applied each time, which limits the number of leaves taken per faculty member.

Employers outside the academic world have begun offering sabbatical leaves of absence to employees to further professional development. According to the Society for Human Resource Management, approximately 11 percent of large companies offer paid sabbaticals to employees and another 29 percent offer unpaid sabbaticals.[7] Previously, only large companies were known for offering employees sabbatical leaves. Nowadays, about 16 percent of small companies and 21 percent of midsize companies today offer unpaid sabbaticals.

Outside academia, sabbatical leaves are usually limited to professional and managerial employees who stand to benefit from intensive training opportunities outside the company's sponsorship. Sabbatical leaves are most suitable for employees such as computer engineers whose standards of knowledge or practice are rapidly evolving. Companies establish guidelines regarding qualification, length of leave, and level of pay. An important guideline pertains to minimum length of employment following completion of a sabbatical. For example, companies require employees to remain employed for a minimum of one year following the sabbatical or repay part or all of one's salary received during the sabbatical. This provision is necessary to protect a company's investment and to limit moves to competitors.

As reported in the Conference Board report,[8] a survey of U.S. companies identified five different types of sabbatical leave programs:

1. *Traditional Sabbaticals.* They are always paid leaves and employees expect to return to their same jobs at the end of the leave. Such leaves provide employees a chance to renew or retool themselves in areas related to their work.

2. *Personal Growth Leaves.* These leaves allow employees to further their education or acquire new skills or knowledge that will directly benefit them personally and subsequently be of benefit to the company.

3. *Social Service Leaves.* These are fully paid leaves in which the employee performs a significant public service, either in the local community or in other areas

important to the company. Such leaves not only enhance the employee's personal growth but also the company's image as a responsible corporate citizen.

4. *Extended Personal Leaves.* These are normally unpaid leaves that provide a significant break of two years or more with return-to-work guarantees. These leaves are commonly taken by employees with young children.

5. *Voluntary Leaves to Meet Business Needs.* These are leaves that are intended to serve the company in times of downsizing or low production in which the company offers employees extended time-off in the form of unpaid leaves.

Volunteerism

Volunteerism refers to giving one's time to support a meaningful cause. More and more companies are providing employees with paid time-off to contribute to causes of their choice. From a company's standpoint, a meaningful cause is associated with the work of nonprofit organizations such as the United Way to help improve the well-being of people. A multitude of meaningful causes exist throughout the world, such as improving literacy, providing comfort to terminally ill patients, serving food at shelters for individuals who cannot afford to feed themselves, serving as a mentor to children who do not have one or more parents, and spending time with elderly or disabled residents of nursing homes who may no longer have living friends or family. Companies generally do not dictate the causes for which employees would receive paid time-off, except that they exclude political campaign and political action groups for eligibility because of possible conflicts of interest with company shareholders and management.

Companies favor providing paid time-off for volunteer work for three reasons. First, volunteer opportunities allow employees to balance work and life demands. Second, giving employees the opportunity to contribute to charitable causes on company time represents positive corporate social responsibility, thus enhancing the company's overall image in the public eye. Third, paid time-off to volunteer is believed to help promote retention. Employees are likely to feel that the employer shares similar values, possibly boosting commitment to the company. Ultimately, the amount of time-off varies considerably from company to company, ranging anywhere between one hour per week to several weeks (the latter employed in limited cases for long-service employees).

LEAVE UNDER THE FAMILY AND MEDICAL LEAVE ACT OF 1993

The **Family and Medical Leave Act (FMLA)** provides employees job protection in cases of family or medical emergency.[9] The basic thrust of the act is guaranteed leave, and a key element of that guarantee is the right of the employee to return either to the position he or she left when the leave began or to an equivalent position with the same benefits, pay, and other terms and conditions of employment. This job restoration clause has certain provisions, which we will discuss later in this chapter. Exhibit 9.3 summarizes employee rights under FMLA.

EXHIBIT 9.3 Your Rights under the Family and Medical Leave Act of 1993

Source: U.S. Department of Labor, Employment Standards Administration, Wage and Hour Division, *WH Publication 1420,* Washington, DC: U.S. Government Printing Office, 1993.

FMLA requires covered employers to provide up to 12 weeks of unpaid, job-protected leave to "eligible" employees for certain family and medical reasons.

Employees are eligible if they have worked for a covered employer for at least one year, and for 1,250 hours over the previous 12 months, and if there are at least 50 employees within 75 miles.

Reasons for Taking Leave:

Unpaid leave must be granted for *any* of the following reasons:

- To care for the employee's child after birth or placement for adoption or foster care;
- To care for the employee's spouse, son or daughter, or parent, who has a serious health condition; or
- For a serious health condition that makes the employee unable to perform the employee's job.

At the employee's or employer's option, certain kinds of *paid* leave may be substituted for unpaid leave.

Advance Notice and Medical Certification:

The employee may be required to provide advance leave notice and medical certification. Taking of leave may be denied if requirements are not met.

- The employee ordinarily must provide 30 days' advance notice when the leave is "foreseeable."
- An employer may require medical certification to support a request for leave because of a serious health condition, and may require second or third opinions (at the employer's expense) and a fitness for duty report to return to work.

Job Benefits and Protection:

- For the duration of FMLA leave, the employer must maintain the employee's health coverage under any "group health plan."
- Upon return from FMLA leave, most employees must be restored to their original or equivalent positions with equivalent pay, benefits, and other employment terms.
- The use of FMLA leave cannot result in the loss of any employment benefit that accrued prior to the start of an employee's leave.

Unlawful Acts by Employers:

FMLA makes it unlawful for any employer to:

- Interfere with, restrain, or deny the exercise of any right provided under FMLA;
- Discharge or discriminate against any person for opposing any practice made unlawful by FMLA or for involvement in any proceeding under or relating to FMLA.

Enforcement:

- The U.S. Department of Labor is authorized to investigate and resolve complaints of violations.
- An eligible employee may bring a civil action against an employer for violations.

FMLA does not affect any federal or state law prohibiting discrimination, or supersede any state or local law or collective bargaining agreement that provides greater family or medical leave rights.

For Additional Information:

Contact the nearest office of the Wage and Hour Division, listed in most telephone directories under U.S. Government, Department of Labor.

The FMLA does not require employers to pay employees while on family leave; most companies choose not to pay them. However, the FMLA does require employers to maintain group health insurance coverage for an employee on FMLA leave whenever such insurance was provided before the leave was taken. In addition, employers must provide insurance protection on the same terms as if the employee had continued to work.

Under certain circumstances, employees may choose to substitute paid leave for unpaid FMLA leave. Where an employee has earned or accrued paid vacation, personal, or family leave, that paid leave may be substituted for all or part of any (otherwise) unpaid FMLA leave relating to a birth, placement of a child for adoption or foster care, or care for a spouse, child, or parent who has a serious health condition. This provision is important to many employees who cannot afford to take *unpaid* FMLA.

For example, let's assume an employee named John Smith has just learned that his spouse has become critically ill and will need extensive care at home. John has accumulated (i.e., he has not used) 13 days of paid vacation and 12 days of paid personal sick leave. Under FMLA, John may take up to 12 weeks of unpaid leave. Because John has accumulated 25 days of paid leave time by combining his unused paid sick and vacation leave, he will be paid for up to five weeks (i.e., 25 days of paid leave divided by 5 workdays per week) of his 12-week FMLA leave.

The Family and Medical Leave Act applies to all local, state, and federal government employers in addition to private sector companies with 50 or more workers employed during 20 or more weeks in the preceding or current calendar year. Employees of covered employers qualify for FMLA leave if they have worked at least 1,250 hours over the previous 12 months in the United States or in any territory or possession of the United States where at least 50 employees are employed by the employer within 75 miles.

Employees eligible for leave may take up to a total of 12 workweeks of unpaid leave during any 12-month period for one or more of the following reasons:

- Birth and care of the newborn child of the employee.
- Placement with the employee of a son or daughter for adoption or foster care.
- Care for an immediate family member (spouse, child, or parent) with a serious health condition.
- Medical leave when the employee is unable to work because of a serious health condition.

Spouses employed by the same employer are jointly entitled to a combined total of 12 workweeks of family leave for the birth and care of the newborn child, placement of a child for adoption or foster care, and care for a parent who has a serious health condition.

Circumstances warranting the leave determine whether employees may take the entire 12-week leave on a consecutive basis or intermittently. Employers give approval for intermittent leave for the birth and care of a child or placement for adoption or foster care. Medical circumstances trigger intermittent leave to care for a seriously ill family member or in the event of serious personal illness.

Employees must give employers a minimum 30-day advance notification of leave when the event is expected (e.g., birth of a child).

The first major revisions to the FMLA were instituted in January 2009. The changes create leave opportunities for the military and require employees to adhere to stricter guidelines for taking leave. Relatives of seriously injured members of the military may take up to 26 weeks off to care for their injured military family members. In addition, relatives of members of the National Guard or reserves who are called to active duty may receive up to 12 weeks of leave to attend military programs (official send-off of the family member's troop), arrange child care, or make financial arrangements. Nonmilitary workers who claim to have chronic health conditions (for example, ongoing back pain) must see their doctor at least twice per year for documentation. In addition, approved FMLA leave is considered absenteeism from the standpoint of disqualifying employees from perfect-attendance awards or bonuses. For instance, an employer awards a $500 bonus to employees who do not miss scheduled workdays during a continuous six-month period. Employers may count approved FMLA leave as absences against the perfect attendance goal. Additional revisions to the FMLA may be on the horizon. For example, President Barack Obama may ask Congress to extend coverage by including companies that employ at least 25 workers. As noted, the current law applies to companies that employ at least 50 workers.

One final comment about family and medical leave warrants mention. As discussed, the FMLA provides *unpaid* leave. On September 23, 2002, the California governor signed legislation that allows employees to take partially paid family leave beginning after July 1, 2004. This paid family leave program allows workers to take up to six weeks off to care for a newborn, a newly adopted child, or an ill family member. Under this new law, employees are eligible to receive 55 percent of their wages during their absence. Unlike the unpaid family leave program that exists under the California Family Rights Act, all employers are covered by this legislation, not just those with 50 or more employees. However, also unlike the unpaid family leave program, businesses with under 50 employees are not required to hold a job for a worker who goes on paid family leave because doing so would likely cause financial hardship.

Employers possess the right to ask employees to furnish:

- Medical certification supporting the need for leave due to a serious health condition affecting the employee or an immediate family member.
- Second or third medical opinions paid by the employer and periodic recertification issued by a licensed health care provider.
- Periodic reports during FMLA leave regarding the employee's status and intent to return to work.

Upon return from FMLA leave, an employee must be restored to the original job, or to an equivalent job with equal pay, benefits, and other terms and conditions of employment. The FMLA also guarantees that employees retain all their benefits (e.g., seniority in the retirement system) earned prior to the leave. Employers possess the right not to restore employment for a limited set of employees if doing so would cause considerable and severe economic burden.

This exception applies only to the highest-paid 10 percent of employees within 75 miles of the work site when the employer fulfills the following obligations:

- Notifies the employee of his or her ineligibility in response to the employee's notice of intent to take FMLA leave.
- Notifies the employee as soon as the employer decides it will deny job restoration, and explain the reasons for this decision.
- Offers the employee a reasonable opportunity to return to work from FMLA leave after giving this notice.
- Makes a final determination whether reinstatement will be denied at the end of the leave period if the employee requests restoration.

FLEXIBLE SCHEDULING

Flexible scheduling allows employees the leeway to take time-off during work hours to care for dependent relatives or react to emergencies. Flexible scheduling, which includes programs such as compressed workweeks (such as four 10-hour days or three 12-hour days), flextime, and job sharing enable companies to help employees balance the demands of work and family.[10] As an aside, some companies allow employees to take paid leave or extend their legally mandated leave sanctioned by the Family and Medical Leave Act. Under extended leave, employers typically continue to provide fringe compensation like insurance and promise to secure individuals comparable jobs upon their return.

Many companies now offer flexible work schedules to employees to help them balance work and family responsibilities. Flextime and compressed workweek schedules are the most prominent flexible work schedules used in companies. Flexible work schedules generally apply to permanent, full-time employees rather than to contingent employees. Flextime, compressed workweeks, and telecommuting should provide single parents or dual-career parents with the opportunity to spend more time with their children. Flextime gives parents the opportunity to schedule work around special events at their children's schools. Compressed workweeks enable parents on limited incomes to save on day care costs by reducing the number of days at the office. Parents can benefit from telecommuting in a similar fashion. Likewise, dual-career couples living apart also benefit from flexible work schedules. Compressed workweeks and telecommuting reduce the time spouses have to spend away from each other.

Flextime Schedules

Flextime schedules allow employees to modify work schedules within specified limits set by the employer. Employees adjust when they will start work and when they will leave. However, flextime generally does not lead to reduced work hours. For instance, an employee may choose to work between 10 a.m. and 6 p.m., 9 a.m. and 5 p.m., or 8 a.m. and 4 p.m.

All workers must be present during **core hours**—certain workday hours when business activity is regularly high. The number of core hours may vary from company to company, by departments within companies, or by season. Although employees are relatively free to choose start and completion times that fall outside core hours, management must carefully coordinate these times to avoid under-staffing. Some flextime programs incorporate a **banking hours** feature. The banking hours feature enables employees to vary the number of work hours daily as long as they maintain the regular number of work hours on a weekly basis.

Employers can expect three possible benefits from using flextime schedules. First, flextime schedules lead to lower tardiness and absenteeism. Flexibly defining the workweek better enables employees to schedule medical and other appointments outside work hours. As a result, workers are less likely to be late or miss work altogether.

Second, flexible work schedules should lead to higher work productivity. Employees have greater choice about when to work during the day. Individuals who work best during the morning hours may schedule morning hours, while individuals who work best during the afternoons or evenings will choose those times. In addition, possessing the flexibility to attend to personal matters outside work should help employees focus on doing their jobs better.

Third, flexible work schedules benefit employers by creating longer business hours and better service. Staggering employee schedules should enable businesses to stay open longer hours without incurring overtime pay expenses. Also, customers should perceive better service because of expanded business hours. Companies that conduct business by telephone on national and international bases will more likely be open during the normal operating hours of customers in other time zones.

Two possible limitations of flexible work schedules include increased overhead costs and coordination problems. Maintaining extended operations leads to higher overhead costs including support staff and utilities. In addition, flexible work schedules may lead to work coordination problems when some employees who work together are not present at the same time.

Compressed Workweek Schedules

Compressed workweek schedules enable employees to perform their work in fewer days than a regular five-day workweek. As a result, employees may work four 10-hour days or three 12-hour days. These schedules can promote a company's recruitment and retention successes by:

- Reducing the number of times employees must commute between home and work.
- Providing more time together for dual-career couples who live in different cities.

However, employers may face challenges when implementing compressed workweek benefits. More employees than can feasibly be accommodated may wish to work on compressed schedules. For example, parents of young children may favor schedules that allow them to be at home before the end of the school day.

Employers and employees often wonder whether the Fair Labor Standards Act (Chapter 4) addresses overtime pay issues for employees who work on flexible schedules. The FLSA does not regulate flexible work schedules. Alternative work arrangements such as flexible work schedules are a matter of agreement between the employer and the employee (or the employee's representative). Relatedly, the FLSA does not regulate job-sharing arrangements where two (or more) workers share the duties of one full-time job, each working part time; or two or more workers who have unrelated part-time assignments. As is the case with flexible work scheduling, the FLSA does not address job sharing. Rather, it is a matter of agreement between an employer and an employee (or the employee's representative).

Telecommuting

Telecommuting represents alternative work arrangements in which employees perform work at home or some other location besides the office. More than 19.8 million people telecommuted in May 2001 (the most recent national data available at the time of this text's publication).[11] Telecommuters generally spend part of their time working in the office and other times working at home. This alternative work arrangement is appropriate for work that does not require regular, direct interpersonal interactions with other workers. Examples include accounting, systems analysis, and telephone sales. Telecommuters stay in touch with co-workers and superiors through electronic mail, telephone, and fax. Exhibit 9.4 lists a variety of possible telecommuting arrangements.

Potential benefits for employers include increased productivity and lower overhead costs for office space and supplies. Telecommuting also serves as an effective recruiting and retention practice for employees who strongly desire to perform their jobs away from the office. Employers may also increase the retention of valued employees who choose not to move when their companies relocate.

Employees find telecommuting beneficial. Telecommuting enables parents to be near their infants or preschool-age children, and to be home when older children finish their school days. In addition, telecommuting arrangements minimize commuting time and expense, which are exceptional in such congested metropolitan areas as Boston, Los Angeles, and New York City. Travel time may increase

EXHIBIT 9.4   **Alternative Telecommuting Arrangements**

Source: Adapted from Bureau of National Affairs, "Telecommuting," *Compensation & Benefits* (Washington, DC: Bureau of National Affairs, 2001). CD-ROM.

- *Satellite work center:* Employees work from a remote extension of the employer's office that includes a clerical staff and a full-time manager.
- *Neighborhood work center:* Employees work from a satellite office shared by several employers.
- *Nomadic executive office:* Executives who travel extensively maintain control over projects through use of telephone, fax, and electronic mail.

In addition:

- Employees sometimes work entirely outside the office. Others might work off-site only once a month, or two to three days a week.
- Telecommuters can be full- or part-time employees.
- Telecommuting arrangements can be temporary or permanent. A temporarily disabled employee may work at home until fully recovered. A permanently disabled employee may work at home exclusively.

threefold during peak "rush hour" traffic periods. Parking and toll costs can be hefty. Monthly parking rates alone often exceed a few hundred dollars a car. Finally, employee involvement in office politics will be reduced, which should promote higher job performance.

Telecommuting programs may also lead to some disadvantages for employers and employees. Often, employers are concerned about not having direct contact with employees, which makes conducting performance appraisals more difficult. Employees sometimes feel that work-at-home arrangements are disruptive to their personal lives. In addition, some employees feel isolated because they do not interact personally as often with co-workers and superiors.

Telecommuting provides tax benefits to employees when employer-provided property or services qualify as a working condition fringe benefit. In the case of telecommuting, copier machines and express mail service are examples of working condition fringe benefits. Specifically, employers exclude these costs from a telecommuter's gross income. Employer-provided equipment does not qualify as a working condition fringe outside a formal telecommuting arrangement. For instance, a copier machine is not a working condition fringe when employees choose to work extra hours at home.

Summary

This chapter reviewed the fundamental concepts of paid time-off policies and flexible work schedules. Most paid time-off benefits and flexible work schedules are offered on a discretionary basis. Federal and state laws play a role in some of these discretionary offerings, as do mandates for family and medical leave.

Key Terms

paid time-off, 232	bereavement leave, *241*	sabbatical leave, *244*
floating holidays, *235*	funeral leave, *241*	volunteerism, *245*
exempt, *237*	jury duty, *241*	Family and Medical Leave
nonexempt jobs, *237*	witness duty, *241*	Act (FMLA), *245*
carryover provisions, *238*	Jury Systems Improvement	flexible scheduling, *249*
"use it or lose it"	Act of 1978, *241*	flextime schedules, *249*
provision, *238*	Uniformed Services	core hours, *249*
cashout provisions, *238*	Employment and	banking hours, *250*
sick leave, *239*	Reemployment Rights Act	compressed workweek
integrated paid time-off	of 1994 (USERRA), *242*	schedules, *250*
policies, *240*	nonproduction time, *243*	telecommuting, *251*
paid time-off banks, *240*	on-call time, *243*	

Discussion Questions

1. Discuss the pros and cons of choosing an integrated paid time-off policy instead of multiple specific paid time-off policies—for example, sick leave, vacation, and so forth.
2. Most companies award vacation and sick-leave time according to seniority. Should companies base the allocation of these benefits on employee performance? Discuss the rationale for your answer.

3. Should the U.S. government mandate similar paid time-off benefits for all employees? Please explain.

4. Are carryover provisions in paid sick leave and vacation benefits unfair to some employees? If yes, for whom are these provisions unfair? In either case, explain the rationale for your answer.

Endnotes

1. U.S. Bureau of Labor Statistics. February 2009. *Vacations, Holidays, and Personal Leave: Access, Quantity, Costs, and Trends* (Issue 2). Online at www.bls.gov/opub/perspectives/issue2for11by17.pdf. Accessed May 30, 2009.

2. 5 U.S. Code 6103(a).

3. 29 Code of Federal Regulations §1605.1.

4. M. M. Markowich. 2007. *Paid Time-Off Banks*. Phoenix, AZ: WorldatWork Press.

5. 38 U.S.C. §4301.

6. *Owens v. Local No. 169*, 30 WH Cases 1634, California 9, July 29, 1992.

7. Society for Human Resource Management. 2007. News bit. Online at www.shrm.org. Accessed April 10, 2007.

8. H. Helen Axel. 1992. "Redefining Corporate Sabbaticals for the 1990s," *The Conference Board Report No. 1005.*

9. 29 C.F.R. §825.

10. U.S. Bureau of Labor Statistics. 2002. *Work at Home in 2001*. USDL 02–107. Online at http://stats.bls.gov/newsrels.htm. Accessed July 22, 2004.

11. J. D. Goodstein. 1994. "Institutional pressures and strategic responsiveness: Employer involvement in work-family issues," *Academy of Management Journal 37*, pp. 350–82.

Accommodation and Enhancement Benefits

Learning Objectives

In this chapter, you will gather
information about:

1. Five categories of accommodation
   and enhancement benefits and
   corresponding objectives.

2. Specific accommodation and
   enhancement benefits for each
   category.

3. Reasons many companies offer
   accommodation and enhancement
   benefits.

4. Tax benefits for employers and
   employees.

5. Legal issues pertaining to
   accommodation and enhancement
   benefits.

You recall the conversations about the challenging work deadlines and travel itineraries from your recent job interview. Suddenly, you begin feeling overwhelmed at the prospects of trying to balance work and family demands. In the future, you hope to have children, and these challenges will be even greater because your spouse also has a demanding career. Then you realize your employee benefits include a variety of programs to help manage the stress that invariably arises when trying to balance work and family considerations.

Increasingly, employees face greater challenges as they try to fulfill work and family obligations, and so they often seek education to minimize skills obsolescence. Pressures to perform well at work intensify when economic conditions decline and companies begin to reduce their staffing levels. With a decline in job security come worries about meeting financial obligations.

Many companies offer accommodation and enhancement benefits to promote effective coping skills, as well as educational opportunities for employees and, sometimes, family members. Although accommodation and enhancement benefits represent a more recent phenomenon (compared to insurance and retirement benefits), ever-changing environments often make them a business necessity.

DEFINING ACCOMMODATION AND ENHANCEMENT BENEFITS

As a discretionary benefit, **accommodation benefits** and **enhancement benefits** promote one or more of the following four objectives:

- The mental and physical well-being of employees and family members.
- Family assistance programs.
- Educational benefits for employees.
- Support programs for daily living.

Following a discussion of the rationale for these benefits, we will review a variety of accommodation and enhancement benefits for each objective.

Rationale for Accommodation and Enhancement Benefits

The decision to provide accommodation and enhancement benefits is based on three considerations. First, in the long run, the cost of absenteeism and tardiness is usually much higher than offering accommodation and enhancement benefits that will increase the timely attendance of employees at work. Programs that promote two particular objectives—the mental and physical well-being of employees and family members, and family assistance programs—contribute to this attendance imperative. After all, ill or dependent family members often rely on other family members (most of whom are also employees) to care for them, necessitating absence from work. The fourth objective—support programs for daily living—also promotes regular attendance. For example, commute times in congested areas vary considerably based on the occurrence of accidents and traffic volume. As we discuss later, employers may offer transportation services such as vanpooling benefits which, in conjunction with local laws, permit travel on express lanes.

Second, many employees are not sufficiently productive for a variety of health-related reasons. For example, excessive smoking tends to limit physical capacity because of impaired lung function. Too much alcohol consumption may inhibit an employee's ability to make sound decisions or impair physical coordination. Excess body weight may reduce an employee's stamina, leading to lower job performance. Employers may sponsor alcohol treatment programs and weight-control programs to promote better health. As we learned in Chapters 3 and 6, health insurance companies are likely to charge substantially more for health care coverage when there has been a history of employees making insurance claims for serious ailments attributed to smoking and excessive alcohol consumption.

Third, promoting educational opportunities for employees yields benefits to both employers and employees. For example, scholarships and tuition reimbursement programs reduce the financial barriers to education by sponsoring employees' pursuit of general equivalency diplomas, college courses, or college degrees. Employees benefit from acquiring greater credentials to compete for higher-level jobs in the company. Employers benefit from staffing flexibility because employees possess a wider range and depth of knowledge and skills. As technology changes the nature of work, skills and knowledge updates minimize the problem of obsolescence.

Tax Benefits for Employers and Employees

In many cases, employers receive tax benefits for offering accommodation and enhancement benefits by deducting the costs as a normal business expense. Employees often enjoy tax benefits for participation. There is wide variation in tax benefits across offerings. We review noteworthy tax benefits for each program.

THE MENTAL AND PHYSICAL WELL-BEING OF EMPLOYEES AND FAMILY MEMBERS

Companies may offer one or two broad programs to promote the mental and physical well-being of employees and family members: employee assistance programs (EAPs) and wellness programs. Employers may offer wellness benefits as EAP services or as separate benefits. The decision is based largely on costs.

Employee Assistance Programs

Employee assistance programs (EAPs) help employees cope with personal problems that may impair their personal lives or job performance. Examples of these problems include alcohol or drug abuse, domestic violence, the emotional impact of AIDS and other diseases, clinical depression, and eating disorders. EAPs also assist employers in helping troubled employees identify and solve problems that may be interfering with their job or personal lives.

EXHIBIT 10.1
Drug-Free
Workplace
Act:
Requirements
for Employers

Employers must meet three main requirements of this act to qualify for contracts with the federal government:

- A written policy informs employees that the unlawful manufacture, distribution, possession, or use of an illicit substance is prohibited in the workplace.
- An employer must inform employees of available resources for counseling and rehabilitation and make employees aware of an EAP when it is part of the company's benefits program.
- Either requirement puts restrictions on employees who sustain a conviction for a criminal drug offense or mandates participation in drug rehabilitation programs.

EAPs are widely used. The term *EAP* did not become popular until the 1970s. Alcohol abuse programs preceded contemporary EAPs that offer multiple services.

Companies offer EAPs because, at any given time, an estimated 10 to 15 percent of any company's employees experience difficulties that interfere with their job performance.[1] Since 1995, there has been a 28 percent increase in the number of substance abuse and mental health care facilities because of the rising prevalence of such conditions throughout society.[2] In 2008, 42 percent of workers in private establishments were eligible for an EAP (U.S. Department of Labor, 2008). Although EAP costs are substantial, the benefits seem to outweigh the costs. For example, the annual cost per employee of an EAP is approximately $50 to $60. However, anecdotal evidence indicates that employers' gains outweigh their out-of-pocket expenses for EAPs: savings from reduced employee turnover, absenteeism, medical costs, unemployment insurance rates, workers' compensation rates, accident costs, and disability insurance costs. One analysis of EAP effectiveness demonstrated that 78 percent of EAP users found resolutions to their problems.[3] Unfortunately, current large-scale evaluation studies are virtually nonexistent.

The federal government has contributed to the rise in EAPs with the **Drug-Free Workplace Act of 1988.**[4] Specifically, this act mandates that companies holding federal contracts (worth at least $25,000) or grants (in any amount) promote a drug-free workplace. Exhibit 10.1 lists the main requirements of the Drug-Free Workplace Act.

EAP Services

Employee assistance programs include a variety of services; the specific services contained in any EAP depend on employer choice. Also, if a company is unionized, negotiations through collective bargaining determine some of the EAP services. Employers rely on staff members to develop and implement EAPs, or they establish contracts with third-party providers. Sometimes, employers use a combination of these methods. The choice rests on keeping costs to acceptable amounts. Exhibit 10.2 lists the most common types of EAP services.

The inclusion of outplacement assistance programs in EAPs represents a relatively recent phenomenon because of ever-changing business conditions (listed in the following).

EXHIBIT 10.2
Typical
Services of
Employee
Assistance
Programs

- Orientation meetings and educational materials to familiarize managers and employees with EAP services and procedures for supervisory referrals or employee self-referrals.
- Problem identification and assessment by interviewing an apparently troubled employee.
- Short-term counseling when appropriate instead of long-term, intensive therapy.
- Referrals to health professionals and community resources when short-term counseling is insufficient to address a troubled employee's problems.
- Follow-up meetings to determine the effectiveness of treatment and make additional plans (e.g., weekly counseling sessions for six months).
- Usually staff crisis hotlines to help employees in urgent situations that require immediate attention.

Many companies use outplacement assistance programs to provide technical and emotional support to employees who are being laid off or terminated. Companies assist through a variety of career and personal programs designed to develop an employee's job-hunting skills and self-confidence. A variety of factors lead to employee termination, factors to which outplacement assistance programs are best suited:

- Elimination of specific positions, often the result of changes in technology.
- Massive layoffs amounting to hundreds of thousands of jobs across industry sectors since the recent deep economic recession began in 2008.
- Changes in management.
- Mergers and acquisitions.
- Plant closings.
- Outsourcing manufacturing, customer service, and professional services (for example, information technology, accounting) to countries with lower pay scales and fewer labor protection.

Outplacement assistance provides such services as personal counseling, career assessment and evaluation, training in job search techniques, résumé and cover letter preparation, interviewing techniques, and training in the use of basic workplace technology such as computers.[5] Employers also receive benefits from offering outplacement assistance to employees: Outplacement assistance programs may promote a positive image of the company among those being terminated, their families, and friends by assisting these employees as they prepare for new employment opportunities. Employers receive tax benefits.

EAP Delivery Options

Employers may choose from two main delivery options when establishing EAPs. The first option, **referral EAPs,** lists the names and contact information for a variety of professional help services, ranging from crisis hotlines to alcohol and substance abuse treatment programs. Under this arrangement, the employer usually does not have a contractual relationship with service providers. Sometimes, large employers negotiate a reduced rate with service providers owing to the volume of referrals.

The second option, **full-service EAPs,** includes service providers such as alcohol treatment programs. Employers offer full-service EAPs through in-house services, third-party providers, or through participation in a consortium EAP. Staff members of **in-house EAPs** are employees of the company. Employers decide between offering in-house EAPs within work facilities (in-house), or somewhere outside these facilities through an independent EAP provider. Oftentimes, employers establish in-house EAPs outside the work facilities to enhance employee willingness to use them. Employees may be more likely to use EAPs when they cannot be seen by co-workers at large.

Employers establish contracts with third-party providers for full-service EAPs. **Third-party providers** are independent companies that offer EAP services to one or more employers. Contracts specify the services and the cost for each one. Larger employers usually pay lower prices for services than smaller employers.

Consortium EAPs establish contracts with sets of numerous smaller employers. Smaller companies combine limited resources to establish a contract with a third-party provider. Compared to larger companies, a smaller company alone generally pays a substantially higher fee per employee. Consortium EAP arrangements reduce this amount by increasing the number of employees who may take advantage of the EAP services.

Procedures for Employee Participation in EAPs

An employee participates in EAPs based on self-initiative or a referral by someone else. Employees initiate participation in an EAP when they recognize a problem and possess a desire to remedy it. Oftentimes, employees either do not recognize how problems adversely affect their work and personal lives or do not subscribe to the view that EAPs are appropriate or worthwhile. Three forces may lead employees to judge participation negatively. Some employees may mistrust employer sponsorship of EAPs. For example, they may view EAPs as a method to gather evidence for discharge. A number of employees may hold the view that personal problems are just that—problems not to be shared in the workplace. Some employees may simply feel strong shame about their problems to the point of denial.

Referrals direct troubled employees to EAPs. Supervisors or co-workers make the most referrals. Less often, family members may do so. Most frequently, supervisory referrals follow a period of poor job performance, excessive absenteeism, or disruptive behavior in the workplace (e.g., aggressive behavior toward co-workers). Companies usually address poor job performance and excessive absenteeism through performance appraisals, and disruptive behavior through disciplinary procedures. However, recognition of a problem (e.g., alcohol use at home or work that appears to diminish job performance) may warrant an EAP referral. Before making a referral, the supervisor should engage in constructive confrontation.

Constructive confrontation entails discussing incidents of poor performance with the troubled employee, citing the necessity of improving job performance within a designated period. In many instances, employees recognize that personal problems are responsible for poor performance; these employees voluntarily seek help through an EAP. When employees do not voluntarily seek help, the supervisor extends the referral to the EAP as a condition of employment because poor job performance is one of the strongest reasons for discipline or discharge.

Co-worker referrals almost always take place when troubled employees do not have direct supervision. In this circumstance, co-workers are in the best position to observe a decrease of quality in performance. Examples of these situations include field sales representatives and appliance repair personnel.

It is worth noting that supervisors and co-workers are responsible for describing the signs of trouble—for example, describing the number of days excessively absent and the frequency of these occurrences during the previous three months. Their responsibilities do not extend to making diagnoses. For instance, it is inappropriate to conclude that a troubled employee is an alcoholic. Quite simply, most co-workers and supervisors do not possess the necessary training to make diagnoses of medical or psychological problems.

Confidentiality

Confidentiality of information is essential to the success of employee assistance programs. Employees are not likely to seek help from EAPs when they believe that information about their status will be shared with supervisors and co-workers. The greatest concern about confidentiality is possible job loss, loss of opportunities for promotion and pay increases, and damage to both personal and professional reputation.

These concerns require that employers take measures to protect confidentiality and communicate these procedures to employees. Troubled employees must feel confident that there will be no oral or written disclosure of information to anyone outside the EAP staff. Exhibit 10.3 contains a list of methods for protecting employee confidentiality.

Release of Confidential Information

Protecting confidentiality does not necessarily mean that EAPs always conceal information from employers and co-workers. In most cases, EAP service providers must obtain the employee's written consent before they release information to supervisors, treatment facilities, or family members. Some situations require EAPs to disclose confidential information about participants to legal entities. Most situations require

---

EXHIBIT 10.3
Protecting Confidentiality in EAP Practice

Source: www. eapassociation.com.

Employee assistance plans:

- Maintain files in separate folders in a secured place away from personnel folders.
- Establish codes to identify employees interpretable only to authorized EAP staff members.
- Expressly inform employees who will be advised of their initial interactions with EAP staff members as well as the types of information based on written consent. Generally, EAPs limit disclosure to an employee's manager, indicating only whether the employee contacted the EAP, whether treatment is warranted, and whether the employee consented to treatment.
- Offer places or times to meet when or where co-workers and management are unlikely to be present.

signed consent for information disclosure from employees. In any event, sound policy includes a promise of confidentiality, except when employees provide written consent, granting permission to release information to designated individuals or when required by law.

Every state includes laws that force the release of confidential information to the appropriate authorities without written consent. EAPs must universally release information about reports of child abuse and neglect. Also, EAPS are obligated to release confidential information about evidence or strong professional judgments that troubled individuals pose a risk to the health and welfare of themselves or others.

Evaluating Employee Assistance Programs

We just reviewed circumstances that necessitate an EAP's release of confidential information. The health and safety of troubled employees, family members, coworkers, and others justifies release of confidential information. Employers seek information to evaluate the effectiveness of these programs and to get answer several questions:

- Are troubled employees aware of their employer's EAP?
- Do co-workers and supervisors understand the importance of, and procedures for, referring troubled employees to EAPs?
- Do the benefits of EAPs (e.g., helping troubled employees, higher productivity, and lower absenteeism) outweigh the costs? Of course, it is difficult to ascribe monetary value to helping others.
- Based on available information, should the EAP be modified in any particular ways, offered as is, or dropped altogether?

Evaluating EAPs requires a variety of complex tasks—for example, survey development and implementation. A significant part of the challenge centers on knowing the right questions to ask and how to reliably measure EAP outcomes. Companies may rely on a professional association for advice about EAPs. The **Employee Assistance Professionals Association (EAPA)** developed an evaluation system for EAPs (www.eapassn.org). Methods of evaluation include interviews, peer review, and case analysis.

Employer Liability

Employers may be legally responsible for inappropriate actions of employee assistance programs just as health care professionals may be held liable for similar inappropriate actions. Possible trouble spots for employers include:

- Misdiagnosis of condition that refers an employee to the wrong facility.
- Negligent referral to providers who do not have proper credentials.
- Abandonment either because a provider stops treatment prematurely or a worker's employment is terminated during the course of treatment, making him or her ineligible for further treatment.
- Inappropriate relationships with a client. The ethics code of virtually every health or social service professional organization prohibits sexual involvement with

clients, and in some jurisdictions it also is illegal. Most ethics codes also prohibit social relationships and business relationships between therapists and clients.

- Defaming an employee's character with libelous or slanderous statements due to participation in an EAP.

Relationship with Employee Benefits Laws

The Employee Retirement Income Security Act of 1974 (ERISA) and the Consolidated Omnibus Budget Reconciliation Act of 1985 (COBRA) may influence EAP practices.

The essence of ERISA is to provide protection of employee benefits rights in pension plans and welfare plans. As described in Chapter 4, ERISA defines a welfare plan as

> any plan, fund or program which was heretofore or is hereafter established or maintained by an employer or by an employee organization, or by both, to the extent that such plan, fund, or program was established or is maintained *for the purpose of providing for its participants or their beneficiaries through the purchase of insurance or otherwise* [emphasis added].[6]

The earlier phrase in italics means that not all EAPs are subject to ERISA's reporting and disclosure requirements for welfare plans. As discussed earlier, some EAPs are referral services only. In this case, employers neither fund EAP services directly nor fund these services indirectly through the purchase of insurance, exempting referral services only from ERISA requirements.

COBRA amended ERISA by providing employees and beneficiaries the right to elect continuation coverage under group health plans if they would lose coverage due to a qualifying event. COBRA usually applies to EAPs under two circumstances: (1) the EAP qualifies as a welfare benefit plan under ERISA, and (2) the EAP qualifies as a health care plan by providing counseling for a medical condition.

Tax Obligations

Employers treat the cost of EAPs as a normal business expense. Employees may exclude the cost of treatment from gross income only when such treatment is to alleviate medical and mental conditions.

Wellness Programs

In the 1980s, employers began sponsoring **wellness programs** to promote and maintain the physical and psychological health of employees. Wellness programs vary in scope. They may emphasize weight loss only, or they may emphasize a range of activities, including:

- Back care
- Smoking cessation
- Stress management
- Weight control and nutrition
- Health risk appraisals

Employers may choose to offer wellness programs on-site or off-site. While some companies may invest in staffing professionals for wellness programs, others contract with external vendors like community health agencies or private health clubs. Although wellness programs are relatively new, some evidence already indicates that these innovations can save companies money and reduce employees' need for health care. For every $1 invested in preventive health care programs, companies can expect to save as much as $6 in medical insurance costs.[7] One study showed a strong relationship between health habits such as smoking and health care costs.[8]

Back Care

Employers sponsor **back care programs** to reduce back injuries through worker training, exercise programs, ergonomic evaluations of the work environment, and relaxation techniques. Apart from containing health care and workers' compensation claims, back care programs presumably reduce frequent absenteeism. The prevalence of injuries to the shoulders and back and its links to absence are substantial. In 2007, 35.4 percent of nonfatal occupational injuries and illnesses within U.S. private industry required recuperation away from work beyond the day of the incident.[9] Problems with the trunk (back and shoulders) were stated to account for most (33.2 percent) of time lost, followed by upper extremities (i.e., wrists, hands, and fingers, 23.2 percent) and lower extremities (i.e., knees, feet, and toes, 22.4 percent).

Clearly, the costs to employers for back-related injuries and illnesses are extremely high based on health care benefits, workers' compensation claims, and lost productivity. Failure to provide reasonable accommodation to qualified individuals with back-related disabilities through the Americans with Disabilities Act of 1990 (ADA) has also added to employer cost burdens. About 11 percent of the 272,000 ADA violations (between July 26, 1997, and September 30, 2008) were due to back impairments.[10]

Smoking Cessation Programs

Employers may invest in **smoking cessation** programs as simple as information campaigns that emphasize the negative aspects of smoking to intensive programs geared toward helping individuals stop smoking. Many employers offer courses and treatment to help and encourage smokers to quit. For example, employers may sponsor the participation of employees in a Smokenders education program. Other options include offering nicotine replacement therapy, such as nicotine gum and patches, and self-help services. Many companies endorse antismoking events, such as the American Cancer Society's "Great American Smoke-Out" during which companies distribute T-shirts, buttons, and literature that discredit smoking, with slogans such as "Commit to Quit."

Employer-sponsored smoking cessation programs usually operate on a reimbursement basis. Employees pay a fee for the program. Upon successful completion of the program, employers reimburse employees for part or all of the cost. Employees are not reimbursed if they fail to complete the program.

Employers deduct their contributions to smoking cessation programs as a normal business expense. Employees generally enjoy tax benefits as well. For example, they may deduct the costs of smoking cessation programs and prescription drugs for nicotine withdrawal, unless reimbursed by the employer or health insurance plan.[11] Employees may pay for nonprescription drugs to assist with smoking cessation with money from a flexible spending account (FSA, Chapter 6), but an individual who does not have an FSA may not deduct the cost of nonprescription drugs for smoking cessation from their income taxes.[12]

Stress Management Programs

Stress management programs can help employees cope with many factors inside and outside work that contribute to stress. For instance, job conditions, health and personal problems, and personal and professional relationships can make employees anxious and thus less productive. Symptoms of stressful workplaces include low morale, chronic absenteeism, low productivity, and high turnover rates. Employers offer stress management programs to teach workers coping skills. Seminars focus on recognizing signs of stress and burnout. Stress reduction techniques can improve the quality of life inside and outside the workplace. Employers benefit from increased employee productivity, reduced absenteeism, and lower health care costs.

Weight-Control and Nutrition Programs

Weight-control and nutrition programs educate employees about proper nutrition and weight loss to promote sound health. Information from the medical community has clearly indicated that excess weight and poor nutrition are significant risk factors in cardiovascular disease, diabetes, high blood pressure, and cholesterol levels. Over time, these employee programs should yield better health, increased morale, and improved appearance. For employers, these programs should result in improved employee productivity and lower health care costs.

Companies can contribute to employee weight control and proper nutrition in different ways. For example, some employers sponsor memberships in weight-loss programs such as Weight Watchers. Employers may also reinforce the positive results of weight-loss programs through support groups, counseling, and competitions. In addition, companies sometimes actively attempt to influence employee food choices by including nutritional foods and beverages as options in vending machines. Further, companies may occasionally offer health screenings on location for diabetes, high blood pressure, and cholesterol level. Employers treat the costs of wellness programs as a normal business expense; however, employees do not receive any tax benefits for costs (e.g., fees to participate in a weight-control program). Finally, as we discuss later, employers may offer physical fitness opportunities on-site or off-site.

Health Risk Appraisals

Employer-sponsored **health risk appraisals** inform employees of potential health risks based on a physical examination, responses to questions about certain habits (e.g., diet, amount of exercise, and review of family members' health histories).

In many cases, the results of health risk appraisals help employees minimize risks whenever possible. Exhibit 10.4 lists common elements of health risk

EXHIBIT 10.4
Elements of
Health Risk
Appraisals

- Analysis of blood chemicals such as cholesterol, triglycerides, glucose, and uric acid levels.
- Blood pressure check.
- Body measurements: height, weight, percentage of body fat.
- Colorectal cancer screening.
- Diabetes screening.
- Electrocardiogram.
- Examination for breast cancer.
- Glaucoma screening.
- Hearing tests.
- Kidney and liver functions.
- Lung function.
- Medical history.
- Physical capacity.
- Physical fitness.
- Stress tests.

appraisals. Follow-through helps employers control health insurance claims. Employers generally pay for health risk appraisals, permitting the deduction of these costs as a business expense. As a result, employees do not receive tax benefits. When wellness programs and EAPs are integrated programs within a company, the results of health risk appraisals can encourage employees to utilize EAP services on a confidential basis. For example, it is not uncommon for many individuals who are overweight to recognize this fact; however, recognizing the issue is often easier than resolving it. The use of such appraisals can remind employees of the health risks associated with excess body weight and, when combined with recommendations for an action plan and referrals to EAP resources, the employee is probably going to be more likely to seek resolution.

FAMILY ASSISTANCE PROGRAMS

Family assistance programs help employees provide care to young children and dependent elderly relatives. Presumably, employees are likely to attend work regularly and work productively when these family members receive the necessary attention. A variety of employer programs and benefits can help employees cope with their family assistance responsibilities. The programs range from making referrals to on-site child or elder care centers, to company-sponsored day care programs, and vary in the amount of financial and human resources needed to administer them. Generally, the least expensive and least labor-intensive programs are referral services. Referral services are designed to help workers identify and take advantage of available community resources, conveyed through media such as educational workshops, videos, employee newsletters and magazines, and EAPs.

Elder care programs provide physical, emotional, or financial assistance for aging parents, spouses, or other relatives who are not fully self-sufficient because they are too frail or disabled. **Child care** programs focus on supervising pre-school-age dependent children whose parents work outside the home. Many employees now rely on elder care and child care programs due to the increasing longevity of their parents[13] and the growing numbers of dual-income families.[14] Child care needs arise from the growing number of single parents and dual-career households with children.

Day care is another possible benefit. Some companies subsidize child or elder day care in community-based centers. Elder care programs usually provide self-help, meals, and entertainment activities for the participants. Child care programs typically offer supervision, preschool preparation, and meals. Facilities must usually maintain state or local licenses. Other companies choose to sponsor on-site day care centers, offering services that are similar to community-based centers.

ADOPTION ASSISTANCE PROGRAMS

Approximately 1.6 million children under 18 years old in the United States are adopted.[15] The U.S. Department of Health and Human Services reports that 51,000 children were adopted with public agency involvement in fiscal year 2005. The cost of adopting a child can range from $5,000 to $40,000, depending on the agency and source. In 2007, 11 percent of all private industry workers had access to employer-provided adoption assistance.

Adoption benefits include direct financial assistance or reimbursement for expenses related to the adoption of a child and/or the provision for paid or additional unpaid leave (other than what is required by the Family and Medical Leave Act of 1993) for the adoptive parent employee.

A recent study[16] revealed that more U.S. companies are creating or improving upon adoption benefits packages they offer employees in an effort to remain competitive. There has been steady growth in the number of large employers willing to provide financial adoption benefits. Moreover, the average adoption-friendly employer has had their adoption benefit in place for eight years, provides up to $5,000 in benefits, and allows five weeks of paid time-off. Finally, among the primary reasons that employers provide adoption benefits were to offer competitive work-life benefits packages, provide a family-friendly image, and establish equity for adoptive parents on a par with what is available for biological parents at companies.

Employers and employees receive tax benefits through employer-sponsored programs. For purposes of both the tax credit and the employer-sponsored programs, IRC Section 23(a) defines **qualified adoption expenses** as reasonable and necessary adoption fees, court costs, attorneys' fees, and other expenses, which do the following:

- Are directly related to, and the principal purpose of which is for, the legal adoption of an eligible child by the taxpayer.
- Are not incurred in violation of state or federal law or in carrying out any surrogate parenting arrangement.

- Are not expenses in connection with the adoption by an individual of a child who is the child of such individual's spouse.
- Are not reimbursed under another program.

Some additional notes: Eligible children are those younger than age 18 or who are physically or mentally incapable of caring for themselves. Also, qualified adoption expenses do not include foreign adoptions, unless the adoption becomes final.

EDUCATIONAL BENEFITS FOR EMPLOYEES

Many companies offer educational benefits to employees and, sometimes, their children. Educational benefits enable employees to pursue educational opportunities that they would otherwise be unable to afford or be unwilling to pay for. Also, educational benefits assist employees by providing them with a college education or advanced degree such as an MBA or executive MBA, particularly at a time when tuition costs are rising rapidly.

Companies stand to benefit from sponsoring employee education. Many companies, however, do not benefit because they often fail to develop and implement career development programs that allow employees to seek promotions with greater responsibility and compensation. The lack of follow-up may lead these educated employees to seek promotions by taking jobs elsewhere.

Three specific types of educational benefits are:

1. Section 127 educational assistance programs.
2. Tuition reimbursement.
3. Scholarship programs.

Educational Assistance Programs

Educational assistance programs allow employees to exclude as much as $5,250 of annual gross income for educational assistance.[17] The Internal Revenue Service currently offers two definitions of educational assistance, based on amendments to Section 127 of the Internal Revenue Code.[18] Tax-free educational assistance benefits include payments for tuition, fees and similar expenses, books, supplies, and equipment. The payments may be for either undergraduate- or graduate-level courses and do not have to be for work-related classes. Educational assistance benefits do not include payments for the following items: meals, lodging, or transportation; tools or supplies (other than textbooks) that may be kept after completing the course of instruction; and courses involving sports, games, or hobbies unless these are related to the business of the employer or are required as part of a degree program.

The Internal Revenue Service permits employers to establish a program under which every employee can exclude as much as $5,250 a year of educational assistance from their gross income, regardless of whether the courses are job-related. Educational assistance programs may qualify for tax benefits. Besides conforming to educational assistance program definitions (described earlier), employers must meet three additional requirements:

1. Describe an educational assistance program in a separate written document.
2. Offer these programs exclusively for the benefit of employees.
3. Satisfy nondiscrimination requirements.

Exhibit 10.5 contains additional details about these requirements.

In general, employees pay taxes on educational amounts that exceed $5,250. There is one exception to this limit: Educational benefits that qualify as a working condition fringe, as described earlier, are not subject to this limit. Employees receive tax benefits on total eligible expenses.

Tuition Reimbursement Programs

Tuition reimbursement programs fully or partially reimburse an employee for expenses incurred for education or training. Oftentimes, tuition reimbursement programs and **pay-for-knowledge programs** are treated synonymously. Tuition reimbursement programs fall under the category of employee benefits. Under these programs, employees usually choose the courses they wish to take when they want to take them. Many employers allow employees to enroll in courses that are not directly related to their work. The main goal of pay-for-knowledge programs is to train employees to meet changing job requirements due to technology and global competitive pressures. Pay-for-knowledge is one kind of direct or monetary compensation. Companies establish set curricula that employees should take, and they generally award pay increases to employees upon successfully completing courses within the curricula. Pay increases are not directly associated with tuition reimbursement programs.

Employers treat the cost of tuition reimbursement as a tax-deductible business expense. Employees receive tax benefits for tuition reimbursement when these plans meet the criteria for a **working condition fringe:**

> Any property or services provided to an employee of the employer to the extent that, if the employee paid for such property or services, such payment would be allowable as a deduction under section 162 [trade or business expenses] or 167 [depreciation of the property used in the trade or business].[19]

Specifically, tuition reimbursement plans qualify as working condition fringe benefits either when instruction or training must maintain or improve essential job skills or when instruction or training is required by employers, by law, for employees to work in their jobs, or to keep their same status or rate of compensation.

Scholarship Programs

Employer-sponsored **scholarship programs** cover some or all of the tuition and related expenses for employees or family members pursuing undergraduate degrees in two- or four-year colleges. In most cases, these programs extend only to the children of employees. Employer-sponsored scholarship programs are the least common educational benefit, perhaps because companies are less likely to

EXHIBIT 10.5 Tax Qualification Requirements for Educational Assistance Programs

Source: Treasury Regulations §1.127-2.

Separate Written Plan

The program must be a separate written plan of the employer. This requirement means that the terms of the program must be set forth in a separate document or documents providing only educational assistance within the meaning of the next paragraph. The requirement for a separate plan does not, however, preclude an educational assistance program from being part of a more comprehensive employer plan that provides a choice of nontaxable benefits to employees.

Educational Assistance Defined

The benefits provided under the program must consist solely of educational assistance. The term *educational assistance* means:

- The employer's payment of expenses incurred by, or on behalf of, an employee for education.
- The employer's provision of education to an employee.

Exclusive Benefit of Employees

The program must be established for the exclusive benefit of the employer's "employees." The definition of *employee* includes retired, disabled, or laid-off employees; present employees on leave (e.g., employees in the military); or self-employed individuals as defined by the tax code. Spouses or dependents of employees are not employees and cannot be included in the program.

Prohibited Discrimination

The program must benefit the employer's employees generally. Among those benefited may be employees who are officers, shareholders, self-employed, or highly compensated. A program is not for the benefit of employees generally, however, if the program discriminates in favor of employees described in the preceding sentence (or in favor of their spouses and dependents who are themselves employees) in requirements relating to eligibility for benefits. Thus, although a program need not provide benefits for all employees, it must benefit those employees who qualify under a job classification that does not illegally discriminate against protected class employees (e.g., Hispanics). The classification of employees to be considered benefited will consist of that group of employees who are actually eligible for educational assistance under the program, taking into account the eligibility requirements set forth in the written plan, the eligibility requirements reflected in the types of educational assistance available under the program, and any other conditions that may affect the availability of benefits under the program. Thus, for example, if an employer's plan provides that all employees are eligible for educational assistance, yet limits that assistance to courses of study leading to postgraduate degrees in fields relating to the employer's business, then only those employees able to pursue such a course of study are considered actually eligible for educational assistance under the program.

A program shall not be considered discriminatory under this paragraph merely because:

- Different types of educational assistance available under the program are utilized to a greater degree by employees with respect to whom discrimination is prohibited than by other employees.
- With respect to a course of study for which benefits are otherwise available, successful completion of the course, attaining a particular course grade, or satisfying a reasonable condition subsequently (such as remaining employed for one year after completing the course) are required or considered in determining the availability of benefits.

benefit directly from educating the children of employees than the employees themselves.

Employers treat the cost of scholarships as a normal business expense. In some cases, employees receive tax benefits for the scholarship amounts. Section 117 of the Internal Revenue Code describes **qualified scholarship programs** that grant tax benefits to employees for their own, or their children's, education below graduate-level work. The tax benefit equals the amount of qualified tuition reduction plus related expenses (e.g., fees, books, supplies). **Qualified tuition reductions** include the reduction in tuition granted by the employer's program. However, not all tuition reductions and related expenses qualify for tax benefits. Specifically, tuition reductions that discriminate in favor of highly compensated employees* do not qualify for favorable tax treatment.

SUPPORT PROGRAMS FOR DAILY LIVING

Employers may offer one or more support programs designed to help employees manage daily challenges. Two common examples include transportation services and opportunities either to become fit or to maintain physical fitness.

Transportation Services

Some employers sponsor **transportation services** to facilitate travel from home to work and back. They may sponsor public transportation subsidies, vanpools, or employer-sponsored vans or buses that transport employees between their homes and the workplace. In general, employers offer transportation services to promote recruitment and retention and to reduce tardiness and absenteeism due to transportation issues.

Employers provide transit subsidies to employees working in metropolitan and suburban areas served by various forms of mass transportation like buses, subways, and trains. Companies may offer transit passes, tokens, or vouchers. Practices vary from partial subsidy to full subsidy.

Many employers must offer transportation services to comply with the Clean Air Act of 1990.[20] Increasingly, local and state governments request that companies reduce the number of single-passenger automobiles commuting to their workplace each day because of government mandates for cleaner air. The **Clean Air Act Amendments of 1990** require employers in smoggy metropolitan areas like Los Angeles to comply with state and local laws concerning commuter trip reduction. Employers may also offer transportation services to recruit individuals who do not care to drive themselves in rush-hour traffic. Further, transportation services enable companies to offset for deficits in parking space availability, particularly in congested metropolitan areas.

Employees obviously stand to benefit from these transportation services. For example, using public transportation or joining a vanpool often saves money by

*See Chapter 4 for definition of highly compensated employee.

eliminating commuting costs such as gas, insurance, car maintenance and repairs, and parking fees. Moreover, commuting time can be quite lengthy for some employees. By leaving the driving to others, employees can use the time more productively—for instance, reading, completing paperwork, or "unwinding."

Employers subsidize transportation services either through salary reduction agreements or on a reimbursement basis. Under salary reduction arrangements, employers pay the provider directly. Employees must provide evidence of payment for approved transportation services before employers issue reimbursements.

Employers deduct the cost of transportation benefits, based on fair market valuation, as a business expense. Section 132 of the Internal Revenue Code specifies tax benefits for employees. Employees may deduct a monthly maximum of $230 (for the 2009 tax year) for employer-subsidized transit passes or vanpools.[21] For employer-subsidized parking, employees also may deduct a monthly maximum of $230 (for the 2009 tax year).[22] Amounts that exceed these limits are subject to federal income tax withholding and taxation under FICA and FUTA.

Physical Fitness

Some employers support physical fitness activities by incorporating an on-site fitness center or by sponsoring memberships in nearby health clubs. Presumably, employees who take advantage of these benefits tend to be absent less often, manage stress more effectively, and control weight. Employers benefit from lower absenteeism and lower health insurance claims.

Employers deduct the cost of these benefits as a normal business expense. Employees may exclude the value of facility usage from income (thus, exemption of this amount from FICA and FUTA requirements) under the Internal Revenue Service **certain benefits** section for on-premises athletic facilities under the control of the employer.[23] These include any gym or other athletic facility (e.g., swimming pool, tennis court, or golf course) that is located on the premises of the employer, is operated by the employer, and is used almost entirely by employees of the employer, their spouses, and their dependent children.

The word *on-premises* is somewhat misleading. On-premises requires that a gym or other athletic facility be located on an employer's property. An employer's property is not restricted to business locations (e.g., field offices, corporate headquarters, or manufacturing facilities). The concept of employer control refers to either of the following: First, the employer operates the facility; second, the employer has a contract with a facility, but the operation is still under the employer's control.[24]

Summary

This chapter reviewed the fundamental concepts of company-sponsored accommodation and enhancement benefits. We started with a review of the objectives of accommodation and enhancement benefits, followed by a description of several benefits. Tax regulations and various laws have a significant impact on the design of most accommodation and enhancement benefits. Changing pressures often justify the expense of these benefits to promote a stable and productive workforce.

Key Terms

accommodation benefits, *256*
enhancement benefits, *256*
employee assistance programs (EAPs), *257*
Drug-Free Workplace Act of 1988, *258*
outplacement assistance, *259*
referral EAPs, *259*
full-service EAPs, *260*
in-house EAPs, *260*
third-party providers, *260*
consortium EAPs, *260*
constructive confrontation, *260*
Employee Assistance Professionals Association (EAPA), *262*

wellness programs, *263*
back care programs, *264*
smoking cessation, *264*
stress management, *265*
weight control and nutrition programs, *265*
health risk appraisals, *265*
family assistance programs, *266*
elder care, *266*
child care, *267*
day care, *267*
adoption benefits, *267*
qualified adoption expenses, *267*
educational assistance programs, *268*

tuition reimbursement programs, *269*
pay-for-knowledge programs, *269*
working condition fringe, *269*
scholarship programs, *269*
qualified scholarship programs, *271*
qualified tuition reductions, *271*
transportation services, *271*
Clean Air Act Amendments of 1990, *271*
certain benefits, *272*

Discussion Questions

1. Describe the differences between health insurance benefits and employee assistance programs (EAPs).
2. Identify additional reasons companies should offer accommodation and enhancement benefits.
3. Discuss one or more reasons why companies should *not* offer accommodation and enhancement benefits.
4. Some companies do not include educational benefits in their benefits plans. Discuss reasons for this position.
5. Companies always face budget constraints, preventing them from offering every possible benefit. Identify one accommodation and enhancement benefit that you believe is most important and another that is least important.

Endnotes

1. Bureau of National Affairs. 2005. Employee Assistance Programs. *Compensation and Benefits*. Washington, DC: Bureau of National Affairs.
2. U.S. Department of Census. 2008. *Statistical Abstracts of the United States: 2009* (128th edition). Online at www.census.gov. Accessed April 18, 2009.
3. F. Luthans and R. Waldersee. 1989. "What do we really know about EAPs?" *Human Resource Management*, 28, pp. 385–401.
4. 41 U.S. Code §701.
5. V. M. Gibson. 1991. "The ins and outs of outplacement," *Management Review*, 80, pp. 59–61.
6. ERISA §3(1), 29 U.S.C. §1002(1).
7. S. Tully. 1995. "America's healthiest companies," *Fortune*, June 15, pp. 98–100 ff.
8. K. R. Parkes. 1987. "Relative weight, smoking, and mental health as predictors of sickness and absence from work," *Journal of Applied Psychology*, 72, pp. 275–86.

9. U.S. Bureau of Labor Statistics 2008. *Nonfatal Occupational Injuries and Illnesses Requiring Days Away from Work, 2007.* Release 08-1716. Online at www.bls.gov. Accessed April 18, 2009.

10. U.S. Equal Employment Opportunity Commission. *Americans with Disabilities Act of 1990 (ADA) Charges, FY 1997–FY 2008.* Online at www.eeoc.gov/stats/ada.html. Accessed April 18, 2009.

11. I.R.C. §213; I.R.S. Ruling 99–28, June 21, 1999.

12. I.R.S. information release 2003-103, September 3, 2003.

13. G. Spencer. November 1992. Projection of the Population of the United States, by Age, Sex, Race, and Hispanic Origin: 1992 to 2050. *Current Population Reports* P-25, no. 1092. Washington, DC: U.S. Government Printing Office.

14. U.S. Department of Census. 2008. *Statistical Abstracts of the United States: 2009.*

15. Ibid.

16. Dave Thomas Foundation for Adoption (2008). *Adoption-Friendly Benefits Study, 2008.* Online at www.DaveThomasFoundationforAdoption.org. Accessed April 19, 2009.

17. I.R.C. §127.

18. I.R.C. §127(c)(1) following amendment by Public Law 107–16, §411(b).

19. I.R.C. §132(d).

20. 42 U.S.C. §85.

21. I.R.C. §132(f)(2)(A).

22. I.R.C. §132(f)(2)(B), amended by Public Law 105–178.

23. I.R.C. §132(j)(4)(B).

24. Ibid.

Extending Employee Benefits: Design and Global Issues

Managing the Employee Benefits System

Learning Objectives

In this chapter, you will gather information about:

1. Methods for managing benefits costs.
2. Differences between the traditional and flexible approaches to benefits designs.
3. Essentials of communicating the benefits program.
4. Outsourcing employee benefits.
5. Issues for the future of employee benefits.

You've reviewed virtually all the benefits included in your employee benefits plan. You thought that while particular benefits may be useful to some employees, other components may not fulfill the needs or interests of others. For example, day care benefits for young children may not fulfill the needs of employees who do not have children, or who have adult children. Many companies have adopted flexible benefits plans that permit employees to customize the benefits program to their needs and interests, of course, within the scope of the employer's offerings.

Besides the issues of choice, you want to learn how your new employer will communicate features of the benefits plans to you in the future, including changes to offerings [for example, adding new investment opportunities for the 401(k) plan], when you may switch health insurers, and so forth.

Following the last presentation, you plan to ask your benefits representative several questions about issues reported in newspapers and newscasts that may affect employee benefits offerings in companies.

A COMPARISON OF TRADITIONAL BENEFITS PLANS AND FLEXIBLE BENEFITS PLANS

Traditional benefits plans contain the same set of benefits for each employee. Offering the same benefits to all employees creates administrative ease and represents a one-size-fits-all approach. Increasingly, companies are replacing fixed benefits plans with cafeteria benefits plans, which give employees a choice of benefits. We discuss these two approaches to benefits design. Exhibits 11.1 and 11.2 depict the structures of traditional and flexible benefits plans. The flexible plan design represents a Section 125 cafeteria plan, which we will discuss shortly.

A One-Size-Fits-All Approach

Traditionally, a company offered its employees a predetermined set and level of benefits based largely on cost considerations. For example, every employee of Company A received the same set of benefits, including medical insurance and life insurance. In addition, every employee received the same level of benefits regardless of need or preferences—for instance, all employees of Company A received life insurance coverage equal to their annual salary or wage (computed over a one-year period). From an employee's perspective, life insurance benefits in any amount are better than no life insurance benefit at all.

EXHIBIT 11.1
Traditional Benefit Plan Structure

Source: J. S. Rosenbloom. 2001. *Handbook of Employee Benefits*. New York: McGraw-Hill.

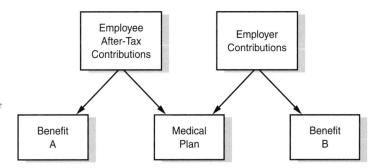

However, differences in employee needs and preferences strongly influence the adequacy of this company-sponsored benefit. Oftentimes, relatively young employees without dependent children or a spouse (or life partner) do not believe life insurance is relevant or valuable. Quite simply, these employees do not have any responsibility for ensuring the financial welfare of family members in the event of death. However, employees with dependents will usually deem company-sponsored life insurance an essential benefit.

Employer Choice to Customize Benefits

Benefits professionals consider several factors when developing strategic benefits plans. As discussed earlier, traditionally a company offered the same set of benefits to most or all employees. However, the increasing diversity of the work- and labor forces has made standardized benefits offerings less practical: Demographic diversity is associated with greater differences in needs and preferences for particular benefits. In addition, since 1978, Internal Revenue Code Section 125 created tax benefits to companies that permitted employee choice.

EXHIBIT 11.2
Comprehensive Cafeteria Plan

Source: J. S. Rosenbloom. 2001. *Handbook of Employee Benefits*. New York: McGraw-Hill.

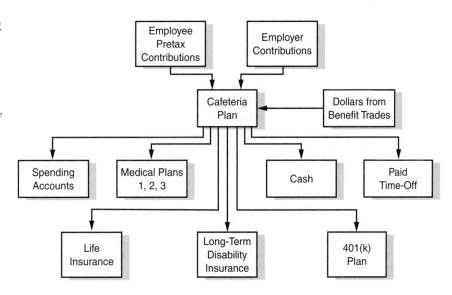

Flexible benefits or **cafeteria plans** enable employees in a company to choose from among a set of benefits and different levels of these benefits. Under these plans, employers grant employees the opportunity to accept or reject benefits (e.g., day care benefits, life insurance coverage). For instance, a single parent chooses day care benefits to supervise young children during the workday, or a nonsmoker chooses not to participate in smoking cessation programs. Companies implement cafeteria plans to meet the challenges of diversity. Limited evidence suggests positive reactions to flexible plans, including benefit satisfaction, overall job satisfaction, pay satisfaction, and understanding of benefits, increased after the implementation of the flexible benefits plan.

Cafeteria Plans under Section 125

Section 125 of the Internal Revenue Code permits an employer to offer employees the choice between taxable pay or to allocate some of their income to purchase qualified benefits through a cafeteria plan. The term *qualified benefit* exists independently of cafeteria plans. **Qualified benefits** refer to any employer-sponsored benefits for which an employee may exclude the cost from federal income tax calculation. For example, an employee's monetary contribution to an employer-sponsored medical insurance plan is excluded from the calculation of annual federal taxes.

Section 125 distinguishes between allowable and prohibited qualified benefits. Exhibit 11.3 lists the allowable qualified benefits and the prohibited qualified benefits in Section 125 plans. The corresponding sections of the Internal Revenue Code that created tax advantages are listed by each benefit.

Additional Guidelines for Section 125 Plans

Besides including only permissible benefits as described, employers have to follow several guidelines to maintain a Section 125 cafeteria plan. Specifically, the plan must:

- Be in writing.
- Allow employees the opportunity to choose between two or more benefits, consisting of at least one nontaxable benefit and at least one taxable benefit such as cash.

EXHIBIT 11.3
Allowable and Prohibited Qualified Employee Benefits Allowed or Prohibited in Section 125 Cafeteria Plans

Allowable Qualified Benefits

- Employer-provided accident or health plan (Sections 105 and 106).
- Group term life insurance (Section 79).
- Elective contributions under a qualified cash or deferred arrangement [Section 401(k)].
- Dependent care assistance (Section 129).
- Adoption assistance (Section 137).

Prohibited Qualified Benefits

- Medical savings accounts (Section 106b).
- Scholarships (Section 117).
- Educational assistance programs (Section 127).
- Fringe benefits such as employer-sponsored transportation services (Section 132).

Note: The information contained in parentheses or brackets indicates the section of the Internal Revenue Code that established these benefits.

- Permit only current and former employees to participate as long as the plan is not established principally for the benefit of former employees.
- Require participants to make yearly benefit choices before the beginning of the plan year (except making changes in benefit choices necessitated by changes in life circumstances, such as electing additional medical insurance coverage immediately following the birth of a child).
- Meet nondiscrimination requirements.
- Prohibit any benefit that defers an employee's receipt of compensation from year to year.

The first four requirements are relatively straightforward. However, the last two requirements are more complex, warranting further discussion.

Nondiscrimination Rules

Nondiscrimination rules prohibit employers from giving preferential treatment to highly compensated participants and key employees. For example, employer contributions to retirement plans that amount to 15 percent of highly compensated or key employees' annual salaries (as defined in Chapter 4) violate nondiscrimination rules when employer contributions to other employees are only 6 percent of salaries. In Section 125 plans, satisfying nondiscrimination rules permits plan participants to take tax deductions for qualified benefits. Failure to meet nondiscrimination rules eliminates tax benefits for one or both groups. The nature of the violation determines which group forfeits tax benefits. Three possible violations relate to eligibility, benefits, and concentration. They are:

- *Eligibility.* The company grants eligibility to highly compensated employees for participation with shorter waiting periods than employees who are not highly compensated. The maximum allowable waiting period following employment is three years.
- *Benefits.* Highly compensated participants with regard to an employer's contributions and benefits levels.
- *Concentration.* Key employees regarding the kinds of benefits and benefits levels provided under the plan.

The Internal Revenue Service applies a separate test to determine whether a cafeteria plan is discriminatory for each criterion—eligibility, benefits, and concentration. Exhibit 11.4 describes these tests.

More on Deferring an Employee's Receipt of Compensation

The last criterion, concentration, is the most complex. Two hypothetical situations illustrate how companies may violate this deferral of income criterion. First, employees elect to contribute a designated amount of wages or salary through salary reduction agreements (discussed shortly in this chapter), established prior to the beginning of a benefits plan year. It is possible that an employee's choice of benefits costs less than the designated amount. Cafeteria plans under Section 125 prohibit employers from allowing participants to carry over unused elective

EXHIBIT 11.4 Eligibility Test

The cafeteria plan must meet the following guidelines for participation eligibility:

- No employee is required to complete more than three years of employment with the employer as a condition of participation in the plan.
- The length of service requirement is the same for each employee.
- Employees are permitted to participate no later than the first day of the first plan year beginning after they satisfy the length-of-service requirement.

Benefits Test

A cafeteria plan is nondiscriminatory under the benefits and contributions test if the plan's nontaxable and total benefits do not discriminate in favor of highly compensated participants.

For cafeteria plans that provide health benefits, Section 125 provides a special safe harbor rule for testing employer contributions for discriminatory effects. Safe harbors refer to compliance guidelines in a law or regulation; cafeteria plans that fall in safe harbors automatically fulfill the nondiscrimination rules. Under this rule, a plan is not discriminatory if the employer contribution, including salary reductions, on behalf of each participant equals:

- 100 percent of the health benefit cost for the majority of highly compensated participants who are similarly situated—such as those who have single or family coverage, or
- 75 percent of the cost of the most expensive health benefit coverage elected by any similarly situated participant.

Contributions exceeding either of these two limits also are nondiscriminatory as long as they bear a uniform relationship to a participant's compensation.

The Concentration Test

The concentration test provides that a cafeteria plan is discriminatory where the nontaxable qualified benefits provided to key employees exceed 25 percent of the total nontaxable qualified benefits provided for all employees under the plan. This calculation can be based on the premium value of the coverage provided, rather than on actual benefits or reimbursements received by employees under the plan.

contributions to pay for benefits in later years. For example, in 2007 an employee signed a salary reduction agreement to contribute $2,000 toward the purchase of benefits in 2008. At the end of 2008, she spent only $1,500 of the allocated $2,000. Cafeteria plans under Section 125 prohibit using this $500 difference to purchase benefits on a pretax basis.

Second, employees may not use elective contributions designated for a chosen year to purchase any benefit for receipt in later years—specifically, benefits such as disability or long-term care insurance coverage. Although employees would pay each year to receive such protection, the actual payouts typically follow years into the future. For example, disability benefits provide monthly income to employees for multiple years following enrollment.

Types of Flexible Benefit Plan Arrangements

Employers design cafeteria plans in a variety of ways. The four most common types of cafeteria plans include salary reduction plans, modular plans, core-plus-option plans, and mix-and-match plans. The designs vary in two ways: flexibility

EXHIBIT 11.5 Flexible Benefit Plans

Source: M. W. Barringer and G. T. Milkovich. 1998. "A Theoretical Explanation of the Adoption and Design of Flexible Benefits Plans," *Academy of Management Review,* 23, no. 2, pp. 305–24.

Low Flexibility			High Flexibility
Low Cost			High Cost
Salary Reduction Only	**Modular Options**	**Core Plus Options**	**Mix and Match**
Premium conversion The employee pays a premium for insurance with a pretax salary reduction.	The employee can choose from among several different combinations of benefits (usually the same types of benefits but different levels of benefits).	*Core* The employee receives basic coverage in certain areas (e.g., health, life, and/or disability insurance).	Flexible credits are provided, and the employee can purchase any type and level of coverage offered.
Flexible spending account Pretax salary reductions fund an account for paying uncovered medical or dependent care bills.		*Plus* The employee has flexible credits to purchase additional coverage in the core area or in supplemental areas, such as child care, vacation days, or a trade-in for cash.	

Notes: Flexible spending accounts may be included in any of the plans described. Medical plan options may include multiple types (HMOs, fee for service) and levels (e.g., high/medium/low deductible and coinsurance rates), or they may be limited to a choice between a single fee-for-service plan and an HMO.

of employee choice and cost to the employer. An employer's cost generally rises as the level of flexibility increases. Exhibit 11.5 summarizes these four plans and displays their relative flexibility and cost.

Pretax Salary Reduction Plans

In general, **pretax salary reduction plans** permit employees to set aside a portion of wages or salary each year on a pretax basis for qualified benefits expenses. In other words, employees exclude allocated wages or salaries from the calculation of annual federal income tax or state income tax (except for New Jersey). This exclusion creates a strong incentive for participation. Employees enter into annual salary reduction agreements before the start of each benefits plan year.

Two well-known versions of salary reduction agreements are available: flexible spending accounts and premium-only plans. **Flexible spending accounts** permit employees to pay for certain benefits expenses (e.g., dental, medical, vision, or day care expenses) or to pay the premium or cost for at least one of these benefits. Usually, flexible spending accounts apply to expenses that exceed regular benefits limits. Prior to each plan year, employees elect the amount of salary-reduction dollars they wish to allocate to this kind of plan. Employers then use these moneys to reimburse employees for expenses incurred during the plan year that qualify for repayment. Exhibit 11.6 illustrates the features typical of flexible spending accounts

EXHIBIT 11.6   Flexible Spending Account (FSA) Program

The Flexible Spending Account (FSA) program is an optional benefit that gives State of Illinois employees the opportunity to use tax-free dollars to pay eligible dependent and/or medical care expenses. The FSA program offers two plans:

- **The Medical Care Assistance Program (MCAP)** allows you to use pretax dollars to pay eligible, medically necessary expenses that you, your spouse, and your dependents incur during the plan year.
- **The Dependent Care Assistance Program (DCAP)** enables you to use pretax dollars to pay eligible dependent care expenses you incur during the plan year.

How Flexible Spending Works

Employees may contribute up to a maximum of $5,000 in pretax dollars for each program. Contributions are deducted from your paycheck and deposited into your FSA account before state, federal, and Social Security taxes are withheld. This amount does not appear on your W-2 Form as taxable income, so it lowers your taxable income, leaving more money to spend and fewer taxes to pay.

Savings from participation in the FSA program can vary greatly depending on income, contribution amount, number of dependents, adjustments or itemizations on federal taxes, and the total of your medical/dependent care expenses. If you have both medical and dependent care expenses, participating in both plans will provide the maximum savings benefit.

How to Enroll

Read the FSA booklet to ensure your expenses meet the IRS/FSA requirements and are eligible for MCAP/DCAP. During the benefit choice period, enroll in MCAP/DCAP by completing the appropriate forms and submitting them to your group insurance representative. New employees, or employees who have an eligible change in status, may enroll within 60 days of their date of hire or change in status. Enrollment and changes in enrollment are not permitted outside the benefit choice period unless an employee experiences an eligible change in status. For enrollment forms and FSA booklets, contact your group insurance representative or the FSA unit. Specific claim eligibility questions should be directed to the claim processor, Fringe Benefits Management Company (FBMC).

How FSA Reimburses

MCAP/DCAP reimbursement can be made through a check payable to the participating member and mailed to the address of record in the FSA system, or through direct deposit.

FSA direct deposit is fast and easy. To enroll, visit the Illinois comptroller's Web site at www.ioc.state.il.us or contact the comptroller's Electronic Commerce Unit at (217) 555-0390. Once electronic payment has been established, all reimbursements paid to you by the comptroller's office, with the exception of your payroll check and income tax refund, will be deposited to your bank account directly. For example, if you elect direct deposit for your FSA reimbursement via the comptroller's Web site, your FSA reimbursements, as well as travel reimbursements, workers' compensation payments, and so forth, will be made by direct deposit.

If you have questions about how direct deposit works, visit the comptroller's Web site or contact the Electronic Commerce Unit as listed above.

Remember: Annual reenrollment in FSA is not automatic. If you currently have a Medical Care Assistance Plan and/or Dependent Care Assistance Plan account(s), and wish to continue participating in the program, you must reenroll during the benefit choice period.

FSA Savings Example

The following is an example of how FSA works:

Married with 2 Dependents	Not Participating in MCAP	Participating in MCAP
Annual gross income	$60,000	$60,000
Standard deductions and exemptions	18,550	18,550
MCAP contribution	0	5,000
Taxable income	41,450	36,450
Taxes (federal, state, and FICA)	11,611	10,320
After-tax medical expenses	5,000	0
Remainder of income	43,389	44,672
Increased spendable income	0	1,283

used in private and public sector companies, using the state of Illinois as an example. **Premium-only plans** enable employees to pay their share of the cost to receive health insurance, dental insurance, and other company-sponsored health insurance.

Modular Plans

With **modular plans,** an employer offers numerous fixed benefits packages to meet the life-cycle needs and priorities of different employee groups. Examples of groups include single employees with no dependents, single parents, married workers with dependents, and employees nearing retirement.

Under this arrangement, the costs of these benefits packages vary based on which benefits are included and the prices. An employer decides upon a fixed amount of money it will spend each year to provide a benefits package. Usually, the fixed amount equals the lowest cost among the available modular packages. Employees contribute the cost difference between a more extensive benefits package and the lowest-cost package.

Core-plus-Option Plans

Core-plus-option plans extend a preestablished set of benefits such as medical insurance and retirement plans as a program core. More often than not, core benefits are mandatory for all employees. Beyond the core, employees may choose from a collection of optional benefits that suit their personal needs. Companies establish upper limits of benefits values available to each employee. If employees do not choose the maximum amount of benefits, employers may offer an option of trading extra benefits credits for cash. Exhibit 11.7 illustrates the choices of a typical core-plus plan.

Mix-and-Match Plans

An employer decides the annual amount it will spend to fund each employee's benefits package. **Mix-and-match plans** permit employees to purchase any benefit (and benefit level). Companies award flexible credits to purchase these plans. Each credit equals $1.00, and the costs of each benefit are clearly communicated to

EXHIBIT 11.7
A Sample Core-plus-Option Plan

The core-plus-option plan contains two sets of benefits: *core benefits* and *optional benefits.* All employees receive a minimum level of *core benefits:*

- Term life insurance equal to 1 times annual salary.
- Health protection coverage (indemnity plan, self-funded, HMO, PPO) for the employee and dependents.
- Disability insurance.

All employees receive credits equal to 4 to 7 percent of salary, which can be used to purchase *optional benefits:*

- Dental insurance for employee and dependents.
- Vision insurance for employee and dependents.
- Additional life insurance coverage.
- Paid vacation time up to 10 days per year.

If an employee has insufficient credits to purchase the desired optional benefits, he or she can purchase these credits through payroll deduction.

employees. For instance, a company grants each employee 3,500 flexible credits. An employee chooses to purchase standard health insurance coverage for the year (1,800 credits) with additional coverage for his spouse and child (750 credits) for a total of 2,550 credits. This employee may use the remaining 950 credits to purchase additional benefits or trade in the credits for dollars.

COMMUNICATING THE EMPLOYEE BENEFITS PROGRAM

Benefits communication is an essential feature of effective plans. The law and good business sense establish the necessity for benefits communication. Sound communication programs facilitate these objectives. It is obvious to say that employees who are not aware of particular discretionary benefits will not gain from these offerings. And simply communicating the existence of these benefits is insufficient. The elements of sound benefits communication programs include:

- What is communicated?
- Who are the recipients of benefits information?
- How are benefits communicated?
- How often are benefits communicated?

We address these questions in this section.

Legal Considerations in Benefits Communication

Legally, employers must satisfy disclosure requirements set forth in the Employee Retirement Income Security Act of 1974. Employers satisfy these requirements by providing employees with written (1) summary plan descriptions and (2) summaries of material modifications. Written notices should not presume expert knowledge about design features. ERISA specifies that written notices be written so the "average" participant can understand them.

Summary Plan Description
Summary plan descriptions describe the following information:

- Names and addresses of the employees responsible for developing and administering the benefits plan.
- A description and explanation of the benefits such as health insurance and retirement plans.
- Disclosure of employee rights under ERISA.
- Eligibility criteria for participating in the benefits program.
- Conditions under which an employee becomes disqualified for benefits or is suspended.
- Claims procedures for receiving payments (e.g., reimbursement for medical expenses) and for appealing denial of claims.
- Whether a retirement plan is insured by the Pension Benefit Guarantee Corporation. The PBGC issues insurance to protect an employee's vested retirement savings when the retirement plan becomes insolvent or the retirement plan is terminated (Chapter 3).

EXHIBIT 11.8   Health Plan Overview

Source: *State of Illinois Benefits Handbook*, Fiscal Year July, 2007–June, 2008. By the Central Management Services in 2007.

Depending on residence, there may be several types of health plans from which to choose. The offerings change each year. Refer to the benefit choice options booklet for the current offerings.

Types of Health Plans

- Indemnity plan
  Quality Care Health Plan (QCHP)
- Managed care plans
  Health Maintenance Organizations (HMOs)
  Point-of-Service (POS) plans

Each plan provides medical, pharmaceutical, and mental health/substance abuse treatment benefits. However, the covered services, benefit levels, exclusions, and restrictions on service providers differ.

In making choices, consider the following: health status, coverage needs, and service preferences. Premiums differ among the various plans, too. Dependents must have the same health and dental plan as the member under whom they are covered.

Indemnity Plan

QCHP, the traditional health plan, offers a comprehensive range of benefits. Under the QCHP, plan participants are free to choose any provider (physician, specialist, or hospital) and change providers at any time. Benefit enhancements are available by utilizing Preferred Provider Organization (PPO) hospitals (for inpatient and outpatient services), the pharmacy network, and mental health/substance abuse network providers. Transplant benefits are available through the Transplant PPO (TPPO) Network.

Managed Care Plans

Over the years, as health care costs continue to rise, more and more employers offer managed health care plans. Individuals receiving medical care under a managed care plan are encouraged to have annual preventive physicals and seek early treatment if they become ill.

Managed care plans negotiate rates with participating network physicians, hospitals, and pharmacies. In turn, the plans offer cost-effective medical care with lower out-of-pocket costs.

HMO and POS plans both provide comprehensive medical benefits. Premium and copayment amounts may vary among the HMO and POS plans offered. When considering a managed care plan, special attention should be directed to the participating physicians and hospitals that plan participants are required to use for maximum benefits.

HMO plan participants choose a doctor or provider location from those participating in the plan's provider network. This doctor or location becomes the primary care provider (PCP). HMO plans provide a comprehensive network for care. All routine medical care, hospitalizations, and referrals for specialized medical care must be coordinated under the direction of the PCP. Services provided without approval/referral from a PCP will not be covered. Plan participants are responsible for 100 percent of the cost of out-of-network care. Coverage outside the HMO area is limited to emergency services only.

A point-of-service plan combines HMO-like benefits and traditional health coverage. POS plan participants choose a PCP from those participating in the plan's provider network. Care received in-network under the direction of the PCP is provided at maximum benefits. A POS plan participant also has the option to go out of network for eligible services and receive reduced benefits with deductibles and coinsurance. Managed care plans contract with a network of physicians and hospitals to deliver or arrange for the delivery of covered services. If the designated PCP leaves the managed care plan's network, three options are available:

- Choose another PCP with that plan.
- Change managed care plans.
- Enroll in the QCHP.

The opportunity to change plans applies only to the PCP leaving the network. It does not apply to hospitals, specialists, or women's health care providers who are not the designated PCP.

Summary plan descriptions may be very lengthy depending on the number of benefits. Exhibit 11.8 shows an excerpt from a company's summary plan description of its indemnity and managed care health insurance plans.

Employers are obligated to distribute summary plan descriptions to employees and the U.S. Department of Labor within 120 days of the plan becoming subject to ERISA's reporting and disclosure requirements (Chapter 3). ERISA also requires that employees or their beneficiaries receive a summary plan description within 90 days of becoming a plan participant. Employers must supply participants with completely updated summary plan descriptions no later than 210 days following every fifth plan year even when the benefits remain unchanged.

Summary of Material Modification

A **summary of material modification** describes important (i.e., material) changes to the benefits plan. Material information applies to changes in the benefits program, including plan administrators, claims procedures, eligibility rules, and vesting provisions of retirement plans. ERISA obligates employers to distribute summaries of material modifications within 210 days after the end of the plan year in which the material change occurred. Summaries of material modifications go to employees and the Department of Labor.

The "Good Business Sense" of Benefits Communication

An effective communication program should have three primary objectives:

- To create an awareness of, and appreciation for, the way current benefits improve the financial security as well as the physical and mental well-being of employees.
- To provide a high level of understanding about available benefits.
- To encourage the wise use of benefits.

A variety of media can be used to communicate such information to employees. Printed brochures that abstract the key features of the benefits program are useful for conveying the "big picture" and help potential employees compare benefits offerings with other companies they may be considering. Once employees join the company, initial group meetings with benefits administrators or audiovisual presentations can detail the elements of the company's benefits program. Shortly after group meetings or the audiovisual presentations (usually within a month), new employees should meet individually with benefits administrators, sometimes known as counselors, to select benefits options. Increasingly, companies are moving away from this approach by eliminating group or individual meetings with benefits counselors, expecting new employees to make their choices based on written explanations of benefits or audiovisual presentations. In any event, after selecting benefits, the company should provide personal benefits statements that detail the scope of coverage and value of each component for the current year. Exhibit 11.9 illustrates a personal statement of benefits.

More recent communications methods include a company's intranet and an interactive phone system. A company intranet is a useful way to communicate benefits information to employees on an ongoing basis beyond the legally required written

EXHIBIT 11.9 Employee Benefits Statement

Source: University of Illinois Office of Human Resources, Urbana–Champaign.

Benefits Statement
Employee Name:　　　　　　Brown, Michael
Date Employed:　　　　　　05–21–1995

The following benefit information is based on the pay period from 10–21–2007 through 11–20–2008.

Health Section

Medical:　　　　　　Personal Care

(Includes vision care plan)

Monthly Cost Breakdown

For You Only	For 0 Dependent(s)	Total You Pay	State Pays	Total Cost
243.14	0	35.50	207.64	243.14

Dental:　　　　　　Quality Care Dental (Employee Only)

Monthly Cost Breakdown

For You Only	For 0 Dependent(s)	Total You Pay	State Pays	Total Cost
16.32	0	7.50	8.82	16.32

Insurance Section

State Basic Life:　　　　　　Minnesota Life Insurance

Monthly Cost Breakdown

Coverage Amount	Total You Pay	State Pays	Total Cost
105,000.00	0	43.06	43.06

State Optional Life:　　　　　　Minnesota Life Insurance 3 × Salary

Monthly Cost Breakdown

Coverage Amount	Total You Pay	State Pays	Total Cost
315,000.00	28.35	0.00	28.35

SURS Disability:　　　　　　SURS

Monthly Cost Breakdown

Coverage Amount	Total You Pay	State Pays	Total Cost
50% of salary (52,500.00)	0.00	87.50	87.50

Tax-Deferred Retirement Plans Section

457 Plans:
Vendor Name	Pay Check Deduction

You are not enrolled in any 457 Tax-Deferred Options.

403b Plans:
Vendor Name	Contribution %	Pay Check Deduction

You are not enrolled in any 403b Tax-Deferred Options.

Flexible Spending Accounts Section

You are not enrolled in any flexible spending programs.

Note: Any changes made during the Benefit Choice enrollment period will not be shown on your benefits statement until after the first payroll calculation in July. If you would like to review the changes you made, you can go to the *Benefit Choice* section.

EXHIBIT 11.10 **Employee Benefits Overview**

Source: University Office of Human Resources, University of Illinois, Urbana–Champaign.

This section is designed to provide detailed information regarding your benefits as a University of Illinois employee. It will give you a comprehensive explanation of each benefit and the resources you will need to initiate enrollment, make changes, or find answers to questions regarding your benefits.

Please select from the following categories:

- *Announcements.* Provides announcements of upcoming sign-up periods or events and updated information relating to your benefits.
- *Benefits Directory.* Provides a listing of staff members, including addresses, phone numbers, and e-mail addresses for the Benefits Service Center and each campus.
- *Benefit Choice.* Benefit Choice is an annual open enrollment period that allows employees to make changes to their State of Illinois health, dental, and life insurance coverages and enroll or reenroll in flexible spending accounts.
- *Benefit Forms.* Provides links to printable and online benefit forms.
- *Benefits on Call.* Provides an explanation and step-by-step instructions on how to access your benefits information by calling the Benefits On Call voice response system.
- *Benefits Statement.* Provides a statement outlining your current benefit enrollments and instructions for accessing that information.
- *Benefits Summary.* Provides a detailed, comprehensive description of each benefit plan and its provisions.
- *Change in Illinois State Plan (CMS) Coverages.* Provides guidelines and required documentation on when and how you can make changes to your state insurance plans.
- *Frequently Asked Questions.* Provides a list of commonly asked questions relating to your benefits.
- *Leave Information.* Provides time-off related information for benefits such as family medical leave, sick leave, and vacation leave.
- *Retirement Planning Seminars.* Provides dates and sign-up information.
- *Shared Benefits.* Provides information on the sharing of sick leave between eligible employees and the process to apply for, or donate time to, the shared sick leave pool.
- *SURS Information.* Provides links to information on the State University Retirement System.
- *University Plans.* Provides plan information and enrollment procedures for university-administered benefit plans.

documents. In an era of the paperless office, employees are less likely to have written materials readily available. Employees can review general information about the benefits program whenever they want. Exhibit 11.10 lists general information about the kinds of available information. Each paragraph contains a hyperlink (e.g., announcements, benefits directory) that leads to more detailed information.

Interactive phone systems communicate descriptive information about benefits, representing an alternative way to stay abreast of basic benefits information. Employees use the telephone to contact a user-friendly voice response system. These phone systems go a step further by allowing employees to make common transactions virtually 24/7, eliminating the need to visit the company's benefits office. For example, employees may request insurance claim forms for delivery by mail or fax. Interactive phone systems are particularly helpful to employees who work in the field or in remote facilities too small to warrant a separate benefits office. Exhibit 11.11 shows a summary of an interactive phone system used by the University of Illinois, Urbana–Champaign, to enroll in or change benefits.

EXHIBIT 11.11 Benefits On Call

Source: University Office of Human Resources, University of Illinois Urbana–Champaign.

BENEFITS ON CALL   (217) 555-8422   1-800-555-1451

Benefits On Call is an interactive voice response system developed to provide employees with benefit information virtually 24 hours a day, seven days a week. By calling the Benefits On Call system, benefit-eligible employees are able to obtain their specific benefit information and eliminate the need to visit or call the Benefit Center.

Benefits On Call is available 24 hours a day, except for the following times:

- Between 4:00 a.m. and 6:00 a.m., Monday through Saturday
- Between 10:00 p.m. Saturday and 8:00 p.m. Sunday

Benefits On Call can be used to:

- Request items to be mailed or faxed to you, such as:
  - A personal benefits statement
  - Claim forms
  - Enrollment forms
- Receive confirmation of health and dental plan enrollments, including dependent coverage.
- Confirm insurance coverage amounts for the state term-life plan and the accidental death and dismemberment plan.
- Verify enrollment and payroll deduction amounts for the tax-deferred retirement plans and flexible spending accounts.
- Hear responses to frequently asked questions, such as:
  - When can I change plans?
  - When can I add a dependent?
  - How long are dependents eligible for coverage?

To use Benefits On Call, you will need:

- A touch-tone telephone.
- A Social Security number.
- A four-digit Personal Identification Number (PIN). You will choose your PIN the first time you call Benefits On Call. This will be your PIN that you use every time you call.

To access your information through Benefits On Call:

- Dial (217) 555-UIBC 8422 or 1-800-555-1451
- After the welcome message, enter your Social Security number, followed by the # sign.
- Enter your PIN, followed by the # sign.
- Select from the menu of topics by pressing the appropriate numbers on your telephone keypad.

After becoming familiar with the system, you will be able to take shortcuts from the main menu by pressing a series of numbers as outlined in the following table.

Shortcuts from Main Menu					
Benefits Statement or Forms		**Health Insurance**		**Life Insurance**	
Benefits statement faxed	21	Health plan enrollment	111	Employee life insurance	1211
Benefits statement mailed	22	Changing plans	411	Spouse life insurance	1212
Forms faxed	31	Adding dependents	412	Child life insurance	1213

(continued)

EXHIBIT 11.11 Benefits On Call (*Continued*)

Shortcuts from Main Menu					
Benefits Statement or Forms		**Health Insurance**		**Life Insurance**	
Forms mailed	31	Children covered until. . .	413	Accidental death insurance	122
		Filing claims	4151		

Shortcuts from Main Menu					
Tax Deferred Plans		**Dental Insurance**		**Medical and/or Dependent Care Assistance Plans**	
403(b) enrollment	131	Enrollment	112	Enrollment, contribution amount	14
457 enrollment	132	Changing plans	411		
		Filing claims	4152	Disability coverage	123

MANAGING THE COSTS OF EMPLOYEE BENEFITS

As we have discussed throughout this book, managing the costs of benefits programs is essential because the already high costs continually increase. In this section, we introduce alternative methods to assist companies in managing benefits costs:

- Employee contributions
- Waiting periods
- High-deductible plans
- Utilization reviews
- Case management
- Provider payment systems
- Lifestyle interventions

We have already introduced two of these methods as basic design features of company-sponsored programs in Chapter 1: employee contributions and waiting periods. Employee contributions help companies save money by requiring that employees pay a nominal amount of the costs paid by the employer to provide particular benefits. As we have also noted in this book, employees typically share the cost of benefits with pretax contributions or after-tax contributions. As we note throughout this chapter, various tax regulations permit employees to exclude contributions from annual income before calculating federal and state income tax obligations. These are called **pretax contributions. After-tax contributions** do not reduce the amount of annual income subject to income tax. For instance, companies expect employees to share the cost of medical insurance coverage with pretax contributions; these companies base employee contributions on their total annual earnings, as shown in the following example.

Annual Pay	Monthly Employee Contribution
Less than $20,000	$35.00
$20,000–$29,999	$45.00
$30,000–$44,999	$55.00
$45,000–$59,999	$65.00
$60,000 or more	$70.00

Second, companies impose one or more waiting periods to limit participation in the benefits program. **Waiting periods** specify the minimum number of months or years an employee must remain employed before becoming eligible for one or more benefits. Waiting periods often correspond with the length of probationary periods. Companies impose probationary periods to judge a newcomer's job performance, and they explicitly reserve the right to terminate employees who demonstrate low job performance. The use of waiting periods helps companies control costs.

Also, in Chapter 6, we discussed the role of high-deductible health care plans in cost control that shift more of the expense of health care from the employer to employee in the form of higher annual deductibles. The premium for high-deductible plans is substantially lower, which creates immediate cost savings for employers. The idea of high-deductible plans has found its way into the workers' compensation (Chapter 8) arena. As we discussed in that chapter, employers are responsible for providing workers' compensation insurance. Traditionally, companies purchased guaranteed coverage, which means that the insurance company would administer the program, undertake all risk, and be responsible for all financial obligations. Under this approach, companies would not have any deductible costs. With high-deductible plans, companies pay substantially less in premiums than they would for guaranteed coverage in exchange for agreeing to pay up to a predetermined deductible amount. The guaranteed approach ensures a substantial expenditure regardless of whether any workers become injured or ill. Under the same scenario, a company's expenditures for workers' compensation stand to be substantially less with high-deductible programs.

In this chapter, we introduce three additional cost-control methods: utilization reviews, case management, and provider payment systems. These methods apply mainly to health insurance benefits. Employers and insurance companies set up cost-control programs to limit unnecessary costs while promoting the highest-quality health care. Without these methods, insurance companies would necessarily charge employers even higher premium amounts. Separate premiums usually apply to health, dental, and life insurance protection.

COST-CONTROL METHODS

Employers and insurance companies set up cost-control programs to limit unnecessary costs while promoting the highest-quality care. Deductibles, coinsurance, copayments, and maximum benefits amounts are regular cost-control features.

Additional methods include employee education, utilization reviews, case management, and provider payment systems. For the purposes of this discussion, the term *health care and health insurance* encompasses prescription drugs, mental health, vision, dental, and medical care.

Employee Education

Educating employees about the cost of health care is essential to controlling the rising costs of health care insurance because past employer and insurance company practices of not educating employees about costs may have inadvertently led them to overutilize health insurance benefits for at least two reasons. First, since the 1940s and 1950s, most medium- and large-scale employers have offered health insurance coverage to employees as part of a benefits package. Offering health insurance coverage provided companies with lucrative tax breaks, and including health insurance in the benefits package helped companies recruit and retain valued employees. Most employees viewed health care coverage, along with other benefits such as paid time-off, as a privilege because it was included as a standard benefit and employees often did not pay to have employer-sponsored health insurance protection. Second, indemnity plans were quite common decades ago. By design, these plans provided individuals with substantial freedom to go directly to doctors of their choice, oftentimes to very expensive medical specialists even when the situation did not actually require the expertise of a specialist.

Even as the costs of health care led insurance companies to raise health insurance premiums in the 1980s and 1990s, employers continued to offer generous insurance coverage while absorbing the cost for higher premiums. Since the U.S. economy began weakening substantially in 2000 compared to the 1990s, and competitive pressures forced more companies to carefully audit their costs, employers began to shift health-related costs to employees by having them pay a greater share. Educating employees about health care costs and the reasons for rising costs should promote cost containment. Moreover, educating employees about the costs of health care as well as the benefits of seeking lower-cost preventative health care should enable them to get the most from consumer-driven health care approaches (Chapter 6).

Utilization Reviews

Utilization reviews serve various purposes. Health care providers conduct **utilization reviews** to evaluate the quality of specific health care services. Employers offering group health benefits, and also insurers, depend on utilization reviews to ensure that medical treatments received by participants are medically appropriate. Sponsors of these reviews hire medical doctors and registered nurses to carry out utilization reviews. These medical professionals rely on professional practice standards established by medical associations to judge the medical appropriateness of treatment and quality of patient care.

Three types of utilization reviews may be conducted. The first, **prospective reviews** or **precertification reviews,** evaluate the appropriateness of proposed medical treatment as a condition for authorizing payment. Specifically, prospective reviews entail:

- Verifying a patient's coverage.
- Determining whether the health plan covers the treatment.

- Judging whether the proposed treatment is medically appropriate.
- Specifying whether a second surgical opinion is necessary.

The use of prospective reviews differs somewhat between indemnity plans and managed care plans. Managed care plans require prospective reviews more often and rely on a participating physician's judgment. Prospective reviews are less common for indemnity plans because the plans incur the cost of hiring outside expertise to conduct these reviews. In aggregate, the costs of hiring external expertise can exceed the savings from conducting these reviews.

The second type, **concurrent reviews,** focuses on current hospital patients. Insurers conduct concurrent reviews to judge whether additional inpatient hospitalization is medically necessary. Concurrent reviews take place approximately one day before a patient is scheduled to be discharged from the hospital when a physician recommends extending hospitalization. Alternatively, insurers conduct utilization reviews shortly after admission to the hospital following emergency treatment. Physicians may appeal these decisions by providing further medical justification for treatment.

The third type, **retrospective reviews,** takes place prior to an insurance company's disbursement of benefits. Retrospective reviews have two main objectives, starting with a determination of whether the health insurance program covers the patient, the medical conditions, and the medical treatment. These reviews also judge that claims are not fraudulent by confirming that medical treatments were actually given and were appropriate for the medical condition.

Case Management

Many health insurance plans use the services of independent **case management** companies to ensure that participants with serious health problems receive essential medical attention on a cost-effective basis. Usually, registered nurses or social workers, who are employed as case managers, collaborate with physicians to balance the medical needs of the patient and to contain costs for health insurers. Serious health problems arising from injuries or illnesses may be acute (short-term) or chronic (ongoing). Exhibit 11.12 lists examples of serious health conditions that may warrant case management.

EXHIBIT 11.12 **Serious Health Conditions Warranting Case Management**		
Acquired immune deficiency syndrome	Multiple sclerosis
Alzheimer's disease	Muscular dystrophy
Amputations	Neurological disorders
Cancer	Organ transplants
Cardiovascular conditions	Paralysis
Cerebral palsy	Pregnancy complications
Cerebral vascular accident (stroke)	Premature birth
Chemical dependency	Psychiatric disorders
Congenital anomaly	Renal failure
Head injuries	Respiratory ailments
Major burns	Spinal cord injuries

Provider Payment Systems

Provider payment systems refer to payment arrangements between managed care insurers and health care providers. Managed care plans establish provider payment systems to control the costs of health care. Fee-for-service plans do not include this feature because health care providers seek reimbursement after rendering services.

Provider payment systems begin with negotiations over amounts the system will pay participating physicians, health care facilities, and pharmacies for the duration of the managed care plan's contract with these providers (in effect for up to a few years). Agreements may include one or more cost saving features, including percentage discounts, capped fee schedules, partial capitation, and full capitation.

As the term implies, **percentage discounts** are fees that are discounted from the amounts health care providers would usually charge. Under this arrangement, health care providers agree to the percentage of discount. Percentage discounts are not the most cost-effective methods for two reasons. First, managed care plans do not enforce a limit on the number of services, making it difficult to anticipate total costs. Second, health care providers are free to increase their "regular" fees, adding to total costs.

Capped fee schedules set maximum dollar amounts for each service. Similar to percentage discount systems, capped fee schedules do not limit the volume of services, making it difficult to anticipate total costs. Managed care plans use usual, customary, and reasonable fees as a starting point for establishing capped fee schedules. From there, they set maximums by limiting payments to a percentage of usual, customary, and reasonable fees.

Partial capitation systems apply to primary care physicians. These systems pay primary care physicians a fixed dollar amount for each patient assigned to them. It is not uncommon for current patients to change primary care physicians, leave the managed care plan altogether, or for new patients to join managed care plans. As a result, the number of patients associated with each primary care physician varies over time. Partial capitation systems render payments to primary care physicians on a monthly basis to account for variability in patient load. These payment systems make it easier for managed care plans to anticipate total costs because physicians are rewarded for the total number of assigned patients, not the number of services rendered in a given amount of time.

Full capitation systems also pay primary care physicians a fixed amount for each assigned patient; however, the actual amount may vary from patient to patient. Under this system, managed care plans hold primary care physicians accountable for the cost of services rendered to each assigned patient. Managed care plans deduct all, or a percentage of, the costs from the allotted maximum amount. Full capitation systems effectively control costs because total outlay does not increase with the volume of services. Unlike percentage discount systems and capped fee schedules, full capitation systems create financial disincentives for primary care physicians to authorize treatments and referrals to specialists.

Lifestyle Interventions

Lifestyle interventions refer to any activity that changes how a person lives life. For example, stopping cigarette smoking is an example of a lifestyle change that can be brought on by participation in a smoking cessation program. In Chapter 10 we discussed a variety of wellness programs that, if followed by employees, should lead to lifestyle changes, and fit with the idea of lifestyle intervention. In virtually all companies, employees *choose* whether to participate in one or more wellness programs (e.g., weight control and stress management), thus initiating a lifestyle intervention. However, some companies believe they should decide whether employees require lifestyle interventions to promote better health and, subsequently, lower the costs of employer-sponsored life and health insurance. In such companies, employers are considering policy to terminate employees who do not make adequate progress. In 2007, Scotts Miracle-Gro Company made controversial news headlines by setting policy to terminate employees who do not quit smoking or lose weight. Terminated employees are claiming wrongful discharge and plan to file suit against the company in court, claiming that it is illegal for a company to impose lifestyle changes (in this situation, use of tobacco and eating in excess). Companies around the U.S. will be watching for the outcome of any suits against Scotts Miracle-Gro. If this company's lifestyle policies are not deemed to be illegal, it is possible other companies will follow suit as a means to control expenditures on insurance and improve productivity.

OUTSOURCING THE BENEFITS FUNCTION

Until now, we presumed that employers manage and administer the entire benefits function internally with a staff of benefits professionals, including managers and support staff. Some employers have chosen to outsource some or all of the benefits function (and other HR functions, for that matter). **Outsourcing** refers to a contractual agreement by which an employer transfers responsibility to a third-party provider. In the case of benefits, third-party providers are independent companies with expertise in benefits design and administration. Outsourcing agreements remain in effect from a few months to a few years.

Outsourcing HR functions is on the rise. Most companies outsource at least one function; many of them typically outsource four functions. Employee benefits is the most outsourced HR function. Among benefits practices, companies tend to outsource 401(k) programs, pension program administration, and health insurance benefits.

Two factors drive the decision to outsource, including reductions in workforce size and the complexity of benefit plan administration. Increasingly, shortages make it difficult for companies to devote staff employee time to only one function. Employers expect staff members to help out in multiple areas, abandoning a specialist role in favor of a generalist one. Assuming more generalist responsibilities makes it difficult to stay abreast of the ever-changing laws and regulations that influence discretionary benefits practices.

Outsourcing some or all benefits administration can be very expensive in the short run because most or all contract fees are due up front. Over time, efficient arrangements can be less costly than devoting several employees to benefits administration, especially when staff member flexibility allows companies to bolster critical functions by adding more employees to customer service during peak demand.

THE FUTURE OF EMPLOYEE BENEFITS

Our consideration of the forces that shape employee benefits today suggests that this realm of human resource (HR) practice is in a state of flux. There are no signs indicating that the future of employee benefits is bleak. Instead, this realm of HR practice will provide exciting challenges to practitioners as they strive to design and implement optimal employee benefits programs in their companies. Adding to the excitement is the challenge of predicting how current and anticipated changes in society and the economy will influence employee benefits practice. At least six influences will be in play:

- Changing employment contract.
- Accountability to shareholders.
- Recent and proposed legislation.
- Domestic partner benefits and same-sex marriage issues.
- Generational diversity and workplace conflict.
- Presidential-year politics.

Changing Employment Contract

The traditional employment relationship was characterized by an expectation of mutual long-term commitment between employers and employees, strong internal promotion and employee development practices, and interest in promoting equitable compensation. Times have changed. Nowadays, competitive pressures encourage employees and employers to share a mutual expectation that the employment relationship is temporary.

For example, many companies are adopting pension programs that by design discourage long-term employment. Specifically, there is a shift in many companies from the use of traditional defined benefit pension plans to defined contribution plans. Typically, companies contribute an amount equal to a fixed percentage of an employee's annual pay. Over time, an employee's pay will rise as he or she receives permanent pay increases for earning promotions, better performance, or gaining new knowledge or skills. As a result, the actual dollar amount contributed to an employee's retirement plan increases, though the percentage remains constant. Defined contribution plans are much like a savings account balance that is invested in a variety of ways chosen by employees. Employers are not required to make contributions to these plans, nor are they responsible for guaranteeing a minimum account balance or income from the plan at any time. These features make it easy for employees to move from one company to the next without any consequence for investment growth over time.

The changing employment contract also has implications for the relevance of particular benefits to younger employees who are not likely to have expectations of long-term employment. For example, younger employees stand to view life insurance and health insurance benefits as less valuable because the likelihood of using such benefits is not as great as it is for older workers who, statistically speaking, are more likely to die or become seriously ill. Instead, younger workers are likely to consider benefits that address priorities fitting their life stage to possess greater value—for instance, day care assistance and tuition reimbursement programs.

Accountability to Shareholders

Shareholders delegate control to management to represent their ownership interests. Ultimately, shareholders' interests are realized through positive returns on their investment. Ideally, compensation and benefits professionals should demonstrate how investments in such benefits as paid vacation, day care services, and medical insurance translate into higher productivity. Unfortunately, accounting procedures to demonstrate the return on benefits expenditures are not readily available and the norm is to account for costs rather than for the benefits. For instance, while it is expected that a healthier workforce translates into higher productivity, there simply is no definitive evidence to show fiscal or productivity returns on such benefits as medical coverage.

Even if such accounting procedures were available, conventional treatment of benefits by management would probably show small positive or negative returns. Companies typically offer an array of discretionary benefits to employees without regard to the costs. Often in the past, companies competed for the best individuals partly through the number and kinds of benefits, making no adjustments later for the quality of an employee's job performance. Nowadays, many employers recognize that employees must earn discretionary benefits if their companies are to sustain competitive advantage. "The 'new economy' has focused firms on survival. No longer are benefits plans designed against the backdrop of assumed profitability and enterprise continuation. Job entitlement has been replaced by performance measurement."[1] As we discussed in Chapter 5, various companies have terminated their defined pension plans and transferred responsibility to the Pension Benefit Guaranty Corporation because of desperate financial conditions. Also, the recent rise of consumer-driven health care and high-deductible health insurance plans has shifted substantially more of the cost of health insurance from the employer to employee.

Recent and Proposed Legislation

Regulatory changes have created alternatives to employment-based benefits. For instance, the **Economic Growth and Tax Relief Reconciliation Act of 2001** eased deductible contributions to individual retirement accounts for taxpayers who are active participants in employer-sponsored retirement plans. The **Taxpayer Relief Act of 1997** introduced a tax-free nondeductible individual retirement account (IRA), referred to as the **Roth IRA.** The **traditional IRA** provides for a deduction when a contribution is made and is taxable in its entirety when distributed. The Roth IRA is nondeductible and withdrawals are nontaxable, including the account's earnings if distributions meet certain criteria.

The **Health Insurance Portability and Accountability Act (HIPAA) of 1996** could be a blow to employee retention. Until recently, thousands of employees in the United States experienced the **job-lock phenomenon.** Job-lock occurs whenever an employed individual experiences a medical problem, and this individual is "locked" into the current job because most health insurance plans contain preexisting conditions clauses. A **preexisting condition** is defined as a condition for which medical advice, diagnosis, care, or treatment was received or recommended during a designated period preceding the beginning of coverage. Although an employee's current medical plan covered the chronic medical condition because it surfaced while covered, another health insurance plan offered by a different employer was not likely to cover the same medical or preexisting condition. Until HIPAA, individuals with chronic health conditions such as AIDS faced the strong possibility of not qualifying for health insurance coverage with a new employer. Since the passage of HIPAA, however, it is easier for individuals to move from employer to employer.

From time to time, lawmakers in Washington propose new legislation that affects employee benefits practices. In 2001, President George W. Bush signed the *Economic Growth and Tax Relief Reconciliation Act* into law. This piece of legislation introduced several measures that permit greater tax-qualified retirement savings in many company-sponsored retirement plans. Perhaps the most noteworthy changes allow increased employee and employer contributions to many types of retirement plans on a tax-deferred basis and provisions for increasing these limits further in future years. Human resource professionals and employees should keep abreast of proposed legislative changes to anticipate how these changes may influence benefit practices.

In 2006, President George W. Bush signed the *Pension Protection Act of 2006* into law. This act is supposed to help shore up the financial solvency of defined benefit plans in private sector companies and to automatically enroll employees in defined contribution plans. From the employee's perspective, defined contribution plans are much riskier than defined benefit plans because the amount and duration of retirement income depends mainly on the performance of investments.

Domestic Partner Benefits and Same-Sex Marriage Issues

Over the past several decades, more companies have offered domestic partner benefits for unmarried employees that are similar to benefits for married employees. Domestic partner benefits may entail as little as extending employee discounts to their partners or as much as having domestic partners and children covered under company-sponsored health insurance. Offering domestic partner benefits is largely done on a discretionary basis to recruit and retain highly qualified applicants and employees, but some states do require that companies offer these benefits. For example, California mandates under state law that companies grant registered domestic partners of employees the same rights and benefits extended to married spouses. New Jersey requires all health insurers to offer domestic partner coverage and prohibits employers from discriminating based on domestic partnership status. However, New Jersey does not require employers to provide domestic partner coverage under employee health plans. If such coverage is offered, employers can have employees pay part, or all, of the premium. In 2007, the New Jersey Attorney General issued an opinion concluding that same-sex marriages and civil unions from out-of-state jurisdictions will be afforded "all of the rights and benefits of marriage" under New Jersey's civil union law. Same-sex civil unions recognized by Vermont and Connecticut, as well as same-sex partnerships under California law, will be treated as equivalents of civil unions in New Jersey.

Not all companies and states define domestic partners similarly. In some cases, employers offer domestic partner benefits to unmarried partners (in heterosexual relationships) and children of all employees, while others limit this coverage to same-sex couples. In any event, employers require endorsement of the domestic partnership through proof of shared residence, signed statements attesting to a long-term relationship, or other information to show that the domestic partnership is not a short-term relationship (e.g., joint bank accounts and being the beneficiary of a partner's life insurance policy can establish that a long-term relationship is in place).

Limiting domestic partner benefits to same-sex partners has raised substantial criticism from unmarried heterosexual couples. This criticism has led to legal challenges that allege discrimination against unmarried heterosexual couples. Thus far, the courts have disagreed with these claims of discrimination because unmarried heterosexual partners would have the same benefits if they were to become married—currently not much of an option for same-sex partners.

The issue of same-sex benefits has become (and will continue to be) more complex as the debate continues in the United States about whether same-sex partners may become legally married. For example, in 2003, the Massachusetts Supreme Judicial Court determined that denying same-sex couples the right to marry violated the state constitution.[2] Then, in 2006, the same court ruled that a proposed state constitutional amendment that would ban same-sex marriage can be placed on the ballot for voter approval if the amendment is approved by the state legislature.[3] In 2007, the Washington State House of Representatives approved a domestic partnership bill (SB 5336) that grants same-sex couples hospital visitation rights, inheritance rights when there is no will, and the power to authorize medical procedures, such as organ donation and autopsies. Although the legislation does not legalize same-sex marriage, this bill represents a significant step toward the legalization of same-sex marriage. Also, in 2007, the Michigan Court of Appeals ruled that an amendment to the state constitution defining marriage as between a man and a woman also prohibits Michigan public employers from offering benefits, such as health insurance, to same-sex partners of gay or lesbian employees.[4] The appeals court overturned a lower court decision finding no conflict between the 2004 amendment and providing the benefits. Employers and employee benefits professionals will be faced with many questions regarding employers' obligations under employee benefit plans, many of which cannot yet be anticipated.

In 2008, same-sex marriage became legal in California only to be struck down by a referendum in November of that year. In April 2009, both Iowa and Vermont decided to recognize same-sex marriage as legal. At the time of publication of this book, only two other states—Connecticut and Massachusetts—permit same-sex couples to become legally married. Proponents of same-sex marriage hope that the U.S. Supreme Court will accept a case in which they argue that a ban on same-sex marriage is unconstitutional. Both socially conservative and liberal political commentators do not expect the U.S. Supreme Court to take a case such as this one. In the 1970s, the U.S. Supreme Court ruled in *Roe v. Wade* that abortion was legalized. Since then, the issue has become divisive and has led to intimidation and even deaths of dozens of doctors who performed abortions. The Court is concerned that legalizing same-sex marriage could potentially result in social upheaval as has been the case following the legalization of abortion.

While some companies may choose to extend benefits to same-sex spouses, ERISA does not address this issue. Currently, ERISA relies on the federal definition of marriage, which occurs only between two individuals of the opposite sex. Federally mandated legally required benefits such as Social Security do not recognize same-sex spouses for the same reason. It is unlikely that the federal definition of spouse will change anytime soon with so few states having legalized same-sex marriages.

Generational Diversity and Workplace Conflict

As we've learned in this book, employers are required by law to provide particular benefits to employees, and can choose to offer other benefits because of tax incentives, and also to attract and retain the best-qualified individuals. A recent report suggests that employee benefits and reward systems are among the top 10 critical concerns facing organizations today.[5] These reports suggest that although companies recognize the importance of their benefits programs for attracting talent, few companies have ascertained employee expectations regarding their benefits programs or have measured the return on investment from their benefit offerings.

A more extensive "rewards dialogue" between employers and employees is likely to make reward and benefits systems more responsive to employee needs. Also, companies hope that the set of employee benefits will motivate employees to perform their jobs as well as possible. This hope is based on a scientific assumption that employees have similar attitudes toward, and will be motivated similarly by, benefits systems. However, several demographic trends in the U.S. workforce call into question this assumption. Consider, for instance, the increasing median age of the working population, the growing dependency ratios—defined as the number of children and elderly per 100 working aged individuals—and the increasing life expectancy of present-day workers.[6] These trends may influence employee attitudes regarding benefits and call for greater scrutiny of these systems and their ability to address the changing needs and expectations of employees.

To motivate employees and elicit desired performance outcomes, companies need to take a more audience-driven approach to their benefits systems (i.e., employees form the audience). Such an approach would involve a greater scrutiny of the motivational potential of these systems in relation to the varying needs and expectations of employees.[7] In the present business environment, a one-size-fits-all approach or flexible benefits programs under Section 125 may not be conducive to this audience-driven approach to employee benefits.

Scientific models of employee motivation (e.g., goal setting theory, expectancy theory, equity theory) have shown to be effective in explaining and predicting behavior where the context has been held constant. However, given changing demographics of the U.S. workforce, the context has changed, and many of the assumptions underlying our reward and motivation theories may not be applicable in all organizational contexts. For instance, due in part to variation across generations in norms regarding the appropriate age of marriage, the age at which an employee becomes concerned with life insurance has likely increased over time. Thus, it is possible that employee benefits systems do not effectively motivate all employees to strive for or attain first-rate job performance. For example, older employees without dependent children are unlikely to set higher work goals, put forth greater effort, or feel that the benefits offerings are equitable because their employer provides various family-friendly programs. In short, although the demographic composition of the U.S. labor force has undergone a major transformation in the 20th century, assumptions underlying employee benefits policies remain largely unchanged.

Presidential-Year Politics

Throughout this book, we have mentioned the escalating costs of employee benefits, particularly health care benefits. The rampant inflation in health care costs and health insurance made this topic a point of contention in the 2008 presidential election between presidential candidates Senators John McCain and Barack Obama. In general, Republican candidates suggested ways to address the high cost of health insurance such as tax credits for small businesses and low-income families. The Republicans are likely to continue advocating methods to support consumer-driven health care insurance because these methods help shift the burden for the cost of insurance from employers to employees. The Democrats, on the other hand, will probably advocate more extensive health care coverage and at lower costs to the employed and unemployed. The issue of multiple- versus single-payer health care systems lies at the heart of these ideological differences.

A variety of forces have contributed to the current multiple-payer health care system in the United States, including tax incentives to employers that provide insurance to employees, and employers' recognition that healthier workforces are likely to be more productive. However, the dramatically rising costs of health care services have made it cost-prohibitive for many employers (particularly small employers) to provide health insurance coverage because insurance companies continually raise their rates to maintain profits. In addition, the rampant rate of inflation in health care costs and insurance has far outpaced the rise in employee wages and salaries, forcing most companies that can still afford to offer health insurance to employees to reduce the level of insurance coverage by increasing deductibles or to contribute more to receive group coverage. Effectively, changes such as these continue to put health care out of the reach of millions of individuals (adults and children). In fact, the number of uninsured Americans has risen noticeably during the past several years to nearly 50 million. As an aside, other societal forces have contributed to the rise in the number of uninsured Americans; among them are the outsourcing of high-paying jobs to other countries, the decline of high-paying unionized jobs such as in the automobile industry, and the rise of lower-paying jobs typical of the expanding service sector of the economy. The confluence of these and other unmeasured forces makes it difficult to isolate the effects of a single source on the uninsured problem. Nevertheless, this problem of more and more people becoming uninsured has caught the attention of politicians, business executives, and the labor movement. These groups are calling for government intervention and collaborative efforts between the groups to reduce the number of uninsured. Extreme proposals advocate a single-payer health care system such as in Canada, based on the belief that access to quality health care is a basic right, rather than a privilege available only to those who can afford to pay for it.

For example, in early 2007, the executives from four major U.S. corporations (Wal-Mart, Intel, AT&T, and Kelly Services) and the leadership from the Service Employees International Union held a national press conference to express the desperate need for a system that provides universal health care coverage for every person in the United States. This coalition, named Better Health Care Together, advocated several goals during the press conference. Specifically, by the year 2012, they hope to see "quality, affordable health insurance coverage" for every American and "having businesses, governments, and individuals all contribute to managing and financing a new American health care system." Critics from other large labor unions such as the United Food and Commercial Workers union argue that large nonunion employers such as Wal-Mart and others that hope to limit union influence are simply attempting to improve their public image by expressing concern about the uninsured problem in America. In any event, the coalition does not address how to fund a universal health care system—that is, who becomes the single payer. At least for now, their objective is to raise awareness of the problem.

President George W. Bush advanced a plan in early 2007 to place the burden of health insurance costs on individuals by offering tax breaks to everyone who purchases health insurance coverage. Currently, the tax laws make employer-sponsored health insurance tax-free for workers and employers. That is, contributions to purchase health insurance are not included in an employer's or employees' taxable income. However, because employers pay the majority of the health insurance premium, typically, the tax deduction for employees is relatively small.

Needless to say, debates about the issue of moving toward a single-payer system in the United States will continue for some time to come for a variety of reasons. Since his election as president of the United States, President Barack Obama authorized the establishment of the White House Office of Health Reform. President Obama has pledged to provide all Americans access to affordable and high-quality health care. This office is charged with establishing policies, priorities, and objectives for the federal government's comprehensive efforts to improve access to health care, the quality of such health care, and the sustainability of the health care system.

Notwithstanding Obama's commitment, Democratic and Republican candidates offer widely different proposals about how to reach President Obama's goal. And, as you read this chapter, the story has already progressed. Nevertheless, some fundamental issues will be at the heart of single-payer health care systems in the United States for many years to come. Among those issues, insurance companies are for-profit businesses and many hospitals are funded by for-profit investment companies. The shareholders and owners of these businesses would strongly resist a transition to a single-payer system akin to Canada's system. Also, the U.S. system focuses on the micromanagement of billions of individual expenditures on health care, questioning the cost-effectiveness of health care practitioners' judgments. The Canadian system, on the other hand, focuses on the negotiation of health budgets with the provinces and typically does not scrutinize health care providers' judgment. Also, regulating access to, and the cost of, health care could potentially stifle innovation that has led to many lifesaving pharmaceuticals and medical procedures because profits to support future research and development would be hindered. Ultimately, establishing a universal health care program in the United States that is akin to the current Canadian single-payer system is unlikely to happen any time soon. This change would require a fundamental culture shift in the operation of health insurance practices, the "business" of health care, and the way millions of people in the United States are accustomed to receiving health care.

Summary

This chapter described the importance of linking benefits program design to overall strategic considerations and included company examples to illustrate this business imperative. Building effective benefits programs requires a review and interpretation of internal information (e.g., the needs and preferences of the workforce) and external information (e.g., the competition). Companies continually balance the needs and preferences of employees with cost considerations, leading to a brief look at cost-control methods. Increased diversity of the workforce and tax incentives have encouraged companies to offer flexible benefits programs. Flexible benefits programs represent a departure from offering the same set of benefits to all employees. Our treatment of benefits communications emphasized their necessity and basic approaches for setting up communications plans. We concluded with a review of outsourcing and pointed out some of the broad issues that employee benefits will have to face.

Key Terms

flexible benefits, *280*
cafeteria plans, *280*
qualified benefits, *280*
nondiscrimination rules, *281*
pretax salary reduction plans, *283*
flexible spending accounts, *283*
premium-only plans, *285*
modular plans, *285*
core-plus-option plans, *285*
mix-and-match plans, *285*
summary plan descriptions, *286*
summary of material modification, *288*

pretax contributions, *292*
after-tax contributions, *292*
waiting periods, *293*
utilization reviews, *294*
prospective reviews, *294*
precertification reviews, *294*
concurrent reviews, *295*
retrospective reviews, *295*
case management, *295*
provider payment systems, *296*
percentage discounts, *296*
capped fee schedules, *296*

partial capitation, *296*
full capitation, *296*
outsourcing, *297*
Economic Growth and Tax Relief Reconciliation Act of 2001, *299*
Taxpayer Relief Act of 1997, *299*
Roth IRA, *299*
traditional IRA, *299*
Health Insurance Portability and Accountability Act (HIPAA) of 1996, *299*
job-lock phenomenon, *299*
preexisting condition, *300*

Discussion Questions

1. Respond to the following statement: Flexible benefits plans are more trouble than they are worth. Do you agree or disagree with this statement? Provide a rationale for your answer.

2. Discuss how Section 125 plans create advantages for employees and employers.

3. What is the "good business sense" of benefits communications?

4. List and describe three specific ways insurance providers control costs. Which is most effective and why?

5. Identify one or more additional issues that may influence employees' benefits practice in the future.

Endnotes

1. D. L. Salisbury, ed. 1998. *Do Employers/Employees Still Need Employee Benefits?* Washington, DC: Employee Benefit Research Institute, p. viii.

2. *Goodridge v. Mass. Department of Public Health*, 440 Mass. 309, 798 NE2d 941 (November 18, 2003).

3. *Schulman v. Attorney General*, 447 Mass. 189, 850 NE2d 505 (July 10, 2006).

4. *National Pride at Work, Inc. v. Governor of Michigan and City of Kalamazoo*, 265 Mich. 870 (February 1, 2007) lc no. 05-000368-CZ.

5. CAHRS. 2006. "CAHRS top ten list, July 2006," Center for Advanced Human Resource Management Research. Online at www.cahrs.org. Accessed August 30, 2006.

6. J. Day. 1996. *Population Projections of the United States by Age, Sex, Race, and Hispanic Origin: 1995 to 2050.* Washington, DC: U.S. Bureau of the Census, Current Population Reports, P25-1130.

7. CAHRS. "CAHRS top ten list, July 2006."

Chapter **Twelve**

Global Employee Benefits at a Glance*

Learning Objectives

In this chapter, you will gather information about:

1. The differences between benefits in the United States and around the world.

2. Paid time-off benefits in various continents and countries.

3. Protection benefits such as retirement, health care, and social security in various continents and countries.

4. Legal and regulatory influences on employee benefits practices.

5. Other practices that distinguish various countries' benefits programs.

* This chapter was prepared by Professor Niti Pandey, Krannert School of Management, Purdue University, and edited for this edition by Joseph Martocchio.

Now you feel confident in your understanding of benefits—what they are and why employers or government offers them. But wait. Though you have developed a solid foundation of employee benefits practices at U.S. companies, in a year or so you will be taking a work assignment in another country. You wonder how employee benefits are structured in other countries and ask yourself, "Will my counterparts in other countries receive the same amount of paid time-off? Do they have similar choices in health care? Are their retirement plans the same or similar to the options here in the United States?"

Let's find out!

NOT ALL EMPLOYEE BENEFITS ARE ALIKE

In his bestseller *The World Is Flat,* Thomas L. Friedman talks about how the current state of technology-driven globalization has resulted in a high level of interconnections between the economies of various parts of the world. This means U.S. employers will be increasingly required to do business with entities in many other countries as erstwhile underdeveloped parts of the world experience tremendous economic, trade, and standard-of-living growth. Additionally, the move from traditional manufacturing to knowledge- and service-based employment also means jobs as well as markets are more likely to be geographically dispersed. As the need increases for employers to interact globally, human resource management professionals will have increased opportunities to develop employment practices for U.S. employees in foreign assignments, as well as deal with indigenous employees in the parent company's foreign offices. While most employers may choose to offer attractive benefits above and beyond the minimum required by the host nations, so as to attract the desired talent, it's important to first know the basic legal employment context and the minimum statutory employment standards of the country where they propose to do business—just as we've discussed throughout this book for U.S. employment (e.g., recall the Employee Retirement Income Security Act). In this chapter, we provide a glimpse of the wide variety of employment practices around the world. For each country listed in the chapter outline, we peruse basic benefits issues, including paid time-off, protection programs (e.g., retirement, health care), and stand-out benefits in particular regions. We start off each review with a brief treatment of that country's governmental structure, norms, and historical events to help shed light on its version of employee benefits.

NORTH AMERICA

This section offers a brief glimpse at employment relationships and employee benefits in Mexico and Canada. Both countries, along with the United States, are part of a trade bloc known as **NAFTA—the North American Free Trade Agreement.**

According to the Office of the United States Trade Representative, NAFTA allowed trade and investment flows in North America to skyrocket, with the International Monetary Fund estimating a doubling of trade between the three countries from 1993 to 2002.[1] Under NAFTA, trade restrictions were removed from industries such as motor vehicles and automotive parts, computers, textiles, and agriculture. In addition, the treaty also delineated the removal of investment restrictions between the three countries. As a result of supplemental agreements signed in 1993, worker and environmental protection provisions were added.

The labor side of NAFTA is the **North American Agreement on Labor Cooperation** (NAALC), which was created to promote cooperation between trade unions and social organizations to champion improved labor conditions.[2] While there has definitely been a convergence of labor standards in North America as a result of NAALC, there has been no convergence in employment, productivity, or salary trends.[3] Overall, NAFTA is reported as having been good for Mexico, which saw a fall in poverty rates and a rise in real income as a result of the trade agreement.[4] This section presents a brief overview of the employment relationship in Canada and Mexico and some basic employee benefits required by law in these countries.

Canada

According to *The CIA World Factbook*, Canada is a constitutional monarchy that is also a parliamentary democracy and a federation consisting of 10 provinces and three territories.[5] With a **per capita gross domestic product (GDP)*** of $39,300 and an 18.18-million-strong labor force, the Canadian economy is very similar to the U.S. market-based economy. And while Canada has enjoyed a trade surplus and balanced budgets for many years, recent concern and debate has grown over the increasing cost of the publicly funded health care system.

Employment law researchers report that the basic rule of Canadian law holds that labor and employment law fall within the exclusive jurisdiction of the provinces.[6] Thus, both individual and collective employment relationships are controlled at the province level, and federal legislation cannot override provincial laws, even when the industry or employer primarily conducts business overseas (except in the cases where the industries are expressly assigned to federal jurisdiction). The origins of the common law governing individual employment contracts are in the **English Statute of Labourers** of 1562, which established working hours and wages. This statute was eventually repealed in the early 19th century but became part of the English common law and later part of the common law governing all the provinces besides Quebec. Quebec, instead, operates under the Civil Code of Quebec (instituted in 1866), whose modernized version became effective January 1, 1994.

---

*Gross domestic product (GDP) describes the size of a country's economy. Size is expressed as the market value of all final goods and services produced within the country over a specified period. The GDP is typically calculated by the country's national statistical agency. GDP per capita generally indicates the standard of living within a country; the larger the per capita GDP, presumably the better is the standard of living. Exhibit 12.1 lists per capita GDP and labor force sizes for the countries reviewed in this chapter. Clearly, the United States shows the largest per capita GDP and India reports the lowest amount. These differences are evident in the extent of government-sponsored benefits offered in those countries.

EXHIBIT 12.1
Per Capita
Expenditures
and Labor
Force Sizes by
Country

Source: *The World Factbook*, www .cia.gov/library/ publications/the- world-factbook/ index.html, 2008 estimates.

Country	Per Capita GDP ($)	Labor Force Size (millions)
United States of America	47,000	155.2
Canada	39,300	18.18
Mexico	14,200	45.5
Brazil	10,100	100.9
Argentina	14,200	16.27
France	32,700	28.5
Germany	34,800	43.62
Spain	34,600	23.1
United Kingdom	36,600	31.2
The Netherlands	40,300	7.75
Italy	31,000	25.09
Poland	17,300	16.95
Sweden	38,500	4.9
Russia	15,800	75.7
People's Republic of China	6,000	807.7
Hong Kong	43,800	3.67
Japan	34,200	66.15
South Korea	26,000	24.35
India	2,800	523.5
Saudi Arabia	20,700	6.74*
South Africa	10,000	18.22
Australia	38,100	11.21

Note: About one-third of the Saudi population in the 15–64 age group is non-national.

Paid Time-Off Benefits

Canadian employment law holds that employees are entitled to between eight and nine annual paid holidays.[7] Employees are also entitled to two weeks' paid vacation time, along with a sum of money as vacation pay (increasing to three weeks after six years of employment).[8] The amount of vacation pay is equal to 2 percent of the employee's pay for the preceding year per week of vacation. Slight variations exist from province to province. Maternity and paternity leave provisions are coordinated under the Federal Employment Insurance Act. Employees are permitted to take job-protected, unpaid paternal and maternity leave up to 52 weeks in most provinces and 70 weeks in Quebec.[9] Employees are eligible for a total of 17 weeks' benefits during pregnancy and after childbirth. Most recently, the Canadian government introduced compassionate care leave, which provides eight weeks of unpaid leave to care for a seriously ill family member. For the purposes of this leave, family members include spouse, common law partner, children, and parents.[10] No laws require the granting of time-off for military service.

Protection Benefits

Pensions and Retirement Benefits   Canada has two state pension plans, one for Quebec residents only and one for the rest of Canada. Both are funded by matching contributions from employers and employees and are fully portable upon employment changes, much like 401(k) plans in the United States.[11] In addition to the public plans, many employers provide supplementary pension plans that are regulated by provincial or federal legislation, which establishes minimum funding standards, specifies the types of investments the plans may make, and deals with matters such as portability, benefit vesting, and locking-in contributions. Employers frequently have different plans for executive, managerial, and other employees.

Health and Disability Benefits   Medical and basic hospital care in Canada are paid for by provincial medical insurance plans with compulsory coverage for all residents, and funding revenue derived from both general federal taxation and provincial taxes.[12] While public health plans normally do not provide employed persons with prescription drugs except while they are hospitalized, additional benefits are provided by private supplementary insurance by employers, including dental and vision care. Employers also provide long- and short-term disability benefits for sickness or injury as part of a benefits package.[13]

Canada's per capita expenditure on health (the sum of Public Health Expenditure and Private Expenditure on Health) as of 2006 at international dollar rates was $3,672.[14] Exhibit 12.2 presents the per capita health care expenditure of the countries reviewed in this chapter.

EXHIBIT 12.2
Per Capita Health Expenditure in Dollars and as Percentage of GDP

Source: The World Health Organization, www.who.int/countries/en/, 2006 estimates.

Country	Per Capita Health Expenditure ($)	Total Health Expenditure as % of GDP
United States of America	6,714	15.3
Canada	3,672	10.0
Mexico	756	6.2
Brazil	765	7.5
Argentina	1,665	10.1
France	3,554	11.1
Germany	3,328	10.4
Spain	2,388	8.1
United Kingdom	2,784	8.4
The Netherlands	3,383	9.3
Italy	2,623	9.0
Poland	910	6.2
Sweden	3,119	8.9
Russia	638	5.3
People's Republic of China	342	4.5
Hong Kong	—	—
Japan	2,514	7.9
South Korea	1,487	6.5
India	109	4.9
Saudi Arabia	607	3.4
South Africa	869	8.6
Australia	3,122	8.7

Mexico

Mexico is a federal republic,[15] and Mexican labor law is based on the Mexican Federal Labor Law.[16] *The CIA World Factbook* reports that Mexico's labor force is about 45.5 million strong and its per capita GDP is $14,200.[17] A free market economy is comprised of agriculture and a mix of new and old industries, which have become increasingly dominated by the private sector. The **Labor and Social Security article** of the constitution is still in effect.[18] Employment relationships in Mexico fall under the Federal Labor Law, which clearly defines the terms *worker* and *employer* for the purpose of individual employment.[19] Some of the employee benefits ensured under federal jurisdiction in Mexico are discussed in the following.

Paid Time-Off Benefits

Mexican employment laws stipulate certain paid time-off benefits for all employees, as reported in publications on international employment laws.[20] Workers are entitled to paid time-off during public holidays, and workers required to work during a mandatory holiday are entitled to double pay. Female employees are entitled to maternity leave—six weeks' leave prior to giving birth, and six weeks' leave after birth on full salary.[21] Maternity leave can also be extended with half pay for as long as necessary and does not affect seniority rights. Employees are entitled to six vacation days after being employed for one year, and get two more days for each subsequent year, up to a maximum of 12 days. As of the fifth year, the worker is entitled to 14 days vacation, and for each additional group of five years, two more vacation days are added. Employers must pay workers a vacation premium equivalent to 25 percent of the salary earned during scheduled vacation days; vacations must be taken on the date indicated by the employer, within the six months following the end of the work year.

Protection Benefits

Social Security Social security programs in Mexico are administered by the Mexican Social Security Institute, which protects employees in the matters of occupational accidents and illnesses, maternity, sicknesses, incapacitation, old age, retirement and survivor pensions, day care for children of insured workers, and social services.[22] The system is financed by contributions from workers, employers, and the government, with contributions based on salary levels (workers earning the minimum salary are exempt from making contributions), while employers bear the bulk of the contributions to the different insurance funds.[23]

The benefits for employees are laid out as follows.[24] Workers with at least 52 weeks' worth of payments into the system who withdraw are entitled to continue making voluntary payments. Should they return to salaried employment again, they may return to the system and maintain all benefits, which may be in cash or in kind. Cash benefits take the form of transfer payments in the early stages of illness or incapacitation, depending on the medical condition and its effects on work and pensions. In-kind benefits take the form of medical attention, including surgery and medicines, hospitalization services, and so forth.

Pensions and Retirement Benefits The U.S. Social Security Administration (SSA) Office of Policy reports that as of July 1, 1997, all workers must join the mandatory individual account system, slowly replacing the former social insurance system.[25] At retirement, employees covered by the social insurance system before 1997 can choose to receive benefits from either the social insurance system or the mandatory individual account system.

Health Benefits   Medical services are normally provided directly to patients (including old age pensioners covered by the 1997 law) through the health facilities of the Mexican Social Security Institute.[26] Benefits include general and specialist care, surgery, maternity care, hospitalization or care in a convalescent home, medicines, laboratory services, dental care, and appliances, and are payable for 52 weeks and may be extended in some cases to 78 weeks.[27] In addition, the wife of an insured man also receives postnatal benefits in kind, and medical services are provided for dependent children up to age 16 (age 25 if a student, no limit if disabled).[28] Mexico's per capita expenditure on health (the sum of the Public Health Expenditure and the Private Expenditure on Health) as of 2006 at the international dollar rate was $756.[29]

Other Benefits[30]   A national system of worker housing exists, paid for by employer contributions in the form of payroll tax fixed at 5 percent, and helps workers obtain sufficient credit for the acquisition of housing. Workers not employed after age 50 are entitled to receive the full balance of contributions made in their name to the housing fund.

SOUTH AMERICA

According to the International Monetary Fund's World Economic Outlook Database, Brazil, Argentina, Colombia, and Chile are the largest economies in South America.[31] Venezuela and Peru are experiencing economic development as well. On the other hand, Argentina and Uruguay have the best **HDI (human development index**—a comparative measure of life expectancy, literacy, and standard of living measured by the United Nations),[32] and Venezuela has large oil reserves that have turned the nation into an important player in world trade. The biggest trade bloc in South America used to be Mercosur, or the Southern Common Market, comprised of Argentina, Brazil, Paraguay, Uruguay, and Venezuela as its main members, and Bolivia, Chile, Colombia, Ecuador, and Peru as associate states.[33] The second-biggest trade bloc was the Andean Community of Nations, made up of Bolivia, Colombia, Ecuador, Peru, Venezuela, and Chile.[34]

These two trade blocs merged in a declaration signed on December 8, 2004, at the Third South American Summit and formed one large trade bloc known as the South American Community of Nations, which plans to model itself on the European Union.[35] This section takes a brief look at the two largest economies in the potentially formidable global economic bloc: Brazil and Argentina.

Brazil

The CIA World Factbook reports that Brazil is a federal republic with a 100.9-million-strong workforce and a per capita GDP of $10,100, and that its economy is by far the strongest in South America. This country has a well-developed mining, manufacturing, agricultural, and services sector, and is increasingly taking on a larger share of global trade and work.[36] The **Consolidation of Labor Laws** *(Consolidacao das Leis do Trabalho)* accords many employee benefits the status of fundamental constitutional rights, and in general the employment relationship in Brazil is highly regulated by statute.[37] For example, Brazilian law states that any and all benefits habitually granted by the employer, whether expressly or tacitly, are considered part of the employee's salary for all legal purposes and cannot be abolished. The status of employment contracts is based on the country's legal principle of continuity. This principle applies to all employment contracts—written and oral. However, in practice, employers discharge employees arbitrarily because there is a substantial supply of readily available workers who are willing to accept lower pay.[38] There simply is not enough incentive provided for employers to engage in good-faith labor relations, and job security is often lacking for most employees.[39]

Paid Time-Off Benefits[40]

Brazilian labor law stipulates an annual 30-day vacation with pay plus a bonus equivalent to one-third of the employee's monthly salary. Maternity leave is 120 days and paid for by social security. In addition, paternity leave of five consecutive days is allowed as of a child's date of birth.

Protection Benefits

Social Security   The social security system that went into effect in 1991 details various benefits for workers in Brazil.[41] Comprehensive social security benefits are provided by law to all workers regarding retirement for illness, old age, or length of service; death benefit pensions; assistance during imprisonment of the worker; savings funds; social services; professional rehabilitation assistance; work accident payments; maternity leave payments; family salary support; accident insurance; and sick leave benefits.

Pensions   The U.S. SSA Office of Policy reports that social insurance is provided to employed persons in industry, commerce, and agriculture, domestic servants, some categories of casual workers, elected civil servants, and the self-employed.[42]

There is also voluntary coverage for students, housewives, the unemployed, and other categories and a special system for public sector employees and military personnel. Monthly benefits are equal to 70 percent of the average earnings plus 1 percent of the average earnings for each year of contributions, up to a maximum of 100 percent. Employees contribute between 7.65 percent and 11 percent of gross earnings, while members of cooperatives contribute 20 percent of declared earnings. These contributions also finance sickness and maternity benefits and family allowances.

Employers are required to contribute 20 percent of payroll. There are no maximum monthly earnings for contribution purposes. Small-enterprise employers may contribute from 1.8 percent to 7.83 percent of monthly declared earnings, depending on annual earnings declared in the last year.

Health Benefits   In Brazil, medical services are provided directly to patients in rural and urban areas through the Unified Health System and include such benefits as general, specialist, maternity, and dental care; hospitalization; medicines (some cost-sharing is required); and necessary transportation.[43] Brazil's per capita expenditure on health (the sum of the Public Health Expenditure and the Private Expenditure on Health) as of 2006 at the international dollar rate was $765.[44]

Argentina

The CIA World Factbook reports that Argentina, a democratic republic, enjoys an economy that benefits from high education and rich natural resources.[45] With a current per capita GDP of $14,500 and a labor force of 16.27 million, Argentina suffered economic decline and depression in the 1990s—a huge fall from being one of the world's wealthiest countries 100 years ago. With various successive governments trying to revive the economy with IMF aid and measures to cut the fiscal deficit, in 2002 the president finally devalued the peso compared to the dollar (and froze utility tariffs, curtailed creditors' rights, imposed high taxes on exports) and helped the economy rebound strongly. Real GDP has been growing at 9 percent annually since 2003. Most recently (late 2008), the government of President Kirchner nationalized private pension funds. The employment relationship is governed by the Employment Contract Law and employees in Argentina are entitled to various statutory protections.[46]

Paid Time-Off Benefits[47]

Employees are entitled to 14 days of paid annual vacation when seniority does not exceed 5 years, 21 days when seniority is between 5 and 10 years, 28 days for between 10 and 20 years, and 35 days for more than 20 years. Employees are also entitled to between three and six months of sick leave based on seniority. Female employees are entitled to maternity leave for 45 days before birth and 45 days after birth, and the employee is entitled to cash benefits paid out by the social security funds. All employees are entitled to short leaves of absence for familial events or for examinations. There are 12 national paid holidays and employees who work on these days must be paid overtime at a 100 percent rate based on the regular hourly rate.

Protection Benefits

Pensions   A mandatory retirement and pension system exists, and all employees must be covered by the social security system.[48] The U.S. SSA Office of Policy reports that both employees and employers are required to pay into the system as a percentage of the employee's gross wages—11 percent of covered earnings which also finance disability and survivor benefits and administrative fees (limited to 1 percent of covered earning), if opting into the individual account system.[49] Voluntary contributions are the same as those for the insured person. The employer contributes 10.17 percent or 12.71 percent of the payroll, according to the type of enterprise. (Additional contributions are made on behalf of workers in hazardous or unhealthy occupations.)

Health Benefits   Employee health insurance is mandated by statute, and the cost of health insurance is financed by a 7.2 percent employer contribution of the gross payroll. Employers must also hire and pay the premium for collective life insurance in favor of the employees.[50] The SSA reports on the workers' medical benefits as follows.[51] Benefits include medical, hospital, dental, and palliative care; rehabilitation; prostheses; and transportation. Benefits are defined by the schedule in law issued by the Ministry of Health and Environment. Pharmaceutical products for chronic diseases are either free or require a 30 percent copayment; 60 percent for other diseases. Pharmaceutical products are free during pregnancy, childbirth, and for postnatal care; for children until age 1; and in cases of hospitalization. Argentina's per capita expenditure on health (the sum of the Public Health Expenditure and the Private Expenditure on Health) as of 2006 at the international dollar rate was $1,665.[52]

EUROPE

The **European Union (EU)** is a unique international organization that aims to become an economic superpower while retaining quintessential European practices, such as high levels of employment, social welfare protection, and strong trade unions.[53] While the EU has its own legal powers and performs executive, legislative, and judicial functions like any other governing body, it has limited authority in the area of labor and employment laws. While the EU does not attempt to harmonize the employment laws of member states, under the laws of all **member states,** employers must provide employees with a written document about the terms of the employment contract. The concept of "employment at will" does not exist in the EU as in the United States. The EU makes use of directives and community legislations to ensure some minimum standards are adopted by member states. All member states either have specific legislation or unfair dismissal or general civil code provisions that apply to termination of employment contracts. They all provide employees with a substantive basis for challenging employment dismissal and procedural mechanisms for adjudicating claims.[54]

The EU Web site reports that community labor law was designed with the aim of ensuring that the creation of the Single Market did not result in a lowering of labor standards or distortions in competition.[55] But it has also been increasingly called upon to play a key role in making it easier for the EU to adapt to evolving forms of work organization. On the basis of article 137 of the Treaty of Maastricht, the European Community shall support and complement the activities of the member states in the area of social policy. In particular, it defines minimum requirements at the EU level in the fields of working and employment conditions, and the information and consultation of workers. Improving living and working conditions in member states depends on national legislation, but also to a large extent on agreements concluded by the social partners at all levels (country, sector, and company). This section briefly presents some of the basic employee benefits practices in the EU member states of France, Germany, Spain, United Kingdom, the Netherlands, Italy, Poland, and Sweden. In addition, the practices in Russia are also examined—Russia is not a member of the EU.

France

According to *The CIA World Factbook,* France, a democratic republic, is currently transitioning from the traditional model (in which government ownership and intervention were strongly featured) to greater reliance on market mechanisms.[56]

France's per capita GDP is $32,700 and its labor force is 28.5 million strong. The government has recently given up stakes in such large companies as Air France, Renault, and Thales, while still maintaining a strong presence in public transport and defense. The population, however, has resisted reforms targeted at labor market flexibility. Also, with the highest tax burden in Europe at nearly half the GDP, the French economy is slacking off.

With 35-hour-long workweeks and five weeks of paid vacation, French workers typically get better benefits than their U.S. counterparts.[57] Employment laws are incorporated in the **French Labor Code (***Code du Travail*) and reflect the social-democratic ideology that has guided the employment relationship. Employees must be informed in writing about essential aspects of employment, including working hours and amount of paid leave. Such features as mandatory profit sharing and greater employee participation in management as well as "just cause dismissal" (as opposed to "employment at will") make French employment relationships different from the United States.

Paid Time-Off Benefits[58]

French law grants every employee the right to a minimum of five weeks' paid leave after one year of employment. Employees are paid during statutory holidays. The only mandatory public holiday in France is Labor Day (May 1), and employees who work on this day must be paid double time. Paid vacation cannot exceed 24 working days; a period of vacation is decided by the employer after consultation with employee representatives or based on mutual agreement; paid leave cannot be replaced by a cash payment. Employees between the ages of 18 and 21 receive an additional benefit of a 30-day annual leave regardless of the time they have served in a company. Maternity leave is provided to female employees at a minimum of 16 weeks, at least 10 weeks of which should be after a child is born. The employer has no legal obligation to pay an employee during maternity leave. Following a mother's return to work, the employer will grant the employee an interview to help place her in an equivalent activity. Companies must provide employees with at least 24 months of employment, half of which is with the current employer, to pursue training opportunities not included in the company's training program.

Protection Benefits

Retirement[59]   Effective August 21, 2003, the government mandated that employees must work longer before they may receive full government pensions. The increase from 40 to 41 years will take effect by 2012. Retirees will also be prohibited from receiving their pensions while working on a part-time basis because the pension amount is set at a generous level—85 percent of annual earnings prior to retirement.

Social Security[60]   Social security benefits granted to employees contain three components: health insurance, unemployment insurance, and retirement insurance. A base regime of social insurance applies equally to all employees, with rules on reimbursement rates for medical expenses, rules on calculation of unemployment allowance, or the right to a retirement allowance. Each is the same for all employees. Also, private employers can provide company benefits such as additional medical coverage and additional retirement benefits. Furthermore, French law provides for mandatory profit sharing for employers with more than 50 employees. Employers and employees may also enter into a variety of voluntary profit-sharing programs. The use of either voluntary or mandatory schemes is encouraged by the government.

Health Insurance   Organization of medical services for employees is the responsibility of the employer, who must bear the costs. Also, a doctor selected by the employer conducts medical examinations.[61] France's per capita expenditure on health (the sum of the Public Health Expenditure and the Private Expenditure on Health) as of 2006 at the international dollar rate was $3,554.[62] The SSA Office of Policy reports that workers' medical benefits include general and specialist care, hospitalization, laboratory services, medicines, optical and dental care, maternity care, appliances, and transportation.[63] The insured normally pays for services and is reimbursed by the local sickness fund. A €1 flat-rate contribution is paid for each medical service up to an annual ceiling (pregnant women or women on maternity leave, hospitalized persons, and persons with low income are exempt). After the deduction of the flat-rate contribution, the sickness insurance reimburses fully or in part the cost incurred by the insured. The amount reimbursed depends on the type of service: 100 percent of the medical service cost for certain severe illnesses, for work injury beneficiaries who are assessed as 66.6 percent or more disabled, and for pregnant women from the sixth month of pregnancy up to the 12th day after childbirth, regardless of whether the costs are related to the pregnancy or not; 70 percent for medical services; 60 percent for paramedic services; 35 percent or 65 percent for pharmaceuticals; 60 percent or 70 percent for laboratory services; 65 percent for optical and appliance fees up to an annual ceiling; and 80 percent for hospitalization after the deduction of a flat-rate daily contribution of €15 (€16 in 2007) (1 USD = 0.744 euro).

Other Benefits[64]   As an exception to the general rules, French law provides more flexible rules for management-level employees. Executive managers (*cadres dirigeants*) or top executives are not subject to French regulation; integrated managers (*cadres integers*) such as office managers or foremen are subject to regulations similar to those for regular employees; autonomous managers (*cadres autonomes*) or managers whose work schedules cannot be determined in advance can enter into individual agreements with the employer.

Germany

Germany is a federal republic with the fifth largest economy in the world as indicated by a per capita GDP of $34,800, according to *The CIA World Factbook*.[65] The

German labor force has about 43.62 million workers. The integration of the former East German economy is a strain on the overall economy of unified Germany, and unemployment rates have been very high. Germany has been recently pushing labor market reforms such as increasing the retirement age and increased female workforce participation. There have been increasing concerns about the aging workforce and high unemployment bankrupting the social security system, but for now Germany has managed to bring the deficit to within the EU debt limit. Germany's employment laws provide considerable voice to labor and job security to employees, while the **German Civil Code** provides numerous statutes that deal with individual employment as well as collective agreements.[66]

Paid Time-Off Benefits[67]

Employees cannot be required to work on official holidays; they range from 10 holidays per year in Northern Germany to 13 in Southern Germany. The statutory minimum vacation has been set at 24 working days (or four weeks since Saturdays are counted). Younger workers have a right to a vacation of 25 to 30 working days; disabled workers receive an additional 5 days of vacation. A minimum of six months of employment is necessary to be eligible for vacation. Under the terms of the **Maternity Leave Law,** time away from work as a result of maternity leave or other limits on work by pregnant women and mothers must be counted as time worked for the purpose of determining entitlement to vacation time. Employees may take 5 days annually or 10 days every two years (under individual state-level statutes) as paid holidays for continuing education purposes at only state-approved institutions. An employee retains his job if he is drafted into the military or called for military exercises, creating a suspended employment relationship. Employees receive regular pay during an illness for a period of six weeks.

Expectant mothers can take six weeks leave before their due date and take an additional eight weeks after giving birth. During this time, the employee must be paid at least an average salary or wages calculated on the basis of the last 13 weeks before commencement of leave. An employee can request up to three years of child-rearing leave, and employers must guarantee their return to the same job following completion of this leave. Any payments for child-rearing leave are made solely by the national health authority.

Protection Benefits

Pensions[68] Germany has a statutory pension system analogous to the Social Security system of the United States. In addition, employers offer the company pension plan and a tax-favored investment plan. Employees have three different sources for their pension benefits: statutory pension insurance, company pension plans, and private life insurance.

Health Insurance German laws stipulate guidelines for the minimal health welfare of workers.[69] For blue-collar workers (and some white-collar workers) mandatory state health insurance premiums are borne 50 percent by the insured and 50 percent by the employer. The employer is required to collect the employees' contributions and pay the entire amount to the appropriate collector. Employees whose income exceeds a certain amount can opt out of the state plan and purchase private health insurance. In such cases, employees may request that the employer's health insurance contribution be included in their salary. Germany's per capita expenditure on health (the sum of the Public Health Expenditure and the Private Expenditure on Health) as of 2006 at the international dollar rate was $3,328.[70]

Spain

According to *The CIA World Factbook,* Spain has a parliamentary monarchy and a mixed capitalist economy.[71] With a workforce of 23.1 million and a per capita GDP of $34,600, the Spanish economy has a solid growth rate, yet is plagued by economic uncertainties due to changing demographics and increased competition. The 1980 **Statute of Workers** set out the employment relationship as well as various employer requirements in terms of the employment relationship.[72]

Paid Time-Off Benefits[73]

Employers must provide employees with at least 30 days per year of paid time-off, and vacation time may not be suppressed or reduced in exchange for pay. Employees get 14 official paid holidays, 8 of which are national holidays, while the rest are determined by regional or local authorities. For birth, adopting, or fostering, employees get 16 weeks of paid leave. Six of the 16 weeks is an obligatory rest period that must be taken after childbirth. If both parents work, the mother can opt for the father to take 10 of the 16 weeks either simultaneously or consecutively. Social Security provides a benefit to cover risks during pregnancy. Nursing mothers are entitled to a daily one-hour leave. Employees are entitled to unpaid leave of absence for up to three years from birth. If both parents are employed, then only one qualifies for this benefit. An employee retains the right to the job prior to starting parental leave (subject to the leave), lasting no longer than 18 months or less, depending upon family size.

Protection Benefits

Social Security[74]   Social security benefits cover all risks related to health care, disability, dependents' coverage, retirement, unemployment, death and survivor benefits, pregnancy, and maternity leave. Contributions made on behalf of the employee are based on the aggregate monthly salary received by the employee and withheld by the employer.

Workers' Compensation[75]   Employees who have temporary or permanent disability due to a work-related accident are covered by the social security system and receive financial compensation. A temporary disability cannot exceed 12 months.

Pensions[76]   Pension funds are regulated under the social security system and fall into three categories: Labor system funds are created by any corporation or entity. Associate system funds are established by trade unions or associations. Individual system funds are established and managed by financial entities—thus, participation is open. The maximum annual contribution to a pension fund is set at €7,215.15 per person, and this limit may be increased for employees older than 52.

Health Benefits   The SSA reports about workers' health benefits in Spain, which include general and specialist care, hospitalization, medicines, dental care, laboratory services, appliances, and transportation.[77] A limit to duration may exist in certain cases. Previously insured workers who are no longer in insured employment may receive medical benefits up to 52 weeks after leaving, according to the number of contributions made in the last year and their family status. Medical services are provided to patients directly through the facilities of the National Health Management Institute, the regional autonomous health services, or by doctors and hospitals under contract. The patient normally pays 40 percent of the cost of prescribed medicines, according to the schedule in law; for some specific and chronic listed diseases, the patient pays 10 percent of the cost up to a maximum of €2.64 for each item. Medicines are free for pensioners and when dispensed by social security facilities. When the cost of the prescribed medicine is higher than the scheduled cost, the beneficiary pays the difference. Spain's per capita expenditure on health (the sum of the Public Health Expenditure and the Private Expenditure on Health) as of 2006 at the international dollar rate was $2,388.[78]

United Kingdom

The CIA World Factbook describes the United Kingdom (U.K.) as a constitutional monarchy and one of the biggest economies in Europe.[79] With a labor force of 31.2 million and a per capita GDP of $36,600, the government has been scaling back on public ownership of businesses and social welfare programs. The employment relationship in the U.K. is governed by a variety of common law and statutory provisions.[80] The most recent reforms instituted by the Labour government resulted in the **Employment Relations Act of 1999.** Employers are generally free to agree to the employment relationship with their employees at their discretion, with a few statutory restrictions.

Paid Time-Off Benefits[81]

Workers are entitled to four weeks' paid annual leave, including statutory and public holidays. Employers are allowed to introduce an accrual system to help manage leave during the first year of employment. The employee is entitled to 28 weeks of statutory sick pay in any three-year period. The employer can recover the money paid as sick pay if the payment exceeds 13 percent of the employer's liability to pay **National Insurance Contributions** in the income tax month in question. The employer reserves the right to require the employee to undergo a medical examination to verify an illness.

Employers cannot permit women to work in the two weeks immediately following birth. Employees can get a leave of 26 weeks, which may not begin prior to 11 weeks before birth. Contractual benefits other than remuneration, such as health insurance, are preserved during maternity leave. The employee also has a right to statutory maternity pay. Employees with one year of service are entitled to take 13 weeks of unpaid leave with respect to child care. Fathers can get paid paternity leave within eight weeks of the child's birth. An employee is entitled to take a reasonable amount of time-off during working hours to take care of dependents, a term which includes the spouse, children, parents, or relatives living under the same roof. Parents of young children have the right to flexible work arrangements in relation to hours/times/place of work, though requests can be refused by disruption (if such arrangements were to cause disruptions to the employer). Employees must have 26 weeks of qualifying service to be eligible for these benefits, and a sufficient relationship with the child and responsibility for child care. The cut-off is two weeks before the child's sixth birthday (or age 18 if the child is disabled).

Protection Benefits

Pensions[82]   All employees with the requisite National Insurance Contributions are entitled to a basic state pension. However, this is a small amount and employees must supplement it in one of four ways:

- State Second Pension—Pays a certain proportion of lifetime average earnings over a quite limited band.
- Company pension—Occupational plans such as defined contribution and defined benefit plans are available from individual employers.
- Personal pension—Established arrangements between employees and insurance companies; employer need not be directly involved, although it may choose to contribute.
- Stakeholder pension—May be operated by insurers and other providers in much the same way as personal pensions, or established by employers and administered by trustees as occupational pension plans and are defined contribution arrangements with strict statutory limits.

Workers' Compensation[83]   Every employer is required to maintain liability insurance under an approved policy with an authorized insurer. This indemnifies the employer against claims for civil liability that may arise as a result of injury and/or disease.

Health Benefits   The U.K.'s per capita expenditure on health (the sum of the Public Health Expenditure and the Private Expenditure on Health) as of 2006 at the international dollar rate was $2,784.[84] Employment relationship–based health benefits are as follows.[85] Medical services are provided by public hospitals and by doctors and dentists under contract with, and paid directly by, the **National Health Service.** Benefits include general practitioner care, specialist services, hospitalization, maternity care, dental care, medicines, appliances, home nursing, and family planning. Patients pay £6.40 for each prescription and 80 percent of the cost of any dental work, up to a maximum of £390. Those receiving means-tested benefits and their adult dependents, children younger than age 16 (age 19 if a student), pregnant women, and nursing mothers are exempt from dental and prescription charges. Persons older than the state pension age and certain other groups are exempt from prescription charges. The National Health Service's Low Income Scheme exempts certain individuals with low income from prescription charges (1 USD = £0.68). Exhibit 12.3 presents the monetary exchange rates against the U.S. dollar for the countries covered in this chapter.

The Netherlands

A constitutional monarchy with an open economy, the Netherlands has a 7.75-million-strong workforce with a per capita GDP of $41,300 and enjoys stable industrial relations and moderate unemployment and inflation as hallmarks of the Dutch

EXHIBIT 12.3
Monetary
Exchange
Rates for U.S.
Dollar by
Country, April
2009

Source: www
.exchangerate.com/.

Country	Currency	Dollar Exchange Rate for US$1
Canada	Canadian dollars (C$)	1.23
Mexico	New pesos (NP)	13.17
Brazil	Real	2.18
Argentina	Pesos	3.72
France	Euros (€)	0.76
Germany	Euros (€)	0.76
Spain	Euros (€)	0.76
United Kingdom	Pounds (£)	0.68
The Netherlands	Euros (€)	0.76
Italy	Euros (€)	0.76
Poland	Zloty	3.31
Sweden	Kronor	8.32
Russia	Ruble	33.66
People's Republic of China	Yuan	6.83
Hong Kong	Hong Kong dollars (HK$)	7.75
Japan	Yen	100.44
South Korea	Won	1322.69
India	Rupees	49.84
Saudi Arabia	Riyal	3.75
South Africa	Rand	9.09
Australia	Australian dollar (A$)	1.40

economy.[86] The **Employment Agreement *Act (Wet op de arbeidsovereenkomst)* of 1907** is the civil code that contains the specific employment relationship rules.[87]

Paid Time-Off Benefits[88]

Law provides for paid leave for vacation, bank holidays, sickness, pregnancy, childbirth, and duties associated with works council* membership. Every employee is entitled to annual vacation at least four times the number of days regularly worked per week. Employees are also allowed to make more flexible arrangements. Employees get paid sick leave for a maximum of 104 weeks at 70 percent of the wages last earned. A woman has a right to pregnancy and childbirth leave of 16 weeks with full pay, and for nine months after childbirth; a breast-feeding mother has the right to feed the child during working hours with full pay to a maximum of one quarter of working time. A works council member has the right to conduct business during working time with full pay for a minimum of 60 hours per year. A maximum of 10 days in a 12-month period is granted to employees who wish to care for a sick relative; the employee is entitled to receive 70 percent of their wages during this time.

*Works councils permit labor to participate in management decisions. Councils entail representation by groups other than labor unions, and the chair of a company's works council is a member of management. Companies with 50 or more employees must establish works councils based on the Works Council Act of 1950 as amended in 1998. Works councils possess codetermination rights (sharing decision making with management) on some issues.

Protection Benefits

Social Security[89] The social security system (*Sociale Verzekeringen*) consists of employee insurance schemes (*werknemersverzekeringen*), national insurance schemes (*volksverzekeringen*), and social assistance schemes (*sociale voorzieningen*). Employee insurance schemes cover only employees in the private sector and include short-term sickness benefits covering illness up to 104 weeks, disability benefits covering illness for more than 104 weeks, and another scheme where unemployment insurance and employees must pay differentiated contributions. These schemes are financed by employer and employee contributions, which are a specified percentage of the employee's gross salary. The national insurance programs apply to all residents of the Netherlands and include general old age benefits and disability benefits, and are financed by income tax and pay wage tax.

Pensions[90] The **State Old Age Pensions Act** provides old age benefits. Supplementary pensions such as occupational or private pensions also exist. Employers are not under any legal obligation to provide supplementary pensions to employees. Occupational pensions or mandatory participation in pension funds exists for the majority of those employed in the Netherlands. Employers can also arrange for private insurance companies to provide pensions for all employees. Supplementary pensions can reach a level that is a maximum of either 70 percent of the employees' last earned salary or the average salary.

Health Benefits The SSA Office of Policy reports that depending on the contract between the health care insurer and the insured, health service benefits in the Netherlands are provided by doctors, hospitals, and pharmacists under contract with the insurer.[91] The insurer reimburses the insured for medical costs. Benefits include general and specialist care, hospitalization, laboratory services, medicines, limited dental care, maternity care, appliances, rehabilitation, and transportation. Specific cost-sharing arrangements exist for long-term hospitalization, artificial limbs, and transportation. There is no limit on duration (except for physiotherapy). Exceptional medical expenses insurance finances the cost of hospitalization from the 366th day. The Netherlands' per capita expenditure on health (the sum of the Public Health Expenditure and the Private Expenditure on Health) as of 2006 at the international dollar rate was $3,383.[92]

Italy

The Italian Republic has a diversified industrial economy with a well-developed and industrial north dominated by industries and a less-well-developed agricultural south dependent on welfare, according to *The CIA World Factbook*.[93] With a 25.09-million-strong labor force and a per capita GDP of $31,000, Italy's total and per capita output equals that of France and the U.K. Italy has moved slowly with regard to reforming their high tax burden and overgenerous pension system, mainly because of the current economic slowdown and opposition from labor unions. The **Civil Code,** enacted in 1942, and a legislatively implemented EU directive cover the employment relationship.[94]

Paid Time-Off Benefits[95]

Depending on the category of the worker and their seniority within the business, employees are entitled to between three and five weeks of paid vacation, which should, if possible, be taken consecutively. Italy has approximately 11 public holidays and an additional four days that used to be public holidays but are now working days on which employees are paid double time. In the event of illness or accident, employees are entitled to full compensation for the first month and one-half thereof for the next two months, when they have less than 10 years' seniority. With more than 10 months' seniority, workers get full pay for the first two months and one-half thereof for the next four months. Blue-collar workers receive a percentage of their compensation for a period established by the collective bargaining agreement.

Pregnant employees have the right to time-off during working hours for medical appointments. Maternity leave with salary is allowed two months before birth and three months after birth; in addition, an optional six months with reduced salary is offered until the child is 8 months old; if there is only one parent, a working mother is entitled to two hours' paid leave per day (to feed the baby) for a maximum of 10 days until the child is one year old. Fathers are allowed to take leave for three months if they possess sole custody of the child, or the child's mother dies or is seriously ill. Employers are obligated to preserve the worker's position during the entire time of conscription and for 30 days after discharge; no payment is required.

Protection Benefits

Pensions[96]   Pension plans are of two types: compulsory and complementary. Compulsory pensions are granted to all workers (including the self-employed) by the Institute for Social Security or other government entities. Complementary pension plans, also granted to all workers and the self-employed, ensure that retirees maintain approximately the same standard of living prior to retirement. Over time, complementary plans increase payments to retirees to adjust for increases in the cost of living. Two different types of complementary pension schemes are available: collective pension schemes and individual pension schemes and life insurance.

Health Benefits   Italy's per capita expenditure on health (the sum of the Public Health Expenditure and the Private Expenditure on Health) as of 2006 at the international dollar rate was $2,623.[97] The SSA Office of Policy reports on workers' medical benefits that health care is provided to patients by doctors, hospitals, and pharmacists under contract with sickness funds.[98] Benefits include comprehensive medical and dental care, preventive examinations and treatment, laboratory tests, maternity care with a midwife or doctor, hospitalization, surgery, appliances, and prescribed medicines. Individuals are responsible for cost sharing in the form of copayment for certain benefits (including medicines, medical equipment, ambulatory care, hospitalization, and transportation). Copayments are waived for certain individuals and for persons with certain medical conditions.

Poland

The Republic of Poland has been pursuing economic liberalization since 1990 and is a great example of a successful transition economy. With a labor force of 16.95 million and a per capita GDP of $17,300, it has a strong private sector that is creating a large number of jobs.[99] The employment relationship in Poland is contained under the Polish Labor Code, and many benefits are provided for under the new constitution that came into effect in July 1997.[100]

Paid Time-Off Benefits[101]

Employees are entitled to an annual continuous paid vacation of 20 days if the length of employment has been less than 10 years, and 26 days if more than 10 years. All employees, irrespective of seniority, are entitled to a maternity leave of 18 weeks for the first birth, 20 weeks for each subsequent birth, and 28 weeks for the birth of more than one child. At least two weeks of the maternity leave may be taken before the birth of the child. Employers are also required to grant unpaid child care leave upon request. Employees are also entitled to take paid time-off from work for personal reasons recognized by labor law regulations such as marriage, the birth of a child, the marriage of a child, death, and funerals.

Protection Benefits

Pensions[102] Poland has a **three-pillar system of pensions.** The first pillar is government-administered and secures a minimum pension level through various funds like the retirement fund, the disability pension fund, the sickness fund, and the accident fund. Contributions are limited by a maximum amount per annum, equal to 30 times the average monthly remuneration predicted in the national economy in a given year. The second pillar is based on several open-pension funds managed commercially by strong financial institutions (pension societies) to create secure full pensions utilizing private fund management and employee-directed contributions. The third pillar is voluntary in nature and is intended to institutionalize pension plans provided by employers who offer employees the opportunity to participate in personal savings programs. The employer withholds contributions for individual accounts from net salary.

Health Insurance Benefits Poland's per capita expenditure on health (the sum of the Public Health Expenditure and the Private Expenditure on Health) as of 2006 at the international dollar rate was $910.[103] The Office of Policy of the SSA reports that medical services are provided directly to patients by private health care providers under contract to the National Health Fund.[104] Benefits include general and specialist care; hospitalization; surgeries specified by the Ministry of Health; laboratory services; dental care, including dental prostheses; ophthalmology and optician services; functional and vocational rehabilitation; free transportation; and basic prescription drugs. Patients may choose the doctor and hospital. No limit exists as to the duration of their stay if employed; if employment ceases, coverage continues for 26 weeks (and may be extended to 39 weeks). There is no cost sharing for basic health care. Government provides a partial subsidy for basic prescription drugs.

Sweden

The CIA World Factbook reports that Sweden is a constitutional monarchy, characterized by capitalism, combined with extensive social welfare benefits (helped along by peace and neutrality throughout the 20th century), which has made

Sweden a model for an enviable standard of living.[105] With a labor force of only 4.9 million, yet a per capita GDP of $38,500, Sweden's economy relies on a skilled labor force. Privately owned firms account for almost 90 percent of output. Interestingly, because of generous sick leave benefits, Sweden has the largest number of workers in Europe reporting sick. The employment relationship is partly covered by the law with the Employment Protection Act of 1982, which helps bind employers to minimum standards.[106]

Paid Time-Off Benefits[107]

The annual work year in Sweden is among the shortest in the world at a total of only 1,600 hours. Childbirth and childcare leave is the oldest plan for time-off. The government actively promotes parental leave. A minimum period of 14 weeks of maternity leave applies and parents are entitled to compensation of 80 percent of wages. The **1977 Act on Vacation** applies to the entire labor market, private and public. It entitles employees to a total of five weeks' paid leave per annum. The work year has 12 holidays, along with a certain number of nonworking afternoons that precede them. Additionally, provisions on time are given to pursue education, take care of sick relatives, conduct job hunting, start a business, hold elected political office, and perform military service.

Protection Benefits

Pensions[108] Two statutory pension plans exist. One provides old age pensions to every person with a close connection to Sweden, regardless of previous employment and individual contribution. The total amount is somewhat low, below the poverty level, but those who are entitled to no other retirement payments receive additional benefits. The second plan provides a pension to employees based on previous earning. This additional pension is fully paid for by contributions from employers and is fully portable. Finally, in addition to these statutory plans, there are private pension plans mostly based on collective agreements; two master agreements cover virtually the entire private sector, one for blue-collar and one for white-collar workers. Benefits are financed by employer contributions and are portable and vested.

Health Insurance Benefits The SSA Office of Policy reports that workers' medical benefits include a refund of part of travel costs, free medical and dental care for children up to age 20, subsidies for basic and preventive dental care, a high-cost limit for prosthetic treatment, and free insulin.[109] A fee of 60 to 300 kronor is paid for each doctor's consultation, up to a maximum of 900 kronor in a 12-month period. For inpatient treatment (including in a maternity ward) in a public hospital, the patient pays a maximum of 80 kronor a day (reduced for low-income earners). Patients pay the full cost of other medicines up to 900 kronor in a 12-month period; thereafter, the partial cost met by patients for other medicines must not exceed 1,800 kronor a year. Sweden's per capita expenditure on health (the sum of the Public Health Expenditure and the Private Expenditure on Health) as of 2006 at the international dollar rate was $3,119.[110] (1 USD = 6.37 kronor.)

Russia

The Federation of Russia has been experiencing a 6.7 percent annual growth rate since the economic crisis of 1998, with a labor force of 75.7 million and a per capita GDP of $15,800. It remains slow in building the rule of law and seems poised on the brink of a return to greater state control over the economy.[111] Labor relations have been established in the **Labor Code of the Russian Federation,** which was implemented on February 1, 2002.[112] The Constitution of the Russian Federation (approved on December 12, 1993) contains articles that deal with various aspects of the employment relationship.[113]

Paid Time-Off Benefits[114]

Ten nonworking days, corresponding with nine national holidays, are provided to employees, and holidays that occur on the weekend roll over into the following week. Workers are entitled to 28 days' annual paid leave, during which they are paid their average wages. A paid annual leave must be granted at least every two years and may accumulate and carry over into the second year. Federal law also provides partially paid leave for various reasons, including education, maternity, child care, and adoption.

Protection Benefits

Pensions   The SSA Office of Policy reports that everyone in Russia is guaranteed social insurance adequate for their age in the event of disease or disability.[115] Employer contribution is 20 percent of the payroll. If each employee's annual earnings range from 280,000 to 600,000 rubles, the contribution is equal to 72,800 rubles plus 10 percent of annual earnings exceeding 280,000 rubles. If each employee's annual earnings exceed 600,000 rubles, the contributions are equal to 104,800 rubles plus 2 percent of annual earnings exceeding 600,000 rubles. The employer's contributions also finance sickness and maternity benefits, medical benefits, and family allowances. Employers may finance supplementary benefits out of their own budgets. Government pensions are paid out of a federal budget (1 USD = 33.66 rubles).

Health Insurance Benefits[116]   Compulsory medical insurance covers medical services provided directly to patients by public and private health providers. Benefits include general, preventive, and emergency care; hospitalization; laboratory services; dental care; maternity care; vaccination; and transportation. Cost sharing: Medicines prescribed during hospitalization are provided free or at reduced rates to persons with certain categories of illness, as well as to the disabled and war veterans. Voluntary medical insurance covers specialized care, expensive medicines, and appliances. In accordance with legislative reform in 2006 in which special in-kind social benefits were replaced by cash compensation, some categories of the population (including the elderly), persons with disabilities, and war veterans may receive cash compensation for some medicines. Russia's per capita expenditure on health (the sum of the Public Health Expenditure and the Private Expenditure on Health) as of 2006 at the international dollar rate was $638.[117]

ASIA

As of 2007, China is the largest economy in Asia, followed by India and Japan.[118]

Although the Japanese economy in the 1980s and 1990s used to be larger than that of the entire continent combined, since then the Chinese economy has grown and become the second largest and is expected to surpass Japan.[119] Asia has several trade blocs, such as the **Asia-Pacific Economic Cooperation,** the **Asia-Europe Economic Meeting,** the **Association of Southeast Asian Nations,** the **South Asian Association for Regional Cooperation,** to name a few. However, given the wide variation and diversity in the world's largest and most populous continent, there is no unifying economic body (like the EU or NAFTA) that represents all the countries of Asia. This section examines a representative sample of the relatively more developed/developing economies in Asia—China, India, Japan, South Korea, Hong Kong, and Saudi Arabia. A bloc of countries that is not examined here, but that nonetheless deserves mention since considerable jobs are being outsourced there, are those in southeast Asia—Thailand, Vietnam, Singapore, Malaysia, Philippines, Cambodia, and Laos. These economies are seeing a current influx of foreign investment, though they are not close to the countries discussed here in terms of annual growth rates.

The People's Republic of China

The People's Republic of China (PRC), as reported by *The CIA World Factbook,* is a communist state characterized by a fast-growing economy, which over the past couple of decades has shifted from a centrally planned system to a more market-oriented one.[120] With a massive labor force of 807.7 million and a per capita GDP of $6,000, the PRC has been experiencing continuously high annual GDP growth at around 10 percent. While the purchasing power parity of the PRC has vaulted to the top in the world, the lower per capita GDP is an indication of income disparity within various strata of society. One of the key challenges for the government has been in sustaining adequate job growth for tens of millions of workers laid off from state-owned enterprises, finding work for migrants, as well as for new entrants to the workforce.

The PRC Labor Law was established in 1995, resulting in a break from the traditional "iron rice bowl" system of employment, with a shift from state-owned enterprises to private ones, a move which has given rise to new employment relationship issues.[121] Under the older welfare system, the workforce was considered the property of the state and many benefits such as housing, medical, and retirement schemes were payable directly by state-owned enterprises to the employees. With the introduction of the PRC Labor Law, the employment relationship is now defined by individual contracts.[122]

Paid Time-Off Benefits[123]

The length of an employer-approved medical treatment period generally depends on the employee's age and length of service and can range from 3 to 24 months. During this period, the salary paid to the employee may not be less than 80 percent of the local minimum wage. Employees who have worked for one or more years are entitled to paid annual leave but no binding laws exist about this;

national policy guidelines recommend 7 to 14 days. Employees who have worked for more than one year are entitled to "home leave" if they do not live in the same place as their spouse or parents. Employees earn normal wages during this period, and employers are obligated to pay all travel expenses for employees visiting their spouse and for unmarried employees visiting their parents. Women are entitled to no less than 90 days of paid maternity leave starting 15 days prior to birth.

Protection Benefits

Pensions The Office of Policy of the SSA reports there has been a new law to decouple the employment relationship from the social insurance system, setting up a unified basic pension system.[124] The system now has social insurance and mandatory individual accounts. (Provincial and city/county social insurance agencies and employers adapt central government guidelines to local conditions.) Coverage includes employees in urban enterprises, and urban institutions managed as enterprises, and the urban self-employed. In some provinces, coverage for the urban self-employed is voluntary. (Urban enterprises comprise all state-owned enterprises, regardless of their location.) Old age provision in rural areas is based mainly on family support, as well as community and state financial support. Pilot schemes in the form of individual accounts, supported at the town and village level, and subject to preferential support by the state, operate in some rural areas. Employees of government and communist party organizations, as well as those in cultural, educational, and scientific institutions (except for institutions financed off-budget), are covered under a government-funded, employer-administered system. Enterprise-based pension systems cover some employees (including the self-employed) in cities.

An employee contribution to mandatory individual accounts is 8 percent of their gross insured earnings. (The contribution rate is higher in some provinces.) The minimum earnings for employee contribution and benefit purposes are equal to 60 percent of the local average wage for the previous year. The maximum earnings for employee contribution and benefit purposes vary but may be as much as 300 percent of the local average wage of the previous year. There are no employer contributions to mandatory individual accounts. Central and local government subsidies are provided to city/council retirement pension pools as needed.

Health Insurance[125] China has a unified medical insurance system with all employers and workers participating in the system; employers contribute 6 percent of the payroll, while employees contribute 2 percent of their salary. Health insurance is based on a **Basic Medical Insurance Fund** consisting of a **Pooled Fund** and **Personal Accounts.** Employees' contributions go directly to their Personal Accounts, and 30 percent of employer contributions are paid into this account. Covered workers receive medical benefits at a chosen accredited hospital or clinic on a fee-for-service basis. The individual account is used to finance medical benefits only, up to a maximum equal to 10 percent of the local average annual wage. The social insurance fund reimburses the cost of the medical benefit from 10 percent up to 400 percent of the local average annual wage, according to the schedule. Medical treatment in high-grade hospitals results in lower percentage reimbursements, and vice versa. Reimbursement for payments beyond 400 percent of the local average annual wage must be covered by private insurance or public supplementary schemes. Contract workers receive the same benefits as permanent workers. The per capita expenditure on health (the sum of the Public Health Expenditure and the Private Expenditure on Health) as of 2006 at the international dollar rate was $342.[126]

Hong Kong

The CIA World Handbook reports that Hong Kong is a limited democracy and a special administrative region of the PRC since reverting from British rule on July 1, 1997.[127]

With a small labor force of only 3.67 million, Hong Kong is nevertheless a highly developed free market economy based on international trade and has a per capita GDP that exceeds that of the four biggest economies of Western Europe at $43,800. Through numerous external challenges—two recessions (one because of the Asian financial crisis of 1997–98 and one because of the global economic downturn of 2001–02) and the SARS ("bird flu") outbreak of 2003—Hong Kong has maintained a steady GDP growth for close to two decades and continues to enjoy economic prosperity with a rise in trade, a rise in tourism directed away from the more restrictive PRC, and by becoming the financial hub of the region.

Under the governing constitution of Hong Kong, known as the **Basic Law,** the **Hong Kong Special Administrative Region** has the authority to make employment laws as well as alter current laws. All employment relationships in Hong Kong are contractual, and the **Employment Ordinance** provides minimum standards relating to wages and leaves and applies to all employees.[128]

Paid Time-Off Benefits[129]

Employees working for at least one year are entitled to paid annual leave of up to 14 days, depending on their length of service. If employed for three months, employees are entitled to statutory holidays with pay and may contract to take statutory holidays on other days. Banks, educational institutions, and public and government offices observe additional public holidays as well. Employees get paid 80 percent of regular pay for sick days, and there is a provision for accrual of sick leave with medical certification requirements and ceilings on maximum duration. Employees who have worked for at least 40 weeks are entitled to 10 weeks of maternity leave with pay at 80 percent of their normal salary. After that, unpaid leave is available for an additional four weeks. An employer cannot terminate an employee after she has given notice that she will be taking maternity leave.

Protection Benefits

Worker's Compensation[130]   Employers are required to pay medical expenses for on-the-job injuries and occupational diseases. Employers are also required to provide valid health insurance for each employee.

Pensions[131]   Universal old age and disability pensions, mandatory occupational benefits (mandatory provident fund schemes), and social assistance (comprehensive social security assistance) systems are the key retirement protection schemes. The mandatory occupational schemes operating under the name of mandatory provident fund schemes are privately run and should not be confused with publicly run national provident funds found in other countries. All employees holding a contract of 60 days or more (employees in the catering and construction industry who are employed for periods shorter than 60 days or who are covered on a daily basis) and the self-employed between ages 18 and 65 are covered. Exclusions include self-employed roadside vendors, domestic employees, persons covered by statutory pension or provident fund schemes (such as civil servants or teachers), members of occupational retirement schemes who are granted exemption certificates, and foreign citizens working in Hong Kong for less than 13 months or who are covered by another country's retirement system.

Employees' contributions to mandatory occupational systems include a minimum 5 percent of their monthly earnings. Voluntary additional contributions are permitted. The minimum and maximum earnings levels for contribution purposes are HK$5,000 a month and HK$20,000 a month, respectively. Contributions are tax-deductible up to HK$12,000 a year. Employer contributions to the mandatory occupational system are a minimum of 5 percent of monthly payroll. Voluntary additional contributions are permitted. There is no minimum earnings level for contribution purposes. The maximum earnings for contribution purposes are HK$20,000 a month (1 USD = 7.75 HKD).

Health Benefits[132]   Free medical care in public hospitals is available for recipients of social assistance cash benefits. Sickness benefits include 80 percent of the employee's wages in the last month before the onset of the sickness, are payable for the number of paid sick days accumulated by the employee, and are accumulated at the rate of 2 days for each completed month of employment during the first 12 months of employment and 4 days for each month of employment thereafter, up to a maximum of 120 days. The benefit is payable after a three-day waiting period. Maternity benefits include 80 percent of the employee's wages in the last month before beginning maternity leave, and are payable for 10 weeks. The benefit is payable from two to four weeks before the expected date of childbirth or from the date of childbirth if it occurs earlier. Social assistance includes HK$2,010 a month for a person living alone, or HK$1,820 a month if living with other family members, subject to the assessed degree of reduced working capacity and whether constant attendance is needed. Added in are special grants to meet the specific individual needs of recipients.

Japan

Japan, according to *The CIA World Handbook,* is a constitutional monarchy with a parliamentary government, a labor force of 66.15 million, and a per capita GDP of $34,200.[133] The Japanese economy is the second most technologically powerful in the world after that of the United States, and the third largest in terms of purchasing power parity after the United States and China. The Japanese economy is also characterized by government-industry cooperation, a strong work ethic, mastery of high technology, and a comparatively small defense allocation (1 percent of GDP). A unique characteristic of the Japanese economy used to be *keiretsu,* or the close-knit relations between manufacturers, suppliers, and distributors representing a guarantee of lifetime employment for a substantial portion of the urban labor force—a system that has now been eroded considerably.

The employment relationship[134] is based on the traditional notion of freedom of contract, and some basic provisions for individual employment are contained in the Civil Code of 1896. However, the outdated Civil Code has been replaced, and there are currently numerous laws enacted post-WWII that deal with labor standards, unions, minimum wages, child care, and family leave—just to name a few—as well as employee benefits laws. Employee benefits laws include various insurance schemes, participation in which is mandatory, with premiums borne either solely by the employer or by a combination of the employer and employee.

Paid Time-Off Benefits[135]

Annual paid leave is allowed for 10 days after six months of consecutive service, and 1 additional day for each additional full year, for a total service of three years and six months. Thereafter, workers are granted 2 additional days for each full year of service, up to a maximum of 20 days. Menstruation leave is available to females when they find attendance at work difficult, and employers are not required to pay employees during this period. Maternity leave is granted if requested within six weeks of giving birth. Postbirth leave of eight weeks is mandatory, although an employee may return to work after six weeks with the approval of a physician. Employer-specific contracts determine the rate of pay during maternity leave; if the employer does not pay anything, then employment insurance pays for 42 days before birth and 56 days after birth at the rate of 60 percent of standard wages. Employees must be granted child care leave upon request for the duration of one year if the child is less than one year old. Family care leave for three months is allowed to care for family members. Employers are not required to pay wages; however, employment insurance provides up to 40 percent of regular wages. There is no military leave granted; employers must give time-off for civic duties such as voting in political elections.

Protection Benefits

Pensions[136]   Japan has a social insurance system involving a flat-rate benefit for all residents under the national pension program and earnings-related benefits under the employees' pension insurance program or other employment-related program; residents aged 20 to 59; voluntary coverage for residents aged 60 to 64 (aged 65 to 69 in special cases); and for citizens residing abroad (aged 20 to 64). The national pension program is one in which the contribution is included in the insured person's contribution to the employees' pension insurance or other employment-related program. A proportionate amount is transferred to the national pension program. All other insured persons contribute 14,410 yen a month. Low-income spouses of workers insured under the employment-related program may apply for exemption from payment. Employees' pension insurance includes 7.675 percent of basic monthly earnings and salary bonuses before tax for most employees; miners and seamen contribute 8.1 percent of basic monthly earnings, including salary bonuses before tax, accorded for most employees. If the employee is contracted out, the contribution is between 5.47 and 5.77 percent of monthly earnings, including salary bonuses before tax. The minimum monthly earnings for contribution and benefit purposes are 98,000 yen. The maximum monthly earnings for contribution and benefit purposes are 620,000 yen. The minimum and maximum earnings levels are adjusted on an ad hoc basis in line with any increases in the national average wage. The government covers 36.53 percent of the cost of benefits, plus 100 percent of administrative costs (1 USD = 100.44 yen).

Health Benefits   Japan's per capita expenditure on health (the sum of the Public Health Expenditure and the Private Expenditure on Health) as of 2006 at the international dollar rate was $2,514.[137] The SSA reports that the National Health Insurance program covers medical care and treatment that is usually provided by clinics, hospitals, and pharmacists under contract with, and paid by, the insurance carrier (some carriers provide services directly through their own clinics and hospitals).[138] Benefits include medical treatment, surgery, hospitalization, nursing care, dental care, maternity care (only for a difficult childbirth), and medicines.

There is no limit to duration. The cost sharing amount depends on the person's age: under age 3, 20 percent of the cost; ages 3 to 69, 30 percent of the cost; ages 70 or older, 10 to 20 percent based on income. Japan's national program is available to all individuals unless they are covered by an employer health plan. Employees' health insurance benefits are similar to those provided under the country's national health insurance program.

South Korea

South Korea is a republic that, since the 1960s, has achieved considerable economic growth and become a member of the high-technology global economy, according to *The CIA World Handbook*.[139] With a labor force of 24.35 million and a per capita GDP of $26,000, the South Korean economy achieved its current developed status by pursuing a system of close government/business ties, including directed credit, import restrictions, sponsorship of specific industries, and a strong labor effort, and continues to be a strong and stable economy in current times. Most aspects of employment in South Korea are governed by laws, and violations of mandatory provision are treated as a criminal offense; and a free enterprise economic system allows for the existence of individual, collective, and collaborative systems of employment law designed to protect employees and regulate working conditions.[140]

Paid Time-Off Benefits[141]

Employees are entitled to paid holidays designated by the company and are also entitled to 10 days' paid leave for those who have worked one year without absence, and 8 days off for employees who have worked 90 percent or more of the year. Female employees are entitled to 90 days' paid maternity leave, of which 45 days must be used after childbirth, with the final 30 days compensated by the **Unemployment Insurance Fund.** Sick leave is statutorily required only in connection with occupational injuries or diseases. Males spend 26 months on active duty in the military and are called back after that for training. Employers cannot penalize any employee for being away on military training. Special leave may be granted to perform civic duties, and there is no specific legal provision for paternity leave.

Protection Benefits

Pensions[142] Peoples' Pension covers most workers, while Local Pension covers public workers, military personnel, and private schoolteachers. Participants must contribute for at least 20 years to be entitled to retirement benefits. Employers and employees each contribute 4.5 percent of an employee's monthly salary. Expatriate employees are not required to contribute to the pension program.

Health Benefits All employers are required to subscribe to the national health insurance plan, pursuant to the National Health Insurance Act as of July 1, 2001, and as of 2004, a premium rate of 5.08 percent of the subscriber's standard monthly salary has been fixed with employer and employee making equal contributions.[143] SSA reports that workers' medical benefits include medical treatment, surgery, hospitalization, and medicines.[144] Medical services are provided by doctors, clinics, hospitals, and pharmacists under contract to the National Health Insurance Corporation (NHIC). Maternity care is provided, with no limit on the number of children. There are no cash maternity benefits. The insured pays 20 percent of hospitalization costs and between 30 and 50 percent of outpatient care (50 percent if provided by a specialized general hospital, 50 percent if provided by a general hospital, 35 to 40 percent if provided by a hospital, or 30 percent if provided by a clinic). The overall limit paid by each patient is 2,000,000 won every six months (1 USD = 1322.69 won). South Korea's per capita expenditure on health (the sum of the Public Health Expenditure and the Private Expenditure on Health) as of 2006 at the international dollar rate was $1,487.[145]

India

According to *The CIA World Handbook,* India is a democratic federal republic with a diverse economy ranging from traditional farming to high-technology industries.[146] India's labor force is composed of 523.5 million individuals with a per capita GDP of only $2,800. The Indian economy, though steadily growing at a nearly 8 percent annual rate, is plagued with income disparity and developmental challenges similar to China's. More than half of India's output is created with less than one-quarter of its labor force, and services are the major source of economic growth. Strong economic growth combined with easy consumer credit and a real estate boom are fueling inflation concerns, and the huge and growing population poses fundamental social, economic, and environmental problems. Basic constitutional legislation governs the employment relationship for all employees, ensuring equality of opportunity to public employment and prohibition of child labor.

The **Directive Principle of State Policy** has statutes that affect various aspects of the employment relationship, such as working conditions and participation in management.[147] Some of the key employee benefits provided by employers in India are provident fund, gratuity (bonus), pension (either defined benefit or defined contribution), housing, car, loans, life insurance protection for dependents, health/disability benefits, medical benefits for employees and their families, and leave encashment.[148] The Employees' Provident Fund Organization is one of the world's largest social security programs, with more than 35 million members. Gratuities apply to most employees in India, and these are funded through employer contributions totaling 4.5 percent of the payroll.

Wide variations exist between the public and private sectors, with the **Ministry of Labour** and labor laws governing employment relationships in the public sector and more employer discretion allowed in the private sector. Additionally, all blue-collar employees and factory workers are governed under existing labor laws.

Paid Time-Off Benefits[149]

Leave is usually calculated for each year based on the number of days worked in the previous year, and if the worker does not take all the accumulated leave, a maximum of 30 days is allowed to roll over to the succeeding calendar year. There is no statutory provision of paternity leave, but maternity leave is allowed in the form of paid time-off and a possible medical bonus. All employees get paid time-off for various public and national holidays.

Protection Benefits

Pensions[150]   The first and current laws regarding pensions were passed in 1952 (employees' provident funds), with amendments in 1972 (payment of gratuity), 1976 (employees' deposit-linked insurance), and 1995 (employees' pension scheme and the national social assistance program). Pension benefits include provident fund with survivor (deposit-linked) insurance and pension fund, gratuity schemes for industrial workers, and social assistance system. In 2004, a voluntary old age, disability, and survivors' benefits scheme was enacted. This program is part of the Unorganized Sector Social Security Scheme for employees and self-employed persons aged 36 to 50 with monthly earnings of 6,500 rupees or less but without mandatory coverage, and was introduced as a pilot program in 50 districts. Contributions are income-related and flat-rate. Coverage includes employees (such as casual, part-time, and daily wage workers and those employed through contractors) with monthly earnings of 6,500 rupees or less working in establishments with a minimum of 20 employees in one of the 182 categories of covered industry (the establishment remains covered even if the number of employees falls below 20).

Employees covered by equivalent occupational private plans may contract out. Voluntary coverage exists for employees of covered establishments with monthly earnings of more than 6,500 rupees, with the agreement of the employer and for establishments with fewer than 20 employees if the employer and a majority of the employees agree to contribute. Provident fund contributions include 12 percent of basic wages (10 percent of basic wages in five specified categories of industry) in covered establishments with fewer than 20 employees and some other specific cases. The maximum monthly earnings for contribution purposes are 6,500 rupees (1 USD = 49.84 rupees).

Health Benefits   SSA reports that state governments arrange for the provision of medical care on behalf of the **Employees' State Insurance Corporation.**[151] Services are provided in different states through social insurance dispensaries and hospitals, state government services, or private doctors under contract. Benefits include outpatient treatment, specialist consultations, hospitalization, surgery and obstetric care, imaging and laboratory services, transportation, and the free supply of drugs, dressings, artificial limbs, aids, and appliances. The duration of benefits is from three months to one year, according to the insured's contribution record. India's per capita expenditure on health (the sum of the Public Health Expenditure and the Private Expenditure on Health) as of 2006 at the international dollar rate was $109.[152]

Saudi Arabia

According to *The CIA World Handbook,* among the countries of the Middle East, the monarchy of Saudi Arabia is a thriving oil economy. This country's per capita GDP is $20,700 with a labor force of 6.74 million. More than 35 percent of the population is non-national.[153] Saudi Arabia is a leading member of OPEC (Organization of the Petroleum Exporting Countries); the petroleum sector contributed half the GDP and nearly all the export earnings. Saudi Arabia acceded to the WTO in December 2005 after many years of negotiations to diversify its economy and attract foreign investment. High oil revenues and, consequently, large budget surpluses, have allowed government spending on job training and education, infrastructure development, and government salaries. Plans to establish six "economic cities" in different regions of the country to promote development and diversification have been recently announced.

Numerous legal obligations rest on the employer regarding the employment relationship that must be strictly complied with, and employment laws are proposed and approved by the **Council of Ministers and the King** and the **Ministry of Labor and Social Affairs,** which regulates employment issues, the legal context of which rests in the Saudi legal system as founded in the Islamic Shari'a law. A new labor law became effective September 27, 2005.[154] Some very basic employer requirements are discussed next.

Paid Time-Off Benefits[155]

After 1 year of service, a worker is entitled to an annual vacation of 15 days at full wages, and vacation time increases to 21 days after 10 continuous years of service. An employee is entitled to three days' marriage leave, and one day of paid leave for the birth of a child or death of a spouse or relative. Two official holidays exist, during which business ceases for about one week. The first is Eid Al-Fitr, a customary 10-day holiday to celebrate the end of Ramadan, the month of fasting, while the second is Eid Al-Adha, which also lasts 10 days. In addition, September 23, the Saudi National Day, is also a designated official holiday. Each is observed by both the government and private businesses alike. If illness is confirmed by a medical certificate, sick leave with pay is available for 30 days and with three-quarters pay for the next 60 days in any given year. A female worker is entitled to maternity leave of four weeks before birth and six weeks after birth with half pay if she has been an employee for more than one year, and full pay if she has been an employee for more than three years.

Protection Benefits

Pensions[156]   Saudi Arabia has a comprehensive social insurance system that automatically covers Saudi employees in the public and private sectors. Others, including self-employed persons, those working abroad, and those who no longer satisfy the conditions for compulsory coverage, may elect voluntary coverage. The following groups of individuals are excluded: agricultural workers, fishermen, domestic servants, family labor, and foreign workers. Employers and employees each pay 9 percent of gross earnings. The government provides the cost of administration during the initial phase and an annual subsidy, and fills any operating deficit.

Health Insurance All necessary medical, dental, and diagnostic treatment, hospitalization, medicines, appliances, transportation, and rehabilitation are covered under the social insurance system.[157] Saudi Arabia's per capita expenditure on health (the sum of the Public Health Expenditure and the Private Expenditure on Health) as of 2006 at the international dollar rate was $607.[158]

Other Benefits[159] Employers are obligated to provide adequate living quarters, suitable camps for living if needed, three meals per day when needed, special food as needed, as well as medical, social, and cultural services. Cash allowance for transportation is part of the wages, but transportation to and from work must be provided in the absence of public transportation.

AFRICA

According to the United Nations' Human Development Report of 2003, the bottom 25 ranked nations in the world were all in Africa.[160] This is due to corrupt governments, despotism, and constant conflict, making the entire continent of Africa—the second largest and second most populous—the world's poorest place. Economic conditions in Africa have stagnated and moved backward in many cases, plagued by low per capita income, lack of foreign trade and investment, poverty, low life expectancy, violence and instability, and a debilitating spread of HIV/AIDS. Some areas of economic success are South Africa and Botswana in the southern part of the continent. Some comparable success is also being made by Ghana, Kenya, Cameroon, Egypt, and most notably Nigeria, which has large proven oil reserves as well as the highest population in Africa and is expected to boom economically. In this section, we take a brief look at the most developed of the African economies, South Africa.

South Africa

The CIA World Handbook notes South Africa as a republic and one of the few relatively more developed economies in Africa.[161] It has an active labor force of 18.22 million, but a high unemployment rate of 25.5 percent, a per capita GDP of $10,000, and 50 percent of the population living in poverty. South Africa is a middle-income, emerging market with an abundant supply of natural resources, well-developed financial, legal, communications, energy, and transport sectors, a stock exchange that ranks among the 10 largest in the world, and a modern infrastructure supporting an efficient distribution of goods to major urban centers throughout the region. This disparity is a daunting economic problem held over from the apartheid era, with continued poverty and lack of economic empowerment among the disadvantaged groups.

Labor rights in South Africa stem from its constitution and its newest legislation, the **Labour Relations Act of 1995,** under which there is no distinction between union and nonunion employees and all employment relationships are dealt with under this law. For example, "unfair labor practice" as a term applies to individual employment contracts, as opposed to collective contracts in the United States.[162]

Paid Time-Off Benefits[163]

All employees are entitled to 21 consecutive days' annual leave for every 12 months' employment cycle, and there are 12 paid public holidays. Sick leave is calculated over a 36-month period at the same employer, and an employee is entitled to paid sick leave equal to the number of days an employee would normally work during a period of six weeks. The employee is entitled to four months of unpaid maternity leave and may not work for six weeks after the birth of a child. Employees are also entitled to family responsibility leave if they have been employed for longer than four months and work at least four days a week. Leave entitlement is three days' paid leave per year for child care, or in the event of the death of a family member, and does not carry over from one leave cycle to another.

Protection Benefits

Pensions[164]   State pensions are available to all persons of relevant age, but the payout is very modest. Bargaining councils have pension or provident schemes to which employers and employees make equal contributions. The social assistance system provides coverage for citizens with limited means, and the government bears the total cost. Government contributions also finance medical benefits.

Health Insurance   Many private medical plans exist in South Africa and those employers who do have health insurance plans require equal contribution from employees. Retirees are entitled to subsidized medical care at provincial hospitals, with such benefits as hospitalization and medication.[165] South Africa's per capita expenditure on health (the sum of the Public Health Expenditure and the Private Expenditure on Health) as of 2006 at the international dollar rate was $869.[166]

AUSTRALIA

The CIA World Factbook reports that the Commonwealth of Australia, a federal parliamentary democracy, has a labor force of 11.21 million and a per capita GDP of $38,100, which is on a par with that of the four largest Western economies.[167] With an economy fueled by high export prices for raw materials and agricultural products, Australia has also emphasized growing ties with China, and has utilized conservative fiscal policies to sustain its high economic standards. As far as employment regulations[168] are concerned, variations exist between each of the states, as well as the Commonwealth, and the vast majority of large employers are now covered by federal legislation as a result of the 2005 Work Choices Act. Employment contracts are affected by awards or industrial agreements that detail working conditions and various employee benefits (paid time-off, training, and so on), and a full 50 percent of all Australian workers are employed under awards made by the **Australian Industrial Relations Commission.** Some of the basic employee rights in Australia are discussed next.

Paid Time-Off Benefits[169]

Full-time employees are entitled to 10 days of paid personal time-off per year. Employees are also entitled to annual leave of 20 days at the end of every year of service, with unused leave accumulating from year to year. Long-service leave accrues after a period of continuous service. A minimum entitlement to unpaid parental leave exists for permanent employees, and maternity leave entitlement is for a period of up to 52 weeks.

Protection Benefits

Pensions Employers are required to make annual contributions to help support the government pension.[170] The SSA reports that the mandatory pension requires voluntary employee contributions that are tax deductible up to a maximum of A$5,000 plus 75 percent of contributions in excess of this amount, or the age-based contribution (younger than age 35, A$15,260; aged 35 to 49, A$42,385; aged 50 or older, A$105,113), whichever is lower.[171] There is no upper limit for voluntary contributions. Employer contributions are 9 percent of basic wages, up to a maximum of A$35,240 a quarter. Employer contributions are tax deductible up to certain limits, depending on the age of the employee. For an employee younger than age 35, the maximum annual tax deductible wage is A$15,260; if aged 35 to 49, A$42,385; or if aged 50 or older, A$105,113. The government matches voluntary contributions made by the insured on the basis of A$1.50 for each A$1.00 contributed, up to A$1,500 a year for low-income earners (1 USD = 1.40 AUD).

Health Benefits[172] Workers' medical benefits include free care by staff doctors in public hospitals. The patient pays 15 percent of the scheduled fee for outpatient ambulatory care or A$50.10, whichever is less (indexed annually for price changes). Private benefit organizations pay for private hospital stays, or public hospitals charge for those who choose treatment by their own physician in public hospitals. A fee of up to A$22.40 per prescription applies to most prescribed medicines. Pensioners, benefit recipients, and low-income persons pay a A$3.60 fee per prescription. Australia's per capita expenditure on health (the sum of the Public Health Expenditure and the Private Expenditure on Health) as of 2006 at the international dollar rate was $3,122.[173]

Summary

We reviewed benefits offerings mandated by the governments of several countries around the world. Extensive variation exists in minimum standards. A striking difference between the United States and other countries is the less-generous family leave benefits in the United States and the relatively fewer paid days off. Governments in other countries mandate paid time-off, reflecting the importance of family and religion. Most countries offer social security pensions and, in many cases, these benefits are not lucrative. We also noted that the cost of health care is a concern in all countries. Various health care delivery systems, single-payer and multiple-payer, struggle with rising health care costs and adequate coverage.

Key Terms

North American Free Trade Agreement (NAFTA), *308*

North American Agreement on Labor Cooperation, *309*

per capita gross domestic product (GDP), *309*

English Statute of Labourers, *309*

Labor and Social Security article (Mexico's constitution), *312*

human development index (HDI), *313*

Consolidation of Labor Laws (Brazil), *314*

European Union (EU), *316*

member states (European Union), *316*

French Labor Code (Code du Travail), *317*

German Civil Code, *319*

Maternity Leave Law (Germany), *319*

Statute of Workers (Spain), *320*

Employment Relations Act of 1999 (United Kingdom), *321*

National Insurance Contributions (United Kingdom), *321*

National Health Service (United Kingdom), *322*

Employment Agreement Act (*Wet op de arbeid-sovereenkomst*) of 1907, *323*

State Old Age Pensions Act (The Netherlands), *324*

Civil Code (Italy), *324*

three-pillar system of pensions (Poland), *326*

1977 Act on Vacation (Sweden), *327*

Labor Code of the Russian Federation, *328*

Asia-Pacific Economic Cooperation, *329*

Asia-Europe Economic Meeting, *329*

Association of Southeast Asian Nations, *329*

South Asian Association for Regional Cooperation, *329*

Basic Medical Insurance Fund (People's Republic of China), *330*

Pooled Fund (People's Republic of China), *330*

Personal Accounts (People's Republic of China), *330*

Basic Law (Hong Kong), *331*

Hong Kong Special Administrative Region, *331*

Employment Ordinance (Hong Kong), *331*

Unemployment Insurance Fund (South Korea), *334*

Directive Principle of State Policy (India), *335*

Ministry of Labour (India), *336*

Employees' State Insurance Corporation (India), *336*

Council of Ministers and the King (Saudi Arabia), *337*

Ministry of Labor and Social Affairs (Saudi Arabia), *337*

Labour Relations Act of 1995 (South Africa), *339*

Australian Industrial Relations Commission, *340*

Endnotes

1. www.ustr.gov/Trade_Agreements/Regional/NAFTA/Section_Index.html.

2. www.worldtradelaw.net/nafta/.

3. D. A. Floudas and L. F. Rojas. 2000. "Some thoughts on NAFTA and trade integration in the American continent," *International Problems*, 4. www.diplomacy.bg.ac.yu/mpro_sa00_4.htm.

4. Ibid.

5. https://www.cia.gov/library/publications/the-world-factbook/geos/ca.html.

6. P. L. Benaroche. 2008. In P. M. Berkowitz, A. E. Reitz, and T. Muller-Bonnani (eds.), *International Labor and Employment Law*, 2nd edition, Volume II, 53.

7. www.hrsdc.gc.ca/eng/lp/spila/clli/eslc/27statutory_holidays_synoptic_table.shtml.

8. www.canadaone.com/ezine/july07/inoutvacation.html.

9. www.osler.com/uploadedFiles/Resources/Publications/.CanLabourEmpLaw2007.pdf.

10. www.servicecanada.gc.ca/eng/ei/types/compassionate_care.shtml.

11. www.ssa.gov/policy/docs/progdesc/ssptw/2006-2007/americas/canada.html.

12. Ibid.
13. Ibid.
14. www.who.int/countries/can/en/.
15. https://www.cia.gov/library/publications/the-world-factbook/geos/mx.html.
16. V. Escoto-Zubiran. 2008. In P. M. Berkowitz, A. E. Reitz, and T. Muller-Bonnani (eds.), *International Labor and Employment Law*, 2nd edition, Volume II, 157.
17. https://www.cia.gov/library/publications/the-world-factbook/geos/mx.html.
18. www.helplinelaw.com/law/mexico/constitution/constitution06.php.
19. www.fredlaw.com/articles/international/Mexico.pdf.
20. V. Escoto-Zubiran, 158–160.
21. N. de Buen Lozano and C. de Buen Unna. 2003. In W. L. Keller and T. J. Darby (eds.), *International Labor and Employment Laws*, 2nd edition, Volume I, 22–60
22. www.ssa.gov/policy/docs/progdesc/ssptw/2006-2007/americas/mexico.html.
23. Ibid.
24. N. de Buen Lozano and C. de Buen Unna, 22–68.
25. www.ssa.gov/policy/docs/progdesc/ssptw/2006-2007/americas/mexico.html.
26. Ibid.
27. Ibid.
28. Ibid.
29. www.who.int/countries/mex/en/.
30. N. de Buen Lozano and C. de Buen Unna, 22-69–22-70.
31. www.imf.org/external/pubs/ft/weo/2008/02/pdf/c2.pdf.
32. http://hdr.undp.org/en/statistics/.
33. www.bilaterals.org/rubrique.php3?id_rubrique 165.
34. www.comunidadandina.org/endex.htm.
35. http://news.bbc.co.uk/2/hi/business/4079505.stm.
36. https://www.cia.gov/library/publications/the-world-factbook/geos/br.html.
37. P. R. F. Pires and L. C. M. Gomes. 2003. In W. L. Keller and T. J. Darby (eds.), *International Labor and Employment Laws*, 2nd edition, Volume I, 30-2–30-19.
38. Ibid. 30-3.
39. Ibid. 30-3.
40. I. C. Franco and C. Pizzotti. 2008. In P. M. Berkowitz, A. E. Reitz, and T. Muller-Bonnani (eds.), *International Labor and Employment Law*, 2nd edition, Volume II, 39.
41. www.ssa.gov/policy/docs/progdesc/ssptw/2006-2007/americas/brazil.html.
42. Ibid.
43. Ibid.
44. www.who.int/countries/bra/en/.
45. https://www.cia.gov/library/publications/the-world-factbook/geos/ar.html.
46. J. D. Orlansky. 2008. In W. L. Keller and T. J. Darby (eds.), *International Labor and Employment Laws*, 3rd edition, Volume IIB, 76-11.
47. Ibid. 76-48–76-50.
48. Ibid. 76-55.

49. www.ssa.gov/policy/docs/progdesc/ssptw/2006-2007/americas/argentina.html.

50. J. D. Orlansky. *International Labor and Employment Laws*, 76-57.

51. www.ssa.gov/policy/docs/progdesc/ssptw/2006-2007/americas/argentina.html.

52. www.who.int/countries/arg/en/.

53. J. Kenner. 2003. In W. L. Keller and T. J. Darby (eds.), *International Labor and Employment Laws*, 2nd edition, Volume I, 1-1–1-2.

54. Ibid. 1-68.

55. www.europa.eu/scadplus/leg/en/s02300.htm.

56. https://www.cia.gov/library/publications/the-world-factbook/geos/fr.html.

57. https://www.cfe-eutax.org/taxation/labor-law/france.

58. Ibid.

59. B. Grinspan and F. Sauvage. 2005. In W. L. Keller and T. J. Darby (eds.). *International Labor and Employment Laws*, Cumulative Supplement, Volume I, 3-10.

60. Ibid. 3-75–3-76.

61. Ibid.

62. www.who.int/countries/fra/en/.

63. www.socialsecurity.gov/policy/docs/progdesc/ssptw/2008-2009/europe/france.html.

64. S. E. Tallent, B. Grinspan, and F. Sauvage. 2003. In W. L. Keller and T. J. Darby (eds.), *International Labor and Employment Laws*, 2nd edition, Volume I, 3-65.

65. https://www.cia.gov/library/publications/the-world-factbook/geos/gm.html.

66. www.fedee.com/natlaw.html#germany.

67. R. Lutringer and M. S. Dichter. 2003. In W. L. Keller and T. J. Darby (eds.), *International Labor and Employment Laws*, 2nd edition, Volume I, 4-86–4-91

68. Ibid.

69. Ibid. 4-103.

70. www.who.int/countries/deu/en/.

71. https://www.cia.gov/library/publications/the-world-factbook/geos/sp.html.

72. L. M. Florez and M. M. Gonzalez. 2003. In W. L. Keller and T. J. Darby (eds.), *International Labor and Employment Laws*, 2nd edition, Volume I, 6-10.

73. Ibid. 6-69–6-72.

74. Ibid. 6-78–6-79.

75. Ibid. 6-77.

76. Ibid. 6-82–6-83.

77. www.socialsecurity.gov/policy/docs/progdesc/ssptw/2008-2009/europe/spain.html.

78. www.who.int/countries/esp/en/.

79. https://www.cia.gov/library/publications/the-world-factbook/geos/uk.html.

80. K. Jack. 2003. In W. L. Keller and T. J. Darby (eds.), *International Labor and Employment Laws*, 2nd edition, Volume I, 7-1–7-9.

81. Ibid. 7-104–7-121.

82. Ibid. 7-151–7-153.

83. Ibid. 7-151.

84. www.who.int/countries/gbr/en/.

85. K. Jack. *International Labor and Employment Laws*, 7-154.

86. https://www.cia.gov/library/publications/the-world-factbook/geos/nl.html.

87. E. G. Van Arkel and C. J. Loonstra. 2008. In W. L. Keller and T. J. Darby (eds.), *International Labor and Employment Laws*, 3rd edition, Volume IIA, 16-19.

88. Ibid. 16-69–16-72.

89. Ibid. 16-84–16-85.

90. Ibid. 16-87–16-89.

91. www.socialsecurity.gov/policy/docs/progdesc/ssptw/2008-2009/europe/netherlands .html.

92. www.who.int/countries/nld/en/.

93. https://www.cia.gov/library/publications/the-world-factbook/geos/it.html.

94. P. Mandruzzato. 2003. In W. L. Keller and T. J. Darby (eds.), *International Labor and Employment Laws*, 2nd edition, Volume I, 5-6.

95. Ibid. 5-86–5-87.

96. Ibid. 5-86–5-87.

97. www.who.int/countries/ita/en/.

98. www.socialsecurity.gov/policy/docs/progdesc/ssptw/2008-2009/europe/ italy.html.

99. https://www.cia.gov/library/publications/the-world-factbook/geos/pl.html.

100. A. Czopski. 2008. In W. L. Keller and T. J. Darby (eds.), *International Labor and Employment Laws*, 3rd edition, Volume IIA, 17-4.

101. Ibid. 17-51–17-55.

102. Ibid. 17-69–17-71.

103. www.who.int/countries/pol/en/.

104. www.socialsecurity.gov/policy/docs/progdesc/ssptw/2008-2009/europe/ poland.html.

105. https://www.cia.gov/library/publications/the-world-factbook/geos/sw.html.

106. R. Fahlbeck. 2008. In W. L. Keller and T. J. Darby (eds.), *International Labor and Employment Laws*, 3rd edition, Volume IIA, 19-21.

107. Ibid. 19-85–19-86.

108. Ibid. 19-99–19-100.

109. www.socialsecurity.gov/policy/docs/progdesc/ssptw/2008-2009/europe/sweden .html.

110. www.who.int/countries/swe/en/.

111. https://www.cia.gov/library/publications/the-world-factbook/geos/rs.html.

112. E. G. Barikhnovskaya. 2008. In W. L. Keller and T. J. Darby (eds.), *International Labor and Employment Laws*, 3rd edition, Volume IIA, 41-6.

113. Ibid. 41-2.

114. Ibid. 41-60–41-64.

115. www.socialsecurity.gov/policy/docs/progdesc/ssptw/2008-2009/europe/russia .html.

116. Ibid.

117. www.who.int/countries/rus/en/.

118. www.imf.org/external/pubs/ft/weo/2006/02/data/index.aspx.

119. www.britannica.com/eb/article-48208/Asia.

120. https://www.cia.gov/library/publications/the-world-factbook/geos/ch.html.

121. A. W. Lauffs et al. 2003. In W. L. Keller and T. J. Darby (eds.), *International Labor and Employment Laws*, 2nd edition, Volume I, 31-5.

122. Ibid.

123. Ibid. 31-38–31-39.

124. www.socialsecurity.gov/policy/docs/progdesc/ssptw/2008-2009/asia/china.html.

125. A. W. Lauffs et al. 2003. In W. L. Keller and T. J. Darby (eds.), *International Labor and Employment Laws*, 2nd edition, Volume I, 31-47–31-48.

126. www.who.int/countries/chn/en/.

127. https://www.cia.gov/library/publications/the-world-factbook/geos/hk.html.

128. J. W. Cowman and S. McKeating. 2003. In W. L. Keller and T. J. Darby (eds.), *International Labor and Employment Laws*, 2nd edition, Volume I, 31-105–31-107.

129. Ibid. 31-128–31-130.

130. Ibid. 31-134.

131. www.socialsecurity.gov/policy/docs/progdesc/ssptw/2008-2009/asia/hongkong.html.

132. Ibid.

133. https://www.cia.gov/library/publications/the-world-factbook/geos/ja.html.

134. J. S. Siegel, M. Ogawa, and G. J. Bengoshi. 2003. In W. L. Keller and T. J. Darby (eds.), *International Labor and Employment Laws*, 2nd edition, Volume I, 32-3–32-4.

135. Ibid. 32-48–32-50.

136. www.socialsecurity.gov/policy/docs/progdesc/ssptw/2008-2009/asia/japan.html.

137. www.who.int/countries/jpn/en/.

138. www.socialsecurity.gov/policy/docs/progdesc/ssptw/2008-2009/asia/japan.html.

139. https://www.cia.gov/library/publications/the-world-factbook/geos/ks.html.

140. C. W. Hyun, S. C. Yuh, and J. Y. Yu. 2008. In W. L. Keller and T. J. Darby (eds.), *International Labor and Employment Laws*, 3rd edition, Volume IIB, 59-5–59-6.

141. Ibid. 59-65–59-68.

142. Ibid. 59-79–59-80.

143. Ibid. 59-83–59-84.

144. www.socialsecurity.gov/policy/docs/progdesc/ssptw/2008-2009/asia/southkorea.html.

145. www.who.int/countries/kor/en/.

146. https://www.cia.gov/library/publications/the-world-factbook/geos/in.html.

147. R. Singhania. 2008. In W. L. Keller and T. J. Darby (eds.), *International Labor and Employment Laws*, 3rd edition, Volume IIB, 57-11–57-13.

148. www.watsonwyatt.com/asia-pacific/localsites/india/services/ebcas.asp.

149. R. Singhania. *International Labor and Employment Laws*, 57-64–57-65.

150. www.socialsecurity.gov/policy/docs/progdesc/ssptw/2008-2009/asia/india.html.

151. Ibid.

152. www.who.int/countries/ind/en/.

153. https://www.cia.gov/library/publications/the-world-factbook/geos/sa.html.

154. D. M. Nabhan. 2008. In W. L. Keller and T. J. Darby (eds.), *International Labor and Employment Laws*, 3rd edition, Volume IIB, pp. 66-7–66-11.

155. Ibid. 66-51–66-56.

156. www.socialsecurity.gov/policy/docs/progdesc/ssptw/2008-2009/asia/saudiarabia .html.

157. Ibid.

158. www.who.int/countries/sau/en/.

159. D. M. Nabhan. *International Labor and Employment Laws*, 66-65–66-66.

160. http://hdr.undp.org/en/statistics/.

161. https://www.cia.gov/library/publications/the-world-factbook/geos/sf.html.

162. S. Stelzneer. 2008. In P. M. Berkowitz, A. E. Reitz, and T. Muller-Bonnani (eds.), *International Labor and Employment Law*, 2nd edition, Volume II, 221.

163. Ibid. 224–225.

164. E. J. Lubbe and H. J. Datz. 2003. In W. L. Keller and T. J. Darby (eds.), *International Labor and Employment Laws*, 2nd edition, Volume I, 33-94–33-95.

165. www.ssa.gov/policy/docs/progdesc/ssptw/2006-2007/africa/southafrica.html.

166. www.who.int/countries/zaf/en/.

167. https://www.cia.gov/library/publications/the-world-factbook/geos/as.html.

168. J. Cooper et al. In W. L. Keller and T. J. Darby (eds.), *International Labor and Employment Laws*, 3rd edition, Volume IIB, pp. 70-1–70-6.

169. Ibid. 70-71–70-73.

170. Ibid. 70–87.

171. www.ssa.gov/policy/docs/progdesc/ssptw/2008-2009/asia/australia.html.

172. Ibid.

173. www.who.int/countries/aus/en/.

Glossary

133 $\frac{1}{3}$ percent rule   Guards against backloading in retirement plans. The annual accrual rate cannot exceed 133$\frac{1}{3}$ percent of the rate of accrual for any prior year.

1-in-20 test   A criterion specified in the Federal Unemployment Tax Act (FUTA) to determine whether employers must participate in state unemployment insurance programs.

A

accidental death and dismemberment insurance (AD&D)   Covers death or dismemberment as a result of an accident. Dismemberment refers to the loss of two limbs or the complete loss of sight (i.e., blindness). Compared to life insurance, AD&D generally does not pay survivor benefits in the case of death by illness.

accommodation and enhancement benefits Promote opportunities for employees and their families such as educational scholarships and transportation services.

accrual rules   Specify the rate at which participants accumulate (or earn) retirement benefits.

accrued benefits   The benefit amount that a participant has earned under the plan's terms at a specified time or account balances for key employees.

accumulated benefit obligation   The present value of benefits based on a designated date. Actuaries determine a defined benefit plan's accumulated benefit obligation by making assumptions about the return on investment of assets and characteristics of the participants and their beneficiaries, including expected length of service and life expectancies.

adverse selection   The tendency of an insurance pool to disproportionately attract "bad risks" and discourage the participation of "good risks."

after-tax contributions   Do not enable employees to exclude contributions from annual income before calculating federal and state income tax obligations.

Age Discrimination in Employment Act of 1967 (ADEA)   A federal Equal Employment Opportunity law, protects older workers age 40 and over from illegal discrimination in the workplace.

age-weighted profit-sharing plan   A type of hybrid retirement plan; fundamentally a defined contribution plan because benefit amounts fluctuate according to how well the investments of plan assets perform. Consideration of age in these plans is similar to defined benefit plans because employers contribute disproportionately more to the accounts of older employees based on a projected hypothetical benefit at normal retirement age.

American Recovery and Reinvestment Act of 2009 (ARRA)   Provides for a 65 percent reduction in COBRA premiums for certain assistance eligible individuals for up to nine months.

Americans with Disabilities Act (ADA)   Prohibits discriminatory employment practices against qualified individuals with disabilities.

Americans with Disabilities Act Amendments Act of 2008   Makes important changes to the definition of the term *disability*. These changes make it easier for an individual seeking protection under the ADA to establish that he or she has a disability within the meaning of the ADA.

annual addition   The annual maximum allowable contribution to a participant's account in a defined contribution plan, including employer contributions allocated to the participant's account, employee contributions, and forfeitures allocated to the participant's account.

annuities   A series of payments for the life of the participant and beneficiary. Annuity contracts are usually purchased from insurance companies, which make payments according to the contract.

automatic cost-of-living adjustments (COLAs) Annual increases to Social Security benefits that approximate rises in the cost of goods and services such as items regularly purchased (e.g., food, medical care).

average benefit test   A test for coverage requirements that determines whether qualified plans benefit a "nondiscriminatory classification" of employees and possess an "average benefit percentage" for non–highly compensated employees that is at a minimum 70 percent of the average benefit percentage for highly compensated employees covered by the plan.

averaged index monthly earnings   Refer to a factor in determining a person's Social Security benefits, specifically, age 62, disability, or death, adjusted for changes in the person's earnings over the course of his or her employment and changes in average wages in the economy over the same period.

B

backing-in approach   A reactive process for making possible changes to benefits. Companies evaluate the benefits program only when unexpected problems arise.

backloading   Occurs whenever benefits accrue at a substantially higher rate during the years close to an employee's eligibility to earn retirement benefits. The Internal Revenue Service discourages backloading; employers must follow one of three rules to ensure regular accumulation of retirement benefits: three percent rule, 133 $\frac{1}{3}$ percent rule, or fractional rule.

back care programs   Educational programs designed to help workers reduce back injuries through training, exercise programs, ergonomic evaluations of the work environment, and relaxation techniques.

banking hours   A feature of flextime schedules that enables employees to vary the number of work hours daily as long as they maintain the regular number of work hours on a weekly basis.

base benefit percentage   The percentage of pay at which employees earn employer-provided benefits on their compensation, up to (and including) the plan's integration level (for integrating defined benefit plans using the excess approach).

base contribution percentage   The rate of employer contributions allocated to individual accounts at or below the integration level (for defined contribution plans using the excess approach).

base pay   The monetary compensation employees earn on a regular basis for performing their jobs. Hourly pay and salary are the main forms.

base period   The minimum period of time an individual must be employed before becoming eligible to receive unemployment insurance under the Social Security Act of 1935.

benefits strategy   The use of benefits practices that support total compensation strategies, human resource strategies, and competitive strategies.

bereavement leave   Provides paid time-off for employees, usually following the death of a relative. A bereavement policy specifies the relatives whose death qualifies employees for leave. Also known as *funeral leave.*

board of directors   Represents the interests of company shareholders by weighing the pros and cons of decisions made by top executives. Boards of directors contain approximately 15 members. These members include CEOs and top executives of other successful companies, distinguished community leaders, well-regarded professionals (e.g., attorneys), and possibly a few top-level executives of the company.

bona fide executive   In the context of the mandatory retirement age for employer-sponsored retirement plans, this person primarily manages the overall company and directs the work of two or more people.

business necessity   A legally acceptable defense against charges of alleged discriminatory employment practices in Title VII of the Civil Rights Act of 1964 and the Civil Rights Act of 1991 claims. Under the business necessity defense, an employer proves that the suspect practice prevented irreparable financial damage to the company.

C

cafeteria plans   Enable employees within a company to choose from among a set of benefits and different levels of these benefits. Also known as *flexible benefits.*

capital gain   The difference between the company stock price at the time of purchase and the lower stock price at the time an executive receives stock options.

capped fee schedules   Set maximum dollar amounts for each service covered in managed care health plans.

carryover provision   Permits employees to take unused vacation time awarded for a calendar or fiscal year during a subsequent calendar or fiscal year.

carve-out plans Insurance plans that offer specific kinds of benefits such as dental care, vision care, prescription drugs, mental health and substance abuse, and maternity care.

case management Companies ensure that patients with serious health problems receive essential medical attention on a cost-effective basis.

cash balance plan A type of hybrid retirement plan that defines benefits for each employee by reference to the amount of the employee's hypothetical account balance.

cash or deferred arrangements (CODAs) See *Section 401(k) plans.*

cashout provisions Pay employees an amount equal to the unused vacation days based on regular daily earnings.

Centers for Medicare & Medicaid Services One of two federal agencies with primary responsibility for the programs established by the Social Security Act of 1935 and its subsequent amendments. See also *Social Security Administration.*

certain benefits The Internal Revenue Code allows employees to exclude the value of facilities usage from income (thus, exemption of this amount from FICA and FUTA requirements) for on-premises athletic facilities under the control of the employer. Certain facilities include any gym or other athletic facility (e.g., swimming pool, tennis court, or golf course).

certificate of coverage Exempts an employee from paying FICA taxes on the same earnings in other countries. For example, the U.S. Social Security Administration issues a certificate of coverage to companies for each U.S. citizen or resident alien working outside the United States.

child care Programs that focus on supervising preschool-age dependent children whose parents work outside the home.

Civil Rights Act of 1991 A federal law that shifted the burden of proof of disparate impact from employees to employers, overturning several 1989 Supreme Court rulings. Previously employees were responsible for indicating which employment practices created disparate impact in employment discrimination suits, and demonstrating how the employment practice created disparate impact (intentional discrimination).

Clean Air Act Amendments of 1990 Require employers in smoggy metropolitan areas like Los Angeles to comply with state and local commuter-trip-reduction laws.

cliff vesting Enables employees to earn 100 percent vesting rights after no more than three years of service.

coinsurance A feature of health insurance programs that refers to the percentage of covered expenses or a fixed dollar amount paid by the insured.

collective bargaining agreements Specify terms of employment including pay, benefits, and working conditions. These agreements arise out of negotiations between management and labor unions that represent some or all employees in the company.

company stock Total equity or worth of the company.

company stock shares Equity segments of equal value. Equity interest increases with the number of stock shares.

compensable factors Job attributes that compensation professionals use to determine the value of jobs, and whether jobs are equal for the purposes of the Equal Pay Act of 1963. These factors pertain to skill, effort, responsibility, and working conditions.

compensation committee Contains members of the board of directors within and outside a company. They review alternative recommendations of executive compensation consultants for compensation packages, discuss the assets and liabilities of the recommendations, and recommend the best proposal to the board of directors for their consideration.

competitive advantage Describes a company's success based on employee efforts to maintain market share and profitability over a sustained period of several years.

competitive strategy The planned use of company resources—technology, capital, and human resources—to promote and sustain competitive advantage.

comprehensive major medical plans Replace traditional fee-for-service plans by extending coverage to a broader array of services (similar to supplemental plans).

compressed workweek schedules Enable employees to perform their work in fewer days than a regular five-day workweek.

concurrent reviews Conducted by health insurance companies, determine whether additional hospitalization is medically necessary. The main goal of such reviews is cost control.

Consolidated Omnibus Budget Reconciliation Act of 1985 (COBRA) An amendment to ERISA that provides employees and beneficiaries the right to elect continuation coverage under group health plans if they would lose coverage due to a qualifying event.

consortium EAPs Establish contracts with sets of numerous smaller employers. Smaller companies combine limited resources to establish a contract with a third-party provider.

constructive confrontation Entails discussing incidents of poor performance with the troubled employee, citing the necessity of improving job performance within a designated period. In many instances, employees recognize that personal problems are responsible for poor performance and voluntarily seek help through an EAP.

constructive receipt A legal concept that guides the timing of an executive's obligation to pay income taxes for funded nonqualified deferred compensation plans.

consumer-driven health care The objective of helping companies maintain control over costs while also enabling employees to make greater choices about health care. This approach may enable employers to lower the cost of insurance premiums by selecting plans with higher employee deductibles. The most popular consumer-driven approaches are flexible spending accounts and health reimbursement accounts.

Consumer Price Index (CPI) Indexes monthly price changes of goods and services that people buy for day-to-day living.

continuation coverage Refers to extended health insurance protection mandated by COBRA up to 36 months following a qualifying event.

contributory financing The company and its employees share the costs of discretionary benefits.

copayment Nominal payments individuals make for office visits to their doctors or for prescription drugs.

core hours The time when employees must be present in the workplace; a feature of flextime schedules.

core plus option plans Extend a preestablished set of benefits such as medical insurance and retirement plans as a program core.

corporate-owned life insurance A particular supplemental executive retirement plan based on the use of whole life insurance.

cost-of-living adjustments (COLAs) Periodic base pay increases that are based on changes in prices as indexed by the consumer price index (CPI). COLAs enable workers to maintain their purchasing power and standards of living by adjusting base pay for inflation.

coverage requirements Limit an employer's freedom to exclude employees from qualified plans. Tests to determine whether coverage requirements are met include the ratio percentage test and the average benefit tests.

covered compensation Maximum integration level approved by the Internal Revenue Service. These amounts are based on the participant's year of birth, and increase steadily for younger employees.

current profit-sharing plans Award cash to employees typically on a quarterly or annual basis.

D

day care Programs involving the supervision and care of children or the elderly.

death benefits Awarded in two forms under workers' compensation: burial allowances and survivor benefits. Burial allowances reflect a fixed amount, varying by state.

death claims Workers' compensation claims for deaths that occur in the course of employment or that are caused by compensable injuries or occupational diseases.

deductible The amount an individual pays for services before insurance benefits become active.

deferred compensation Agreement between an employee and a company to render payments to an employee at a future date. Deferred compensation is a hallmark of executive compensation packages.

deferred profit-sharing plans Place cash awards in trust accounts for employees. These trusts are set aside as a source of retirement income on behalf of employees.

defined benefit plans   Guarantee retirement benefits specified in the plan document. This benefit usually is expressed in terms of a monthly sum equal to a percentage of a participant's preretirement pay multiplied by the number of years he or she has worked for the employer.

defined contribution plans   Require employers and employees to make annual contributions to separate retirement fund accounts established for each participating employee, based on a formula contained in the plan document.

deliberate and knowing tort   A type of tort that entails an employer's deliberate and knowing intent to harm at least one employee. See also *torts*.

dental fee-for-service plans   Fashioned after general fee-for-service insurance programs, provide protection against dental health care expenses in the form of cash benefits paid to the insured or directly to the dental care provider.

dental HMOs   Prepaid dental services.

dental insurance   Covers routine preventative procedures and necessary procedures to promote the health of teeth and gums.

dental maintenance organizations   Deliver dental services through the comprehensive health care plans of many health maintenance organizations (HMOs) and preferred provider organizations (PPOs).

dental service corporations   Nonprofit corporations of dentists owned and administered by state dental associations.

Department of Labor Advisory Opinion Letters Help clarify aspects of a regulation for which specific definitions are not stated or when court rulings offer differing opinions on specific aspects of one or more laws. For example, various Letters help companies interpret aspects of the Employee Retirement Income Security Act (ERISA).

discount stock options   A kind of executive deferred compensation; entitle executives to purchase their company's stock in the future at a predetermined price. Discount stock options are similar to nonstatutory stock options with one exception: Companies grant stock options at rates far below the stock's fair market value on the date the option is granted.

disposition   The sale of stock by the stockholder.

distribution   Payment of vested benefits to participants or beneficiaries.

distributive justice   Perceived fairness about how rewards are distributed.

Drug-Free Workplace Act of 1988   A federal law mandating that companies holding federal contracts (worth at least $25,000) or grants (in any amount) promote a drug-free workplace.

dual capacity   A legal doctrine that applies to the relationship between employers and employees. Specifically, a company may fulfill a role for employees that is completely different from its role as employer.

dual-percentage approach   Relies on specified percentages to reduce an employee's company-sponsored disability benefits based on public disability benefits.

E

economic exchange   As with wages and salary, where the nature of the exchange has been specified at the time of employment. (Of course, economic exchange can also be renegotiated at any time during employment, such as yearly pay raises.) Explicit company policies and procedures help to ensure that each party (i.e., the employer and the employee) fulfills the obligations in the exchange relationship. In other words, in exchange for continued employments and wages, employees are obligated to work for the employer.

Economic Growth and Tax Relief Reconciliation Act of 2001   Created tax benefits to individuals and companies in various ways, such as increasing the amount companies and employees can contribute to qualified retirement plans on a pretax basis.

economies of scale   The idea that it is more efficient or less costly to provide the same benefit to larger groups of individuals than smaller groups of individuals.

educational assistance programs   Allow employees to exclude as much as $5,250 of annual gross income for educational assistance.

EEOC v. Chrysler   District court ruling that early retirement programs are permissible when companies offer them to employees on a voluntary basis.

Forcing early retirement upon older workers represents age discrimination.

EEOC v. Madison Community Unit School District No. 12 Circuit court ruling that shed light on judging whether jobs are equal based on four compensable factors: skill, effort, responsibility, and working conditions.

elder care Programs that provide physical, emotional, or financial assistance for aging parents, spouses, or other relatives who are not fully self-sufficient because they are too frail or disabled.

election period Relating to the Consolidated Omnibus Budget Reconciliation Act, refers to the period that begins on or before the occurrence of the qualifying event, and it extends for at least 60 days.

elimination period Minimum amount of time an employee must wait after becoming disabled before disability insurance payments begin. Elimination periods follow the completion of the preeligibility period.

Emergency Unemployment Insurance (EUC) Program established in June 2008 by the *Supplemental Appropriations Act of 2008,* provides 13 additional weeks of federally funded unemployment insurance benefits to the unemployed who have exhausted all state unemployment insurance benefits for which they were eligible.

Employee Assistance Professionals Association (EAPA) A professional organization dedicated to promoting standards for EAPs.

employee assistance programs (EAPs) Help employees cope with personal problems that may impair their personal lives or job performance. Examples of these problems are alcohol or drug abuse, domestic violence, the emotional impact of AIDS and other diseases, clinical depression, and eating disorders. EAPs also assist employers in helping troubled employees identify and solve problems that may be interfering with their job or personal life.

employee benefits Compensation other than hourly wage or salary. Examples include paid vacation, medical insurance coverage, and tuition reimbursement.

employee-financed benefits Employers do not contribute to the financing of discretionary benefits because employees bear the entire cost.

employee-owned annuities Offer executives the greatest degree of financial security because they own the annuities. An executive sets up annuity arrangements with third-party vendors such as mutual fund companies; then, the company pays the cost for an annuity. An executive's vested retirement benefit usually determines the amount of the annuity.

employee (individual) mandates Something that an individual must do because it is required by law.

Employee Plans Compliance Resolution System (EPCRS) A system used by the Internal Revenue Service to ensure that employers comply with Title II provisions of the Employee Retirement Income Security Act (ERISA): minimum participation, vesting, distributions, and funding rules of qualified plans.

Employee Retirement Income Security Act of 1974 (ERISA) Regulates the establishment and implementation of discretionary benefits practices. These include medical, life, and disability programs as well as pension programs.

employee stock option plans (ESOPs) May be the basis for a company's Section 401(k) plan; these plans invest in company securities, making them similar to profit-sharing plans and stock bonus plans. ESOPs provide employees with options to purchase company stock at a future date, presumably when the value of stock has increased.

employer mandates Another expression for legally required benefits, or something that the law requires to be provided to employees.

Employment and Training Administration U.S. Department of Labor agency that oversees unemployment insurance programs.

equal benefit principle or **equal cost principle** Requires employers under the Older Workers Benefit Protection Act (OWBPA) to offer older workers benefits of equal or greater value than the benefits offered to younger workers.

equal employment opportunity (EEO) Federal laws prohibiting illegal discrimination against various protected classes of individuals regarding all employment practices, including employee benefits.

Equal Employment Opportunity Commission (EEOC) Federal government agency that oversees the enforcement of EEO laws.

Equal Pay Act of 1963   A federal EEO law requiring that companies pay women equally when performing equal work as defined by compensable factors. This act does specify permissible exceptions, allowing companies to pay women less than men for jobs of equal worth, based on seniority, merit, quantity of work, or other factors besides sex.

equal payments   Reflect a belief that all employees should share equally in the company's gain to promote cooperation among employees.

establishment funds   Primitive forms of disability insurance created and funded by employers that provided minimal cash payments to workers who became occupationally ill or injured.

excess approach   A method approved by the Internal Revenue Service for integrating qualified defined contribution plans with Social Security benefits. This approach stipulates a compensation amount, which is known as the integration level. Companies contribute to the pension plan or offer benefits at a lower rate for compensation below the integration level than above the integration level.

excess benefit percentage   For integrating defined benefit plan benefits with Social Security benefits using the excess approach, excess benefit percentage is the percentage of pay at which employees earn employer-provided benefits on compensation in excess of the plan's integration level.

excess benefit plans   An executive retirement plan that extends the provisions of existing qualified plans. The objective is to increase retirement benefits by the amount lost due to contribution and annual addition limits set by the Internal Revenue Service.

excess contribution percentage   Rate of employer contributions allocated to individual accounts above the integration level. Each percentage is based on an employee's annual compensation.

exclusion provisions   Of insurance plans, a list of the particular conditions that are ineligible for coverage. For example, most disability insurance plans do not provide coverage for disabilities that result from self-inflicted injuries.

exclusive provider organization (EPO)   A variation of preferred provider organizations (PPOs). EPOs do not offer reimbursement for services provided outside the established network of health care providers. See *preferred provider organization*.

executive compensation consultants   Recommend alternative pay packages to compensation committees.

executive perquisites   Cover a broad range of benefits from free lunches to the use of corporate jets. These benefits help recognize the attained status of executives.

exempt jobs   Not subject to the overtime pay provisions of the Fair Labor Standards Act (FLSA).

exercise of stock option   An employee's purchase of stock using stock options.

expatriates   Using the United States as a frame of reference, expatriates are U.S. citizens employed in U.S. companies with work assignments outside the United States. See also *third-country nationals*.

experience rating   A system that establishes higher contributions (to fund insurance programs) for employers with higher incidences of claims (i.e., more people using the insurance).

experience rating system   Establishes higher contributions to fund unemployment insurance programs for employers with higher incidences of unemployment.

extrinsic compensation   Includes both monetary and nonmonetary rewards.

F

Fair Labor Standards Act of 1938 (FLSA)   Contains provisions for minimum wage, overtime pay, and child labor restrictions.

fair market value   The average value between the highest and lowest reported sales price of a stock on the New York Stock Exchange on any given date.

Family and Medical Leave Act of 1993 (FMLA)   Provides protection in cases of family or medical emergency. FMLA permits eligible employees to take up to a total of 12 workweeks of unpaid leave during any 12-month period for family or medical emergencies.

family assistance programs   Help employees provide care to young children and dependent elderly relatives.

family coverage   Offers health insurance benefits to the covered employee and his or her family members as defined by the plan (usually, spouse and children).

FASB 106   Created by the Financial Accounting Standards Board; a rule that changed the method of how companies recognize the costs of nonpension retirement benefits, including health insurance, on financial balance sheets. This rule effectively reduces a company's net profit amounts listed on the balance sheet.

Federal Employees' Compensation Act   Created a workers' compensation program for federal civilian employees.

Federal Insurance Contributions Act (FICA)   Taxes employees and employers to finance the Social Security Old-Age, Survivor, and Disability Insurance Program (OASDI).

Federal Unemployment Tax Act (FUTA)   Mandates employer contributions to fund state unemployment insurance programs. FUTA also specifies two criteria used to determine whether employers must participate in state unemployment insurance programs: the 1-in-20 test and the wage test.

fee-for-service plans   Provide protection against health care expenses in the form of cash benefits paid to the insured or directly to the health care provider after receiving health care services. These plans pay benefits on a reimbursement basis.

fiduciaries   Individuals who manage employee benefits plans and pension plan funds.

fiduciary responsibilities   The responsible management of employee benefits programs and pension plan funds.

final average compensation   For integrating defined benefit plan benefits with Social Security benefits using the offset approach, final average compensation is the average of an employee's annual compensation for the three-consecutive-year period ending with or within the plan year. For employees with fewer than three years of service, final average compensation is the average of the annual compensation during the period of employment.

Financial Accounting Standards Board (FASB)   Nonprofit company responsible for improving standards of financial accounting and reporting in companies.

fixed first-dollar-of-profits formula   In profit-sharing plans, uses a specific percentage of either pretax or after-tax annual profits (alternatively, gross sales or some other basis), contingent upon the successful attainment of a company goal.

flat benefit formula   In retirement plans, designates either a flat dollar amount per employee (flat amount formula) or dollar amount based on an employee's compensation (flat percentage formula). Annual benefits are usually expressed as a percentage of final average wage or salary.

flexible benefits   See *cafeteria plans.*

flexible scheduling   Allows employees the leeway to take time off during work hours to care for dependent relatives or react to emergencies.

flexible spending accounts   Permit employees to pay for certain benefits expenses (i.e., dental, medical, vision, or day care expenses) or to pay the premium or cost for at least one of these benefits.

flextime schedules   Allow employees to modify work schedules within specified limits set by the employer. Employees adjust when they will start work and when they will leave.

floating holidays   Allow employees to take paid time-off to observe any holiday not included on the employer's list of recognized paid holidays.

foreign affiliate   A non-U.S. business in which the U.S. employer possesses at least a 10 percent ownership interest.

forfeitures   Amounts from the accounts of employees who terminated their employment prior to earning vesting rights.

Form 5500   Guides employers in reporting detailed financial and actuarial data about pension and welfare plans to the U.S. Treasury Department.

formularies   Lists of drugs proven to be clinically appropriate and cost effective. The basis for setting formularies varies for each insurance plan.

fractional rule   Guards against backloading in retirement plans. This rule applies to participants who terminate their employment prior to reaching normal retirement age. Also stipulates that benefit accrual upon termination be proportional to normal retirement benefits.

full capitation   Refers to a system of paying primary care physicians a fixed amount for each assigned patient, but the amount may vary from patient to patient based on the cost of care.

full retirement age   Age at which individuals become eligible to receive full old-age (retirement benefits) Social Security benefits. This age began rising slowly from 65 in 2000 and will reach 67 for individuals born in 1960 or later.

full-integration approach Reduces an individual's company-sponsored disability benefits by the amount of public disability benefits.

full-service EAPs Include service providers such as alcohol treatment programs. Employers offer full-service EAPs through in-house services, third-party providers, or participation in a consortium EAP.

fully insured Status for old-age (retirement program) Social Security benefits that enables individuals to receive Social Security benefits for life. This status depends upon the accumulation of Social Security credits.

funded plans Allocate money or property (i.e., company stock or securities) to trust funds or insurance company contracts established in an executive's name without risk of forfeiture.

funding mechanisms Provide for executive retirement plans, the financial resources for funded or unfunded plans. Funding mechanisms vary according to the level of security, listed from least amount of security to the greatest amount: general asset approach, corporate-owned life insurance, split-dollar life insurance, rabbi trusts, secular trusts, and employee-owned annuities.

funeral leave See *bereavement leave.*

G

Genetic Information Nondiscrimination Act of 2008 (GINA) Protects job applicants, current and former employees, labor union members, and apprentices and trainees from discrimination based on their genetic information by making unlawful the misuse of genetic information to discriminate in health insurance and employment.

Giles v. General Electric Co. A U.S. Court of Appeals for the Fifth District upheld a lower court's decision to award a former General Electric machinist $590,000 for damages, front pay, and attorney fees. Giles injured his back while performing his job.

golden handcuffs The idea that defined benefit pension plans provide strong financial incentive for employees to build seniority because pension income is much more generous for these individuals (compared to those who leave the company usually after a few short years).

golden parachute Refers to a clause in most executive employment agreements that provide pay

and benefits to executives following their termination resulting from a change in control.

gradual vesting schedule Enables employees to earn vesting rights in stages; specifically, employees acquire vesting rights in increments of 20 percent each year beginning with the employee's second year of service, reaching 100 percent vesting rights after no more than six years of service.

graduated first-dollar-of-profits formula In profit-sharing plans, uses a specific percentage based on either pretax or after-tax annual profits (alternatively, gross sales or some other basis); this percentage changes with these levels. For example, a company may choose to share 4 percent of the first $10 million of profits and 7 percent of the profits in excess of that level.

Great Depression During the 1930s scores of businesses failed and masses of employees became chronically unemployed.

group coverage Extends health insurance coverage to a group of employees and their dependents under a single master contract.

group model HMOs Primarily use contracts with established practices of physicians that cover multiple specialties. Each group model HMO contracts exclusively with one practice of physicians at a time. These HMOs do not employ physicians directly. Instead, they compensate physicians according to a preestablished schedule of fees for each service, or on a capitation basis by setting monthly amounts per patient.

group policyholders The entities to which insurance companies issue master contracts that apply to groups of individuals. The most common group policyholders include employers, professional associations, labor unions, and trusts established to provide health insurance to designated individuals.

H

Health Care Financing Administration The previous name for the current Centers for Medicare & Medicaid Services.

health insurance Covers the costs of a variety of services that promote sound physical and mental health, including physical examinations, diagnostic testing (X-rays), surgery, and hospitalization. Companies can choose from two broad classes of health insurance programs including fee-for-service plans and managed care plans.

Health Insurance Portability and Accountability Act of 1996 (HIPAA) An amendment to ERISA, this act imposes requirements on group health and health insurance issuers relating to portability, increased access by limiting preexisting limitation rules, renewability, and health care privacy.

Health Maintenance Organization Act of 1973 (HMO Act) Promoted company use of health maintenance organizations by providing HMOs with financial incentives subject to becoming federally qualified.

health maintenance organizations (HMOs) Sometimes described as providing prepaid medical services because fixed periodic enrollment fees cover HMO members for all medically necessary services only if the services are delivered or approved by the HMO.

health protection programs A host of practices geared toward promoting sound health. Health protection programs subsume health insurance and a variety of programs designed to promote physical and mental health.

health reimbursement accounts Established and funded by employers for employees as a source to cover eligible health care costs.

health risk appraisal A type of wellness program that informs employees of potential health risks based on a physical examination, responses to questions about certain habits (e.g., diet and family members' health histories).

health savings accounts (HSAs) Established by employers for employees as a source to cover eligible health care costs. Employees, employers, or both may make contributions to fund these accounts.

high-deductible health insurance plans Require substantial deductibles and low out-of-pocket maximums.

highly compensated individuals Defined by the Internal Revenue Service as an officer, a shareholder owning more than 5 percent of the voting power or value of all classes of stock, an employee who is highly compensated based on all facts and circumstances, and a spouse or dependent of one of the preceding.

high policy-making position In the context of the mandatory retirement age for employer-sponsored

retirement plans, refers to those who play a significant role in the development of company policy but do not have direct line control (e.g., over business functions such as accounting, finance, human resources).

home leave benefits Enable expatriates and third-country nationals to take paid time-off in the home country.

hospitalization benefits The items that an insurance company will provide coverage for, related to stays in the hospital such as the cost of the room and necessary medical supplies.

hospital insurance tax Supports the Medicare Part A program. Also known as *Medicare tax.*

host-country nationals Using the United States as a frame of reference, foreign national citizens who work in branch offices or manufacturing plants of U.S. companies in their home countries.

hours worked See the *Portal-to-Portal Act of 1947.*

human resource strategy Specifies the use of multiple human resource (HR) practices that are consistent with a company's competitive strategy.

hybrid retirement plan Combines features of defined benefit and defined contribution plans. Four common hybrid retirement plans include cash balance plans, target benefit plans, money purchase plans, and age-weighted profit-sharing plans.

I

illegal bargaining subjects Proposals for contract revisions that are either illegal under the National Labor Relations Act or violate federal or state law.

impairment approach Bases workers' compensation benefit amounts on the physical or mental loss associated with an injury to a bodily function. This approach does not account for loss of future earnings because it ignores the physical and mental capacities necessary to perform the essential functions of one's job.

incentive pay Defined as compensation, other than base wages or salaries, that fluctuates according to employees' attainment of some standard such as a preestablished formula, individual or group goals, or company earnings. Also known as *variable pay.*

incentive stock options Entitle executives to purchase their company's stock in the future at a predetermined price. Usually the predetermined price equals the stock price at the time an executive receives the stock options. Incentive stock options entitle executives to favorable tax treatment.

income annuities   Distribute income to retirees based on retirement savings paid to insurance companies in exchange for guaranteed monthly checks for life.

indemnity plans   Traditional health insurance plans in which the insurance company agrees to pay a designated percentage of the costs for health insurance procedures and the insured (i.e., recipient of the insurance benefit) agrees to pay a designated percentage.

individual coverage   Extends insurance protection to a named employee and possibly to his or her dependents including children and spouse.

individual practice associations   Types of HMOs, which are partnerships or other legal entities that arrange health care services by entering into contracts with independent physicians, health professionals, and group practices. Physicians participate in this type of HMO practice out of their own facilities and continue to see HMO enrollees and patients who are not HMO enrollees. Participating physicians charge fees according to a capped fee schedule.

informational justice   Fairness of the accounts given for certain procedures.

in-house EAPs   Rely on employees of the company to provide EAP services.

injury claims   Workers' compensation claims for disabilities that have resulted from accidents such as falls, injuries from equipment use, or physical strains from heavy lifting.

inpatient benefits   Covered expenses associated with hospital stays.

insurance policy   Contractual relationship between an insurance company and beneficiary that specifies the obligations of both parties. For example, a health insurance company specifies that it will cover the cost of physical examinations, and a life insurance company agrees to pay a spouse an amount equal to double of his deceased wife's annual salary.

insured   Employees covered by an insurance policy.

integrated paid time-off policy   Enables employees to schedule time-off without justifying the reasons.

Internal Revenue Code (IRC)   The set of federal government regulations pertaining to taxation in the United States [e.g., sales tax, company (employer) income tax, individual (employee) income tax, property tax].

Internal Revenue Service (IRS)   Agency of the federal government that establishes and implements tax regulations. The IRS also assesses penalties for violations of these regulations.

interpersonal justice   Perceived fairness of the interpersonal treatment people receive from others.

intrinsic compensation   Employees' psychological mind-sets that result from performing their jobs.

IRS Form 8109   Federal Tax Deposit Coupon, accompanies FUTA deposits of employers.

IRS Form 940   Used by companies to file annual tax returns for FUTA deposits.

J

job-lock phenomenon   Occurs whenever an employed individual experiences a medical problem, and this individual is "locked" into the current job because most health insurance plans contain preexisting condition clauses.

Joint Pension, Profit-Sharing, and Employee Stock Ownership Plan Task Force   An ad hoc committee established by Title III of ERISA for a short duration following the passage of the act in 1974. This committee studied such issues as the means of providing for the portability of pension rights among different pension plans, and the appropriate treatment under Title IV regarding plan termination insurance.

jury duty   Leave and witness duty policies protect employee rights to serve on a jury or as a witness in courts of law. Participation may be paid or unpaid, depending upon various factors. Jury duty is guided by federal and state law; witness duty policy is guided by state law in only about one-third of all states.

Jury Systems Improvement Act of 1978   A federal law recognizing that participation on a jury in federal court is a protected individual's right.

K

key employees   As defined by the Internal Revenue Service, includes any employee who during the current year is an officer of the employer having an annual compensation greater than

$130,000 (indexed for inflation in increments of $5,000 beginning in 2003), a 5 percent owner of the employer, or a 1 percent owner of the employer having an annual compensation from the employer of more than $150,000.

L

leveraged ESOPs ESOPs in which the company borrows money from a financial institution to purchase company stock.

liability management For the purposes of executive retirement plans, liability management speaks to adequate preparation to honor financial obligations to executives as set forth in nonqualified plans.

life insurance Protects the families of employees by paying a specified amount to an employee's beneficiaries upon the employee's death. Most policies pay some multiple of the employee's salary.

Longshore and Harborworkers' Compensation Act Created a workers' compensation program for maritime workers.

long-term disability insurance Provides benefits for extended periods of time anywhere between six months and life.

Lorance v. AT&T Technologies A Supreme Court decision that limited the rights of employees to challenge the use of seniority systems only to within 180 days of the system's implementation date.

loss of wage earning capacity approach Factors in two important issues that are likely to affect an injured worker's ability to compete for employment: human capital (e.g., work experience, age, and education) and the type of permanent impairment.

lump sum distributions Single payments of benefits. In defined contribution plans, lump sum distributions equal the vested amount (sum of all employee and vested employer contributions, and interest on this sum).

M

Mail Order Prescription Drug Program Dispenses expensive medications used to treat chronic health conditions such as HIV infection or neurological disorders such as Parkinson's disease.

managed care plans Emphasize cost control by limiting an employee's choice of doctors and hospitals. They also provide protection against health care expenses in the form of prepayment to health care providers.

mandatory bargaining subjects Employers and unions must bargain on these subjects if either constituent makes proposals about them.

mandatory retirement age Illegal under the Aged Discrimination in Employment Act (ADEA) with the exception of limited circumstances.

maximum benefit limits Maximum amount of money an insurance company expressed on a per health care procedure basis, for a benefits plan year, or for the lifetime of the insured employee.

maximum excess allowance Amount by which the excess benefit percentage exceeds the base benefit percentage for permitted disparity rules involving Social Security OASDI payments and employer-sponsored defined benefit payments.

maximum offset allowance Limits the amount by which benefits may be reduced. The maximum offset allowance may be the lesser of 50 percent of the benefit the employee would have earned without the plan's offset reduction (i.e., gross benefit percentage), or 0.75 percent of the participant's final average compensation multiplied by the participant's years of service (up to a maximum of 35 years).

Medicaid A jointly funded, federal–state health insurance program for low-income people and a variety of people in need, including children, the elderly, blind, or disabled people who are eligible to receive federally assisted income maintenance payments.

medical reimbursement plans Reimburse employees for some or all of the cost of prescription drugs. These plans pay benefits after an employee has met an annual deductible for the plan.

medical savings account (MSA) Refers to a personal savings account set up for employees to pay for medical expenses.

medical underwriting Process by which employees provide information on their past medical history in a questionnaire or physical examination. Insurers use this health information to exclude coverage or to tie premiums more closely to past medical history.

Medicare Programs that serve nearly all U.S. citizens aged at least 65 or disabled Social Security beneficiaries by providing insurance coverage for hospitalization, convalescent care, and major doctor bills.

Medicare Advantage Variety of health insurance coverage options for individuals eligible for Medicare protection who choose not to participate in Parts A and B.

Medicare Advantage or **Medicare Part C** One of four Medicare programs; offers beneficiaries additional choices in health care providers.

Medicare Part A One of four Medicare programs; provides compulsory hospitalization insurance.

Medicare Part B One of four Medicare programs; provides voluntary supplementary medical insurance.

Medicare Prescription Drug, Improvement and Modernization Act of 2003 Led to changes in the Medicare program by adding prescription drug coverage and recognizing health savings accounts (HSAs).

Medicare Select plans Medigap policies that offer lower premiums in exchange for limiting the choice of health care providers.

Medicare tax See *hospital insurance tax.*

Medigap One of four Medicare programs; provides voluntary supplemental insurance to fill in the gaps for Parts A and B. Medicare Select plans are Medigap policies that offer lower premiums in exchange for limiting the choice of health care providers.

mental health and substance abuse plans Cover the costs to treat mental health ailments such as clinical depression and the abuse of alcohol or chemical substances (e.g., addictions to cocaine or prescribed narcotic medications).

Mental Health Parity Act A federal law that established parity requirements for mental health plans being offered in conjunction with a group health plan that contains medical and surgical benefits. It expired in September 2001; lawmakers may resurrect this law in the future.

mergers and acquisitions The combination of once separate business entities or companies into a single business.

merit pay programs Reward employees with permanent increases to base pay according to differences in job performance.

military leave Enables employees who are members of the National Guard to report for military

duty when ordered just as civilians do in the event of a mandatory military draft. Employers choose whether to pay employees while on military leave.

minimum funding standards Ensure that employers contribute the minimum amount of money necessary to provide employees and beneficiaries promised benefits.

mix-and-match plans Permit employees to purchase any benefit (and benefit level).

modular plans Offer numerous fixed benefit packages to meet the life-cycle needs and priorities of different employee groups. Examples include single employees with no dependents, single parents, married workers with dependents, and employees nearing retirement.

money purchase plan A type of hybrid retirement plan that is a defined contribution plan because the benefit is based on the account balance (i.e., the employer contributions plus returns on investment of the employer contributions) at retirement. But these plans possess the funding requirements of defined benefit plans because employers must make annual contributions according to the designated formula for the plan.

morbidity tables Express annual probabilities of the occurrence of health problems. In general, insurance companies set insurance rates higher as the probability of death or the occurrence of health problems increases.

mortality tables Indicate yearly probabilities of death based on factors such as age and sex established by the Society of Actuaries. Insurance companies rely on these tables in the underwriting process.

multiemployer plans Pension plans to which more than one employer is required to contribute based on a collective bargaining agreement.

multiple-payer system Refers to a system in which there is more than one party responsible for covering the cost of health care, including the government, employers, labor unions, employees, or individuals not currently employed (e.g., retirees, the unemployed, and employees whose employer does not pay for health care coverage).

multiple qualifying event rules Entitle employees and their qualified beneficiaries to receive up to 36 months of continuation coverage under the Consolidated Omnibus Budget Reconciliation Act of 1985.

multiple tiers Specified copayment amounts an individual will pay for a specific prescription.

N

Nashville Gas Co. v. Satty A U.S. District Court held that excluding benefits for pregnant women from the company's disability plan did not violate Title VII of the Civil Rights Act of 1964. The court's decision was based on the following rationale: Both men and *nonpregnant women* benefited from the company's disability plan, and there was no reason to believe that men received more benefits than women.

National Association of Insurance Commissioners (NAIC) A nonprofit organization that addresses issues concerning the supervision of insurance within each state. Specifically, the NAIC has three main objectives: maintaining and improving state regulation, ensuring the reliability of insurance companies in matters of financial condition, and promoting fair, just, and equitable treatment of policyholders and claimants.

National Labor Relations Act of 1935 (NLRA) Establishes the right of employees to bargain collectively with employers on such issues as wages, work hours, and working conditions.

National Labor Relations Board (NLRB) Oversees the enforcement of the NLRA.

network model HMOs Contract with two or more independent physicians' practices. These HMOs usually compensate physicians according to a capped fee schedule.

Newborns' and Mothers' Health Protection Act of 1996 Sets minimum standards for the length of hospital stays for mothers and newborn children, and prohibits employers and all insurers (independent and self-funded indemnity plans as well as managed care plans) from using financial incentives to shorten hospital stays.

noncontributory financing The company pays the total costs of each discretionary benefit.

nondiscrimination rules Apply to pension plans. These rules prohibit employers from discriminating in favor of highly compensated employees in contributions or benefits, availability of benefits, rights, or plan features. Also, employers may not amend pension plans to favor highly compensated employees.

nonexempt jobs Subject to the FLSA overtime pay provision.

nonleveraged ESOPs May be the basis for a company's Section 401(k) plan. These plans invest in company securities, making them similar to employee stock option plans and profit-sharing plans. Also known as *stock bonus plans.* Stock bonus plans pay benefits in company stock.

nonproduction time A variety of possible uses of time related to, but not actually performing, an employee's main job duties or to periods of non-work time during a work shift. Nonproduction time related to the performance of job duties includes cleanup, preparation, and travel between job locations. Nonwork time during a work shift includes rest periods or "breaks" and periods to eat a meal.

nonqualified plans Welfare and pension plans that do not meet various requirements set forth by the Employee Retirement Income Security Act of 1974, disallowing favorable tax treatment for employee and employer contributions.

nonscheduled injuries As classified in workers' compensation programs, they are general injuries of the body that make working difficult or impossible. Examples of nonscheduled injuries include back or head damage.

nonstatutory stock options A kind of executive deferred compensation that entitles executives to purchase their company's stock in the future at a predetermined price. Usually the predetermined price equals the stock price at the time an executive receives the stock options. Nonstatutory stock options do not entitle executives to favorable tax treatment.

normal retirement age Lowest age specified in a pension plan. Upon attaining this age, an employee gains the right to retire without the consent of the employer, and to receive benefits based on length of service at the full rate specified in the pension plan.

O

occupational disease claims Workers' compensation claims for disabilities caused by ailments associated with particular industrial trade or processes.

offset approach A method approved by the Internal Revenue Service for integrating qualified pension plans with Social Security benefits. This approach subtracts a particular fraction of the qualified pension plan benefit from the total benefit without integration.

offset provisions Reduce company-sponsored retirement, disability, or life insurance by subtracting a particular percentage of these benefits from workers' compensation and Social Security disability plans.

Old-Age, Survivor, and Disability Insurance (OASDI) Programs that provide retirement income, income to the survivors of deceased workers, and income to disabled workers and their family members under the Social Security Act of 1935.

Older Workers Benefit Protection Act (OWBPA) The 1990 amendment to the Age Discrimination in Employment Act of 1967.

on-call time Requires employees to spend time on or close to the employer's premises so that they cannot use the time effectively for their own purposes. Virtually every employer can demand that nonexempt employees be available on an as-needed basis. In general, on-call time is paid leave.

organizational citizenship behavior Employees' discretionary behavior, not explicitly or directly recognized by the formal reward system of the employer, but in aggregate promoting organizational effectiveness.

out-of-pocket maximum Refers to the maximum amount a policyholder must pay per calendar year or plan year.

outpatient benefits Covered expenses for treatments in hospitals not requiring overnight stays.

outplacement assistance Programs that provide technical and emotional support to employees who are being laid off or terminated. Companies assist through a variety of career and personal programs designed to develop employee job-hunting skills and self-confidence.

outsourcing A contractual agreement by which an employer transfers responsibility to a third-party provider. In the case of benefits, third-party providers are independent companies with expertise in benefits design and administration.

Owens v. Local No. 169 A federal appeals court ruling, holding that the time that pulp mill mechanics spent on call was not compensable under FLSA since the on-call policy of the employer, while giving on-call employees the option of wearing a beeper, did not significantly restrict them from engaging in personal activities.

P

paid time-off Policies that compensate employees when they are not performing their primary work duties. Companies offer most paid time-off as a matter of custom, particularly paid holidays, vacations, and sick leave.

parity requirements Prohibit setting lower annual or lifetime maximums for mental health and substance abuse benefits than for medical and surgical benefits. This act contains a *sunset clause* that discontinues parity requirements for mental health benefits rendered on or after September 30, 2001.

partial capitation Refers to a system of paying primary care physicians a fixed dollar amount for each patient assigned to them.

partial disabilities Provide supplemental benefits in long-term disability plans to cover a portion of income loss associated with part-time employment.

partial disabilities inclusion Refers to a provision of many company-sponsored long-term disability plans. Specifically, this provision offers supplemental benefits to cover a portion of income loss associated with part-time employment.

pay-for-knowledge programs These reward managerial, service, or professional workers for successfully learning specific curricula.

Pension and Welfare Benefits Administration Agency of the U.S. Department of Labor that possesses responsibility for enforcing Title I of ERISA. This agency conducts investigations through its 10 regional offices and 5 district offices located in major cities throughout the country.

Pension Benefit Guarantee Corporation (PBGC) A tax-exempt self-financed corporation that insures nearly 38,000 private defined benefit pension plans covering more than 43 million American workers and retirees.

pension equity plans Hybrid retirement plans that are similar to cash balance plans, except that these plans credit employees' accounts with points based on years of service.

Pension Plan Table Required by the Securities Exchange Act of 1934, this table registers information about estimated annual benefits from defined benefit plans or actuarial plans that base retirement benefits primarily on final compensation and years of service.

pension plans   Provide income to individuals and beneficiaries throughout their retirement. Also called *retirement plans*.

perceived organizational support   Employee's perception of the degree to which the employer values the employee's contributions and well-being.

percentage discounts   Fees that are discounted from the amounts health care providers would usually charge.

per diem (allowance)   Provides expatriates and third-country nationals with allowances to compensate for differences in location (based on cost-of-living and family size).

permanent partial disabilities   Limit the kind of work an individual performs on an enduring basis.

permanent total disabilities   Prevent individuals from ever performing any work.

permissive bargaining subjects   Subjects on which neither the employer nor union is obligated to bargain.

permitted disparity rules   Allow companies to explicitly take into account Social Security OASDI benefits when determining pension benefits. Subject to established limits, qualified plans may reduce benefits based on the benefits owed under the Social Security program. Companies rely on either the excess approach or offset approach to integration. Also known as *Social Security integration*.

person-focused pay plans   General rewards to employees for acquiring job-related competencies, knowledge, or skills rather than for demonstrating successful job performances.

phantom stock   A compensation arrangement whereby boards of directors compensate executives with hypothetical company stock rather than actual shares of company stock. Phantom stock plans are similar to restricted stock plans because executives must meet specific conditions before they can convert these phantom shares into real shares of company stock.

plan termination rules   Specifications set forth by the Pension Benefit & Guaranty Corporation regarding the discontinuation of an employer's defined benefit pension plan.

point-of-service plans (POSs)   Combine features of fee-for-service systems and health maintenance organizations. Employees pay a nominal copayment for each visit to a designated network of physicians; alternatively, they may receive treatment from providers outside the network, but they pay more for this choice.

Portal-to-Portal Act of 1947   Defines the term *hours worked* as the compensable activities that precede and follow the primary work activities. See *hours worked*.

preadmission certification   Certification by a medical professional of a health insurance company may be necessary before a doctor can authorize hospitalization of a policyholder. Failure to ascertain preadmission certification may lead to denial of hospitalization benefits.

precertification reviews   These evaluate the appropriateness of proposed medical treatment as a condition for authorizing payment. Also known as *prospective reviews*.

preeligibility period   Spans from the initial date of hire to eligibility for coverage in a disability insurance program.

preexisting condition   A mental or physical disability for which medical advice, diagnosis, care, or treatment was received during a designated period preceding the beginning of disability or health insurance coverage.

preexisting condition periods   Time periods during which insurance coverage is excluded for preexisting conditions. See *preexisting condition*.

preferred provider organization (PPO)   A type of managed care plan that refers to a select group of health care providers who agree to furnish health care services to a given population (for example, Company B's employees) at a higher level of reimbursement than under fee-for-service plans.

Pregnancy Discrimination Act of 1978 (PDA)   Amendment to Title VII of the Civil Rights Act of 1964. The PDA prohibits discrimination against pregnant women in all employment practices.

premium   Amount of money an individual or company pays to maintain insurance coverage.

premium-only plans   Enable employees to pay their share of the cost to receive health insurance, dental insurance, and other company-sponsored health insurance.

prepaid group practice   A specific type of HMO that provides medical care for a set premium, rather than a fee-for-service basis.

prepaid medical services   Refer to most benefits offered by HMOs because fixed periodic enrollment fees cover HMO members for all medically necessary services only if the services are delivered or approved by the HMO. Also, alternative name for HMOs.

prescription card program   Operates like an HMO by providing prepaid benefits with nominal copayments for prescription drugs.

prescription drug plans   Cover the costs of drugs that state or federal laws require be dispensed by licensed pharmacists.

present value   Refers to the necessary amount of money invested now to achieve a desired amount at a designated future point in time.

pretax contributions   Enable employees, with tax regulation approval, to exclude contributions to benefits from annual income before calculating federal and sometimes state income tax obligations.

pretax salary reduction plans   Permit employees to set aside a portion of wages or salary each year on a pretax basis for qualified benefits expenses. In other words, employees exclude allocated wages or salaries from the calculation of annual federal income tax or state income tax (except for New Jersey).

primary care physicians   Designated by HMOs to determine whether patients require the care of a medical specialist. This functions to control costs by reducing the number of medically unnecessary visits to expensive specialists.

primary insurance amount   Equals the monthly benefit amount paid to a retired worker at full retirement age or to a disabled worker.

probationary period   Initial term of employment (the length of which is set by the employer) during which companies attempt to ensure that they have made sound hiring decisions. Often, employees are not entitled to participate in discretionary benefits programs during their probationary periods.

procedural justice   Perceived fairness of processes.

profitability threshold formula   Funds profit-sharing pools only if profits exceed a predetermined minimum level but fall below some established maximum level.

profit-sharing plans   Pay a portion of company profits to employees, separate from base pay, cost-of-living adjustments, or permanent merit pay increases. Two kinds of profit-sharing plans are used widely today: current profit sharing and deferred profit sharing.

profit-sharing pool   Money earmarked for distribution to employees who participate in profit-sharing plans. Companies may choose to fund profit-sharing plans based on gross sales revenue or some basis other than profits.

proportional payments to employees based on their annual salary   A belief that all employees should share the company's gain in proportion to annual salary.

proportional payments to employees based on their contribution to profits   A belief that employees should share the company's gain based on their contributions to profit generation.

prospective reviews   Also known as precertification reviews. Help control health insurance expenditures by evaluating the appropriateness of proposed medical treatment as a condition for authorizing payment. Specifically, prospective reviews aim to verify a patient's coverage, determine whether the health plan covers the treatment, judge whether the proposed treatment is medically appropriate, and specify whether a second surgical opinion is necessary.

protection programs   Provide family benefits, promote health, and guard against income loss caused by catastrophic factors like unemployment, disability, or serious illnesses.

provider payment systems   Payment arrangements between health care providers and managed care insurers.

psychological contracts   Implicitly establish terms of employment. This is in contrast to more explicit economic exchange agreements such as wage or salary levels.

Q

qualified beneficiary   For the purposes of the Consolidated Omnibus Budget Reconciliation Act, any individual who is a beneficiary under the group health plan such as the spouse of the covered employee or dependent child of the covered employee. Qualified beneficiaries include the covered employee when the qualifying event is termination of employment (other than by reason of misconduct) or a reduction in work hours.

qualified benefits   Any employer-sponsored benefit for which an employee may exclude the cost from federal income tax calculation. For example, an employee's monetary contribution to an employer-sponsored medical insurance plan is excluded from the calculation of annual federal taxes.

qualified domestic relations orders (QDROs)   In qualified plans, QDROs permit a retirement plan to divide a participant's benefits in the event of divorce. Dividing a participant's benefits without a QDRO is a violation of ERISA and the IRC.

qualified individual with a disability   Person who possesses the necessary skills, experience, education, and other job-related requirements and, regardless of reasonable accommodation, can perform the essential functions of the job; related to the ADA.

qualified joint and survivor annuity (QJSA)   In qualified plans, a QJSA is an annuity for the life of the participant with a survivor annuity for the participant's spouse.

qualified plans   Welfare and pension plans that meet various requirements set forth by the Employee Retirement Income Security Act of 1974; these plans entitle employees and employers to favorable tax treatment by deducting the contributions from taxable income. Qualified plans do not disproportionately favor highly compensated employees.

qualified preretirement survivor annuity (QPSA)   In qualified plans, a QPSA provides payments for the life of the participant's surviving spouse if the participant dies before he or she has begun to receive retirement benefits.

qualified scholarship programs   Established by Section 117 of the Internal Revenue code, these programs grant tax benefits to employees for their own or their children's education below graduate-level work. The tax benefit equals the amount of qualified tuition reduction plus related expenses (e.g., fees, books, supplies).

qualified tuition reductions   Reduction in tuition granted by the employer's program of qualified scholarship programs.

qualifying events   Pertain to an employee's right to elect continuation coverage under the Consolidated Omnibus Budget Reconciliation Act.

Qualifying events include the death of the covered employee, termination or reduction in hours of employment (other than by reason of misconduct), divorce or legal separation, dependent child ceasing to meet the health plan's definition of a dependent child, and eligibility for Medicare benefits under the Social Security Act.

R

rabbi trusts   Irrevocable grantor trusts named after an Internal Revenue Service ruling that created them. Grantors of a rabbi trust, in this case, employers, maintain ownership of the trust. Companies establish rabbi trusts to provide executives and key employees or beneficiaries with deferred compensation upon retirement or termination without cause.

ratemaking service organizations   Recommend rates that states charge companies to provide workers' compensation insurance.

rating manuals   In workers' compensation programs, these manuals specify insurance rates based on classifications of businesses.

ratio percentage test   A test for coverage requirements that determines whether qualified plans cover a percentage of non–highly compensated employees that is at least 70 percent of the percentage of highly compensated employees covered by the plan.

readily ascertainable fair market value   Fair market value of stock when traded on established stock exchanges.

referral EAPs   List of names and contact information for a variety of professional help services, ranging from crisis hot lines to alcohol and substance abuse treatment programs.

rehabilitative services   Cover physical and vocational rehabilitation in workers' compensation. Rehabilitative services are available in all states.

relational psychological contracts   Employees' expectations from the employer that might be either economic or noneconomic, but are also emotional, subjective, and intrinsic in nature.

rest and relaxation   Additional paid time-off leave awarded to expatriate and third-country nationals who work in designated hardship locations. The U.S. Department of State lists more than 150 hardship posts where the living conditions are considered unusually harsh.

restoration   An objective of executive retirement plans that addresses the gap between the maximum retirement benefits allowed by the Internal Revenue Service for qualified plans and the more substantial retirement income benefits absent IRS regulations.

restricted stock   A type of long-term executive compensation. Specifically, restricted stock means that executives do not have any ownership control over the disposition of the stock for a predetermined period, often 5 to 10 years.

retirement plans   See *pension plans.*

retrospective reviews   Following medical treatment but prior to disbursement of benefits, help control health insurance expenditures by determining whether the health insurance program covers the patient, the medical condition, and the medical treatment. These reviews also judge whether claims are nonfraudulent by confirming that medical treatments were actually given and appropriate for the medical condition.

risk-of-loss rules (alternatively, uniform coverage requirement)   Rules that require that employers make the full amount of benefits and coverage elected under a flexible spending account (FSA) plan available to employees from the first day the plan becomes effective regardless of how much money an employee has actually contributed.

Roth Individual Retirement Account (Roth IRA) A tax-free, nondeductible IRA introduced by the Taxpayer Relief Act of 1997. Withdrawals are nontaxable, including the account's earnings if distributions meet certain criteria. See also *traditional IRA.*

S

sabbatical leave   Paid time-off for professional development activities such as professional certification, conducting research, and curriculum development.

safe harbors   Compliance guidelines in a law or regulation.

savings incentive match plans for employees (SIMPLEs)   May be the basis for individual retirement accounts or Section 401(k) plans in small companies.

scheduled injuries   The loss of a member of the body, including an arm, leg, finger, hand, or eye, as classified in workers' compensation programs.

scholarship programs   Cover some or all of the tuition and related expenses for employees or family members pursuing undergraduate degrees in two- or four-year colleges.

second-injury funds   Cover a portion or all of the costs of a current workers' compensation claim associated with preexisting conditions from a work-related injury during prior employment elsewhere.

second surgical opinions   A feature of many health insurance plans, reduces unnecessary surgical procedures and costs by encouraging an individual to seek an independent opinion from another doctor.

Section 401(k) plans   Qualified retirement plans named after the section of the IRC that created them. These plans permit employees to defer part of their compensation to the trust of a qualified defined contribution plan. Only private sector or tax-exempt employers are eligible to sponsor 401(k) plans. Also known as *cash or deferred arrangements (CODAs).*

Section 457 plans   Nonqualified retirement plans for government employees; named after the section of the IRC that created them.

secular trusts   Similar to rabbi trusts with one exception: Secular trusts are not subject to a company's creditors in the event of bankruptcy or insolvency.

Securities and Exchange Commission (SEC)   A nonpartisan, quasi-judicial federal government agency with responsibility for administering federal securities laws.

Securities Exchange Act of 1934   Applies to the disclosure of executive compensation in companies that trade stock on public stock exchanges.

Self-Employment Contributions Act (SECA) Requires self-employed individuals to contribute to the OASDI and Medicare programs but at a higher tax rate than required for non-self-employed individuals.

self-funding (self-funded plans)   Refer to health insurance plans that pay benefits directly from an employer's assets.

seniority pay systems   Employees rewarded with permanent additions to base pay periodically according to employees' length of service performing their jobs.

short-term disability   For the purposes of private disability insurance plans, is an inability to perform the duties of one's regular job for a limited period (e.g., six months).

short-term disability insurance   Provides income benefits for limited periods of time, usually less than six months.

sick leave   Benefits that compensate employees for a specified number of days absent due to occasional minor illness or injury.

single coverage   Extends health insurance benefits only to the covered employee.

single-payer system   Refers to a health care system in which the government regulates the health care and uses taxpayer dollars to fund health care such as in Canada and some other economically developed countries. Single-payer systems are often referred to as universal health care systems because the government ensures that all its citizens have access to quality health care regardless of ability to pay.

six-year graduated schedule   Allows workers to become 20 percent vested after two years and to vest at a rate of 20 percent each year thereafter until they are 100 percent vested after six years of service.

small employer   For the purposes of medical savings accounts, refers to companies with an average employment of 50 or fewer employees during the previous two calendar years.

smoking cessation   A type of wellness program designed to help employees quit smoking tobacco products.

social comparison theory   Provides an explanation for executive compensation determination based on the tendency for the board of directors to offer executive compensation packages that are similar to the executive compensation packages in peer companies.

social exchange   The most basic concept explaining social behavior. All social behavior can be seen as an exchange of activity (*work effort*), tangible (*visible performance*) or intangible (*motivation and commitment*), and more or less rewarding or costly (*pay and benefits*), between at least two persons (*employee and employer*).

Social Security Act of 1935   Established four main types of legally required benefits: unemployment insurance, retirement income, benefits for dependents, and medical insurance (Medicare).

Social Security Administration (SSA)   One of two federal agencies with primary responsibility for the programs established by the Social Security Act of 1935 and its subsequent amendments. See also *Centers for Medicare & Medicaid Services.*

Social Security credits   Used by the Social Security Administration to determine whether eligible individuals qualify for benefits. Employees accumulate credits based on their payment of Social Security taxes withheld from earnings.

Social Security integration   See *permitted disparity rules.*

Social Security numbers   The nine-digit numbers used to keep track of employee wages and benefits under the original OASDI and unemployment insurance programs.

Social Security totalization agreements   These agreements between the Social Security Administration and various countries specify the country to which employers and employees pay Social Security taxes for OASDI programs.

spillover effect   Occurs whenever management of a nonunion company offers higher wages and benefits to reduce the chance that employees would seek union representation.

split-dollar life insurance   Policies that provide separate life benefits and death benefits. The employer and executive share the premium payment. An agreement between the employer and executive determines the relative share of the premium and the policy's owner.

staff model HMOs   Medical facilities owned by the HMO that employ medical and support staff on the premises. These practices compensate physicians on a salary basis. Staff physicians treat only HMO members.

state compulsory disability laws   See *workers' compensation laws.*

stock appreciation rights   A type of executive deferred compensation that provides income to executives at the end of a designated period, much like restricted stock options. However, executives never have to exercise their stock rights to receive income. The company simply awards payment to executives based on the difference in stock price from the time the company granted the stock rights at fair market value to the end of the designated period, permitting the executives to keep the stock.

stock bonus plan   See *nonleveraged ESOPs.*

stock grant   A company's offering of stock to employees.

stock options Describe an employee's right to purchase company stock.

strategic benefit plans Detail different scenarios that may reasonably affect the company, and these plans emphasize long-term changes in how a company's benefit plans operate.

Strategic Enforcement Plan (StEP) Announced in April 2000 by the Pension and Welfare Benefits Administration, specifies a general framework for enforcing Title I of ERISA. Usual, customary, and reasonable charges refer to the amounts a fee-for-service plan will pay for specific treatments. In particular, these charges are not more than the physician's usual charge, within the customary range of fees charged in the locality, and reasonable, based on the medical circumstances.

strategic planning Entails a series of judgments, under uncertainty, that companies direct toward achieving specific goals. Companies base strategy formulation on environmental scanning activities. The main focus of environmental scanning is discerning threats and opportunities.

stress management A type of wellness program that helps employees cope with many factors inside and outside work that contribute to stress.

suitable work For purposes of unemployment insurance benefits, suitable work refers to jobs that require skills, knowledge, and ability similar to a person's customary work. Unemployed workers must demonstrate that they are actively seeking suitable work to maintain unemployment insurance benefits.

Summary Compensation Table Discloses compensation information for CEOs and the four most highly paid executives over a three-year period employed by companies whose stock is traded on public stock exchanges. The information in this table is presented in tabular and graphic forms to make information more accessible to the public. Required by the Securities Exchange Act of 1934.

summary of material modification Describes important (i.e., material) changes to the benefits plan. Material information applies to changes in the benefits program, including plan administrators, claims procedures, eligibility rules, and vesting provisions of retirement plans. Required by the Employee Retirement Income Security Act.

summary plan descriptions Specify essential information about employer-sponsored benefits as required by the Employee Retirement Income Security Act. Essential information includes the names and addresses of the employees responsible for developing and administering the benefits plan, disclosure of employee rights under ERISA, eligibility criteria for participating in the benefits program, and conditions under which an employee becomes disqualified for benefits or is suspended, claims procedures for receiving payments and for appealing denial of claims, and whether a retirement plan is insured by the Pension Benefit Guarantee Corporation.

supplemental executive retirement plans (SERPs) Provide executives with supplemental retirement benefits, usually increasing an executive's total retirement benefits to a substantially greater sum than restoration plans.

supplemental retirement benefits Increase an executive's total retirement benefits to a sum that is substantially greater than benefits provided by restoration plans.

supplemental unemployment benefit (SUB) Unemployment insurance usually awarded to individuals who were employed in cyclical industries. This benefit, usually specified in collective bargaining agreements, supplements unemployment insurance required by the Social Security Act of 1935.

T

tactical decisions Support competitive strategy. Managers throughout a company make tactical decisions to specify policy for promoting competitive advantage.

target benefit plan A type of hybrid retirement plan that calculates benefits in a fashion similar to defined benefit plans based on formulas that use income and years of service. But these target benefit plans are fundamentally defined contribution plans, because the benefit amount at retirement may be more or less than the targeted benefit amount based on the investment performance of the plan assets.

taxable wage base Limits the amount of annual wages or payroll cost per employee subject to taxation to fund OASDI programs.

tax-deferred annuity (TDA) Established by Section 403(b) of the Internal Revenue Code, the TDA is a type of qualified retirement plan for employees of public educational institutions (e.g., state colleges and universities) or private tax-exempt organizations (e.g., charitable organizations, state-supported hospitals).

Taxpayer Relief Act of 1997 Introduced a tax-free nondeductible individual retirement account (IRA), referred to as the Roth IRA.

telecommuting Alternative work arrangements in which employees perform work at home or some other location besides the office.

temporary partial disabilities Individuals may perform limited amounts of work until making a full recovery.

temporary total disabilities Prevent individuals performing meaningful work for a limited period. Individuals with temporary total disabilities eventually make full recoveries.

term life insurance The most common type of life insurance offered by companies; provides protection to an employee's beneficiaries only during a limited period based on a specified number of years or maximum age. After that, insurance automatically expires.

termination insurance Protects against the loss of vested pension benefits when plans fail. Employers with eligible defined benefit pension plans must purchase termination insurance.

third-country nationals Using the United States as frame of reference, third-country nationals are foreign national citizens who work in branch offices or manufacturing plants of U.S. companies in foreign countries—excluding the United States and their home countries. See also *expatriates* and *host-country nationals*.

third-party providers Independent companies that offer one or more benefits services to one or more employers. Contracts specify the services and the costs.

three percent rule Guards against backloading in retirement plans. A participant's accrued benefit cannot be less than 3 percent of the normal retirement benefit, assuming the participant began participation at the earliest possible age under the plan and she or he remained employed without interruption until age 65 or the plan's designated normal retirement age.

Title VII of the Civil Rights Act of 1964 A federal equal employment opportunity (EEO) law that makes it an unlawful employment practice for an employer to discriminate against any individual with respect to his compensation, terms, conditions, or privileges of employment, because of such individual's race, color, religion, sex, or national origin.

top-down approach A proactive process for benefits planning. Companies regularly review the entire benefits program or particular parts of the program.

top hat plans Unfunded deferred compensation plans for a select group of managers or highly compensated employees.

top-heavy provisions Apply to minimum benefits accrual and vesting rights. Plans are said to be top-heavy if the accrued benefits or account balances for key employees exceed 60 percent of the accrued benefits or account balances for all employees.

torts Laws offering remedies to individuals harmed by the unreasonable actions of others. Tort claims usually involve state law and are based on the legal premise that individuals are liable for the consequences of their conduct if it results in injury to others. Tort laws involve civil suits, which are actions brought to protect an individual's private rights.

total compensation strategies The use of compensation and benefits practices that support both human resource strategies and competitive strategies.

traditional individual retirement account (IRA) Provides for a tax-free deduction when a contribution is made, and the IRA is subject to income tax in its entirety when distributed. See also *Roth IRA*.

transactional psychological contracts Employees' expectations from the employer are more economic and extrinsic in nature.

transportation services Companies may sponsor public transportation subsidies, vanpools, or employer-sponsored vans or buses that transport employees between their homes and the workplace. These services promote attendance and help retain employees for whom transportation between home and work is either challenging ("heavy traffic or unreliable transportation") or too expensive.

trust Obligation to protect the interests of designated trustees.

trustees Possess exclusive authority to manage and control plan assets, unless otherwise specified in the plan document.

tuition reimbursement programs These programs fully or partially reimburse an employee for expenses incurred for education or training.

U

underwriting Decision process insurance companies rely upon to decide whether to offer insurance.

Unemployment Compensation Act of 2008 Expanded the Emergency Unemployment Compensation Program benefits to 20 weeks nationwide (from 13 weeks) and provided for 13 more weeks of emergency unemployment compensation (for a total of 33 weeks) to individuals who reside in states with high unemployment rates.

unfunded plans Do not guarantee retirement benefits because companies may choose to use any money set aside for an executive's retirement for other purposes and a company's creditors.

Uniformed Services Employment and Reemployment Rights Act of 1994 A federal law that gives individuals the right to employment by the company in which they worked prior to military service (i.e., reemployment rights). Individuals reemployed after military service are entitled to the seniority and other rights and benefits they would have had by remaining continuously employed.

unit benefit formulas Recognize length of service in retirement plans. Typically, employers decide to contribute a specified dollar amount per years worked by an employee. Alternatively, they may choose to contribute a specified percentage amount per years of service.

universal health care Refers to systems in which the government ensures that all its citizens have access to quality health care regardless of ability to pay.

universal life insurance Provides protection to employees' beneficiaries based on the insurance feature of term life insurance and a more flexible savings or cash accumulation plan than is found in whole life insurance plans.

use-it-or-lose-it provision Does not permit employees to have unused vacation time awarded for a calendar or fiscal year during a subsequent calendar or fiscal year.

U.S. Department of Labor A federal government agency that fosters and promotes the welfare of the job seekers, wage earners, and retirees of the United States by improving their working conditions; advancing their opportunities for profitable employment; protecting their retirement and health care benefits; helping employers find workers; strengthening free collective bargaining; and tracking changes in employment, prices, and other national economic measurements. In carrying out this mission, the Department administers a variety of federal labor laws including those that guarantee workers' rights to safe and healthful working conditions; a minimum hourly wage and overtime pay; freedom from employment discrimination; unemployment insurance; and other income support.

usual, customary, and reasonable charges Defined as not more than the physician's usual charge, within the customary range of fees charged in the locality, and reasonable, based on the medical circumstances.

utilization reviews Evaluate the frequency of employee's usage and cost of health insurance based on a review of insurance claims and the quality of specific health care services. Also, employers offering health benefits and insurers depend on utilization reviews to ensure that medical treatments received by participants were medically appropriate.

V

vesting An employee's nonforfeitable rights to pension benefits. There are two aspects of vesting: Employees acquire vesting rights on either a cliff vesting schedule or on a gradual vesting schedule.

violations of an affirmative duty tort Such violations take place when an employer fails to reveal the exposure of one or more workers to harmful substances, or the employer does not disclose a medical condition typically caused by exposure.

vision insurance Covers eye examinations, lenses, frames, and fitting of glasses.

volunteerism Refers to giving of one's time to support a meaningful cause. More and more companies are providing employees with paid time-off to contribute to causes of their choice.

W

wage-loss approach Bases workers' compensation benefits on the actual loss of earnings that results directly from nonscheduled injuries.

Application of this approach requires monitoring of an individual's income following an injury. The objective is to replace a part of or all of the earnings loss due to the injury.

wage test   Criterion specified in the Federal Unemployment Tax Act (FUTA) to determine whether employers must participate in state unemployment insurance programs.

waiting periods   Specify the minimum number of months or years an employee must remain employed before becoming eligible for one or more benefits. Waiting periods often correspond to the length of probationary periods.

wearaway   Some (usually older) employees do not accrue benefits for a period of time following conversion of a defined benefit plan to a cash balance plan, while other (usually younger) employees do not experience an interruption in accruing benefits.

weekly benefit amounts (WBAs)   The amount an individual receives from unemployment insurance programs, usually ranging between 50 to 67 percent of previous earnings.

weight control and nutrition   A type of wellness program that educates employees about proper nutrition and weight loss to promote sound health.

welfare plan   Generally refers to nonpension benefits for the purposes of ERISA.

welfare practices   Historical term for employee benefits: "anything for the comfort and improvement, intellectual or social, of the employees, over and above wages paid, which is not a necessity of the industry nor required by law."

wellness programs   Promote and maintain the physical and psychological health of employees.

whole life insurance   Pays an amount to the designated beneficiaries of the deceased employee. Unlike term life insurance, whole life plans do not terminate until payment to beneficiaries.

witness duty   See *jury duty.*

Women's Health and Cancer Rights Act of 1998 Requires group health plans to provide medical and surgical benefits for mastectomies.

Worker Adjustment and Retraining Notification (WARN) Act   Generally requires that management give at least a 60-day advance notice of a plant closing or mass layoff. An employer's failure to comply with the requirement of the WARN Act entitles employees to recover pay and benefits for the period for which notice was not given, typically up to a maximum of 60 days.

workers' compensation benefits   Include unlimited medical care, disability income, rehabilitation services, and death benefits.

workers' compensation laws   Established state-run insurance programs that are designed to cover medical, rehabilitation, and disability income expenses resulting from employees' work-related accidents. Also known as *state compulsory disability laws.*

working condition fringe   Any property or services provided to an employee of the employer to the extent that, if the employee paid for such property or services, such payment would be allowable as a deduction under Section 162 [trade or business expenses] or 167 [depreciation of the property used in the trade or business] of the Internal Revenue Code.

Index